I0012807

GIMP 2.8 Reference Manual 1/2

A catalogue record for this book is available from the Hong Kong Public Libraries.

This book contains only the first half of the GIMP Documentation Team manual due to book size restrctions. Chapter 1 to 15 are included in this book. Chapter 16-18 and the Appendix are included in the second volume.

Published by Samurai Media Limited.

Email: info@samuraimedia.org

ISBN 978-988-14435-9-5

Copyright 2002 to 2014 The GIMP Documentation Team
Minor modifications for publication Copyright 2015 Samurai Media Limited.

Permission is granted to copy, distribute and or modify this document under the terms of the GNU Free Documentation License, Version 1.2 or any later version published by the Free Software Foundation; with no Invariant Sections, no Front-Cover Texts, and no Back-Cover Texts. A copy of the license is included in the section enphrased GNU Free Documentation License.

Background Cover Image by https://www.flickr.com/people/webtreatsetc/

Contents

List of Examples

Preface

GIMP User Manual Authors and Contributors

Content Writers Alex Muñoz (Spanish) , Alexandre Franke (French) , Alexandre Prokoudine (Russian) , Angelo Córdoba Inunza (Spanish) , Christian Kirbach (German) , Daniel Francis (Spanish) , Daniel Mustieles (Spanish) , Daniel Winzen (German) , Delin Chang (Chinese) , Dimitris Spingos (Greek) , Djavan Fagundes (Brasilian) , Enrico Nicoletto (Brasilian) , Felipe Ribeiro (Brasilian) , Guiu Rocafort (Spanish) , Jiro Matsuzawa (Japanese) , Joe Hansen (Danish) , João S. O. Bueno (Brasilian) , Julien Hardelin (French, English) , Kenneth Nielsen (Danish) , Kolbjørn Stuestøl (Norwegian) , Marco Ciampa (Italian) , María Majadas (Spanish) , Milagros Infante Montero (Spanish) , Milo Casagrande (Italian) , Piotr Drag (Polish) , Rafael Ferreira (Brasilian) , Róman Joost (German, English) , Seong-ho Cho (Korean) , SimaMoto,RyōTa (   ) (Japanese) , Sven Claussner (German, English) , Timo Jyrinki (Finnish) , Ulf-D. Ehlert (German) , Vitaly Lomov (Russian) , Willer Gomes Junior (Brasilian) , Yuri Myasoedov (Russian)

Proof Reading Stéphane Poumaer (French) , Axel Wernicke (German, English) , Alessandro Falappa (Italian) , Manuel Quiñones (Spanish) , Ignacio AntI (Spanish) , Choi Ji-Hui(   ) (Korean) , Nickolay V. Shmyrev (Russian) , Albin Bernharsson (Swedish) , Daniel Nylander (Swedish) , Patrycja Stawiarska (Polish) , Andrew Pitonyak (English) , Jakub Friedl (Czech, English) , Hans De Jonge (Dutch) , Raymon Van Wanrooij (Dutch) , Semka Kuloviæ-Debals (Croatian) , Sally C. Barry (English) , Daniel Egger (English) , Sven Neumann (English, German) , Domingo Stephan (German) , Thomas Lotze (German) , Thomas Güttler (German) , Zhong Yaotang (Chinese) , Calum Mackay (English) , Thomas S Lendo (German) , Mel Boyce (syngin) (English) , Oliver Ellis (Red Haze) (English) , Markus Reinhardt (German) , Alexander Weiher (German) , Michael Hölzen (German) , Raymond Ostertag (French) , Cédric Gémy (French) , Sébastien Barre (French) , Niklas Mattison (Swedish) , Daryl Lee (English) , William Skaggs (English) , Cai Qian (   ) (Chinese) , Yang Hong (   ) (Chinese) , Xceals (Chinese) , Eric Lamarque (Chinese) , Robert van Drunen (Dutch) , Marco Marega (Italian) , Mike Vargas (Italian) , Andrea Zito (Italian) , Karine Delvare (French) , David 'Ilicz' Klementa (Czech) , Jan Smith (English) , Adolf Gerold (German) , Roxana Chernogolova (Russian) , Grigory Bakunov (Russian) , Oleg Fritz (Russian) , Mick Curtis (English) , Vitaly Lomov (Russian) , Pierre PERRIER (French) , Oliver Heesakke (Dutch) , Susanne Schmidt (English, German) , Ben (German) , Daniel Hornung (English) , Sven Claussner (English, German)

Graphics, Stylesheets Jakub Steiner , Øyvind Kolås

Build System, Technical Contributions Kenneth Nielsen , Róman Joost , Axel Wernicke , Nickolay V. Shmyrev , Daniel Egger , Sven Neumann , Michael Natterer (mitch) , Henrik Brix Andersen (brix) , Thomas Schraitle , Chris Hübsch , Anne Schneider , Peter Volkov , Daniel Richard

Part I

Getting Started

Chapter 1

Introduction

1.1 Welcome to GIMP

GIMP is a multi-platform photo manipulation tool. GIMP is an acronym for GNU Image Manipulation Program. The GIMP is suitable for a variety of image manipulation tasks, including photo retouching, image composition, and image construction.

GIMP has many capabilities. It can be used as a simple paint program, an expert quality photo retouching program, an online batch processing system, a mass production image renderer, an image format converter, etc.

GIMP is expandable and extensible. It is designed to be augmented with plug-ins and extensions to do just about anything. The advanced scripting interface allows everything from the simplest task to the most complex image manipulation procedures to be easily scripted.

One of The GIMP's strengths is its free availability from many sources for many operating systems. Most GNU/Linux distributions include The GIMP as a standard application. The GIMP is also available for other operating systems such as Microsoft Windows or Apple's Mac OS X (Darwin). The GIMP is a Free Software application covered by the General Public License [GPL]. The GPL provides users with the freedom to access and alter the source code that makes up computer programs.

1.1.1 Authors

The first version of the GIMP was written by Peter Mattis and Spencer Kimball. Many other developers have contributed more recently, and thousands have provided support and testing. GIMP releases are currently being orchestrated by Sven Neumann and Mitch Natterer and the other members of the GIMP-Team.

1.1.2 The GIMP Help system

The GIMP Documentation Team and other users have provided you with the information necessary to understand how to use GIMP. The User Manual is an important part of this help. The current version is on the web site of the Documentation Team [GIMP-DOCS] in HTML format. The HTML version is also available as context sensitive help (if you installed it) while using GIMP by pressing the **F1** key. Help on specific menu items can be accessed by pressing the **F1** key while the mouse pointer is focused on the menu item. Read on to begin your GIMP journey.

1.1.3 Features and Capabilities

The following list is a short overview of some of the features and capabilities which GIMP offers you:

- A full suite of painting tools including brushes, a pencil, an airbrush, cloning, etc.

- Tile-based memory management, so image size is limited only by available disk space

- Sub-pixel sampling for all paint tools for high-quality anti-aliasing

- Full Alpha channel support for working with transparency

- Layers and channels

- A procedural database for calling internal GIMP functions from external programs, such as Script-Fu

- Advanced scripting capabilities

- Multiple undo/redo (limited only by disk space)

- Transformation tools including rotate, scale, shear and flip

- Support for a wide range of file formats, including GIF, JPEG, PNG, XPM, TIFF, TGA, MPEG, PS, PDF, PCX, BMP and many others

- Selection tools, including rectangle, ellipse, free, fuzzy, bezier and intelligent scissors

- Plug-ins that allow for the easy addition of new file formats and new effect filters.

1.2   What's New in GIMP 2.8?

GIMP 2.8 is another important release from a development point of view, even more that it was for 2.6. It features a big change to the user interface addressing one of the most often received complaints: the lack of a single window mode. Moreover the integration effort of GEGL library had taken a big step forward, reaching more than 90% of the GIMP core, a new powerful transformation tool, layer groups, new common options, new brushes, improved text tool, and more.

User Interface

New single window mode With this new feature it will be possible to work with all the GIMP dialogs inside one big window, usually with the image(s) centered inside. No more floating panels or toolbox but the dialogs could be arranged inside this single window. This mode could be enabled or disabled all the time, even while working, and the option will be remembered through the sessions.

Figure 1.1 The new look of the single window mode

New file save workflow Now Save and Save as work only with xcf formats. If you want to export an image in another format, say jpg or png, you have to explicitly Export it. This enhances the workflow and lets you simply overwrite the original file or export to various other formats.

Figure 1.2 The new image workflow

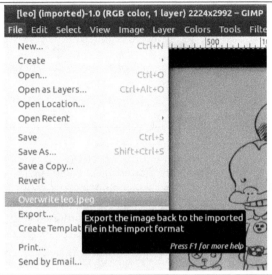

New image bar A new useful image bar comes with the single window mode, which lets you switch easily between open images through the means of a tab bar with image thumbnails.

Figure 1.3 The new image bar

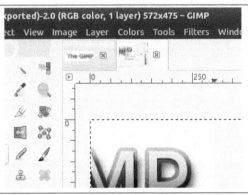

New arrangement options GIMP will make users working with two screens (one for dialogs, the other for images) happy: now it is possible to arrange the dialogs one over the other, in tabs and in columns too.

Figure 1.4 Multi column docks

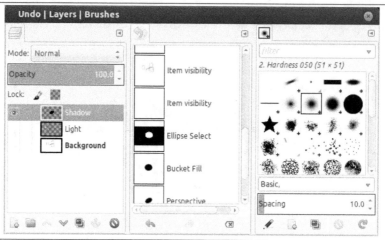

New resources tags GIMP Brushes, Gradients, Pattern and Palettes can be filtered and searched via tags. Tags are text labels that the user can assign to resources. With Tags the user can easily find the resources by means of an input text box. Tags can be manually assigned by the user with the same input box used for searching tags, or they can be automatically tagged using the directory name of the imported items.

Figure 1.5 Resource tags

Simple math in size entries Enhancements have also been made to the size entry widget, which is used for inputting most of the x, y, width, height parameters. For example, in the scale dialog it is now possible to write "50%" in the Width field to scale the image to 50% of the width. Expressions such as "30in + 40px" and "4 * 5.4in" work, too.

Figure 1.6 Math size entries

Minor changes

- The new "Lock Pixels" option in the layers dialog can avoid undesired painting on a layer when working with several layers.

Figure 1.7 The new Lock Pixels option

- Now you can move between images in single and multi window mode using the shortcuts Ctrl-PageUp/PageDown or Alt-Number.

- Add support for F2 to rename items in lists.

- You can now Alt-Click on layers in the Layers dialog to create a selection from it. Add, subtract and intersect modifiers **Click**, **Shift** and Ctrl-Shift keys work too. This makes it easy to compose contents of a layer based on the contents of other layers, without detours.

- Since the keyboard shortcuts Ctrl-E and Ctrl-Shift-E have been redirected to image export mechanisms, new keyboard shortcuts have been setup for "Shrink Wrap" and "Fit in Window", namely Ctrl-J and Ctrl-Shift-J respectively.

- Added Windows → Hide docks menu item that does what "Tab" does and also displays its state, which is now persistent across sessions, too.

- The layer modes have been rearranged into more logical and useful groups based on the effect they have on layers. Layer modes that make the layer lighter are in one group, layer modes that make the layer darker in another group, and so forth.

- In multi-window mode, you can now close the Toolbox without quitting GIMP.

- Allow binding arbitrary actions to extra mouse buttons.

- Now it is possible to change the application language directly from the preference menu.

Tools, Filters and Plug-ins

A new tool: Cage Transform With this new tool is now possible to create custom bending of a selection just moving control points. This is the result of one of our Google Summer of Code 2010 students.

Figure 1.8 Cage Transform

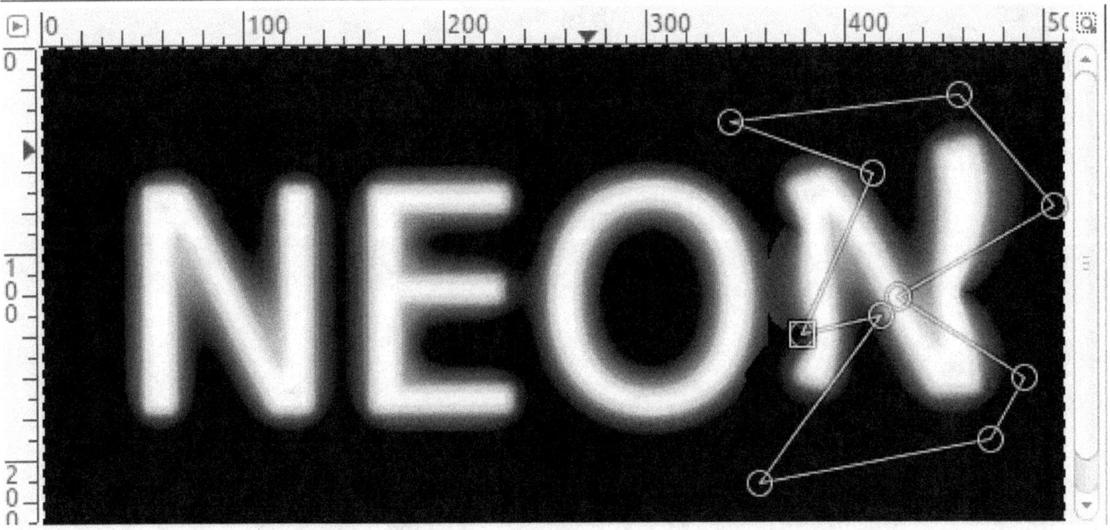

Improved Text Tool The text tool has been enhanced to support on canvas text writing and make possible changing the attributes of a single char.

Figure 1.9 Improved text tool

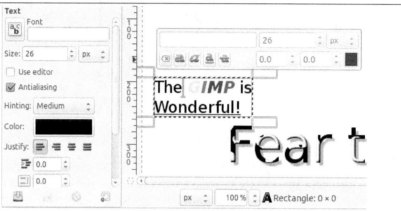

New layer groups It is now possible to group set of layers and treat them like an entity. It is possible to switch a group on or off and to move the group in the layers dialog. It is easy to add / remove existing layers to a group or to create / delete a layer inside the group and it is even possible to create embedded groups of groups. It is possible to apply a layer mode to a group as you do with a single layer. All this greatly improves the workflow with complex multilayer images making them easier to manage.

Figure 1.10 New layer groups

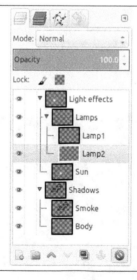

Rotating brushes Brushes can now be rotated at will, acting on the brush option "Angle".

Figure 1.11 Rotating brushes

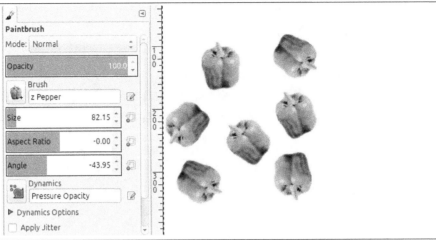

Minor changes

- The default Quick Mask color is now configurable.
- The RTL mode (right to left writing) has been improved in the Text tool.
- You can specify the written language in the Text Tool. This helps choosing an appropriate font, or appropriate glyphs for the selected language.
- Added optional diagonal guides to the crop tool.
- Added "Rule of fifths" crop guide overlay.
- A Cairo based PDF exporter has been implemented. Although being somewhat simplistic, the exporter saves text, embedding fonts into the final PDF file, and attempts to convert bitmaps to vector objects.
- Brush dynamics improved.
- Added plug-in for loading JPEG2000 images.
- Added plug-ins for X11 Mouse Cursor import and export support.
- Added fundamental OpenRaster (.ora) import and export support.
- Added RGB565 support to the csource plug-in.
- Added a new "Create" command that allows loading a Web page directly into GIMP using Webkit.

Under the Hood

GEGL The porting of the GIMP core towards the new high bit-depth and non-destructive editing GEGL [GEGL] library has taken big steps and now more than 90% of the task is already finished.

In addition to porting color operations to GEGL, an experimental GEGL Operation tool has been added, found in the Tools menu. It enables applying GEGL operations to an image and it gives on-canvas previews of the results. The screenshot below shows this for a Gaussian Blur.

Figure 1.12 GEGL operation

Cairo porting Started with GIMP version 2.6, all tools rendering on canvas is now completely ported to [CAIRO]. It provides smooth antialiased graphics and improves GIMP look. Some plug-ins have been upgraded to Cairo as well. Additionally all tools now use an on-canvas progress indicator instead of the one in the statusbar.

Figure 1.13 Progress indicator

Miscellaneous

License change The GIMP license has been changed to (L)GPLv3+.

New script API

- A lot of GIMP APIs have been rebuilt to simplify developing new scripts.
- To further enhances scripting abilities, API changes to support layer groups have been made.

Backwards Compatibility To allow migrating from the old tools presets system to the new one, there is a Python script, which you can download from the GIMP wiki site. However, the old tools presets are not 100% convertible to the new tool presets. For instance, brush scale from 2.6 can't be converted to brush size in 2.8.

Known Problems Working with graphics tablets could be problematic due to the GTK+2 library in use. If in this case either use the older version 2.6 or wait for the up coming version 3.0 for the full GTK+3 support.

Chapter 2

Fire up the GIMP

2.1 Running GIMP

Most often, you start GIMP either by clicking on an icon (if your system is set up to provide you with one), or by typing **gimp** on a command line. If you have multiple versions of GIMP installed, you may need to type **gimp-2.8** to get the latest version. You can, if you want, give a list of image files on the command line after the program name, and they will automatically be opened by GIMP as it starts. It is also possible, though, to open files from within GIMP once it is running.

Most operating systems support file associations, which associates a class of files (as determined by their filename extension, such as .jpg) with a corresponding application (such as GIMP). When image files are properly "associated" to GIMP, you can double click on an image to open it in GIMP.

2.1.1 Known Platforms

The GIMP is the most widely supported image manipulation available today. The platforms on which GIMP is known to work include:

GNU/Linux, Apple Mac OS X, Microsoft Windows, OpenBSD, NetBSD, FreeBSD, Solaris, SunOS, AIX, HP-UX, Tru64, Digital UNIX, OSF/1, IRIX, OS/2, and BeOS.

The GIMP is easily ported to other operating systems because of its source code availability. For further information visit the GIMP developers homepage. [GIMP-DEV].

2.1.2 Language

GIMP automatically detects and uses the system language. In the unlikely event that language detection fails, or if you just want to use a different language, since GIMP-2.8, you can do so through: Edit → Preferences → Interface.

You can also use:

Under Linux *In LINUX*: in console mode, type **LANGUAGE=en gimp** or **LANG=en gimp** replacing en by fr, de, ... according to the language you want. Background: Using **LANGUAGE=en** sets an environment variable for the executed program **gimp**.

Under Windows XP Control Panel → System → Advanced → Environment button in "System Variables" area: Add button: Enter LANG for Name and fr or de... for Value. Watch out! You have to click on three successive OK to validate your choice.

If you change languages often, you can create a batch file to change the language. Open NotePad. Type the following commands (for french for instance):

```
set lang=fr
start gimp-2.8.exe
```

Save this file as GIMP-FR.BAT (or another name, but always with a .BAT extension). Create a shortcut and drag it to your desktop.

Another possibility: Start → Programs → GTK Runtime Environment Then Select language and select the language you want in the drop-down list.

11

Under Apple Mac OS X From System Preferences, click on the International icon. In the Language tab, the desired language should be the first in the list.

Another GIMP instance Use **-n** to run multiple instances of GIMP. For example, use `gimp-2.8` to start GIMP in the default system language, and **`LANGUAGE=en gimp-2.8 -n`** to start another instance of GIMP in English; this is very useful for translators.

2.1.3 Command Line Arguments

Although arguments are not required when starting GIMP, the most common arguments are shown below. On a Unix system, you can use **man gimp** for a complete list.

Command line arguments must be in the command line that you use to start GIMP as **gimp-2.8 [OPTION...] [FILE | URI...]**.

-?, --help Display a list of all commandline options.

--help-all Show all help options.

--help-gtk Show GTK+ Options.

-v, --version Print the GIMP version and exit.

--license Show license information and exit.

--verbose Show detailed start-up messages.

-n, --new-instance Start a new GIMP instance.

-a, --as-new Open images as new.

-i, --no-interface Run without a user interface.

-d, --no-data Do not load patterns, gradients, palettes, or brushes. Often useful in non-interactive situations where start-up time is to be minimized.

-f, --no-fonts Do not load any fonts. This is useful to load GIMP faster for scripts that do not use fonts, or to find problems related to malformed fonts that hang GIMP.

-s, --no-splash Do not show the splash screen while starting.

--no-shm Do not use shared memory between GIMP and plugins.

--no-cpu-accel Do not use special CPU acceleration functions. Useful for finding or disabling buggy accelerated hardware or functions.

--session=`name` Use a different `sessionrc` for this GIMP session. The given session name is appended to the default `sessionrc` filename.

--gimprc=`filename` Use an alternative `gimprc` instead of the default one. The `gimprc` file contains a record of your preferences. Useful in cases where plugins paths or machine specs may be different.

--system-gimprc=`filename` Use an alternate system gimprc file.

-b, --batch=`commands` Execute the set of commands non-interactively. The set of commands is typically in the form of a script that can be executed by one of the GIMP scripting extensions. When the command is **-**, commands are read from standard input.

--batch-interpreter=`proc` Specify the procedure to use to process batch commands. The default procedure is Script-Fu.

--console-messages Do not popup dialog boxes on errors or warnings. Print the messages on the console instead.

--pdb-compat-mode=`mode` PDB compatibility mode (off | on | warn).

--stack-trace-mode=`mode` Debug in case of a crash (never | query | always).

--debug-handlers Enable non-fatal debugging signal handlers. Useful for GIMP debugging.

--g-fatal-warnings Make all warnings fatal. Useful for debug.

--dump-gimprc Output a gimprc file with default settings. Useful if you messed up the gimprc file.

--display=*display* Use the designated X display (does not apply to all platforms).

2.2   Starting GIMP the first time

When first run, GIMP performs a series of steps to configure options and directories. The configuration process creates a subdirectory in your home directory called .gimp-2.8. All of the configuration information is stored in this directory. If you remove or rename the directory, GIMP will repeat the initial configuration process, creating a new .gimp-2.8 directory. Use this capability to explore different configuration options without destroying your existing installation, or to recover if your configuration files are damaged.

2.2.1   Finally . . .

Just a couple of suggestions before you start, though: First, GIMP provides tips you can read at any time using the menu command Help → Tip of the Day. The tips provide information that is considered useful, but not easy to learn by experimenting; so they are worth reading. Please read the tips when you have the time. Second, if at some point you are trying to do something, and GIMP seems to have suddenly stopped functioning, the section Getting Unstuck may help you out. Happy Gimping!

Chapter 3

First Steps with Wilber

3.1 Basic Concepts

Figure 3.1 Wilber, the GIMP mascot

The Wilber_Construction_Kit (in src/images/) allows you to give the mascot a different appearance. It is the work of Tuomas Kuosmanen (tigertATgimp.org).

This section provides a brief introduction to the basic concepts and terminology used in GIMP. The concepts presented here are explained in much greater depth elsewhere. With a few exceptions, we have avoided cluttering this section with a lot of links and cross-references: everything mentioned here is so high-level that you can easily locate it in the index.

Images Images are the basic entities used by GIMP. Roughly speaking, an "image" corresponds to a single file, such as a TIFF or JPEG file. You can also think of an image as corresponding to a single display window (although in truth it is possible to have multiple windows all displaying the same image). It is not possible to have a single window display more than one image, though, or for an image to have no window displaying it.

A GIMP image may be quite a complicated thing. Instead of thinking of it as a sheet of paper with a picture on it, think of it as more like a stack of sheets, called "layers". In addition to a stack of layers, a GIMP image may contain a selection mask, a set of channels, and a set of paths. In fact, GIMP provides a mechanism for attaching arbitrary pieces of data, called "parasites", to an image.

In GIMP, it is possible to have many images open at the same time. Although large images may use many megabytes of memory, GIMP uses a sophisticated tile-based memory management system that allows GIMP to handle very large images gracefully. There are limits, however, and having more memory available may improve system performance.

Layers If a simple image can be compared to a single sheet of paper, an image with layers is likened to a sheaf of transparent papers stacked one on top of the other. You can draw on each paper, but still see the content of the other sheets through the transparent areas. You can also move one sheet in relation to the others. Sophisticated GIMP users often deal with images containing many layers, even dozens of them. Layers need not be opaque, and they need not cover the entire extent of an

15

image, so when you look at an image's display, you may see more than just the top layer: you may see elements of many layers.

Resolution Digital images comprise of a grid of square elements of varying colors, called pixels. Each image has a pixel size, such as 900 pixels wide by 600 pixels high. But pixels don't have a set size in physical space. To set up an image for printing, we use a value called resolution, defined as the ratio between an image's size in pixels and its physical size (usually in inches) when it is printed on paper. Most file formats (but not all) can save this value, which is expressed as ppi — pixels per inch. When printing a file, the resolution value determines the size the image will have on paper, and as a result, the physical size of the pixels. The same 900x600 pixel image may be printed as a small 3x2" card with barely noticeable pixels — or as a large poster with large, chunky pixels. Images imported from cameras and mobile devices tend to have a resolution value attached to the file. The value is usually 72 or 96ppi. It is important to realize that this value is arbitrary and was chosen for historic reasons. You can always change the resolution value inside GIMP — this has no effect on the actual image pixels. Furthermore, for uses such as displaying images on line, on mobile devices, television or video games — in short, any use that is not print — the resolution value is meaningless and is ignored, and instead the image is usually displayed so that each image pixel conforms to one screen pixel.

Channels A Channel is a single component of a pixel's color. For a colored pixel in GIMP, these components are usually Red, Green, Blue and sometimes transparency (Alpha). For a Grayscale image, they are Gray and Alpha and for an Indexed color image, they are Indexed and Alpha.

The entire rectangular array of any one of the color components for all of the pixels in an image is also referred to as a Channel. You can see these color channels with the Channels dialog.

When the image is displayed, GIMP puts these components together to form the pixel colors for the screen, printer, or other output device. Some output devices may use different channels from Red, Green and Blue. If they do, GIMP's channels are converted into the appropriate ones for the device when the image is displayed.

Channels can be useful when you are working on an image which needs adjustment in one particular color. For example, if you want to remove "red eye" from a photograph, you might work on the Red channel.

You can look at channels as masks which allow or restrict the output of the color that the channel represents. By using Filters on the channel information, you can create many varied and subtle effects on an image. A simple example of using a Filter on the color channels is the Channel Mixer filter.

In addition to these channels, GIMP also allows you to create other channels (or more correctly, Channel Masks), which are displayed in the lower part of the Channels dialog. You can create a New Channel or save a selection to a channel (mask). See the glossary entry on Masks for more information about Channel Masks.

Selections Often when modify an image, you only want a part of the image to be affected. The "selection" mechanism makes this possible. Each image has its own selection, which you normally see as a moving dashed line separating the selected parts from the unselected parts (the so-called "marching ants"). Actually this is a bit misleading: selection in GIMP is graded, not all-or-nothing, and really the selection is represented by a full-fledged grayscale channel. The dashed line that you normally see is simply a contour line at the 50%-selected level. At any time, though, you can visualize the selection channel in all its glorious detail by toggling the QuickMask button.

A large component of learning how to use GIMP effectively is acquiring the art of making good selections—selections that contain exactly what you need and nothing more. Because selection-handling is so centrally important, GIMP provides many tools for doing it: an assortment of selection-making tools, a menu of selection operations, and the ability to switch to Quick Mask mode, in which you can treat the selection channel as though it were a color channel, thereby "painting the selection".

Undoing When you make mistakes, you can undo them. Nearly everything you can do to an image is undoable. In fact, you can usually undo a substantial number of the most recent things you did, if you decide that they were misguided. GIMP makes this possible by keeping a history of your actions. This history consumes memory, though, so undoability is not infinite. Some actions use very little undo memory, so that you can do dozens of them before the earliest ones are deleted from this history; other types of actions require massive amounts of undo memory. You can configure the amount of memory GIMP allows for the undo history of each image, but in any situation, you should always be able to undo at least your 2-3 most recent actions. (The most important action that is not undoable is closing an image. For this reason, GIMP asks you to confirm that you really want to close the image if you have made any changes to it.)

Plug-ins Many, probably most, of the things that you do to an image in GIMP are done by the GIMP application itself. However, GIMP also makes extensive use of "plug-ins", which are external programs that interact very closely with GIMP, and are capable of manipulating images and other GIMP objects in very sophisticated ways. Many important plug-ins are bundled with GIMP, but there are also many available by other means. In fact, writing plug-ins (and scripts) is the easiest way for people not on the GIMP development team to add new capabilities to GIMP.

All of the commands in the Filters menu, and a substantial number of commands in other menus, are actually implemented as plug-ins.

Scripts In addition to plug-ins, which are programs written in the C language, GIMP can also make use of scripts. The largest number of existing scripts are written in a language called Script-Fu, which is unique to GIMP (for those who care, it is a dialect of the Lisp-like language called Scheme). It is also possible to write GIMP scripts in Python or Perl. These languages are more flexible and powerful than Script-Fu; their disadvantage is that they depend on software that does not automatically come packaged with GIMP, so they are not guaranteed to work correctly in every GIMP installation.

3.2   Main Windows

The GIMP user interface is now available in two modes:

- multi-window mode,

- single window mode.

When you open GIMP for the first time, it opens in multi-window mode by default. You can enable single-window mode through Windows → >Single-Window Mode) in the image menu bar. After quitting GIMP with this option enabled, GIMP will start in single-window mode next time.

Multi-Window Mode

Figure 3.2 A screenshot illustrating the multi-window mode.

The screenshot above shows the most basic arrangement of GIMP windows that can be used effectively.

You can notice two panels, left and right, and an image window in middle. A second image is partially masked. The left panel collects Toolbox and Tool Options dialog together. The right panel collects layers, channels, paths, undo history dialogs together in a multi-tab dock, brushes, patterns and gradients dialogs together in another dock below. You can move these panels on screen. You can also mask them using the **Tab** key.

1. *The Main Toolbox:* Contains a set of icon buttons used to select tools. By default, it also contains the foreground and background colors. You can add brush, pattern, gradient and active image icons. Use Edit → Preferences → Toolbox to enable, or disable the extra items.

2. *Tool options:* Docked below the main Toolbox is a Tool Options dialog, showing options for the currently selected tool (in this case, the Move tool).

3. *Image windows:* Each image open in GIMP is displayed in a separate window. Many images can be open at the same time, limited by only the system resources. Before you can do anything useful in GIMP, you need to have at least one image window open. The image window holds the Menu of the main commands of GIMP (File, Edit, Select...), which you can also get by right-clicking on the window.

   An image can be bigger than the image window. In that case, GIMP displays the image in a reduced zoom level which allows to see the full image in the image window. If you turn to the 100% zoom level, scroll bars appear, allowing you to pan across the image.

4. The *Layers, Channels, Paths, Undo History* dock — note that the dialogs in the dock are tabs. The Layers tab is open : it shows the layer structure of the currently active image, and allows it to be manipulated in a variety of ways. It is possible to do a few very basic things without using the Layers dialog, but even moderately sophisticated GIMP users find it indispensable to have the Layers dialog available at all times.

5. *Brushes/Patterns/Gradients:* The docked dialog below the layer dialog shows the dialogs (tabs) for managing brushes, patterns and gradients.

Dialog and dock managing is described in Section 3.2.3.

Single Window Mode

Figure 3.3 A screenshot illustrating the single-window mode.

You find the same elements, with differences in their management:

- Left and right panels are fixed; you can't move them. But you can decrease or increase their width. If you reduce the width of a multi-tab dock, there may be not enough place for all tabs; then arrow-heads appear allowing you to scroll through tabs.

As in multi-window mode, you can mask these panels using the **Tab** key.

- The image window occupies all space between both panels.

When several images are open, a new bar appears above the image window, with a tab for every image. You can navigate between images by clicking on tabs or either using Ctrl-PageUp or PageDown or Alt-Number. "Number" is tab number; you must use the number keys of the upper line of your keyboard, not that of keypad (Alt-shift necessary for some national keyboards).

This is a minimal setup. There are over a dozen other types of dialogs used by GIMP for various purposes, but users typically open them when they need them and close them when they are done. Knowledgeable users generally keep the Toolbox (with Tool Options) and Layers dialog open at all times. The Toolbox is essential to many GIMP operations. The Tool Options section is actually a separate dialog, shown docked to the Main Toolbox in the screenshot. Knowledgeable users almost always have it set up this way: it is very difficult to use tools effectively without being able to see how their options are set. The Layers dialog comes into play when you work with an image with multiple layers: after you advance beyond the most basic stages of GIMP expertise, this means *almost always*. And of course it helps to display the images you're editing on the screen; if you close the image window before saving your work, GIMP will ask you whether you want to close the file.

Note

If your GIMP layout is lost, your arrangement is easy to recover using Windows → Recently Closed Docks ; the Windows menu command is only available while an image is open. To add, close, or detach a tab from a dock, click ◁ in the upper right corner of a dialog. This opens the Tab menu. Select Add Tab, Close Tab , or Detach Tab.

The following sections walk you through the components of each of the windows shown in the screenshot, explaining what they are and how they work. Once you have read them, plus the section describing the basic structure of GIMP images, you should have learned enough to use GIMP for a wide variety of basic image manipulations. You can then look through the rest of the manual at your leisure (or just experiment) to learn the almost limitless number of more subtle and specialized things that are possible. Have fun!

3.2.1 The Toolbox

Figure 3.4 Screenshot of the Toolbox

The Toolbox is the heart of GIMP. Here is a quick tour of what you will find there.

Tip

In the Toolbox, as in most parts of GIMP, moving the mouse over something and letting it rest for a moment, usually displays a "tooltip" that describes the thing. Short cut keys are also frequently shown in the tooltip. In many cases, you can hover the mouse over an item and press the **F1** key to get help about the thing that is underneath the mouse.

By default, only the Foreground-background icon is visible. You can add Brush-Pattern-Gradient icons and Active Image icon through Edit → Preferences → Toolbox: Tools configuration.

1. *Tool icons:* These icons are buttons which activate tools for a wide variety of purposes: selecting parts of images, painting an image, transforming an image, etc. Section 14.1 gives an overview of how to work with tools, and each tool is described systematically in the Tools chapter.

2. *Foreground/Background colors:* The color areas here show you GIMP's current foreground and background colors, which come into play in many operations. Clicking on either one of them brings up a color selector dialog that allows you to change to a different color. Clicking on the double-headed arrow swaps the two colors, and clicking on the small symbol in the lower left corner resets them to black and white.

3. *Brush/Pattern/Gradient:* The symbols here show you GIMP's current selections for: the Paintbrush, used by all tools that allow you to paint on the image ("painting" includes operations like erasing and smudging, by the way); for the Pattern, which is used in filling selected areas of an image; and for the Gradient, which comes into play whenever an operation requires a smoothly varying range of colors. Clicking on any of these symbols brings up a dialog window that allows you to change it.

4. *Active Image:* In GIMP, you can work with many images at once, but at any given moment, only one image is the "active image". Here you find a small iconic representation of the active image. Click the icon to display a dialog with a list of the currently open images, click an image in the dialog to make it active. Usually, you click an image window in multi-window mode, or an image tab in single-window mode, to make it the active image.

   You can "Drop to an XDS file manager to save the image". XDS is an acronym for "X Direct Save Protocol": an additional feature for the X Window System graphical user interface for Unix-like operating systems.

Note

At every start, GIMP selects a tool (the brush), a color, a brush and a pattern by default, always the same. If you want GIMP to select the last tool, color, brush and pattern you used when quitting your previous session, check the Save input device settings on exit in Preferences/Input Devices.

Tip

The Toolbox window displays "Wilber's eyes" along the top of the dialog. You can get rid of the "Wilber's eyes" by adding the following line to your `gimprc` file: `(to olbox-wilber no)`. It only affects the toolbox. The eyes in the Image window are only visible when you do not have an open image.

Tip

Drag and drop an image from a file browser into the Toolbox window to open the image in its own Image window or tab.

3.2.2 Image Window

GIMP user interface is now available in two modes: multi-window mode (default), and single-window mode (optional, through Windows → >Single-Window Mode. But, if you quit GIMP with this option enabled, GIMP will open in single mode next time).

In single-window mode, no new window is added: images and dialogs are added in tabs. Please see Single Window Mode.

When you start GIMP without any image open, the image window seems to be absent in single-window mode, while, in multi-window mode, an image window exists, even if no image is open.

We will begin with a brief description of the components that are present by default in an ordinary image window. Some of the components can be removed by using commands in the View menu.

Figure 3.5 The Image Window in Multi-Window Mode

Figure 3.6 The Image Area in Single-Window Mode

Note

 Despite *Single*-window Mode, we will use "image window" for "image area".

---

1. *Title Bar:* The Title Bar in an image window without an image displays "GNU Image Manipulating Program". An image window with an image displays the image name and its specifications in the title bar according to the settings in Preference Dialog. The Title Bar is provided by the operating system, not by GIMP, so its appearance is likely to vary with the operating system, window manager, and/or theme — in Linux systems, this title bar has a button to display the image window on all your desktops. You also have this button in toolbox window and layer window.

   If you have opened a non-xcf image, it is "(imported)" as a .xcf file and its original name appears in the status bar at the bottom of the image window.

   When an image is modified, an asterisk appears in front of title.

2. *Image Menu:* Directly below the Title Bar appears the Menu bar (unless it has been suppressed). The Image Menu provides access to nearly every operation you can perform on an image. You can also right-click on an image to display a pop-up image menu, [1], or by left-clicking on the little "arrow-head" symbol in the upper left corner, called *Menu Button*, described just below. Many menu commands are also associated with keyboard *shortcuts* as shown in the menu. You can define your own custom shortcuts for menu actions, if you enable Use Dynamic Keyboard Shortcuts in the Preferences dialog.

3. *Menu Button:* Click the Menu Button to display the Image Menu in a column,(essential in full screen mode). If you like to use keyboard shortcuts, use Shift-F10 to open the menu.

4. *Ruler:* In the default layout, rulers are shown above and to the left of the image. Use the rulers to determine coordinates within the image. The default unit for rulers is pixels; use the settings described below to use a unit other than pixels.

   One of the most important uses of rulers is to create *guides*. Click and drag a ruler into the image to create a guide. A guide is a line that helps you accurately position things—or verify that another line is truly horizontal or vertical. Click and drag a guide to move it. Drag a guide out of the image to delete it; you can always drag another guide into the image. You can even use multiple guides at the same time.

   In ruler area, the mouse pointer position is marked with two small arrow-heads pointing vertically and horizontally.

5. *QuickMask Toggle:* The small button in the lower left corner of the image toggles the Quick Mask on and off. When the Quick Mask is on, the button is outlined in red. See QuickMask for more details on this highly useful tool.

6. *Pointer Coordinates:* When the pointer (mouse cursor, if you are using a mouse) is within the image boundaries, the rectangular area in the lower left corner of the window displays the current pointer coordinates. The units are the same as for the rulers.

7. *Units Menu:* Use the Units Menu to change the units used for rulers and several other purposes. The default unit is pixels, but you can quickly change to inches, cm, or several other possibilities using this menu. Note that the setting of "Dot for dot" in the View menu affects how the display is scaled: see Dot for Dot for more information.

8. *Zoom Button:* There are a number of ways to zoom the image in or out, but the Zoom Button is perhaps the simplest. You can directly enter a zoom level in the text box for precise control.

---

[1] Users with an Apple Macintosh and a one button mouse can use Ctrl-mousebutton instead.

9. *Status Area:* The Status Area is at the bottom of the image window. By default, the Status Area displays the original name of the image.xcf file, and the amount of system memory used by the image. Please use Edit → Preferences → Image Windows → Title & Status to customize the information displayed in the Status Area. During time-consuming operations, the status area temporarily shows the running operation and how complete the operation is.

> **Note**
>
> Note that the memory used by the image is very different from the image file size. For instance, a 70Kb .PNG image may occupy 246Kb in RAM when displayed. There are two primary reasons the difference in memory usage. First, a .PNG file is compressed format, and the image is reconstituted in RAM in uncompressed form. Second, GIMP uses extra memory, and copies of the image, for use by the Undo command.

10. *Cancel Button:* During complex time-consuming operations, usually a plug-in, a Cancel button temporarily appears in the lower right corner of the window. Use the Cancel button to stop the operation.

> **Note**
>
> A few plug-ins respond badly to being canceled, sometimes leaving corrupted pieces of images behind.

11. *Navigation Control:* This is a small cross-shaped button at the lower right corner of the image display. Click and hold (do not release the mouse button) on the navigation control to display the Navigation Preview. The Navigation Preview has a miniature view of the image with the displayed area outlined. Use the Navigation Preview to quickly pan to a different part of the image—move the mouse while keeping the button pressed. The Navigation Window is often the most convenient way to quickly navigate around a large image with only a small portion displayed. (See Navigation Dialog for other ways to access the Navigation Window). (If your mouse has a middle-button, click-drag with it to pan across the image).

12. *Inactive Padding Area:* When the image dimensions are smaller than the image window, this padding area separates the active image display and the inactive padding area, so you're able to distinguish between them. You cannot apply any Filters or Operations in general to the inactive area.

13. *Image Display:* The most important part of the image window is, of course, the image display or canvas. It occupies the central area of the window, surrounded by a yellow dotted line showing the image boundary, against a neutral gray background. You can change the zoom level of the image display in a variety of ways, including the Zoom setting described below.

14. *Image Window Resize Toggle:* Without enabling this feature, if you change the size of the image window by click-and-dragging border limits, the image size and zoom does not change. If you make the window larger, for example, then you will see more of the image. If this button is pressed, however, the image resizes when the window resizes so that (mostly) the same portion of the image is displayed before and after the window is resized.

Tip

Drag and drop an image into the Toolbox window from a file browser to open the image in its own Image window or tab.

Dragging an image file into the Layer dialog adds it to the image as a new layer.

Image size and image window size can be different. You can make image fit window, and vice versa, using two keyboard shortcuts:

- Ctrl-J: this command keeps the zoom level; it adapts window size to image size. The Shrink Wrap command does the same.

- Ctrl-Shift-J: this command modifies the zoom level to adapt the image display to the window.

3.2.3 Dialogs and Docking

3.2.3.1 Organizing Dialogs

GIMP has great flexibility for arranging dialog on your screen. A "dialog" is a moving window which contains options for a tool or is dedicated to a special task. A "dock" is a container which can hold a collection of persistent dialogs, such as the Tool Options dialog, Brushes dialog, Palette dialog, etc. Docks cannot, however, hold non-persistent dialogs such as the Preferences dialog or an Image window.

GIMP has three default docks:

- the Tool Options dock under the Toolbox in the left panel,

- the Layers, Channels, Paths and Undo dock in the upper part of the right panel,

- the Brushes, Patterns and Gradients dock in the lower part of the right panel.

In these docks, each dialog is in its own tab.

In multi-window mode, the Toolbox is a *utility window* and not a dock. In single-window mode, it belongs to the single window.

Use Windows → Dockable Dialogs to view a list of dockable dialogs. Select a dockable dialog from the list to view the dialog. If the dialog is available in a dock, then it is made visible. If the dialog is not in a dock, the behavior is different in multi and single window modes:

- In multi-window mode, a new window, containing the dialog, appears on the screen.

- In single-window mode, the dialog is automatically docked to the Layers-Undo dock as a tab.

You can click-and-drag a tab and drop it in the wanted place:

- either in the tab bar of a dock, to integrate it in the dialog group,

- or on a docking bar that appears as a blue line when the mouse pointer goes over a dock border, to anchor the dialog to the dock.

In multi-window mode, you can also click on the dialog title and drag it to the wanted place.

Figure 3.7 Integrating a new dialog in a dialog group

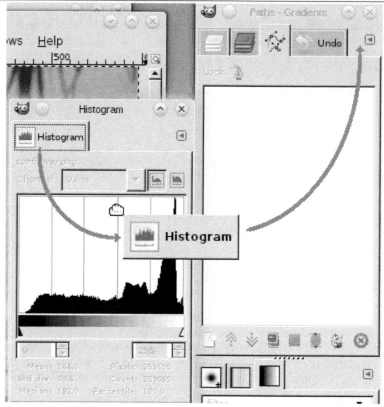

Here, in multi-window mode, the Histogram dialog was dragged to the tab bar of the Layers-Undo dock.

More simple: the **Add tab** command in the Tab menu Section 3.2.3.2.

Figure 3.8 Anchoring a dialog to a dock border

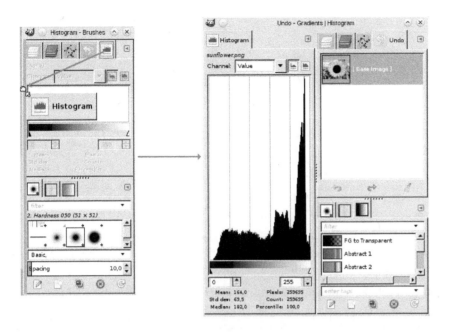

The Histogram dialog dragged to the left vertical docking bar of the right panel and the result: the dialog anchored to the left border of the right panel. This dialog now belongs to the right panel.
So, you can arrange dialogs in a **multi-column** *display, interesting if you work with two screens, one for dialogs, the other for images.*

Tip

Press **TAB** in an Image window to toggle the visibility of the docks. This is useful if the docks hide a portion of the image Window. You can quickly hide all the docks, do your work, then display all the docs again. Pressing **TAB** inside a dock to navigate through the dock.

3.2.3.2 Tab Menu

Figure 3.9 A dialog in a dock, with the Tab menu button highlighted.

In each dialog, you can access a special menu of tab-related operations by pressing the Tab Menu button, as highlighted in the figure above. Exactly which commands are shown in the menu depends on the active dialog, but they always include operations for creating new tabs, closing or detaching tabs.

Figure 3.10 The Tab menu of the Layers dialog.

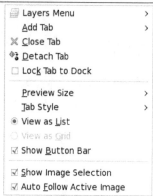

The Tab menu gives you access to the following commands:

Context Menu At the top of each Tab menu, an entry opens the dialog's context menu, which contains operations specific to that particular type of dialog. For example, the context menu for the Layers tab is Layers Menu, which contains a set of operations for manipulating layers.

Add Tab Add Tab opens into a submenu allowing you to add a large variety of dockable dialogs as new tabs.

Figure 3.11 "Add tab" sub-menu

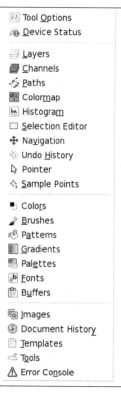

Close Tab Close the dialog. Closing the last dialog in a dock causes the dock itself to close.

Detach Tab Detach the dialog from the dock, creating a new dock with the detached dialog as its only member. It has the same effect as dragging the tab out of the dock and releasing it at a location where it cannot be docked.

It's a way to create a paradoxical new window in single-window mode!

If the tab is locked, this menu item is insensitive and grayed out.

Lock Tab to Dock Prevent the dialog from being moved or detached. When activated, Detach Tab is insensitive and grayed out.

Preview Size

Figure 3.12 Preview Size submenu of a Tab menu.

Many, but not all, dialogs have Tab menus containing a Preview Size option, which opens into a submenu giving a list of sizes for the items in the dialog (see the figure above). For example, the Brushes dialog shows pictures of all available brushes: the Preview Size determines how large the pictures are. The default is Medium.

Tab Style

Figure 3.13 Tab Style submenu of a Tab menu.

Available only when multiple dialogs are in the same dock, Tab Style opens a submenu allowing you to choose the appearance of the tabs at the top (see the figure above). There are five choices, not all are available for every dialog:

Icon Use an icon to represent the dialog type.

Current Status Is only available for dialogs that allows you to select something, such as a brush, pattern, gradient, etc. Current Status shows a representation of the currently selected item in the tab top.

Text Use text to display the dialog type.

Icon and Text Using both an icon and text results in wider tabs.

Status and Text Show the currently selected item and text with the dialog type.

View as List; View as Grid These entries are shown in dialogs that allow you to select an item from a set: brushes, patterns, fonts, etc. You can choose to view the items as a vertical list, with the name of each beside it, or as a grid, with representations of the items but no names. Each has its advantages: viewing as a list gives you more information, but viewing as a grid allows you to see more possibilities at once. The default for this varies across dialogs: for brushes and patterns, the default is a grid; for most other things, the default is a list.

When the tree-view is View as List, you can use tags. Please see Section 15.3.6.

You can also use a list search field:

Figure 3.14 The list search field.

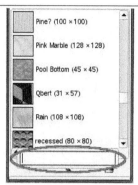

Use Ctrl-F to open the list search field. An item must be selected for this command to be effective.

The list search field automatically closes after five seconds if you do nothing.

> **Note**
>
> The search field shortcut is also available for the tree-view you get in the "Brush", "Font" or "Pattern" option of several tools.

Show Button Bar Some dialogs display a button bar on the bottom of the dialog; for example, the Patterns, Brushes, Gradients, and Images dialogs. This is a toggle. If it is checked, then the Button Bar is displayed.

Figure 3.15 Button Bar on the Brushes dialog.

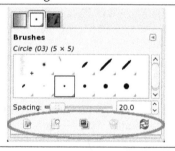

Show Image Selection This option is available in multi-window mode only. This is a toggle. If it is checked, then an Image Menu is shown at the top of the dock:

Figure 3.16 A dock with an Image Menu highlighted.

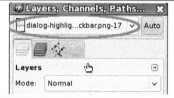

It is not available for dialogs docked below the Toolbox. This option is interesting only if you have several open images on your screen.

Auto Follow Active Image This option is available in multi-window mode only. This option is also
interesting only if you have several images open on your screen. Then, the information displayed
in a dock is always that of the selected image in the Image Selection drop-down list. If the Auto
Follow Active Image is disabled, the image can be selected only in the Image Selection. If enabled,
you can also select it by activating the image directly (clicking on its title bar).

3.3 Undoing

Almost anything you do to an image in GIMP can be undone. You can undo the most recent action
by choosing Edit → Undo from the image menu, but this is done so frequently that you really should
memorize the keyboard shortcut, Ctrl-Z.

Undoing can itself be undone. After having undone an action, you can *redo* it by choosing Edit →
Redo from the image menu, or use the keyboard shortcut, Ctrl-Y. It is often helpful to judge the effect of
an action by repeatedly undoing and redoing it. This is usually very quick, and does not consume any
extra resources or alter the undo history, so there is never any harm in it.

Caution

If you undo one or more actions and then operate on the image in any way except
by using Undo or Redo, it will no longer be possible to redo those actions: they are
lost forever. The solution to this, if it creates a problem for you, is to duplicate the
image and then test on the copy. (Do *Not* test the original, because the undo/redo
history is not copied when you duplicate an image.)

If you often find yourself undoing and redoing many steps at a time, it may be more convenient to
work with the Undo History dialog, a dockable dialog that shows you a small sketch of each point in the
Undo History, allowing you to go back or forward to that point by clicking.

Undo is performed on an image-specific basis: the "Undo History" is one of the components of an
image. GIMP allocates a certain amount of memory to each image for this purpose. You can customize
your Preferences to increase or decrease the amount, using the Environment page of the Preferences
dialog. There are two important variables: the *minimal number of undo levels*, which GIMP will maintain
regardless of how much memory they consume, and the *maximum undo memory*, beyond which GIMP
will begin to delete the oldest items from the Undo History.

Note

Even though the Undo History is a component of an image, it is not saved when
you save the image using GIMP's native XCF format, which preserves every other
image property. When the image is reopened, it will have an empty Undo History.

GIMP's implementation of Undo is rather sophisticated. Many operations require very little Undo
memory (e.g., changing visibility of a layer), so you can perform long sequences of them before they
drop out of the Undo History. Some operations, such as changing layer visibility, are *compressed*, so that
doing them several times in a row produces only a single point in the Undo History. However, there are
other operations that may consume a lot of undo memory. Most filters are implemented by plug-ins, so
the GIMP core has no efficient way of knowing what changed. As such, there is no way to implement
Undo except by memorizing the entire contents of the affected layer before and after the operation. You
might only be able to perform a few such operations before they drop out of the Undo History.

3.3.1 Things That Cannot be Undone

Most actions that alter an image can be undone. Actions that do not alter the image generally cannot
be undone. Examples include saving the image to a file, duplicating the image, copying part of the
image to the clipboard, etc. It also includes most actions that affect the image display without altering

---

the underlying image data. The most important example is zooming. There are, however, exceptions: toggling QuickMask on or off can be undone, even though it does not alter the image data.

There are a few important actions that do alter an image but cannot be undone:

Closing the image The Undo History is a component of the image, so when the image is closed and all of its resources are freed, the Undo History is gone. Because of this, unless the image has not been modified since the last time it was saved, GIMP always asks you to confirm that you really want to close the image. (You can disable this in the Environment page of the Preferences dialog; if you do, you are assuming responsibility for thinking about what you are doing.)

Reverting the image "Reverting" means reloading the image from the file. GIMP actually implements this by closing the image and creating a new image, so the Undo History is lost as a consequence. Because of this, if the image is unclean, GIMP asks you to confirm that you really want to revert the image.

"Pieces" of actions Some tools require you to perform a complex series of manipulations before they take effect, but only allow you to undo the whole thing rather than the individual elements. For example, the Intelligent Scissors require you to create a closed path by clicking at multiple points in the image, and then clicking inside the path to create a selection. You cannot undo the individual clicks: undoing after you are finished takes you all the way back to the starting point. For another example, when you are working with the Text tool, you cannot undo individual letters, font changes, etc.: undoing after you are finished removes the newly created text layer.

Filters, and other actions performed by plugins or scripts, can be undone just like actions implemented by the GIMP core, but this requires them to make correct use of GIMP's Undo functions. If the code is not correct, a plugin can potentially corrupt the Undo History, so that not only the plugin but also previous actions can no longer properly be undone. The plugins and scripts distributed with GIMP are all believed to be set up correctly, but obviously no guarantees can be given for plugins you obtain from other sources. Also, even if the code is correct, canceling a plugin while it is running may corrupt the Undo History, so it is best to avoid this unless you have accidentally done something whose consequences are going to be very harmful.

3.4 Common Tasks

This tutorial is based on text Copyright © 2004 Carol Spears. The original tutorial can be found online: [TUT02].

3.4.1 Intention

GIMP is a powerful image editing program with many options and tools. However, it is also well suited for smaller tasks. The following tutorials are meant for those who want to achieve these common tasks without having to learn all the intricacies of GIMP and computer graphics in general.

Hopefully, these tutorials will not only help you with your current task, but also get you ready to learn more complex tools and methods later, when you have the time and inspiration.

All you need to know to start this tutorial, is how to find and open your image. (File → Open from the Image window).

3.4.2 Change the Size of an Image for the screen

You have a huge image, possibly from a digital camera, and you want to resize it so that it displays nicely on a web page, online board or email message.

Figure 3.17 Example Image for Scaling

The first thing that you might notice after opening the image, is that GIMP opens the image at a logical size for viewing. If your image is very large, like the sample image, GIMP sets the zoom so that it displays nicely on the screen. The zoom level is shown in the status area at the bottom of the Image window. This does not change the actual image.

The other thing to look at in the title-bar is the mode. If the mode shows as RGB in the title bar, you are fine. If the mode says Indexed or Grayscale, read the Section 3.4.7.

Figure 3.18 GIMP Used for Image Scaling

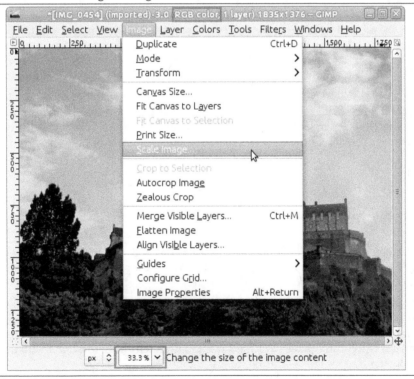

Use Image → Scale Image to open the "Scale Image" dialog. You can right click on the image to open the menu, or use the menu along the top of the Image window. Notice that the "Scale Image" menu item contains three dots, which is a hint that a dialog will be opened.

Figure 3.19 Dialog for Image Scaling in Pixels

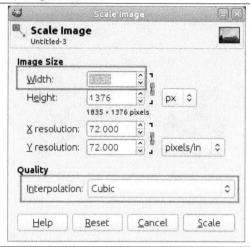

The unit of size for the purpose of displaying an image on a screen is the pixel. You can see the dialog has two sections: one for width and height and another for resolution. Resolution applies to printing only and has no effect on the image's size when it is displayed on a monitor or a mobile device. The reason is that different devices have different pixels sizes and so, an image that displays on one device (such as a smartphone) with a certain physical size, might display on other devices (such as an LCD projector) in another size altogether. For the purpose of displaying an image on a screen, you can ignore the resolution parameter. For the same reason, do not use any size unit other than the pixel in the height / width fields.

If you know the desired width, enter it in the dialog at the top where it says Width. This is shown in the figure above. If you don't have such a number in mind, choose an appropriate width for the desired use. Common screen sizes range between 320 pixels for simpler phones, 1024 pixels for a netbook, 1440 for a wide-screen PC display and 1920 pixels for an HD screen. for the purpose of displaying an image on-line, a width of 600 to 800 pixels offers a good compromise.

When you change one of the image's dimensions, GIMP changes the other dimension proportionally. To change the other dimension, see Section 3.4.5. Bear in mind that when you change the two dimensions arbitrarily, the image might become stretched or squashed.

3.4.3   Change the Size of an Image for print

As discussed before, pixels don't have a set size in the real world. When you set out to print an image on paper, GIMP needs to know how big each pixels is. We use a parameter called resolution to set the ratio between pixels and real-world units such as inches.

By default, most images open with the resolution set to 72. This number was chosen for historical reasons as it was the resolution of screens in the past, and means that when printed, every pixel is 1/72 of an inch wide. When printing images are taken with modern digital cameras, this produces very large but chunky images with visible pixels. What we want to do is tell GIMP to print it with the size we have in mind, but not alter the pixel data so as not to lose quality.

To change the print size use Image → Print Size to open the "Print Size" dialog. Select a size unit you are comfortable with, such as "inches". Set one dimension, and let GIMP change the other one proportionally. Now examine the change in resolution. If the resolution is 300 pixels per Inch or over, the printed image's quality will be very high and pixels will not be noticeable. With a resolution of between 200 and 150 ppi, pixels will be somewhat noticeable, but the image will be fine as long as its not inspected too closely. Values lower than 100 are visibly coarse and should only be used for material that is seen from a distance, such as signs or large posters.

Figure 3.20 Dialog for Setting Print Size

3.4.4 Compressing Images

Figure 3.21 Example Image for JPEG Saving

If you have images that take up a large space on disk, you can reduce that space even without changing the image dimensions. The best image compression is achieved by using the JPG format, but even if the image is already in this format, you can usually still make it take up less space, as the JPG format has an adaptive compression scheme that allows saving in varying levels of compression. The trade-off is that the less space an image takes, the more detail from the original image you lose. You should also be aware that repeated saving in the JPG format causes more and more image degradation.

To save you image as a JPG file, therefore, use File → Save As to open the "Save As" dialog.

Figure 3.22 "Save As" Dialog

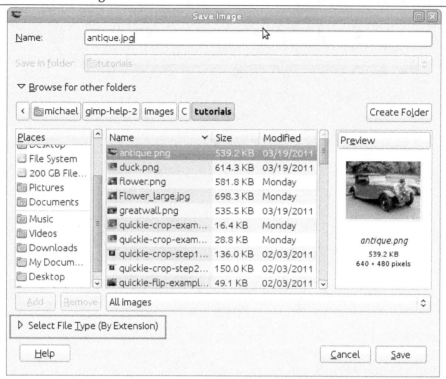

The dialog opens with the file name already typed in the Name box. If the image is not a JPG image, delete the existing extension and type JPG instead, and GIMP will determine the file type from the file extension. Use the file extension list, circled in the figure above, to see the types supported by GIMP. The supported extensions change depending on your installed libraries. If GIMP complains, or if "JPEG" is grayed out in the Extensions menu, cancel out of everything and step through the Section 3.4.7. Once you have done this, click Save. This opens the "Save as" " JPEG dialog that contains the quality control.

The "Save as JPEG" dialog uses default values that reduce size while retaining good visual quality; this is the safest and quickest thing to do.

Figure 3.23 "Save as JPEG" dialog with poor quality.

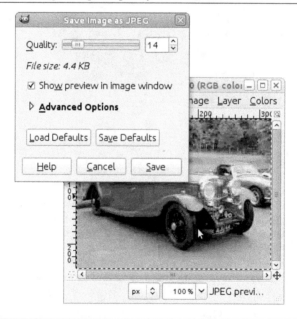

Reduce the image Quality to make the image even smaller. Reduced quality degrades the image, so be certain to check "Show preview in image window" to visually gauge the degradation. As shown in the figure above, a Quality setting of 10 produces a very poor quality image that uses very little disk space. The figure below shows a more reasonable image. A quality of 75 produces a reasonable image using much less disk space, which will, in turn, load much faster on a web page. Although the image is somewhat degraded, it is acceptable for the intended purpose.

Figure 3.24 Dialog for Image Saving as JPEG

Finally, here is a comparison of the same picture with varying degrees of compression:

Figure 3.25 Example for High JPEG Compression

(a) *Quality: 10; Size: 3.4 KiloBytes*   (b) *Quality: 40; Size: 9.3 KiloBytes*

Figure 3.26 Example for Moderate JPEG Compression

(a) *Quality: 70; Size: 15.2 KiloBytes*   (b) *Quality: 100; Size: 72.6 KiloBytes*

3.4.5   Crop An Image

Figure 3.27 Example Image for Cropping

(a) *Source image*   (b) *Image after cropping*

There are many reasons to crop an image; for example, fitting an image to fill a frame, removing a portion of the background to emphasize the subject, etc. There are two methods to activate the crop tool. Click the ✐ button in the Toolbox, or use Tools → Transform Tools → Crop in the image window. This changes the cursor and allow you to click and drag a rectangular shape. The button in the toolbox is the easiest way to get to any of the tools.

Figure 3.28 Select a Region to Crop

Click on one corner of the desired crop area and drag your mouse to create the crop rectangle. You don't have to be accurate as you can change the exact shape of the rectangle later.

Figure 3.29 Dialog for Cropping

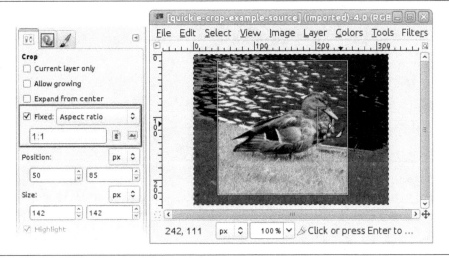

After completing the click and drag motion, a rectangle with special regions is shown on the canvas. As the cursor is moved over the different areas of the selected crop area, the cursor changes. You can then drag the rectangle's corners or edges to change the dimensions of the selected area. As shown in the figure above, as the crop area is resized, the dimensions and ratio are shown in the status bar. See Section 14.4.4 for more information on cropping in GIMP. If you would like to crop the image in a specific aspect ratio, such as a square, make sure the tool options are visible (Windows → Dockable Dialogs → Tool Options). In the Tool Options dockable, check the mark next to Fixed and make sure the drop-down box next to it is set to Aspect Ratio. You can now type the desired aspect ratio on the text box below, such as "1:1". You also have controls to change the aspect from landscape to portrait. After you set the aspect ratio, drag one of the corners of the crop rectangle to update it. The rectangle changes to the chosen ratio, and when you drag it should maintain that ratio.

3.4.6 Find Info About Your Image

Figure 3.30 Finding Info

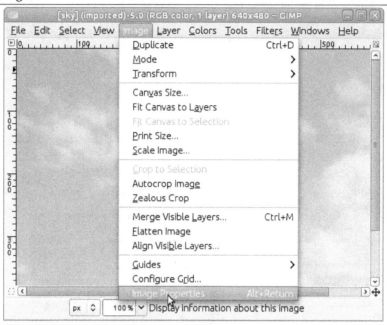

When you need to find out information about your image, Use Image → Image Properties to open the "Image Properties" dialog, which contains information about the image size, resolution, mode and much more.

Figure 3.31 "Image Properties" Dialog

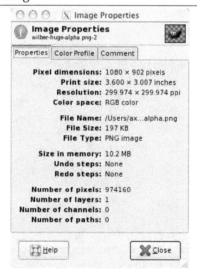

3.4.7 Change the Mode

As with anything else, images come in different kinds and serve different purposes. Sometimes, a small size is important (for web sites) and at other times, retaining a high color depth (e.g., a family portrait) is what you want. GIMP can handle all of this, and more, primarily by converting between three fundamental modes, as seen in this menu. In order to switch your image to one of these modes, you open it and follow that menu and click the mode you want.

Figure 3.32 Dialog for changing the mode

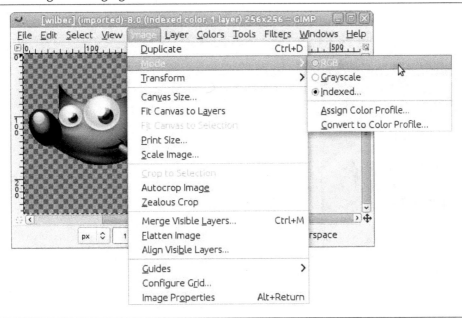

RGB- This is the default mode, used for high-quality images, and able to display millions of colors. This is also the mode for most of your image work including scaling, cropping, and even flipping. In RGB mode, each pixel consists of three different components: R->Red, G->Green, B->Blue. Each of these in turn can have an intensity value of 0-255. What you see at every pixel is an additive combination of these three components.

Indexed- This is the mode usually used when file size is of concern, or when you are working with images with few colors. It involves using a fixed number of colors (256 or less) for the entire image to represent colors. By default, when you change an image to a palleted image, GIMP generates an "optimum palette" to best represent your image.

Figure 3.33 Dialog "Change to Indexed Colors"

As you might expect, since the information needed to represent the color at each pixel is less, the file size is smaller. However, sometimes, there are options in the various menus that are grayed-out for no apparent reason. This usually means that the filter or option cannot be applied when your image is in its current mode. Changing the mode to RGB, as outlined above, should solve this issue. If RGB mode doesn't work either, perhaps the option you're trying requires your layer to have the ability to be transparent. This can be done just as easily via Layer → Transparency → Add Alpha Channel.

Figure 3.34 Add Alpha Channel

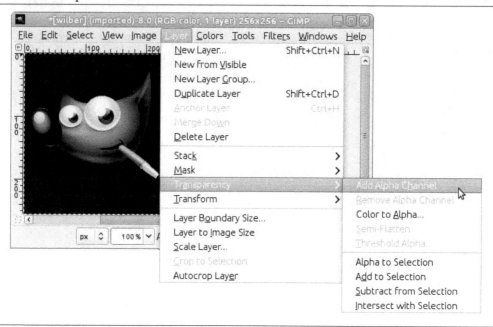

Grayscale- Grayscale images have only shades of gray. This mode has some specific uses and takes less space on the hard drive in some formats, but is not recommended for general use as reading it is not supported by many applications.

There is no need to convert an image to a specific mode before saving it in your favorite format, as GIMP is smart enough to properly export the image.

3.4.8 Flip An Image

Use this option when you need the person in the photo looking in the other direction, or you need the top of the image to be the bottom. Use Tools → Transform Tools → Flip , or use the button on the toolbox. After selecting the flip tool from the toolbox, click inside the canvas. Controls in the Tool Options dockable let you switch between Horizontal and Vertical modes.

Figure 3.35 Dialog "Flip an Image"

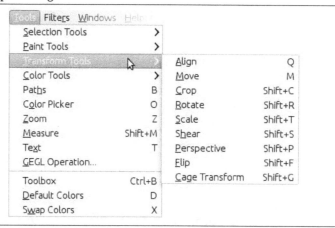

After selecting the flip tool from the toolbox, click inside the canvas. The tool flips the image horizontally. Use the options dialog to switch between horizontal and vertical. If it is not already displayed in the dock under the toolbox, double click the toolbox button. You can also use the **Ctrl** key to switch between horizontal and vertical.

In the images below, all possible flips are demonstrated:

Figure 3.36 Example Image to Flip

Source image

Horizontal flipped image

Vertical flipped image

Horizontal and vertical flipped image

3.4.9 Rotate An Image

Figure 3.37 Menu for "Rotate An Image"

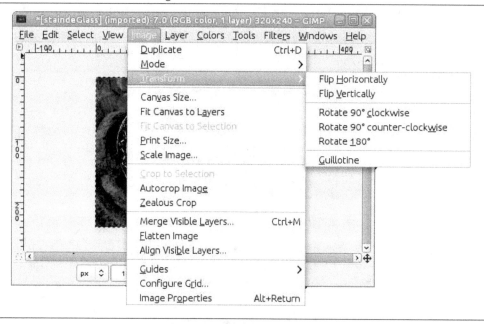

Images that are taken with digital cameras sometimes need to be rotated. To do this, use Image →
Transform → Rotate 90° clockwise (or counter-clockwise). The images below demonstrate a 90 degrees
CCW rotation.

Figure 3.38 Example for "Rotate An Image"

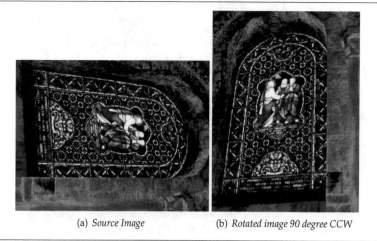

(a) *Source Image*   (b) *Rotated image 90 degree CCW*

3.4.10 Separating an Object From Its Background

Figure 3.39 Object with Background

Sometimes you need to separate the subject of an image from its background. You may want to have the subject on a flat color, or keep the background transparent so you can use it on an existing background, or any other thing you have in mind. To do this, you must first use GIMP's selection tools to draw a selection around your subject. This is not an easy task, and selecting the correct tool is crucial. You have several tools to accomplish this.

The "Free Select Tool" allows you to draw a border using either freehand or straight lines. Use this when the subject has a relatively simple shape. Read more about this tool here: Section 14.2.4

Figure 3.40 Free Select Tool

The "Intelligent Scissors Select Tool" lets you select a freehand border and uses edge-recognition algorithms to better fit the border around the object. Use this when the subject is complex but distinct enough against its current background. Read more about this tool here: Section 14.2.7

Figure 3.41 Intelligent Scissors Select Tool

The "Foreground Select Tool" lets you mark areas as "Foreground" or "Background" and refines the selection automatically. Read more about this tool here: Section 14.2.8

Figure 3.42 Foreground Select Tool

Once you have selected your subject successfully, use Select → Invert. Now, instead of the subject, the background is selected. What you do now depends on what you intended to do with the background.

- To fill the background with a single color:

  Click the foreground color swatch (the top left of the two overlapping colored rectangles) in the toolbox and select the desired color. Next, use Section 14.3.4 to replace the background with your chosen color.

Figure 3.43 Result of Adding a Plain Color Background

- To make a transparent background:

  Use Layer → Transparence → Add Alpha Channel to add an alpha channel. Next, use Edit Clear or hit the **Del** key on the keyboard to remove the background. Please note that only a small subset of file formats support transparent areas. Your best bet is to save your image as PNG.

Figure 3.44 Result of Adding a Transparent Background

- To make a black-and-white background while keeping the subject in color:

  Use Colors → Desaturate. In the dialog that opens, cycle between the modes and select the best-looking one, then click OK.

Figure 3.45 Result of Desaturating the Background

3.5 How to Draw Straight Lines

This tutorial is based on Text and images Copyright © 2002 Seth Burgess. The original tutorial can be found in the Internet [TUT01].

3.5.1 Intention

Figure 3.46 Example of straight lines

This tutorial shows you how to draw straight lines with GIMP. Forcing a line to be straight is a convenient way to deal with the imprecision of a mouse or tablet, and to take advantage of the power of a computer to make things look neat and orderly. This tutorial doesn't use Straight Lines for complex tasks; its intended to show how you can use it to create quick and easy straight lines.

1. Preparations

Figure 3.47 Introducing the **Shift**-key

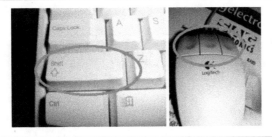

The invention called the typewriter introduced the **Shift** Key. You generally have 2 of them on your keyboard. They look something like the figure above. The keys are located on the left and right sides of your keyboard. The mouse was invented by Douglas C. Engelbart in 1970. These come in different varieties, but always have at least one button.

2. Creating a Blank Drawable

Figure 3.48 New image

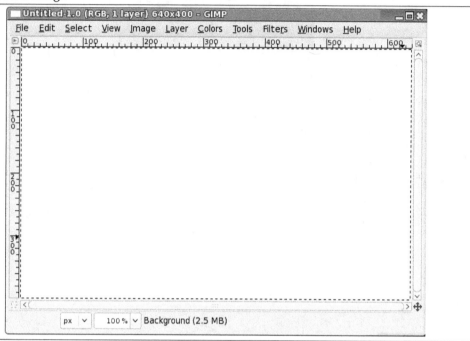

First, create a new image. Any size will do. Use File → New to create a new image.

3. Choose a Tool

Figure 3.49 Paint tools in the toolbox

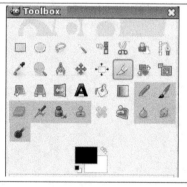

Any of the red-highlighted tools on the above toolbox can do lines.

4. Create a Starting Point

Figure 3.50 Starting point

Click on the paintbrush in the toolbox. Click in the image where you want a line to start or end. A single dot will appear on the screen. The size of this dot represents the current brush size, which you can change in the Brush Dialog (see Section 15.3.2).Now, lets start drawing a line. Hold down the **Shift** key, and keep it down.

5. Drawing the Line

Figure 3.51 Drawing the line

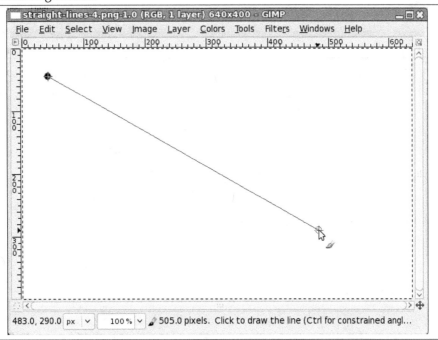

After you have a starting point and while pressing the **Shift**, you will see a straight line that follows the cursor. Press the first button on the Mouse (the leftmost one usually) and let it go. During that whole "click" of the Mouse button, you need to keep the **Shift** Key held down.

6. Final

Figure 3.52 Final Image

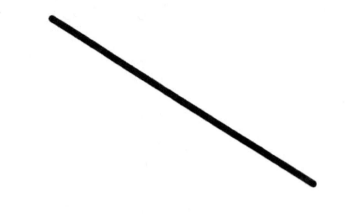

This is a powerful feature. You can draw straight lines with any of the draw tools. You can even draw more lines at the end of this one. Our last step is to let go of the **Shift** key. And there you have it. Some more examples are shown below. Happy GIMPing!

3.5.2 Examples

Figure 3.53 Examples I

(a) *Check Use color from gradient.*   (b) *Select the Clone tool and set the source to "Maple Leaves" pattern.*

Figure 3.54 Examples II

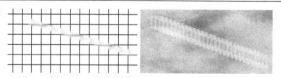

(a) *Use Filters → Render → Pattern → Grid to create a grid. Use the Smudge Tool to draw a cool line with a slightly larger brush.*   (b) *Use Filters → Render → Clouds → Plasma to create the plasma cloud. Use the Erase Tool with a square brush to draw a line.*

Figure 3.55 Example III

Use the rectangle select tool to select a rectangle, and then fill the selection with a light blue color. Select the dodge/burn tool. Set the type to Dodge and paint along the top and left side using an appropriately sized brush. Set the type to Burn and paint along the right and bottom.

Chapter 4

Getting Unstuck

4.1 Getting Unstuck

4.1.1 Stuck!

All right, okay: you're stuck. You're trying to use one of the tools on an image, and nothing is happening, and nothing you try makes any difference. Your fists are starting to clench, and your face is starting to feel warm. Are you going to have to kill the program, and lose all your work? This sucks!

Well, hold on a second. This happens pretty frequently, even to people who've used GIMP for a long time, but generally the cause is not so hard to figure out (and fix) if you know where to look. Lets be calm, and go through a checklist that will probably get you GIMPing happily again.

4.1.2 Common Causes of GIMP Non-Responsiveness

4.1.2.1 There is a floating selection

Figure 4.1 Layers dialog showing a floating selection.

How to tell: If there is a floating selection, many actions are impossible until the floating section is anchored. To check, look at the Layers dialog (making sure it's set to the image you're working on) and see whether the top layer is called "Floating Selection".

How to solve: Either anchor the floating selection, or convert it into an ordinary (non-floating) layer. If you need help on how to do this, see Floating Selections.

4.1.2.2   The selection is hidden

Figure 4.2 Unstuck show selection menu

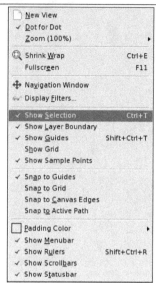

In the View menu, make sure that "Show Selection" is checked.

How to tell: If this is the problem, merely reading this will already have made you realize it, probably, but to explain in any case: sometimes the flickering line that outlines the selection is annoying because it makes it hard to see important details of the image, so GIMP gives you the option of hiding the selection, by unchecking Show Selection in the View menu. It is easy to forget that you have done this, though.

How to fix: If this hasn't rung any bells, it isn't the problem, and if it has, you probably know how to fix it, because it doesn't happen unless you explicitly tell it to; but anyway: just go to the View menu for the image and, if Show Selection is unchecked, click on it..

4.1.2.3   You are acting outside of the selection

Figure 4.3 Unstuck select all

Click "All" in the Select menu to make sure that everything is selected.

How to fix: If doing this has destroyed a selection that you wanted to keep, hit Ctrl-Z (undo) a couple of times to restore it, and then we'll figure out what the problem is. There are a couple of possibilities. If you couldn't see any selection, there may have been a very tiny one, or even one that contained no pixels. If this was the case, it surely is not a selection that you wanted to keep, so why have you gotten this far in the first place? If you can see a selection but thought you were inside it, it might be inverted from what you think. The easiest way to tell is to hit the Quick Mask button: the selected area will be clear and the unselected area will be masked. If this was the problem, then you can solve it by toggling Quick Mask off and choosing Invert in the Select menu.

4.1.2.4   The active drawable is not visible

Figure 4.4 Unstuck layer invisibility

Layers dialog with visibility off for the active layer.

How to tell: The Layers dialog gives you ability to toggle the visibility of each layer on or off. Look at the Layers dialog, and see if the layer you are trying to act on is active (i.e., darkened) and has an eye symbol to the left of it. If not, this is your problem.

    How to fix: If your intended target layer is not active, click on it in the Layers dialog to activate it. (If none of the layers are active, the active drawable might be a channel -- you can look at the Channels tab in the Layers dialog to see. This does not change the solution, though.) If the eye symbol does not appear, click in the Layers dialog at the left edge to toggle it: this should make the layer visible. See the Help section for the Layers Dialog if you need more help.

4.1.2.5   The active drawable is transparent

Figure 4.5 Unstuck layer transparency

Layers dialog with opacity set to zero for the active layer.

How to tell: When the opacity is set 0 on the layer, you cannot see anything which you draw on it. Look the Opacity slider, and see which side the slider placed at. If it is at the leftmost side, that is your problem.

    How to fix: Move the slider.

4.1.2.6   You are trying to act outside the layer

How to tell: In GIMP, layers don't need to have the same dimensions as the image: they can be larger or smaller. If you try to paint outside the borders of a layer, nothing happens. To see if this is happening, look for a black-and-yellow dashed rectangle that does not enclose the area you're trying to draw at.

How to fix: You need to enlarge the layer. There are two commands at the bottom of the Layer menu that will let you do this: Layer to Image Size, which sets the layer bounds to match the image borders; and Layer Boundary Size, which brings up a dialog that allows you to set the layer dimensions to whatever you please.

4.1.2.7   The image is in indexed color mode.

*How to tell:*GIMP can handle three different color modes: RGB(A), Indexed and Grayscale. The indexed colormode uses a colormap, where all used colors on the image are indexed. The color picker in GIMP however, let you choose RGB colors. That means, if you try to paint with a different color than it is indexed in the colormap, you end up in very undetermined results (e.g. it paints with the wrong color or you can't paint).

How to fix: Always use the RGB Color mode to paint on images. You can verify and select another color mode from the Mode menuitem in the Image menu.

Part II

How do I Become a GIMP Wizard?

Chapter 5

Getting Images into GIMP

This chapter is about getting images into GIMP. It explains how to create new images, how to load images from files, how to scan them and how to make screenshots.

But first we want to introduce you to the general structure of images in GIMP.

5.1 Image Types

It is tempting to think of an *image* as something that corresponds with a single display window, or to a single file such as a JPEG file. In reality, however, a GIMP image is a a complicated structure, containing a stack of layers plus several other types of objects: a selection mask, a set of channels, a set of paths, an "undo" history, etc. In this section we take a detailed look at the components of a GIMP image, and the things that you can do with them.

The most basic property of an image is its *mode*. There are three possible modes: RGB, grayscale, and indexed. RGB stands for Red-Green-Blue, and indicates that each point in the image is represented by a "red" level, a "green" level, and a "blue" level; representing a full-color image. Each color channel has 256 possible intensity levels. More details in Color Models

In a grayscale image, each point is represented by a brightness value, ranging from 0 (black) to 255 (white), with intermediate values representing different levels of gray.

Figure 5.1 Components of the RGB and CMY Color Model

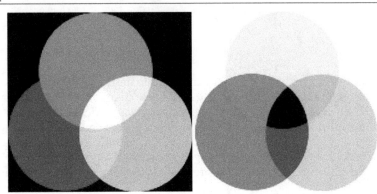

(a) *In the RGB Color Model, mixing Red, Green and Blue gives White, which is what happens on your screen.*

(b) *In the CMY(K) color model, mixing Cyan, Magenta and Yellow gives Black, which is what happens when you print on a white paper. The printer will actually use the black cartridge for economical reasons and better color rendering.*

Conceptually, the difference between a grayscale image and an RGB image is the number of "color channels": a grayscale image has one; an RGB image has three. An RGB image can be thought of as three superimposed grayscale images, one colored red, one green, and one blue.

Actually, both RGB and grayscale images have one additional color channel called the *alpha* channel, which represents opacity. When the alpha value at a given location in a given layer is zero, the layer is completely transparent (you can see through it), and the color at that location is determined by what lies underneath. When alpha is maximal (255), the layer is opaque (you cannot see through it), and the color is determined by the color of the layer. Intermediate alpha values correspond to varying degrees of transparency / opacity: the color at the location is a proportional mixture of color from the layer and color from underneath.

Figure 5.2 Example of an image in RGB and Grayscale mode

(a) *An image in RGB mode, with the channels corresponding to Red, Green and Blue.* (b) *An image in Grayscale mode, with the channel corresponding to Luminosity.*

In GIMP, every color channel, including the alpha channel, has a range of possible values from 0 to 255; in computing terminology, a depth of 8 bits. Some digital cameras can produce image files with a depth of 16 bits per color channel. GIMP cannot load such a file without losing resolution. In most cases the effects are too subtle to be detected by the human eye, but in some cases, mainly where there are large areas with slowly varying color gradients, the difference may be perceptible.

Figure 5.3 Example of an image with alpha channel

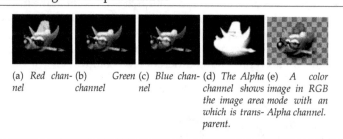

(a) *Red channel* (b) *Green channel* (c) *Blue channel* (d) *The Alpha channel shows the image area which is transparent.* (e) *A color image in RGB mode with an Alpha channel.*

The third type, *indexed* images, is a bit more complicated to understand. In an indexed image, only a limited set of discrete colors are used, usually 256 or less. These colors form the "colormap" of the image, and each point in the image is assigned a color from the colormap. Indexed images have the advantage that they can be represented inside a computer in a way which consumes relatively little memory, and back in the dark ages (say, ten years ago), they were very commonly used. As time goes on, they are used less and less, but they are still important enough to be worth supporting in GIMP. (Also, there are a few important kinds of image manipulation that are easier to implement with indexed images than with continuous-color RGB images.)

Some very commonly used types of files (including GIF and PNG) produce indexed images when they are opened in GIMP. Many of GIMP's tools don't work very well on indexed images–and many filters don't work at all–because of the limited number of colors available. Because of this, it is usually best to convert an image to RGB mode before working on it. If necessary, you can convert it back to indexed mode when you are ready to save it

GIMP makes it easy to convert from one image type to another, using the Mode command in the Image menu. Some types of conversions, of course (RGB to grayscale or indexed, for example) lose information that cannot be regained by converting back in the other direction.

> **Note**
>
>
> If you are trying to use a filter on an image, and it appears grayed out in the menu, usually the cause is that the image (or, more specifically, the layer) you are working on is the wrong type. Many filters can't be used on indexed images. Some can be used only on RGB images, or only on grayscale images. Some also require the presence or absence of an alpha channel. Usually the fix is to convert the image to a different type, most commonly RGB.

5.2 Creating new Files

Use File → New to open the Create a new image dialog. Modify the initial width and height of the file or use the standard values, then create a new image file. More information about the Create a new image dialog can be found in Section 16.2.2.

5.3 Opening Files

There are several ways of opening an existing image in GIMP:

5.3.1 Open File

The most obvious way to open an existing image is the menu. Use File → Open to open the Open Image dialog,allowing you to navigate to the file and click on its name. This method works well if you know the name and location of the file you want to open. Although the Open Image dialog does have a preview pane, it is not convenient (easy) to find an image based on a thumbnail.

> **Note**
>
>
> While opening a file, GIMP must determine the file type. Unfortunately, the file extension, such as .jpg, is not reliable: file extensions vary from system to system; any file can be renamed to have any extension; and there are many reasons why a file name might lack an extension. GIMP first tries to recognize a file by examining its contents: most of the commonly used file formats have "magic headers" that permit them to be recognized. Only if the magic yields no result does GIMP resort to using the extension.

Figure 5.4 The "Open Image" dialog

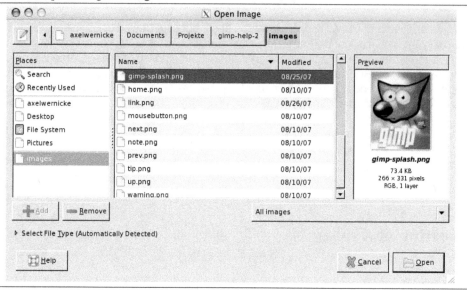

GIMP 2.2 introduced a new Open Image dialog that provides several features to help you navigate quickly to a file. Perhaps the most important is the ability to create "bookmarks", or Places, for folders that you use often. Your list of bookmarks appears on the left side of the dialog. The ones at the top, such as "Desktop", are provided automatically. Use the the Add button to add the current directory to the list. Use the Remove button to remove the selected bookmark. Double-click on a bookmark to navigate directly to that directory.

The center of the dialog contains a listing of the contents of the selected directory. Subdirectories are shown at the top of the list, files below them. By default, all files in the directory are listed, but you can restrict the listing to image files of a specific type using the File Type selection menu that appears beneath the directory listing.

When you select an image file entry in the listing, a preview appears on the right side of the dialog, along with some basic information about the image. Note that previews are cached when they are generated, and there are some things you can do that may cause a preview to be incorrect. If you suspect that this may be happening, you can force a new preview to be generated by holding down the **Ctrl** key and clicking in the Preview area.

By default, a Location text box is present in the File Open dialog. It may be absent: the Ctrl-L key combination toggles this text box. Alternatively, you can click on the icon of the paper and pencil in the upper left corner to toggle the text box.

Note

If you select a file name from the list, and click the "Open" button in the lower right corner or the dialog, it is almost always true that GIMP will automatically determine the file type for you. On rare occasions, mainly if the file type is unusual and the name lacks a meaningful extension, GIMP may fail to correctly identify the file type. Use Select File Type at the bottom of the dialog to manually specify the file type if this is required. More commonly, though, if GIMP fails to open an image file, it is either corrupt or not a supported format.

5.3.2 Open Location

If instead of a file name, you have a URI (i.e., a web address) for the image, you can open it using the menu, by choosing File → Open Location... from an image menu. This brings up a small dialog that allows you to enter (or paste) the URI.

Figure 5.5 The "Open Location" dialog

The "Open Location" dialog.

5.3.3 Open Recent

The easiest way to open an image that was recently open in GIMP, may be using File → Open Recent. This displays a scrollable list of the mostly recently opened images with icons beside them. Select and open the desired image.

5.3.4 Using External Programs

GIMP uses plugins for reading and writing all file formats except XCF. These plugins may use external libraries or programs. For example, GIMP does not directly support PostScript. Instead, for reading (or writing) PostScript files (file extension .ps or .eps), GIMP requires a powerful free software program called Ghostscript.

5.3.4.1 Installing Ghostscript

Linux distributions almost always come with Ghostscript already installed (not necessarily the most recent version). For other operating systems, you may have to install it yourself. Here are instructions for installing it on Windows:

- Go to the Ghostscript project page on Sourceforge [GHOSTSCRIPT].

- Look for the package gnu-gs or ghostscript (for non-commercial use only) and go to the download section.

- Download one of the prepared Windows distributions, such as gs650w32.exe or gs700w32.exe.

- Start the executable and follow the instructions for the installation procedure.

- Set the GS_PROG environment variable to the full file name of the gswin32c binary (e.g. C:\\gs\\gsX.YY\\bin\\gswin32c.exe).

Now you should be able to read PostScript files with GIMP. Please note that you must not move the Ghostscript directories once the installation is complete. The installation creates registry entries which allow Ghostscript to find its libraries. (These instructions courtesy of http://www.kirchgessner.net.)

5.3.5 File Manager

If you have associated an image file type with GIMP, either when you installed GIMP or later, then you can navigate to the file using a file manager (such as Nautilus or Konqueror in Linux, or Windows Explorer in Windows), and once you have found it, double-click on the file. If properly configured, the image will open in GIMP.

5.3.6 Drag and Drop

Drag and drop a file onto the GIMP Toolbox to open the file. Drag an image into an open GIMP image to add dropped file as a new layer, or set of layers, to the already open image.

Many applications support dragging and dropping an image into GIMP; for example, drag an image from Firefox and drop it onto GIMP's toolbox.

5.3.7   Copy and Paste

Use File → Create → From Clipboard to create a new image from the clipboard; alternatively, you can use Edit → Past as → New image. Many applications support copying an image to the clipboard that can then be pasted into GIMP. Many operating systems support copying screens to the clipboard. **Print Screen** typically copies the screen to the clipboard, and ALT-Print Screen copies only the active window. Print screen is not universally supported, and just because your operating system can copy an image to the clipboard, does not mean that GIMP can use the image from the clipboard. Your best bet is to try it and see if it works.

5.3.8   Image Browser

Linux supports an image-management application named gThumb. Besides being an excellent image browser, you can right click an image, choose Open with, then select GIMP from the list of options. You can also drag an image from gThumb onto the GIMP toolbox. See the gThumb home page [GTHUMB] for more information. Other similar applications are : GQview [GQVIEW], and XnView [XNVIEW].

Chapter 6

Getting Images out of GIMP

6.1 Files

GIMP is capable of reading and writing a large variety of graphics file formats. With the exception of GIMP's native XCF file type, file handling is done by Plugins. Thus, it is relatively easy to extend GIMP to support new file types when the need arises.

6.1.1 Save / Export Images

> **Note**
>
> In former GIMP releases, when you loaded an image in some format, let us say JPG or PNG, the image kept its format and was saved in the same format by **Save**. With GIMP-2.8, images are loaded, imported, in the XCF format as a new project. For example, a "sunflower.png" image will be loaded as "*[sunflower] (imported)-1.0 (indexed color, 1 layer)". The leading asterisk indicates that this file has been changed. This image will be saved as "sunflower.xcf" by **Save**. To save this image in a format other than XCF, you must use **Export**.

When you are finished working with an image, you will want to save the results. (In fact, it is often a good idea to save at intermediate stages too: GIMP is a pretty robust program, but we have heard rumors, possibly apocryphal, that it may have been known on rare and mysterious occasions to crash.) Most of the file formats that GIMP can open, can also be used for saving. There is one file format that is special, though: XCF is GIMP's native format, and is useful because it stores *everything* about an image (well, almost everything; it does not store "undo" information). Thus, the XCF format is especially suitable for saving intermediate results, and for saving images to be re-opened later in GIMP. XCF files are not readable by most other programs that display images, so once you have finished, you will probably also want to export the image in a more widely used format, such as JPEG, PNG, TIFF, etc.

6.1.2 File Formats

There are several commands for *saving* images. A list, and information on how to use them, can be found in the section covering the File Menu.

GIMP allows you to *export* the images you create in a wide variety of formats. It is important to realize that the only format capable of saving *all* of the information in an image, including layers, transparency, etc., is GIMP's native XCF format. Every other format preserves some image properties and loses others. It is up to you to understand the capabilities of the format you choose.

Exporting an image does not modify the image itself, so you do not lose anything by exporting. See Export file.

Note

When you close an image (possibly by quitting GIMP), you are warned if the image is "dirty"; that is, if it has been changed without subsequently being saved (an asterisk is in front of the image name).

Figure 6.1 Closing warning

Saving an image in any file format will cause the image to be considered "not dirty", even if the file format does not represent all of the information from the image.

6.1.2.1   Export Image as GIF

Figure 6.2 The GIF Export dialog

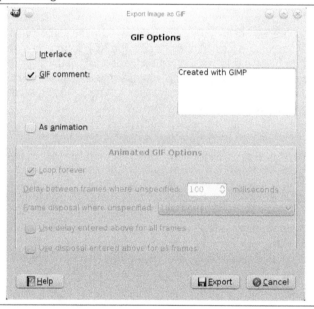

Warning

 The GIF file format does not support some basic image properties such as *print resolution*. If you care for these properties, use a different file format like PNG.

GIF Options

Interlace Checking interlace allows an image on a web page to be progressively displayed as it is downloaded. Progressive image display is useful with slow connection speeds, because you can stop an image that is of no interest; interlace is of less use today with our faster connection speeds.

GIF comment GIF comments support only 7-bit ASCII characters. If you use a character outside the 7-bit ASCII set, GIMP will export the image without a comment, and then inform you that the comment was not saved.

Animated GIF Options

Loop forever When this option is checked, the animation will play repeatedly until you stop it.

Delay between frames where unspecified You can set the delay, in milliseconds, between frames if it has not been set before. In this case, you can modify every delay in the Layer Dialog.

Frame disposal where unspecified If this has not been set before, you can set how frames will be superimposed. You can select among three options :

- I don't care: you can use this option if all your layers are opaque. Layers will overwrite what is beneath.
- Cumulative Layers (combine): previous frames will not be deleted when a new one is displayed.
- One frame per layer (replace): previous frames will be deleted before displaying a new frame.

Use delay entered above for all frames Self-explanatory.

Use disposal entered above for all frames Self-explanatory.

6.1.2.2 Export Image as JPEG

JPEG files usually have an extension .jpg, .JPG, or .jpeg. It is a very widely used format, because it compresses images very efficiently, while minimizing the loss of image quality. No other format comes close to achieving the same level of compression. It does not, however, support transparency or multiple layers.

Figure 6.3 The JPEG Export dialog

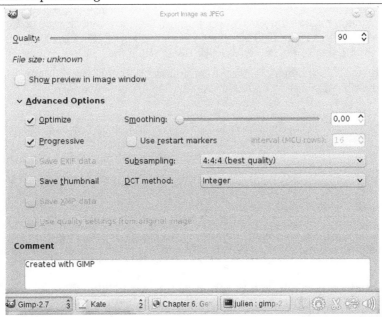

The JPEG algorithm is quite complex, and involves a bewildering number of options, whose meaning is beyond the scope of this documentation. Unless you are a JPEG expert, the Quality parameter is probably the only one you will need to adjust.

Quality When you save a file in JPEG format, a dialog is displayed that allows you to set the Quality level, which ranges from 0 to 100. Values above 95 are generally not useful, though. The default quality of 85 usually produces excellent results, but in many cases it is possible to set the quality substantially lower without noticeably degrading the image. You can test the effect of different quality settings by checking Show Preview in image window in the JPEG dialog.

> Note
>
> Please note, that the numbers for the JPEG quality level have a different meaning in different applications. Saving with a quality level of 80 in GIMP is not necessarily comparable with saving with a quality level of 80 in a different application.

Preview in image window Checking this option causes each change in quality (or any other JPEG parameter) to be shown in the image display. (This does not alter the image: the image reverts back to its original state when the JPEG dialog is closed.)

Advanced settings Some information about the advanced settings:

Optimize If you enable this option, the optimization of entropy encoding parameters will be used. The result is typically a smaller file, but it takes more time to generate.

Progressive With this option enabled, the image chunks are stored in the file in an order that allows progressive image refinement during a slow connection web download. The progressive option for JPG has the same purpose as the interlace option for GIF. Unfortunately, the progressive option produces slightly larger JPG files (than without the progressive option).

Save EXIF data JPEG files from many digital cameras contain extra information, called EXIF data. EXIF data provides information about the image such as camera make and model, image size, image date, etc. Although GIMP uses the "libexif" library to read and write EXIF data, the library is not automatically packaged with GIMP. If GIMP was built with libexif support, then EXIF data is preserved if you open a JPEG file, work with the resulting image, and then export it as JPEG. The EXIF data is not altered in any way when you do this. The EXIF data may indicate things such as image creation time and file name, which may no longer be correct. If GIMP was not built with EXIF support, you can still open JPG files containing EXIF data, but the EXIF data is ignored, and will not be saved when the resulting image is later exported.

Save thumbnail This option lets you save a thumbnail with the image. Many applications use the small thumbnail image as a quickly available small preview image.

> Note
>
> This option is present only if GIMP was built with EXIF support.

Save XMP data XMP data is "meta" data about the image; it is a competing format with EXIF. If you enable this option, the meta data of the image is saved in an XMP-structure within the file.

Use quality settings from original image If a particular quality setting (or "quantization table") was attached to the image when it was loaded, then this option allows you to use them instead of the standard ones.

If you have only made a few changes to the image, then re-using the same quality setting will give you almost the same quality and file size as the original image. This will minimize the losses caused by the quantization step, compared to what would happen if you used different quality setting.

If the quality setting found in the original file are not better than your default quality settings, then the option "Use quality settings from original image" will be available but not enabled. This ensures that you always get at least the minimum quality specified in your defaults. If you did not make major changes to the image and you want to save it using the same quality as the original, then you can do it by enabling this option.

Smoothing JPG compression creates artifacts. By using this option, you can smooth the image when saving, reducing them. But your image becomes somewhat blurred.

Restart markers The image file can include markers which allow the image to be loaded as segments. If a connection is broken while loading the image in a web page, loading can resume from the next marker.

Subsampling The human eye is not sensitive in the same way over the entire color spectrum. The compression can use this to treat slightly different colors that the eye perceives as very close, as identical colors. Three methods are available :

- 1x1,1x1,1x1 (best quality): Commonly referred to as (4:4:4), this produces the best quality, preserving borders and contrasting colors, but compression is less.
- 2x1,1x1,1x1 (4:2:2): This is the standard subsampling, which usually provides a good ratio between image quality and file size. There are situations, however, in which using no subsampling (4:4:4) provides a noticeable increase in the image quality; for example, when the image contains fine details such as text over a uniform background, or images with almost-flat colors.
- 1x2,1x1,1x1 This is similar to (2x1,1x1,1x1), but the chroma sampling is in the horizontal direction rather than the vertical direction; as if someone rotated an image.
- 2x2,1x1,1x1 (smallest file): Commonly referred to as (4:1:1), this produces the smallest files. This suits images with weak borders but tends to denature colors.

DCT Method DCT is "discrete cosine transform", and it is the first step in the JPEG algorithm going from the spatial to the frequency domain. The choices are "float", "integer" (the default), and "fast integer".

- float: The float method is very slightly more accurate than the integer method, but is much slower unless your machine has very fast floating-point hardware. Also note that the results of the floating-point method may vary slightly across machines, while the integer methods should give the same results everywhere.
- integer (the default): This method is faster than "float", but not as accurate.
- fast integer: The fast integer method is much less accurate than the other two.

Image comments In this text box, you can enter a comment which is saved with the image.

6.1.2.3 Export Image as PNG

Figure 6.4 The "Export Image as PNG" dialog

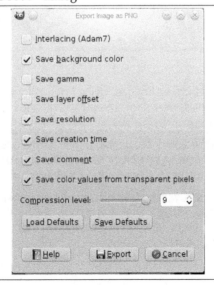

Interlacing Checking interlace allows an image on a web page to be progressively displayed as it is downloaded. Progressive image display is useful with slow connection speeds, because you can stop an image that is of no interest; interlace is of less use today with our faster connection speeds.

Save background color If your image has many transparency levels, the Internet browsers that recognize only two levels, will use the background color of your Toolbox instead. Internet Explorer up to version 6 did not use this information.

Save gamma Gamma correction is the ability to correct for differences in how computers interpret color values. This saves gamma information in the PNG that reflects the current Gamma factor for your display. Viewers on other computers can then compensate to ensure that the image is not too dark or too bright.

Save layer offset PNG supports an offset value called the "oFFs chunk", which provides position data. Unfortunately, PNG offset support in GIMP is broken, or at least is not compatible with other applications, and has been for a long time. Do not enable offsets, let GIMP flatten the layers before saving, and you will have no problems.

Save Resolution Save the image resolution, in ppi (pixels per inch).

Save creation time Date the file was saved.

Save comment You can read this comment in the Image Properties.

Save color values from transparent pixels With this option is checked, the color values are saved even if the pixels are completely transparent.

Compression level Since compression is not lossy, the only reason to use a compression level less than 9, is if it takes too long to compress a file on a slow computer. Nothing to fear from decompression: it is as quick whatever the compression level.

Save Defaults Click to save the current settings. Latter, you can use Load Defaults to load the saved settings.

> **Note**
>
> The PNG format supports indexed images. Using fewer colors, therefore, results in a smaller file; this is especially useful for creating web images; see Section 16.6.6.
>
> Computers work on 8 bits blocks named "Byte". A byte allows 256 colors. Reducing the number of colors below 256 is not useful: a byte will be used anyway and the file size will not be less. More, this "PNG8" format, like GIF, uses only one bit for transparency; only two transparency levels are possible, transparent or opaque.
>
> If you want PNG transparency to be fully displayed by Internet Explorer, you can use the AlphaImageLoader DirectX filter in the code of your Web page. See Microsoft Knowledge Base [MSKB-294714]. Please note, that this is not necessary for InternetExplorer 7 and above.

6.1.2.4   Export Image as TIFF

Figure 6.5 The TIFF Export dialog

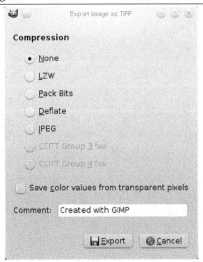

Compression This option allows you to specify the algorithm used to compress the image.

- None: is fast, and lossless, but the resulting file is very large.

- LZW: The image is compressed using the "Lempel-Ziv-Welch" algorithm, a lossless compression technique. This is old, but efficient and fast. More information at [WKPD-LZW].

- Pack Bits: is a fast, simple compression scheme for run-length encoding of data. Apple introduced the PackBits format with the release of MacPaint on the Macintosh computer. A PackBits data stream consists of packets of one byte of header followed by data. (Source: [WKPD-PACKBITS])

- Deflate: is a lossless data compression algorithm that uses a combination of the LZ77 algorithm and Huffman coding. It is also used in Zip, Gzip and PNG file formats. Source: [WKPD-DEFLATE].

- JPEG: is a very good compression algorithm but lossy.

- CCITT Group 3 fax; CCITT Group 4 fax is a black and white format developed to transfer images by FAX.

> **Note**
>
> These options can only be selected, if the image is in indexed mode and reduced to two colors. Use Image → Mode → Indexed to convert the image to indexed. Be certain to check "Use black and white (1-bit) palette".

Save color values from transparent pixels With this option the color values are saved even if the pixels are completely transparent.

Comment In this text box, you can enter a comment that is associated with the image.

6.1.2.5   Export Image as MNG

Figure 6.6 Export MNG File Dialog

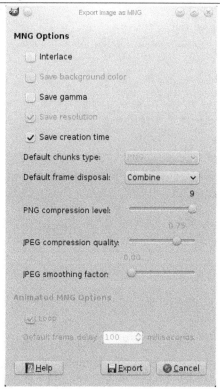

MNG is acronym for "Multiple-Image Network Graphics".

The main problem is that Konqueror is the only Web navigator that recognizes the MNG animation format. Please see http://en.wikipedia.org/wiki/Multiple-image_Network_Graphics.

6.2   Preparing your Images for the Web

One of the most common uses for GIMP, is to prepare images for web sites. This means that images should look as nice as possible while keeping the file size as small as possible. This step-by-step guide demonstrates how to create small files with minimal loss of image quality.

6.2.1   Images with an Optimal Size/Quality Ratio

An optimal image for the web depends upon the image type and the file format. Use JPEG for Photographs because they usually have many colors and great detail. An image with fewer colors, such as a button, icon, or screenshot, is better suited to the PNG format.

1. First, open the image as usual. I have opened our Wilber as an example image.

Figure 6.7 The Wilber image opened in RGBA mode

2. The image is now in RGB mode, with an additional Alpha channel (RGBA). There is usually no need to have an alpha channel for your web image. You can remove the alpha channel by flattening the image.

   A photograph rarely has an alpha channel, so the image will open in RGB mode rather than RGBA mode; and you won't have to remove the alpha channel.

Note

If the image has a soft transition into the transparent areas, you should not remove the alpha channel, since the information used for the transition is not be saved in the file. To export an image with transparent areas that do not have a soft transition, (similar to GIF), remove the alpha channel.

---

3. After you have flattened the image, export the image in the PNG format for your web site.

Note

You can export your image in the PNG format with the default settings. Always using maximum compression when creating the image. Maximum compression has no affect on image quality or the time required to display the image, but it does take longer to export. A JPEG image, however, loses quality as the compression is increased. If your image is a photograph with lots of colors, you should use jpeg. The main thing is to find the best tradeoff between quality and compression. You can find more information about this topic in Section 6.1.2.2.

6.2.2   Reducing the File Size Even More

If you want to reduce the size of your image a bit more, you could convert your image to Indexed mode. That means that all of the colors will be reduced to only 256 values. Do not convert images with smooth color transitions or gradients to indexed mode, because the original smooth gradients are typically converted into a series of bands. Indexed mode is not recommended for photographs because after the conversion, they typically look coarse and grainy.

Figure 6.8 The indexed image

An indexed image can look a bit grainy. The left image is Wilber in its original size, the right image is zoomed in by 300 percent.

1. Use the command described in Section 16.6.3 to convert an RGB image to indexed mode.

2. After you convert an image to indexed mode, you are once again able to export the image in PNG format.

6.2.3   Saving Images with Transparency

There are two different approaches used by graphic file formats for supporting transparent image areas: simple binary transparency and alpha transparency. Simple binary transparency is supported in the GIF format; one color from the indexed color palette is marked as the transparent color. Alpha transparency is supported in the PNG format; the transparency information is stored in a separate channel, the Alpha channel.

Note

The GIF format is rarely used because PNG supports all the features of GIF with additional features (e.g., alpha transparency). Nevertheless, GIF is still used for animations.

Creating an Image with Transparent Areas (Alpha Transparency)

1. First of all, we will use the same image as in the previous tutorials, Wilber the GIMP mascot.

Figure 6.9 The Wilber image opened in RGBA mode

2. To export an image with alpha transparency, you must have an alpha channel. To check if the image has an alpha channel, go to the channel dialog and verify that an entry for "Alpha" exists, besides Red, Green and Blue. If this is not the case, add a new alpha channel from the layers menu; Layer+Transparency → Add Alpha Channel.

3. The original XCF file contains background layers that you can remove. GIMP comes with standard filters that supports creating gradients; look under Filters+Light and Shadow. You are only limited by your imagination. To demonstrate the capabilities of alpha transparency, a soft glow in the background around Wilber is shown.

4. After you're done with your image, you can export it in PNG format.

Figure 6.10 The Wilber image with transparency

Mid-Tone Checks in the background layer represent the transparent region of the exported image while you are working on it in GIMP.

Chapter 7

Painting with GIMP

7.1 The Selection

Often when you operate on an image, you only want part of it to be affected. In GIMP, you make this happen by *selecting* that part. Each image has a *selection* associated with it. Most, but not all, GIMP operations act only on the selected portions of the image.

Figure 7.1 How would you isolate the tree?

There are many, many situations where creating just the right selection is the key to getting the result you want, and often it is not easy to do. For example, in the above image, suppose I want to cut the tree out from its background, and paste it into a different image. To do this, I need to create a selection that contains the tree and nothing but the tree. It is difficult because the tree has a complex shape, and in several spots is hard to distinguish from the objects behind it.

Figure 7.2 Selection shown as usual with dashed line.

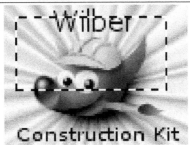

Now here is a very important point, and it is crucial to understand this. Ordinarily when you create a selection, you see it as a dashed line enclosing a portion of the image. The common, not entirely accurate, idea you could get from this, is that the selection is a sort of container, with the selected parts of the image inside, and the unselected parts outside. Although this concept of selection is okay for many purposes, it is not entirely correct.

Actually the selection is implemented as a *channel*. In terms of its internal structure, it is identical to the red, green, blue, and alpha channels of an image. Thus, the selection has a value defined at each pixel of the image, ranging between 0 (unselected) and 255 (fully selected). The advantage of this approach is that it allows some pixels to be *partially selected*, by giving them intermediate values between 0 and 255. As you will see, there are many situations where it is desirable to have smooth transitions between selected and unselected regions.

What, then, is the dashed line that appears when you create a selection?

The dashed line is a *contour line*, dividing areas that are more than half selected from areas that are less than half selected.

Figure 7.3 Same selection in QuickMask mode.

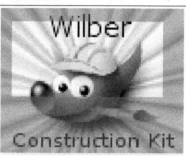

While looking at the dashed line that represents the selection, always remember that the line tells only part of the story. If you want to see the selection in complete detail, the easiest way is to click the QuickMask button in the lower left corner of the image window. This causes the selection to be shown as a translucent overlay atop the image. Selected areas are unaffected; unselected areas are reddened. The more completely selected an area is, the less red it appears.

Many operations work differently in QuickMask mode, as mentioned in the QuickMask overview. Use the QuickMask button in the lower left corner of the image window to toggle QuickMask mode on and off.

Figure 7.4 Same selection in QuickMask mode after feathering.

7.1.1   Feathering

With the default settings, the basic selection tools, such as the Rectangle Select tool, create sharp selections. Pixels inside the dashed line are fully selected, and pixels outside completely unselected. You can verify this by toggling QuickMask: you see a clear rectangle with sharp edges, surrounded by uniform red. Use the "Feather edges" checkbox in the Tool Options to toggle between graduated selections and sharp selections. The feather radius, which you can adjust, determines the distance over which the transition occurs.

If you are following along, try this with the Rectangle Select tool, and then toggle QuickMask. You will see that the clear rectangle has a fuzzy edge.

Feathering is particularly useful when you are cutting and pasting, so that the pasted object blends smoothly and unobtrusively with its surroundings.

It is possible to feather a selection at any time, even if it was originally created as a sharp selection. Use Select → Feather from the image menu to open the Feather Selection dialog. Set the feather radius and click OK. Use Select → Sharpen to do the opposite—sharpen a graduated selection into an all-or-nothing selection.

> **Note**
>
> For technically oriented readers: feathering works by applying a Gaussian blur to the selection channel, with the specified blurring radius.

7.1.2 Making a Selection Partially Transparent

You can set layer opacity, but you cannot do that directly for a selection. It is quite useful to make the image of a glass transparent. Use the following methods to set the layer opacity:

- For simple selections, use the Eraser tool with the desired opacity.

- For complex selections: use Selection → Floating to create a floating selection. This creates a new layer with the selection called "Floating Selection". Set the opacity slider in the Layer Dialog to the desired opacity. Then anchor the selection: outside the selection, the mouse pointer includes an anchor. When you click while the mouse pointer includes the anchor, the floating selection disappears from the Layer Dialog and the selection is at the right place and partially transparent (anchoring works this way only if a selection tool is activated : you can also use the Anchor Layer command in the context menu by right clicking on the selected layer in the layer dialog).

  And, if you use this function frequently: Ctrl-C to copy the selection, Ctrl-V to paste the clipboard as a floating selection, and Layer → New Layer to turn the selection into a new layer. You can adjust the opacity before, or after creating the new layer.

- Another way: use Layer → Mask → Add Layer Mask to add a layer mask to the layer with the selection, initializing it with the selection. Then use a brush with the desired opacity to paint the selection with black, i.e. paint it with transparency. Then Layer/Mask/Apply Layer Mask. See Section 15.2.1.3.

- To *make the solid background of an image transparent*, add an Alpha channel, and use the Magic Wand to select the background. Then, use the Color Picker tool to select the background color, which becomes the foreground color in Toolbox. Use the Bucket Fill tool with the selected color. Set the Bucket Fill mode to "Color Erase", which erases pixels with the selected color; other pixels are partially erased and their color is changed.

  The simplest method is to use Edit → Clear, which gives complete transparency to a selection.

7.2 Creating and Using Selections

7.2.1 Moving a Selection

Rectangular and elliptical selections have two modes. The default mode has handles on the selection. If you click the selection or press the **Enter** key, the handles disappear leaving only the dotted outline (marching ants). The other selection tools have different behaviour.

7.2.1.1 Moving rectangular and elliptical selections

If you click-and drag a selection with handles, you move the selection outline, and you don't move the contents of rectangular or elliptic selections.

Select the Move tool and set the options to move the selection; the tool supports moving the selection, path, or layer.

Figure 7.5 Moving selection outline

Most systems support moving the selection using the arrow keys. The precise behavior is system dependent. If the arrow keys do not cause the selection to move, try hovering the mouse cursor over the selection first. Press and hold the **Alt** (or Ctrl-Alt, Shift-Alt, or **Alt**). One combination may move the selection by one pixel, and another by 25 pixels each step. Hover the mouse cursor over a side or corner handle, and the arrow keys and combinations can change the size of the selection.

If you click-and-drag the selection without handles, you create a new selection! To move the selection contents, you have to

- hold down Ctrl-Alt keys and click-and-drag the selection. This makes the original place empty. A floating selection is created. The required key commands may differ on your system, look in the status bar to see if another combination is specified; for example, Shift-Ctrl-Alt.

Figure 7.6 Moving a selection and its content, emptying the original place

- hold down Shift-Alt keys and click-and-drag the selection to move without emptying the original place. A floating selection is created.

Figure 7.7 Moving a selection and its content without emptying the original place

> **Note**
>
> On some systems, you must push **Alt** before **Shift** or **Ctrl**. On these systems, pressing **Shift** or **Ctrl** first, causes GIMP to enter a mode that adds or subtract from the current selection — after that, the **Alt** key is ineffective!

7.2.1.2 Moving the other selections

The other selections (Lasso, Magic wand, By Color) have no handle. Click-and dragging them doesn't move them. To move their contents, as with rectangular and elliptical selections, you have to hold down Ctrl-Alt keys or Shift-Alt and click-and-drag.

If you use keyboard arrow keys instead of click-and-drag, you move the outline.

7.2.1.3 Other method

> **Note**
>
> You can also use a more roundabout method to move a selection. Make it float-
> ing. Then you can move its content, emptying the origin, by click-and-dragging or
> keyboard arrow keys. To move without emptying, use copy-paste.

7.2.2 Adding or subtracting selections

Tools have options that you can configure. Each selection tool allows you to set the selection mode. The following selection modes are supported:

- Replace is the most used selection mode. In replace mode, a selection replaces any existing selection.

- Add mode, causes new selections to be added to any existing selection. Press and hold the **Shift** key while making a selection to temporarily enter add mode.

- Subtract mode, causes new selections to be removed from any existing selection. Press and hold the **Ctrl** key while making a selection to temporarily enter subtract mode.

- Intersect mode, causes areas in both the new and existing selection to become the new selection. Press and hold both the **Shift** and **Ctrl** key while making a selection to temporarily enter intersect mode.

Figure 7.8 Enlarging a rectangular selection with the Lasso

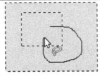

The figure shows an existing rectangular selection. Select the Lasso. While pressing the **Shift** key, make a free hand selection that includes the existing selection. Release the mouse button and areas are included in the selection.

> **Note**
>
> To correct selection defects precisely, use the Quick Mask.

7.3 The QuickMask

Figure 7.9 Image with QuickMask enabled

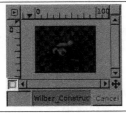

The usual selection tools involve tracing an outline around an area of interest, which does not work well for some complex selections. The QuickMask, however, allows you to paint a selection instead of just tracing its outline.

7.3.1 Overview

Normally, a selection in GIMP is represented by "marching ants" that trace the selection outline, but there may be more to a selection than the marching ants show. A GIMP selection is actually a full-fledged grayscale channel, covering the image, with pixel values ranging from 0 (unselected) to 255 (fully selected). The marching ants are drawn along a contour of half-selected pixels. Thus, what the marching ants show you as either inside or outside the boundary is really just a slice through a continuum.

The QuickMask is GIMP's way of showing the full structure of the selection. QuickMask also provides the ability to interact with the selection in new, and substantially more powerful, ways. Click the small outlined button at the lower left of the image window to toggle QuickMask on and off. The button switches between QuickMask mode, and marching ants mode. You can also use Select → Toggle QuickMask, or Shift-Q, to toggle between QuickMask and marching ants mode.

In QuickMask mode, the selection is shown as a translucent screen overlying the image, whose transparency at each pixel indicates the degree to which that pixel is selected. By default the mask is shown in red, but you can change this if another mask color is more convenient. The less a pixel is selected, the more it is obscured by the mask. Fully selected pixels are shown completely clear.

In QuickMask mode, many image manipulations act on the selection channel rather than the image itself. This includes, in particular, paint tools. Painting with white selects pixels, and painting with black unselects pixels. You can use any of the paint tools, as well as the bucket fill and gradient fill tools, in this way. Advanced users of GIMP learn that "painting the selection" is the easiest and most effective way to delicately manipulate the image.

Tip

 To save a QuickMask selection to a new channel; Make sure that there is a selection and that QuickMask mode is not active in the image window. Use Select → Save to Channel. to create a new channel in the channel dialog called "SelectionMask copy" (repeating this command creates "..copy#1", "...copy#2" and so on...).

Tip

 In QuickMask mode, Cut and Paste act on the selection rather than the image. You can sometimes make use of this as the most convenient way of transferring a selection from one image to another.

You can learn more on Selection masks in the section dedicated to the channel dialog.

7.3.2 Properties

There are two QuickMask properties you can change by right-clicking on the QuickMask button.

- Normally the QuickMask shows unselected areas "fogged over " and selected areas "in clear", but you can reverse this by choosing "Mask Selected Areas" instead of the default "Mask Unselected Areas".

- Use "Configure Color and Opacity" to open a dialog that allows you to set these to values other than the defaults, which are red at 50% opacity.

7.4   Using QuickMask Mode

1. Open an image or begin a new document.

2. Activate QuickMask mode using the left-bottom button in the image window. If a selection is present the mask is initialized with the content of the selection.

3. Choose any drawing tool. Paint on the QuickMask with black to remove selected areas, and paint with white to add selected areas. Use grey colors to partially select areas.

   You can also use selection tools and fill these selections with the Bucket Fill tool; this does not destroy the QuickMask selections!

4. Toggle QuickMask mode off using the left-bottom button in the image window: the selection will be displayed with marching ants.

7.5   Paths

Paths are curves (known as Bézier-curves). Paths are easy to learn and use in GIMP. To understand their concepts and mechanism, look at the glossary Bézier-curve or Wikipedia [WKPD-BEZIER]. The Paths tool is very powerful, allowing you to design sophisticated forms. To use the Paths tool in GIMP, you must first create a path, and then stroke the path.

In GIMP, the term "Stroke path" means to apply a specific style to the path (color, width, pattern...). A Path has two main purposes:

- You can convert a closed path to a selection.

- Any path, open or closed, can be *stroked*; that is, painted on the image in a variety of ways.

Figure 7.10 Illustration of four different path creating

Four examples of GIMP paths: one closed and polygonal; one open and polygonal; one closed and curved; one with a mixture of straight and curved segments.

7.5.1   Path Creation

Start by drawing the outline for your path; the outline can be modified later (see the Paths tool). To start, select the Paths tool using one of the following methods:

- Use Tools → Path from the image menu.

- Use the relevant icon in toolbox.

- Use the hotkey **B**.

When the Paths tool is selected, the mouse cursor changes into a pointer (arrow) with a curve. Left click in the image to create the first point on the path. Move the mouse to a new point and left click the mouse to create another point linked to the previous point. Although you can create as many points as you desire, you only need two points to learn about Paths. While adding points, the mouse cursor has a little "+" next to the curve, which indicates that clicking will add a new point. When the mouse cursor is close to a line segment, the "+" changes into a cross with arrows; like the move tool.

Move the mouse cursor close to a line segment, left-click and drag the line segment. Two events occur.

- The line segment bends and curves as it is pulled.

- Each line segment has a start point and an end point that is clearly labeled. A "direction line" now projects from each end point for the line segment that was moved.

The curved line segment leaves an end point in the same direction that the "direction line" leaves the end point. The length of the "direction line" controls how far the line segment projects along the "direction line" before curving toward the other end point. Each "direction line" has an empty square box (called a handle) on one end. Click and drag a handle to change the direction and length of a "direction line".

Figure 7.11 Appearance of a path while it is manipulated

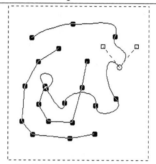

Appearance of a path while it is manipulated using the Path tool.

The path is comprised of two components with both straight and curved segments. Black squares are anchor points, the open circle indicates the selected anchor, and the two open squares are the handles associated with the selected anchor.

7.5.2   Path Properties

Paths, like layers and channels, are components of an image. When an image is saved in GIMP's native XCF file format, any paths it has are saved with it. The list of paths in an image can be viewed and operated on using the Paths dialog. You can move a path from one image to another by copying and pasting using the pop-up menu in the Paths dialog, or by dragging an icon from the Paths dialog into the destination image window.

GIMP paths belong to a mathematical type called "Bezier paths". What this means in practical terms is that they are defined by *anchors* and *handles*. "Anchors" are points the path goes through. "Handles" define the direction of a path when it enters or leaves an anchor point: each anchor point has two handles attached to it.

Paths can be very complex. If you create them by hand using the Path tool, unless you are obsessive they probably won't contain more than a few dozen anchor points (often many fewer); but if you create them by transforming a selection into a path, or by transforming text into a path, the result can easily contain hundreds of anchor points, or even thousands.

A path may contain multiple *components*. A "component" is a part of a path whose anchor points are all connected to each other by path segments. The ability to have multiple components in paths allows you to convert them into selections having multiple disconnected parts.

Each component of a path can be either *open* or *closed*: "closed" means that the last anchor point is connected to the first anchor point. If you transform a path into a selection, any open components are automatically converted into closed components by connecting the last anchor point to the first anchor point with a straight line.

Path segments can be either straight or curved. A path is called "polygonal" if all of its segments are straight. A new path segment is always created straight; the handles for the anchor points are directly on top of the anchor points, yielding handles of zero length, which produces straight-line segments. Drag a handle handle away from an anchor point to cause a segment to curve.

One nice thing about paths is that they use very few resources, especially in comparison with images. Representing a path in RAM requires storing only the coordinates of its anchors and handles: 1K of memory is enough to hold a complex path, but not enough to hold a small 20x20 pixel RGB layer. Therefore, it is possible to have literally hundreds of paths in an image without causing any significant stress to your system; the amount of stress that hundreds of paths might cause *you*, however, is another question. Even a path with thousands of segments consumes minimal resources in comparison to a typical layer or channel.

Paths can be created and manipulated using the Path tool.

7.5.3 Paths and Selections

GIMP lets you transform the selection for an image into a path; it also lets you transform paths into selections. For information about the selection and how it works, see the Selection section.

When you transform a selection into a path, the path closely follows the "marching ants". Now, the selection is a two-dimensional entity, but a path is a one-dimensional entity, so there is no way to transform the selection into a path without losing information. In fact, any information about partially selected areas (i.e., feathering) are lost when a selection is turned into a path. If the path is transformed back into a selection, the result is an all-or-none selection, similar to what is obtained by executing "Sharpen" from the Select menu.

7.5.4 Transforming Paths

Each of the Transform tools (Rotate, Scale, Perspective, etc) can be set to act on a layer, selection, or path. Select the transform tool in the toolbox, then select layer, selection, or path for the "Transform:" option in the tool's Tool Options dialog. This gives you a powerful set of methods for altering the shapes of paths without affecting other elements of the image.

By default a Transform tool, when it is set to affect paths, acts on only one path: the *active path* for the image, which is shown highlighted in the Paths dialog. You can make a transformation affect more than one path, and possibly other things as well, using the "transform lock" buttons in the Paths dialog. Not only paths, but also layers and channels, can be transform-locked. If you transform one element that is transform-locked, all others will be transformed in the same way. So, for example, if you want to scale a layer and a path by the same amount, click the transform-lock buttons so that "chain" symbols appear next to the layer in the Layers dialog, and the path in the Paths dialog; then use the Scale tool on either the layer or the path, and the other will automatically follow.

7.5.5 Stroking a Path

Figure 7.12 Stroking paths

The four paths from the top illustration, each stroked in a different way.

Paths do not alter the appearance of the image pixel data unless they are *stroked*, using Edit → Stroke Path from the image menu or the Paths dialog right-click menu, or the "Stroke Path" button in the Tool Options dialog for the Path tool.

Choosing "Stroke Path" by any of these means brings up a dialog that allows you to control the way the stroking is done. You can choose from a wide variety of line styles, or you can stroke with any of the Paint tools, including unusual ones such as the Clone tool, Smudge tool, Eraser, etc.

Figure 7.13 The Stroke Path dialog

You can further increase the range of stroking effects by stroking a path multiple times, or by using lines or brushes of different widths. The possibilities for getting interesting effects in this way are almost unlimited.

7.5.6 Paths and Text

Figure 7.14 Text converted to a path

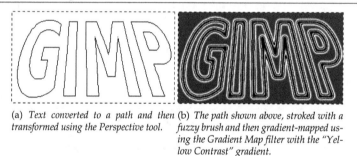

(a) *Text converted to a path and then transformed using the Perspective tool.* (b) *The path shown above, stroked with a fuzzy brush and then gradient-mapped using the Gradient Map filter with the "Yellow Contrast" gradient.*

A text item created using the Text tool can be transformed into a path using the **Path from Text** command in the the context menu of the Text tool. This can be useful for several purposes, including:

- Stroking the path, which gives you many possibilities for fancy text.

- More importantly, transforming the text. Converting text into a path, then transforming the path, and finally either stroking the path or converting it to a selection and filling it, often leads to much higher-quality results than rendering the text as a layer and transforming the pixel data.

7.5.7 Paths and SVG files

SVG, standing for "Scalable Vector Graphics", is an increasingly popular file format for *vector graphics*, in which graphical elements are represented in a resolution-independent format, in contrast to *raster graphics*; in which graphical elements are represented as arrays of pixels. GIMP is mainly a raster graphics program, but paths are vector entities.

Fortunately, paths are represented in SVG files in almost exactly the same way they are represented in GIMP. (Actually fortune has nothing to do with it: GIMP's path handling was rewritten for GIMP 2.0 with SVG paths in mind.) This compatibility makes it possible to store GIMP paths as SVG files without losing any information. You can access this capability in the Paths dialog.

It also means that GIMP can create paths from SVG files saved in other programs, such as Inkscape or Sodipodi, two popular open-source vector graphics applications. This is nice because those programs have much more powerful path-manipulation tools than GIMP does. You can import a path from an SVG file using the Paths dialog.

The SVG format handles many other graphical elements than just paths: among other things, it handles figures such as squares, rectangles, circles, ellipses, regular polygons, etc. GIMP cannot do anything with these entities, but it can load them as paths.

Note

 Creating paths is not the only thing GIMP can do with SVG files. It can also open SVG files as GIMP images, in the usual way.

7.6 Brushes

Figure 7.15 Brush strokes example

A number of examples of brushstrokes painted using different brushes from the set supplied with GIMP. All were painted using the Paintbrush tool.

A *brush* is a pixmap or set of pixmaps used for painting. GIMP includes a set of 10 "paint tools", which not only perform operations that you would normally think of as painting, but also operations such as erasing, copying, smudging, lightening or darkening, etc. All of the paint tools, except the ink tool, use the same set of brushes. The brush pixmaps represent the marks that are made by single "touches" of the brush to the image. A brush stroke, usually made by moving the pointer across the image with the mouse button held down, produces a series of marks spaced along the trajectory, in a way specified by the characteristics of the brush and the paint tool being used.

Brushes can be selected by clicking on an icon in the Brushes dialog. GIMP's *current brush* is shown in the Brush/Pattern/Gradient area of the Toolbox. Clicking on the brush symbol there is one way of activating the Brushes dialog.

When you install GIMP, it comes with a number of basic brushes, plus a few bizarre ones that serve mainly to give you examples of what is possible (i. e., the "green pepper" brush in the illustration). You can also create new brushes, or download them and install them so that GIMP will recognize them.

GIMP can use several different types of brushes. All of them, however, are used in the same way, and for most purposes you don't need to worry about the differences when you paint with them. Here are the available types of brushes:

Ordinary brushes Most of the brushes supplied with GIMP fall into this category. They are represented in the Brushes dialog by grayscale pixmaps. When you paint using them, the current foreground color (as shown in the Color Area of the Toolbox) is substituted for black, and the pixmap shown in the brushes dialog represents the mark that the brush makes on the image.

To create such a brush: Create a small image in gray levels using zoom. Save it with the .gbr extension. Click on Refresh button in the Brush Dialog to get it in preview without it being necessary to restart GIMP.

Color brushes Brushes in this category are represented by colored images in the Brushes dialog. They can be pictures or text. When you paint with them, the colors are used as shown; the current foreground color does not come into play. Otherwise they work the same way as ordinary brushes.

To create such a brush: Create a small RGBA image. For this, open New Image, select RGB for image type and Transparent for fill type. Draw your image and and firs save it as a .xcf file to keep its properties. Then save it in *.gbr* format. Click on the *Refresh* button in Brush Dialog to get your brush without it being necessary to restart GIMP.

Tip

When you do a Copy or a Cut on a selection, you see the contents of the clipboard (that is the selection) at the first position in the brushes dialog. And you can use it for painting.

Figure 7.16 Selection to Brush after Copy or Cut

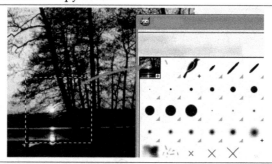

Image hoses / Image pipes Brushes in this category can make more than one kind of mark on an image. They are indicated by small red triangles at the lower right corner of the brush symbol in the Brushes dialog. They are sometimes called "animated brushes" because the marks change as you trace out a brushstroke. In principle, image hose brushes can be very sophisticated, especially if you use a tablet, changing shape as a function of pressure, angle, etc. These possibilities have never really been exploited, however; and the ones supplied with GIMP are relatively simple (but still quite useful).

You will find an example on how to create such brushes in Animated brushes

Parametric brushes These are brushes created using the Brush Editor, which allows you to generate a wide variety of brush shapes by using a simple graphical interface. A nice feature of parametric brushes is that they are *resizable*. It is possible, using the Preferences dialog, to make key presses or mouse wheel rotations cause the current brush to become larger or smaller, if it is a parametric brush.

Now, all brushes have a variable size. In fact, in the option box of all painting tools there is a slider to enlarge or reduce the size of the active brush. You can do this directly in the image window if you have set correctly your mouse wheel; see Varying brush size.

In addition to the brush pixmap, each GIMP brush has one other important property: the brush *Spacing*. This represents the distance between consecutive brush-marks when a continuous brushstroke is painted. Each brush has an assigned default value for this, which can be modified using the Brushes dialog.

7.7 Adding New Brushes

To add a new brush, after either creating or downloading it, you need to save it in a format GIMP can use. The brush file needs to be placed in the GIMP's brush search path, so that GIMP is able to index and display it in the Brushes dialog. You can hit the Refresh button, which reindexes the brush directory. GIMP uses three file formats for brushes:

GBR The .gbr ("*gimp brush*") format is used for ordinary and color brushes. You can convert many other types of images, including many brushes used by other programs, into GIMP brushes by opening them in GIMP and saving them with file names ending in .gbr. This brings up a dialog box in which you can set the default Spacing for the brush. A more complete description of the GBR file format can be found in the file gbr.txt in the devel-docs directory of the GIMP source distribution.

Figure 7.17 Save a .gbr brush

GIH The .gih ("*gimp image hose*") format is used for animated brushes. These brushes are constructed from images containing multiple layers: each layer may contain multiple brush-shapes, arranged in a grid. When you save an image as a .gih file, a dialog comes up that allows you to describe the format of the brush. Look at The GIH dialog box for more information about the dialog. The GIH format is rather complicated: a complete description can be found in the file gih.txt in the devel-docs directory of the GIMP source distribution.

VBR The .vbr format is used for parametric brushes, i. e., brushes created using the Brush Editor. There is really no other meaningful way of obtaining files in this format.

To make a brush available, place it in one of the folders in GIMP's brush search path. By default, the brush search path includes two folders, the system brushes folder, which you should not use or alter, and the brushes folder inside your personal GIMP directory. You can add new folders to the brush search path using the Brush Folders page of the Preferences dialog. Any GBR, GIH, or VBR file included in a folder in the brush search path will show up in the Brushes dialog the next time you start GIMP, or as soon as you press the Refresh button in the Brushes dialog.

> **Note**
>
> When you create a new parametric brush using the Brush Editor, it is automatically saved in your personal brushes folder.

There are a number of web sites with downloadable collections of GIMP brushes. Rather than supplying a list of links that will soon be out of date, the best advice is to do a search with your favorite search engine for "GIMP brushes". There are also many collections of brushes for other programs with painting functionality. Some can be converted easily into GIMP brushes, some require special conversion utilities, and some cannot be converted at all. Most fancy procedural brush types fall into the last category. If you need to know, look around on the web, and if you don't find anything, look for an expert to ask.

7.8   The GIH Dialog Box

When your new animated brush is created, it is displayed within the image window and you would like save it into a gih format. You select File → Save as... menu, name your work with the gih extension in the new window relevant field and as soon as you pressed the Save button, the following window is displayed:

Figure 7.18 The dialog to describe the animated brush

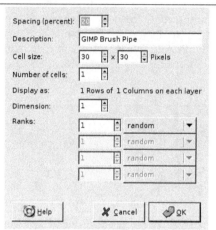

This dialog box shows up, if you save an image as GIMP image hose

---

This dialog box has several options not easy to understand. They allow you to determine the way your brush is animated.

Spacing (Percent) "Spacing" is the distance between consecutive brush marks when you trace out a brushstroke with the pointer. You must consider drawing with a brush, whatever the paint tool, like stamping. If Spacing is low, stamps will be very close and stroke look continuous. If spacing is high, stamps will be separated: that's interesting with a color brush (like "green pepper" for instance). Value varies from 1 to 200 and this percentage refers to brush "diameter": 100% is one diameter.

Description It's the brush name that will appear at the top of Brush Dialog (grid mode) when the brush is selected.

Cell Size That's size of cells you will cut up in layers... Default is one cell per layer and size is that of the layer. Then there is only one brush aspect per layer.

We could have only one big layer and cut up in it the cells that will be used for the different aspects of the animated brush.

For instance, we want a 100x100 pixels brush with 8 different aspects. We can take these 8 aspects from a 400x200 pixels layer, or from a 300x300 pixels layer but with one cell unused.

Number of cells That's the number of cells (one cell per aspect) that will be cut in every layer. Default is the number of layers as there is only one layer per aspect.

Display as This tells how cells have been arranged in layers. If, for example, you have placed height cells at the rate of two cells per layer on four layers, GIMP will display: `1 rows of 2 columns on each layer`.

Dimension, Ranks, Selection There things are getting complicated! Explanations are necessary to understand how to arrange cell and layers.

GIMP starts retrieving cells from each layer and stacks them into a FIFO stack (First In First Out: the first in is at the top of the stack and so can be first out). In our example 4 layers with 2 cells in each, we'll have, from top to bottom: first cell of first layer, second cell of first layer, first cell of second layer, second cell of second layer..., second cell of fourth layer. With one cell per layer or with several cells per layer, result is the same. You can see this stack in the Layer Dialog of the resulting `.gih` image file.

Then GIMP creates a computer array from this stack with the Dimensions you have set. You can use four dimensions.

In computer science an array has a "myarray(x,y,z)" form for a 3 dimensions array (3D). It's easy to imagine a 2D array: on a paper it's an array with rows and columns

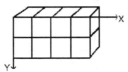

With a 3d array we don't talk rows and columns but Dimensions and Ranks. The first dimension is along x axis, the second dimension along y axis, the third along z axis. Each dimension has ranks of cells.

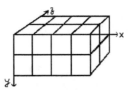

To fill up this array, GIMP starts retrieving cells from the top of stack. The way it fills the array reminds that of an odometer: right rank digits turn first and, when they reach their maximum, left rank digits start running. If you have some memories of Basic programming you will have, with an array(4,2,2), the following succession: (1,1,1),(1,1,2),(1,2,1),(1,2,2),(2,1,1),(2,1,2),(2,2,2),(3,1,1)....(4,2,2). We will see this later in an example.

Besides the rank number that you can give to each dimension, you can also give them a Selection mode. You have several modes that will be applied when drawing:

Incremental GIMP selects a rank from the concerned dimension according to the order ranks have in that dimension.

Random GIMP selects a rank at random from the concerned dimension.

Angular GIMP selects a rank in the concerned dimension according to the moving angle of the brush.

The first rank is for the direction 0°, upwards. The other ranks are affected, clockwise, to an angle whose value is 360/number of ranks. So, with 4 ranks in the concerned dimension, the angle will move 90° clockwise for each direction change: second rank will be affected to 90° (rightwards), third rank to 180° (downwards) and fourth rank to 270° (-90°) (leftwards).[1]

Speed, Pressure, x tilt, y tilt These options are for sophisticated drawing tablets.

Examples

A one dimension image pipe Well! What is all this useful for? We'll see that gradually with examples. You can actually place in each dimension cases that will give your brush a particular action.

Let us start with a 1D brush which will allow us to study selection modes action. We can imagine it like this:

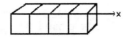

Follow these steps:

1. Open a new 30x30 pixels image, RGB with Transparent fill type. Using the Text tool create 4 layers "1", "2", "3", "4". Delete the "background" layer.

2. Save this image first with `.xcf` extension to keep its properties then save it as `.gih`.

---

[1] For previous GIMP versions you may have to replace "clockwise" with "counter-clockwise".

3. The Save As Dialog is opened: select a destination for your image. OK. The GIH dialog is opened: Choose Spacing 100, give a name in Description box, 30x30 for Cell Size, 1 dimension, 4 ranks and choose "Incremental" in Selection box. OK.

4. You may have difficulties to save directly in the GIMP Brush directory. In that case, save the `.gih` file manually into the `/usr/share/gimp/gimp/2.0/brushes` directory. Then come back into the Toolbox, click in the brush icon to open the Brush Dialog then click on Refresh 🔄 icon button. Your new brush appears in the Brush window. Select it. Select pencil tool for instance and click and hold with it on a new image:

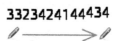

You see 1, 2, 3, 4 digits following one another in order.

5. Take your `.xcf` image file back and save it as `.gih` setting Selection to "Random":

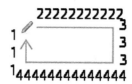

Digits will be displayed at random order.

6. Now select "Angular" Selection:

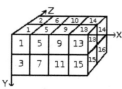

A 3 dimensions image hose We are now going to create a 3D animated brush: its orientation will vary according to brush direction, it will alternate Left/Right hands regularly and its color will vary at random between black and blue.

The first question we have to answer to is the number of images that is necessary. We reserve the first dimension (x) to the brush direction (4 directions). The second dimension (y) is for Left/Right alternation and the third dimension (z) for color variation. Such a brush is represented in a 3D array "myarray(4,2,2)":

```
           Z
       2   6   10  14
     1   5   9   13  14
                    18      X
    1   5   9   13     16
                    15
    3   7   11  15
  Y
```

There are 4 ranks in first dimension (x), 2 ranks in second dimension (y) and 2 ranks in third dimension (z). We see that there are 4x2x2 = 16 cells. We need 16 images.

1. Creating images of dimension 1 (x)

   Open a new 30x30 pixels image, RGB with Transparent Fill Type. Using the zoom draw a left hand with fingers upwards.[2] Save it as `handL0k.xcf` (hand Left 0° Black).

   Open the Layer Dialog. Double click on the layer to open the Layer Attributes Dialog and rename it to handL0k.

   Duplicate the layer. Let visible only the duplicated layer, select it and apply a 90° rotation (Layer/Transform/ 90° rotation clockwise). Rename it to handL90k.

   Repeat the same operations to create handL180k and handL-90k (or handL270k).

2. Creating images of dimension 2 (y)

   This dimension in our example has two ranks, one for left hand and the other for right hand. The left hand rank exists yet. We shall build right hand images by flipping it horizontally.

   Duplicate the handL0k layer. Let it visible only and select it. Rename it to handR0K. Apply Layer/Transform/Flip Horizontally.

---

[2] Ok, we are cheating here: our hand is borrowed from `http://commons.wikimedia.org/wiki/File:Stop_hand.png`.

Repeat the same operation on the other left hand layers to create their right hand equivalent. Re-order layers to have a clockwise rotation from top to bottom, alternating Left and Right: handL0k, handR0k, handL90k, handR90k, ..., handR-90k.

3. Creating images of dimension 3 (z)

   Creating images of dimension 3 (z): The third dimension has two ranks, one for black color and the other for blue color. The first rank, black, exists yet. We well see that images of dimension 3 will be a copy, in blue, of the images of dimension 2. So we will have our 16 images. But a row of 16 layers is not easy to manage: we will use layers with two images.

   Select the handL0k layer and let it visible only. Using Image/Canvas Size change canvas size to 60x30 pixels.

   Duplicate hand0k layer. On the copy, fill the hand with blue using Bucket Fill tool.

   Now, select the Move tool. Double click on it to accede to its properties: check Move the Current Layer option. Move the blue hand into the right part of the layer precisely with the help of Zoom.

   Make sure only handL0k and its blue copy are visible. Right click on the Layer Dialog: Apply the Merge Visible Layers command with the option Expand as Necessary. You get a 60x30 pixels layer with the black hand on the left and the blue hand on the right. Rename it to "handsL0".

   Repeat the same operations on the other layers.

4. Set layers in order

   Layers must be set in order so that GIMP can find the required image at some point of using the brush. Our layers are yet in order but we must understand more generally how to have them in order. There are two ways to imagine this setting in order. The first method is mathematical: GIMP divides the 16 layers first by 4; that gives 4 groups of 4 layers for the first dimension. Each group represents a direction of the brush. Then, it divides each group by 2; that gives 8 groups of 2 layers for the second dimension: each group represents a L/R alternation. Then another division by 2 for the third dimension to represent a color at random between black and blue.

   The other method is visual, by using the array representation. Correlation between two methods is represented in next image:

   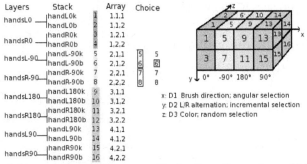

   How will GIMP read this array?: GIMP starts with the first dimension which is programmed for "angular", for instance 90°. In this 90° rank, in yellow, in the second dimension, it selects a L/R alternation, in an "incremental" way. Then, in the third dimension, in a random way, it chooses a color. Finally, our layers must be in the following order:

5. Voilà. Your brush is ready. Save it as .xcf first, then as .gih with the following parameters:

- Spacing: 100
- Description: Hands
- Cell Size: 30x30
- Number of cells: 16
- Dimensions: 3
    - Dimension 1: 4 ranks Selection: Angular
    - Dimension 2: 2 ranks Selection: Incremental
    - Dimension 3: 2 ranks Selection: Random

Place your `.gih` file into GIMP brush directory and refresh the brush box. You can now use your brush.

Figure 7.19 Here is the result by stroking an elliptical selection with the brush:

This brush alternates right hand and left hand regularly, black and blue color at random, direction according to four brush directions.

7.9 Varying brush size

From GIMP-2.4, all brushes have a variable size.

7.9.1 How to vary the height of a brush

You can get the brush size varying in three ways:

1. Using the Scale slider of the tool that uses the brush. Pencil, Paintbrush, Eraser, Airbrush, Clone, Heal, Perspective Clone, Blur/Sharpen and Dodge/Burn tools have a slider to vary brush size.

Figure 7.20 The Scale slider

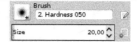

---

2. By programming the mouse wheel:

    (a) In the main window of GIMP, click on Edit → Preferences.

    (b) In the left column of the new window, select Input Devices → Input Controllers.

    (c) You can see Additional Input Controllers, with two columns: Available Controllers and Active Controllers.
    In the column Active Controllers, double-click the Main Mouse Wheel button.

    (d) Then, you see a new window: Configure Input Controller.
    In the left column Event, click Scroll Up to get it highlighted.

    (e) Click the Edit button (at the bottom middle of the list).

(f) You can see the window Select Controller Event Action.

Drop-down the Tools item, by clicking the small triangle on its left.

(g) In the left column Action, click Increase Brush Scale to highlight it, then click the OK button.

(h) Now, in front of Scroll Up is display tools-paint-brush-scale-increase.

(i) Close the window.

(j) With the same method, program Scroll Down with Decrease Brush Scale.

(k) Don't forget to click the OK button of the main window of Preferences.

After these somewhat long explanations, you can use your mouse wheel to vary size brush. For example, choose the pencil tool with the "Circle" brush. Set the pointer in the image window, use the mouse wheel, in the two directions, you can see the "Circle" shrinking or stretching.

3. You can program the "Up" and "Down" arrow keys of the keyboard.

The method is similar to that of the mouse wheel. The only differences are:

- In the column Active Controllers, double-click Main Keyboard.

- In the column Event, click Cursor Up for the first key, and Cursor Down for the second key.

- Then, use the two keys (Up arrow and Down arrow) and the result is the same as you got with the mouse wheel.

7.9.2 Creating a brush quickly

Two methods to create a new brush easily:

1. First, the "superfast" method. You have an image area you want make a brush from it, to be used with a tool like pencil, airbrush... Select it with the rectangular (or elliptical) select tool, then do a Copy of this selection and immediately you can see this copy in the first position of the Brush Dialog, and its name is "Clipboard". It is immediately usable.

Figure 7.21 Selection becomes a brush after copying

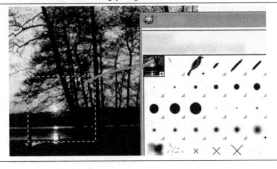

2. The second method is more elaborate.

Do File → New with, for example, a width and a length of 35 pixels and in the advanced options a Color Space in Gray Level and Fill with: white.

Zoom on this new image to enlarge it and draw on it with a black pencil.

Save it with a .gbr extension in the directory /home/name_of_user/.gimp-2.8/brushes/.

In the Brushes dialog window, click on the button Refresh brushes ⟳ .

And your marvellous brush appears right in the middle of the other brushes. You can use it immediately, without starting GIMP again.

Figure 7.22 Steps to create a brush

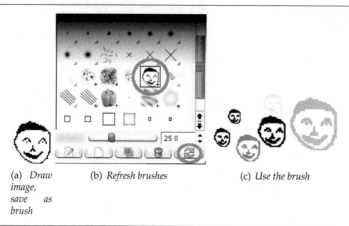

(a) Draw   (b) Refresh brushes   (c) Use the brush
image,
save   as
brush

7.10   Gradients

Figure 7.23 Some examples of GIMP gradients.

Gradients from top to bottom: FG to BG (RGB); Full saturation spectrum; Nauseating headache; Browns; Four bars

A *gradient* is a set of colors arranged in a linear order. The most basic use of gradients is by the Blend tool, sometimes known as the "gradient tool" or "gradient fill tool": it works by filling the selection with colors from a gradient. You have many options to choose from for controlling the way the gradient colors are arranged within the selection. There are also other important ways to use gradients, including:

Painting with a gradient Each of GIMP's basic painting tools allows you the option of using colors from a gradient. This enables you to create brushstrokes that change color from one end to the other.

The Gradient Map filter This filter is now in the Colors menu, and allows you to "colorize" an image, using the color intensity of each point with the corresponding color from the active gradient (the intensity 0, very dark, is replaced by the color at most left end of the gradient, progressively until the intensity is 255, very light, replaced by the most right color of the gradient. See Section 16.8.23 for more information.

When you install GIMP, it comes presupplied with a large number of interesting gradients, and you can add new ones that you create or download from other sources. You can access the full set of available gradients using the Gradients dialog, a dockable dialog that you can either activate when you need it, or keep around as a tab in a dock. The "current gradient", used in most gradient-related operations, is shown in the Brush/Pattern/Gradient area of the Toolbox. Clicking on the gradient symbol in the Toolbox is an alternative way of bringing up the Gradients dialog.

Many quickly examples of working with gradient (for more information see Blend Tool):

- Put a gradient in a selection:

  1. Choose a gradient.

  2. With the Blend Tool click and drag with the mouse between two points of a selection.

3. Colors will distributed perpendicularly to the direction of the drag of the mouse and according to the length of it.

Figure 7.24 How to use rapidly a gradient in a selection

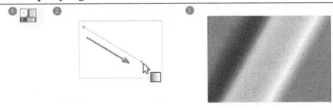

- Painting with a gradient:

  You can also use a gradient with the Pencil, Paintbrush or Airbrush tools if you choose the dynamics Color From Gradient. In the next step choose a suitable gradient from Color options and in the Fade options set the gradients length and the style of the repeating. The chapter Section 14.3.2.6 describes these parameters in more detail.

  The following example shows the impact on the Pencil tool. You see in the upper side of the figure the necessary settings and the lower side of the figure shows the resulting succession of the gradients colors.

Figure 7.25 How to use rapidly a gradient with a drawing tool

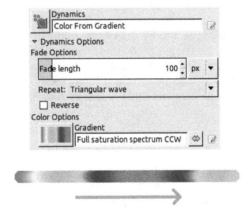

To use the Paint tools with the same settings as they were known as option Use color from gradient in GIMP up to version 2.6 open the Tool Presets Dialog. Then choose one of the items Airbrush (Color From Gradient), Paintbrush (Color From Gradient) or Pencil (Color From Gradient) from it.

- Different productions with the same gradient:

Figure 7.26 Gradient usage

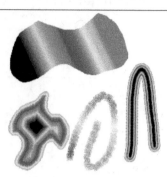

Four ways of using the Tropical Colors gradient: a linear gradient fill, a shaped gradient fill, a stroke painted using colors from a gradient, and a stroke painted with a fuzzy brush then colored using the Gradient Map filter.

A few useful things to know about GIMP's gradients:

- The first four gradients in the list are special: they use the Foreground and Background colors from the Toolbox Color Area, instead of being fixed. FG to BG (RGB) is the RGB representation of the gradient from the Foreground color to the Background color in Toolbox. FG to BG (HSV counter-clockwise) represents the hue succession in Color Circle from the selected hue to 360°. FG to BG (HSV clockwise represents the hue succession in Color Circle from the selected hue to 0°. With FG to transparent , the selected hue becomes more and more transparent. You can modify these colors by using the Color Selector. Thus, by altering the foreground and background colors, you can make these gradients transition smoothly between any two colors you want.

- Gradients can involve not just color changes, but also changes in opacity. Some of the gradients are completely opaque; others include transparent or translucent parts. When you fill or paint with a non-opaque gradient, the existing contents of the layer will show through behind it.

- You can create new *custom* gradients, using the Gradient Editor. You cannot modify the gradients that are supplied with GIMP, but you can duplicate them or create new ones, and then edit those.

The gradients that are supplied with GIMP are stored in a system `gradients` folder. By default, gradients that you create are stored in a folder called `gradients` in your personal GIMP directory. Any gradient files (ending with the extension `.ggr`) found in one of these folders, will automatically be loaded when you start GIMP. You can add more directories to the gradient search path, if you want to, in the Gradients tab of the Data Folders pages of the Preferences dialog.

New in GIMP 2.2 is the ability to load gradient files in SVG format, used by many vector graphics programs. To make GIMP load an SVG gradient file, all you need to do is place it in the `gradients` folder of your personal GIMP directory, or any other folder in your gradient search path.

Tip

 You can find a large number of interesting SVG gradients on the web, in particular at OpenClipArt Gradients [OPENCLIPART-GRADIENT]. You won't be able to see what these gradients look like unless your browser supports SVG, but that won't prevent you from downloading them.

7.11 Patterns

A *pattern* is an image, usually small, used for filling regions by *tiling*, that is, by placing copies of the pattern side by side like ceramic tiles. A pattern is said to be *tileable* if copies of it can be adjoined left-edge-to-right-edge and top-edge-to-bottom-edge without creating obvious seams. Not all useful patterns are tileable, but tileable patterns are nicest for many purposes. (A *texture*, by the way, is the same thing as a pattern.)

Figure 7.27 Pattern usage

Three ways of using the "Leopard" pattern: bucket-filling a selection, painting with the Clone tool, and stroking an elliptical selection with the pattern.

In GIMP there are three main uses for patterns:

- With the Bucket Fill tool, you can choose to fill a region with a pattern instead of a solid color.

Figure 7.28 The checked box for use a pattern

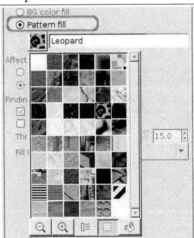

The box for pattern fill is checked and a click on the pattern shows you all patterns in grid mode.

- With the Clone tool, you can paint using a pattern, with a wide variety of paintbrush shapes.

- When you *stroke* a path or selection, you can do it with a pattern instead of a solid color. You can also use the Clone tool as your choice if you stroke the selection using a painting tool.

Tip

 Note: Patterns do not need to be opaque. If you fill or paint using a pattern with translucent or transparent areas, then the previous contents of the area will show through from behind it. This is one of many ways of doing "overlays" in GIMP.

When you install GIMP, it comes presupplied with a few dozen patterns, which seem to have been chosen more or less randomly. You can also add new patterns, either ones you create yourself, or ones you download from the vast number available online.

GIMP's *current pattern*, used in most pattern-related operations, is shown in the Brush/Pattern/Gradient area of the Toolbox. Clicking on the pattern symbol brings up the Patterns dialog, which allows you to select a different pattern. You can also access the Patterns dialog by menu, or dock it so that it is present continuously.

To add a new pattern to the collection, so that it shows up in the Patterns dialog, you need to save it in a format GIMP can use, in a folder included in GIMP's pattern search path. There are several file formats you can use for patterns:

PAT The .pat format is used for patterns which were created specifically for GIMP. You can convert any image into a .pat file by opening it in GIMP and then saving it using a file name ending in .pat.

Caution

 Do not confuse GIMP-generated .pat files with files created by other programs (e.g. Photoshop) – after all, .pat is just a part of an (arbitrary) file name.

(However, GIMP *does* support Photoshop .pat files until a certain version.)

PNG, JPEG, BMP, GIF, TIFF Since GIMP 2.2 you can use .png, .jpg, .bmp, .gif, or .tiff files as patterns.

To make a pattern available, you place it in one of the folders in GIMP's pattern search path. By default, the pattern search path includes two folders, the system patterns folder, which you should not use or alter, and the patterns folder inside your personal GIMP directory. You can add new folders to the pattern search path using the Pattern Folders page of the Preferences dialog. Any PAT file (or, in GIMP 2.2, any of the other acceptable formats) included in a folder in the pattern search path will show up in the Patterns dialog the next time you start GIMP.

There are countless ways of creating interesting patterns in GIMP, using the wide variety of available tools and filters -- particularly the rendering filters. You can find tutorials for this in many locations, including the GIMP home page [GIMP]. Some of the filters have options that allows you to make their results tileable. Also, see Section 17.2.7, this filter allows you to blend the edges of an image in order to make it more smoothly tileable.

Figure 7.29 Pattern script examples

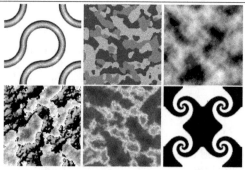

Examples of patterns created using six of the Pattern Script-Fu's that come with GIMP. Default settings were used for everything except size. (From left to right: 3D Truchet; Camouflage; Flatland; Land; Render Map; Swirly)

Also of interest are a set of pattern-generating scripts that come with GIMP: you can find them in the menu bar, through File → Create → Patterns. Each of the scripts creates a new image filled with a particular type of pattern: a dialog pops up that allows you to set parameters controlling the details of the appearance. Some of these patterns are most useful for cutting and pasting; others serve best as bumpmaps.

Figure 7.30 How to create new patterns

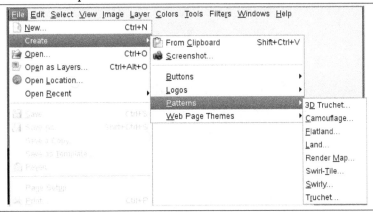

7.12 Palettes

A *palette* is a set of discrete colors. In GIMP, palettes are used mainly for two purposes:

- They allow you to paint with a selected set of colors, in the same way an oil painter works with colors from a limited number of tubes.

- They form the colormaps of indexed images. An indexed image can use a maximum of 256 different colors, but these can be any colors. The colormap of an indexed image is called an "indexed palette" in GIMP.

Actually neither of these functions fall very much into the mainstream of GIMP usage: it is possible to do rather sophisticated things in GIMP without ever dealing with palettes. Still, they are something that an advanced user should understand, and even a less advanced user may need to think about them in some situations, as for example when working with GIF files.

Figure 7.31 The Palettes dialog

When you install GIMP, it comes supplied with several dozen predefined palettes, and you can also create new ones. Some of the predefined palettes are commonly useful, such as the "Web" palette, which contains the set of colors considered "web safe"; many of the palettes seem to have been chosen more or less whimsically. You can access all of the available palettes using the Palettes dialog. This is also the starting point if you want to create a new palette.

Figure 7.32 The Palette Editor

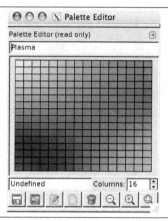

Double-clicking on a palette in the Palettes dialog brings up the Palette Editor, showing the colors from the palette you clicked on. You can use this to paint with the palette: clicking on a color sets GIMP's foreground to that color, as shown in the Color Area of the Toolbox. Holding down the **Ctrl** key while clicking, on the other hand, sets GIMP's background color to the color you click on.

You can also, as the name implies, use the Palette Editor to change the colors in a palette, so long as it is a palette that you have created yourself. You cannot edit the palettes that are supplied with GIMP; however you can duplicate them and then edit the copies.

When you create palettes using the Palette Editor, they are automatically saved as soon as you exit GIMP, in the `palettes` folder of your personal GIMP directory. Any palette files in this directory, or in the system `palettes` directory created when GIMP is installed, are automatically loaded and shown in the Palettes dialog the next time you start GIMP. You can also add other folders to the palette search path using the Palette Folders page of the Preferences dialog.

GIMP palettes are stored using a special file format, in files with the extension `.gpl`. It is a very simple format, and they are ASCII files, so if you happen to obtain palettes from another source, and would like to use them in GIMP, it probably won't be very hard to convert them: just take a look at any `.gpl` and you will see what to do.

7.12.1 Colormap

Confusingly, GIMP makes use of two types of palettes. The more noticeable are the type shown in the Palettes dialog: palettes that exist independently of any image. The second type, *indexed palettes*, form the colormaps of indexed images. Each indexed image has its own private indexed palette, defining the set of colors available in the image: the maximum number of colors allowed in an indexed palette is 256. These palettes are called "indexed" because each color is associated with an index number. (Actually, the colors in ordinary palettes are numbered as well, but the numbers have no functional significance.)

Figure 7.33 The Colormap dialog

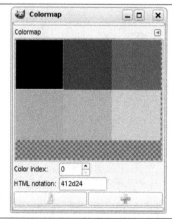

The colormap of an indexed image is shown in the Indexed Palette dialog, which should not be confused with the Palettes dialog. The Palettes dialog shows a list of all of the palettes available; the Colormap dialog shows the colormap of the currently active image, if it is an indexed image – otherwise it shows nothing.

You can, however, create an ordinary palette from the colors in an indexed image—actually from the colors in any image. To do this, choose Import Palette from the right-click popup menu in the Palettes dialog: this pops up a dialog that gives you several options, including the option to import the palette from an image. (You can also import any of GIMP's gradients as a palette.) This possibility becomes important if you want to create a set of indexed images that all use the same set of colors.

When you convert an image into indexed mode, a major part of the process is the creation of an indexed palette for the image. How this happens is described in detail in Section 16.6.6. Briefly, you have several methods to choose from, one of which is to use a specified palette from the Palettes dialog.

Thus, to sum up the foregoing, ordinary palettes can be turned into indexed palettes when you convert an image into indexed mode; indexed palettes can be turned into ordinary palettes by importing them into the Palettes dialog.

Figure 7.34 Colormap dialog (1) and Palette dialog (2)

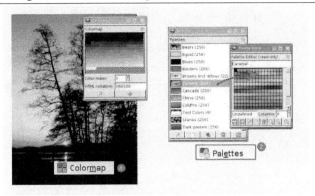

7.13   Presets

If you often use tools with particular settings, presets are for you. You can save these settings and get them back when you want.

Paint tools, which are normally in Toolbox, have a preset system that have been much improved with GIMP-2.8. Color tools (except Posterize and Desaturate), which are not normally in Toolbox, have their own preset system.

Four buttons at the bottom of all tools options dialogs allow you to save, restore, delete or reset presets.

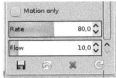

Paint tool presets are described in Section 15.5.1.
Color tool presets are described in Section 14.5.1.1.

7.14   Drawing Simple Objects

In this section, you will learn how to create simple objects in GIMP. It's pretty easy once you figure out how to do it. GIMP provides a huge set of Tools and Shortcuts which most new users get lost in.

7.14.1   Drawing a Straight Line

Let's begin by painting a straight line. The easiest way to create a straight line is by using your favorite brush tool, the mouse and the keyboard.

Drawing a Straight Line

Figure 7.35 A new image

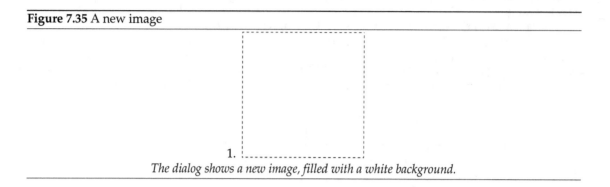

1.
The dialog shows a new image, filled with a white background.

Create a new image. Select your favorite brush tool or use the pencil, if in doubt. Select a foreground color, but be sure that the foreground and background colors are different.

Figure 7.36 The start of the straight line

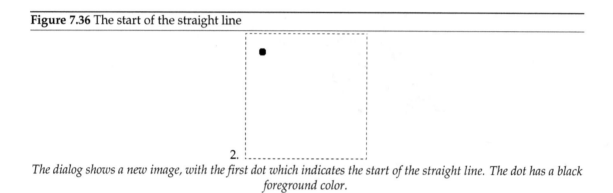

2.
The dialog shows a new image, with the first dot which indicates the start of the straight line. The dot has a black foreground color.

Create a starting point by clicking on the image display area with the left mouse button. Your canvas should look similar to Figure 7.35.

Figure 7.37 The helpline

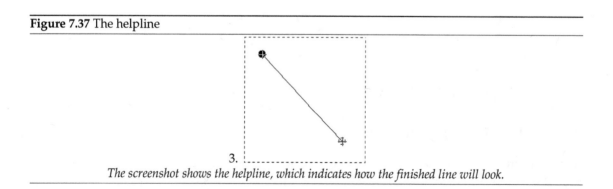

3.
The screenshot shows the helpline, which indicates how the finished line will look.

Now, hold down the **Shift** button on your keyboard and move the mouse away from the starting point you created. You'll see a thin line indicating how the line will look.

Figure 7.38 The line after the second click

4.

*The line created appears in the image window after drawing the second point (or end point), while the **Shift** key is still pressed.*

If you're satisfied with the direction and length of the line, click the left mouse button again to finish the line. The GIMP displays a straight line now. If the line doesn't appear, check the foreground and background colors and be sure that you kept the **Shift** key pressed while painting. You can keep creating lines by continuing to hold the **Shift** key and creating additional end points.

7.14.2   Creating a Basic Shape

1. GIMP is not designed to be used for drawing.[3] However, you may create shapes by either painting them using the technique described in Section 7.14.1 or by using the selection tools. Of course, there are various other ways to paint a shape, but we'll stick to the easiest ones here. So, create a new image and check that the foreground and background colors are different.

Figure 7.39 Creating a rectangular selection

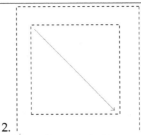

2.

The screenshot shows how a rectangular selection is created. Press and hold the left mouse button while you move the mouse in the direction of the red arrow.

Basic shapes like rectangles or ellipses, can be created using the selection tools. This tutorial uses a rectangular selection as an example. So, choose the rectangular selection tool and create a new selection: press and hold the left mouse button while you move the mouse to another position in the image (illustrated in figure Figure 7.39). The selection is created when you release the mouse button. For more information about key modifiers see selection tools.

Figure 7.40 Rectangular selection filled with foreground color

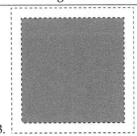

3.

The screenshot shows a rectangular selection filled with the foreground color.

---

[3] Try out e.g. [INKSCAPE] for this purpose.

After creating the selection, you can either create a filled or an outlined shape with the foreground color of your choice. If you go for the first option, choose a foreground color and fill the selection with the bucket fill tool. If you choose the latter option, create an outline by using the Stroke selection menu item from the Edit menu. If you're satisfied with the result, remove the selection.

Chapter 8

Combining Images

8.1 Introduction to Layers

A good way to visualize a GIMP image is as a stack of transparencies: in GIMP terminology, each individual transparency is called a *layer*. There is no limit, in principle, to the number of layers an image can have: only the amount of memory available on the system. It is not uncommon for advanced users to work with images containing dozens of layers.

The organization of layers in an image is shown by the Layers dialog, which is the second most important type of dialog window in GIMP, after the Main Toolbox. The appearance of the Layers dialog is shown in the adjoining illustration. How it works is described in detail in the Layers Dialog section, but we will touch on some aspects of it here, in relation to the layer properties that they display.

Each open image has at any time a single *active drawable*. A "drawable" is a GIMP concept that includes layers, but also several other types of things, such as channels, layer masks, and the selection mask. (Basically, a "drawable" is anything that can be drawn on with painting tools). If a layer is currently active, it is shown highlighted in the Layers dialog, and its name is shown in the status area of the image window. If not, you can activate it by clicking on it. If none of the layers are highlighted, it means the active drawable is something other than a layer.

In the menubar above an image window, you can find a menu called Layer, containing a number of commands that affect the active layer of the image. The same menu can be accessed by right-clicking in the Layers dialog.

8.1.1 Layer Properties

Each layer in an image has a number of important attributes:

Name Every layer has a name. This is assigned automatically when the layer is created, but you can change it. You can change the name of a layer either by double-clicking on it in the Layers dialog, or by right-clicking there and then selecting the top entry in the menu that appears, Edit Layer Attributes.

Presence or absence of an alpha channel An alpha channel encodes information about how transparent a layer is at each pixel. It is visible in the Channel Dialog: white is complete opacity, black is complete transparency and grey levels are partial transparencies.

The background layer is particular. If you have just created a new image, it has still only one layer which is a background layer. If the image has been created with an opaque Fill type, this one layer has no Alpha channel. If you add a new layer, even with an opaque Fill type, an Alpha channel is automatically created, which applies to all layers apart from the background layer. To get a background layer with transparency, either you create your new image with a transparent Fill type, or you use the Add an Alpha Channel.

Every layer other than the bottom layer of an image has automatically an Alpha channel, but you can't see a grayscale representation of the alpha values. See Alpha in Glossary for more information.

Example for Alpha channel

Figure 8.1 Alpha channel example: Basic image

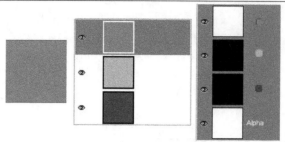

This image has three layers painted with pure 100% opaque Red, Green, and Blue. In the Channel Dialog, you can see that an alpha Channel has been added. It is white because the image is not transparent since there is at least one 100% opaque layer. The current layer is the red one : since it is painted with pure red, there is no green and no blue and the corresponding channels are black.

Figure 8.2 Alpha channel example: One transparent layer

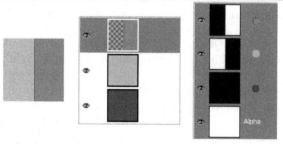

The left part of the first layer has been made transparent (Rectangular selection, Edit/Clear). The second layer, green, is visible. The Alpha channel is still white, since there is an opaque layer in this part of the image.

Figure 8.3 Alpha channel example: Two transparent layers

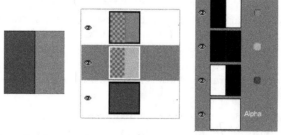

The left part of the second layer has been made transparent. The third layer, blue, is visible through the first and second layers. The Alpha channel is still white, since there is an opaque layer in this part of the image.

Figure 8.4 Alpha channel example: Three transparent layers

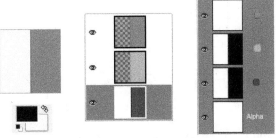

The left part of the third layer has been made transparent. The Alpha channel is still white and the left part of the layer is white, opaque! The background layer has no Alpha channel. In this case, the Clear command works like the Eraser and uses the Background color of Toolbox.

Figure 8.5 Alpha channel example: Alpha channel added to the Background

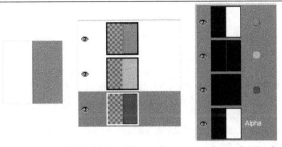

We used the Layer → Transparency → Add Alpha Channel command, on the Background layer. Now, the left part of the image is fully transparent and has the color of the page the image is lying on. The left part of the Alpha Channel thumbnail is black (transparent) in the Channel Dialog.

Layer type The layer type is determined by the image type (see previous section) and the presence or absence of an alpha channel. These are the possible layer types:

- RGB
- RGBA
- Gray
- GrayA
- Indexed
- IndexedA

The main reason this matters is that most filters (in the Filters menu) only accept a subset of layer types, and appear grayed out in the menu if the active layer does not have an acceptable type. Often you can rectify this either by changing the mode of the image or by adding or removing an alpha channel.

Visibility It is possible to remove a layer from an image, without destroying it, by clicking on the symbol in the Layers dialog. This is called "toggling the visibility" of the layer. Most operations on an image treat toggled-off layers as if they did not exist. When you work with images containing many layers, with varying opacity, you often can get a better picture of the contents of the layer you want to work on by hiding some of the other layers.

Tip

 If you *Shift*-click on the eye symbol, this will cause all layers *except* the one you click on to be hidden.

 Linkage to other layers If you click between the eye icon and the layer thumbnail, you get a chain icon, which enables you to group layers for operations on multiple layers (for example with the Move tool or a transform tool).

Figure 8.6 Layer Dialog

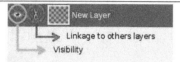

Red: Linkage to others layers. Green: Visibility.

Size and boundaries In GIMP, the boundaries of a layer do not necessarily match the boundaries of the image that contains it. When you create text, for example, each text item goes into its own separate layer, and the layer is precisely sized to contain the text and nothing more. Also, when you create a new layer using cut-and-paste, the new layer is sized just large enough to contain the pasted item. In the image window, the boundaries of the currently active layer are shown outlined with a black-and-yellow dashed line.

The main reason why this matters is that you cannot do anything to a layer outside of its boundaries: you can't act on what doesn't exist. If this causes you problems, you can alter the dimensions of the layer using any of several commands that you can find near the bottom of the Layer menu.

Note

The amount of memory that a layer consumes is determined by its dimensions, not its contents. So, if you are working with large images or images that contain many layers, it might pay off to trim layers to the minimum possible size.

Opacity The opacity of a layer determines the extent to which it lets colors from layers beneath it in the stack show through. Opacity ranges from 0 to 100, with 0 meaning complete transparency, and 100 meaning complete opacity.

Mode The Mode of a layer determines how colors from the layer are combined with colors from the underlying layers to produce a visible result. This is a sufficiently complex, and sufficiently important, concept to deserve a section of its own, which follows. See Section 8.2.

Layer mask In addition to the alpha channel, there is another way to control the transparency of a layer: by adding a *layer mask*, which is an extra grayscale drawable associated with the layer. A layer does not have a layer mask by default: it must be added specifically. Layer masks, and how to work with them, are described much more extensively in the Layer Mask section.

"Lock alpha channel" setting In the upper left corner of the Layers dialog appears a small checkbox that controls the "Lock" setting for the transparency of the layer (see the figure below). If this is checked, then the alpha channel for the layer is locked, and no manipulation has any effect on it. In particular, nothing that you do to a transparent part of the layer will have any effect.

Figure 8.7 Lock Alpha channel

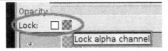

8.2 Layer Modes

GIMP has twenty-one layer modes. Layer modes are also sometimes called "blending modes". Selecting a layer mode changes the appearance of the layer or image, based on the layer or layers beneath it. If there is only one layer, the layer mode has no effect. There must therefore be at least two layers in the image to be able to use layer modes.

You can set the layer mode in the Mode menu in the Layers dialog. GIMP uses the layer mode to determine how to combine each pixel in the top layer with the pixel in the same location in the layer below it.

Note

There is a drop-down list in the Toolbox options box which contains modes that affect the painting tools in a similar way to the layer modes. You can use all of the same modes for painting that are available for layers, and there are two additional modes just for the painting tools. See Section 14.3.3.

Layer modes permit complex color changes in the image. They are often used with a new layer which acts as a kind of mask. For example, if you put a solid white layer over an image and set the layer mode of the new layer to "Saturation", the underlying visible layers will appear in shades of gray.

Figure 8.8 Images (masks) for layer mode examples

(a) *Mask 1*

(b) *Mask 2*

Figure 8.9 Images (backgrounds) for layer mode examples

(a) *Key fob*   (b) *Ducks*

In the descriptions of the layer modes below, the equations are also shown. This is for those who are curious about the mathematics of the layer modes. You do not need to understand the equations in order to use the layer modes effectively, however.

The equations are in a shorthand notation. For example, the equation

Equation 8.1 Example

$$E = M + I$$

means, " For each pixel in the upper (*Mask*)and lower (*Image*) layer, add each of the corresponding color components together to form the *E* resulting pixel's color. " Pixel color components must always be between 0 and 255.

Note

 Unless the description below says otherwise, a negative color component is set to 0 and a color component larger than 255 is set to 255.

The examples below show the effects of each of the modes.

Since the results of each mode vary greatly depending upon the colors on the layers, these images can only give you a general idea of how the modes work. You are encouraged to try them out yourself. You might start with two similar layers, where one is a copy of the other, but slightly modified (by being blurred, moved, rotated, scaled, color-inverted, etc.) and seeing what happens with the layer modes.

Normal

Figure 8.10 Example for layer mode "Normal"

(a) *Both images are blended into each other with the same intensity.*

(b) *With 100% opacity only the upper layer is shown when blending with "Normal".*

Normal mode is the default layer mode. The layer on top covers the layers below it. If you want to see anything below the top layer when you use this mode, the layer must have some transparent areas.

The equation is:

Equation 8.2 Equation for layer mode Normal

$$E = M$$

Dissolve

Figure 8.11 Example for layer mode "Dissolve"

(a) *Both images are blended into each other with the same intensity.*

(b) *With 100% opacity only the upper layer is shown when blending with "dissolve".*

Dissolve mode dissolves the upper layer into the layer beneath it by drawing a random pattern of pixels in areas of partial transparency. It is useful as a layer mode, but it is also often useful as a painting mode.

This is especially visible along the edges within an image. It is easiest to see in an enlarged screen-shot. The image on the left illustrates "Normal" layer mode (enlarged) and the image on the right shows the same two layers in "Dissolve" mode, where it can be clearly seen how the pixels are dispersed.

Figure 8.12 Enlarged screenshots

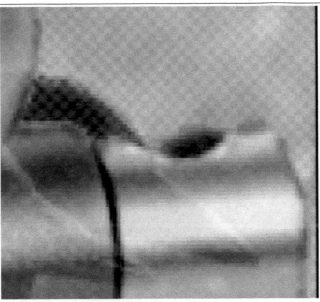

(a) *Normal mode.*

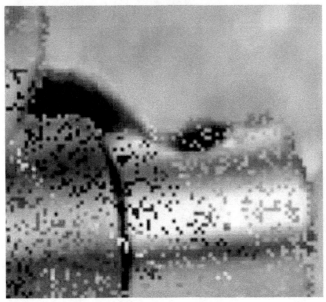

(b) *Dissolve mode.*

Multiply

Figure 8.13 Example for layer mode "Multiply"

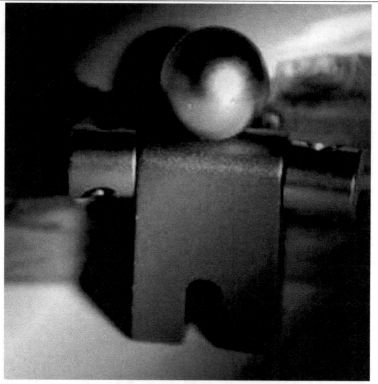

(a) *Mask 1 is used as upper layer with 100% opacity.*

(b) *Mask 2 is used as upper layer with 100% opacity.*

Multiply mode multiplies the pixel values of the upper layer with those of the layer below it and then divides the result by 255. The result is usually a darker image. If either layer is white, the resulting image is the same as the other layer (1 * I = I). If either layer is black, the resulting image is completely black (0 * I = 0).

The equation is:

Equation 8.3 Equation for layer mode Multiply

$$E = \frac{M \times I}{255}$$

The mode is commutative; the order of the two layers doesn't matter.

Divide

Figure 8.14 Example for layer mode "Divide"

(a) *Mask 1 is used as upper layer with 100% opacity.*

(b) *Mask 2 is used as upper layer with 100% opacity.*

Divide mode multiplies each pixel value in the lower layer by 256 and then divides that by the corresponding pixel value of the upper layer plus one. (Adding one to the denominator avoids dividing by zero.) The resulting image is often lighter, and sometimes looks "burned out".

The equation is:

Equation 8.4 Equation for layer mode Divide

$$E = \frac{256 \times I}{M + 1}$$

Screen

Figure 8.15 Example for layer mode "Screen"

(a) *Mask 1 is used as upper layer with 100% opacity.*

(b) *Mask 2 is used as upper layer with 100% opacity.*

Screen mode inverts the values of each of the visible pixels in the two layers of the image. (That is, it subtracts each of them from 255.) Then it multiplies them together, divides by 255 and inverts this value again. The resulting image is usually brighter, and sometimes "washed out" in appearance. The exceptions to this are a black layer, which does not change the other layer, and a white layer, which results in a white image. Darker colors in the image appear to be more transparent.

The equation is:

Equation 8.5 Equation for layer mode Screen

$$E = 255 - \frac{(255 - M) \times (255 - I)}{255}$$

The mode is commutative; the order of the two layers doesn't matter.

Overlay

Figure 8.16 Example for layer mode "Overlay"

(a) *Mask 1 is used as upper layer with 100% opacity.*

(b) *Mask 2 is used as upper layer with 100% opacity.*

Overlay mode inverts the pixel value of the lower layer, multiplies it by two times the pixel value of the upper layer, adds that to the original pixel value of the lower layer, divides by 255, and then multiplies by the pixel value of the original lower layer and divides by 255 again. It darkens the image, but not as much as with "Multiply" mode.

The equation is: [1]

Equation 8.6 Equation for layer mode Overlay

$$E = \frac{I}{255} \times \left(I + \frac{2 \times M}{255} \times (255 - I) \right)$$

Dodge

---

[1] The equation is the *theoretical* equation. Due to Bug #162395 , the actual equation is equivalent to Soft light. It is difficult to fix this bug without changing the appearance of existing images.

Figure 8.17 Example for layer mode "Dodge"

(a) *Mask 1 is used as upper layer with 100% opacity.*

(b) *Mask 2 is used as upper layer with 100% opacity.*

Dodge mode multiplies the pixel value of the lower layer by 256, then divides that by the inverse of the pixel value of the top layer. The resulting image is usually lighter, but some colors may be inverted.

In photography, dodging is a technique used in a darkroom to decrease the exposure in particular areas of the image. This brings out details in the shadows. When used for this purpose, dodge may work best on Grayscale images and with a painting tool, rather than as a layer mode.

The equation is:

Equation 8.7 Equation for layer mode Dodge

$$E = \frac{256 \times I}{(255 - M) + 1}$$

Burn

Figure 8.18 Example for layer mode "Burn"

(a) *Mask 1 is used as upper layer with 100% opacity.*

(b) *Mask 2 is used as upper layer with 100% opacity.*

Burn mode inverts the pixel value of the lower layer, multiplies it by 256, divides that by one plus the pixel value of the upper layer, then inverts the result. It tends to make the image darker, somewhat similar to "Multiply" mode.

In photography, burning is a technique used in a darkroom to increase the exposure in particular areas of the image. This brings out details in the highlights. When used for this purpose, burn may work best on Grayscale images and with a painting tool, rather than as a layer mode.

The equation is:

Equation 8.8 Equation for layer mode Burn

$$E = 255 - \frac{256 \times (255 - I)}{M + 1}$$

Hard light

Figure 8.19 Example for layer mode "Hard light"

(a) *Mask 1 is used as upper layer with 100% opacity.*

(b) *Mask 2 is used as upper layer with 100% opacity.*

Hard light mode is rather complicated because the equation consists of two parts, one for darker colors and one for brighter colors. If the pixel color of the upper layer is greater than 128, the layers are combined according to the first formula shown below. Otherwise, the pixel values of the upper and lower layers are multiplied together and multiplied by two, then divided by 256. You might use this mode to combine two photographs and obtain bright colors and sharp edges.

The equation is complex and different according to the value >128 or ≤ 128:

Equation 8.9 Equation for layer mode Hard light, M > 128

$$E = 255 - \frac{(255 - 2 \times (M - 128)) \times (255 - I)}{256}, \qquad M > 128$$

Equation 8.10 Equation for layer mode Hard light, M ≤ 128

$$E = \frac{2 \times M \times I}{256}, \qquad M \leq 128$$

Soft light

Figure 8.20 Example for layer mode "Soft light"

(a) *Mask 1 is used as upper layer with 100% opacity.*

(b) *Mask 2 is used as upper layer with 100% opacity.*

Soft light is not related to "Hard light" in anything but the name, but it does tend to make the edges softer and the colors not so bright. It is similar to "Overlay" mode. In some versions of

GIMP, "Overlay" mode and "Soft light" mode are identical.

The equation is complicated. It needs Rs, the result of Screen mode :

Equation 8.11 Equation for layer mode Screen

$$R_s = 255 - \frac{(255 - M) \times (255 - I)}{255}$$

Equation 8.12 Equation for layer mode Soft light

$$E = \frac{(255 - I) \times M + R_s}{255} \times I$$

Grain extract

Figure 8.21 Example for layer mode "Grain extract"

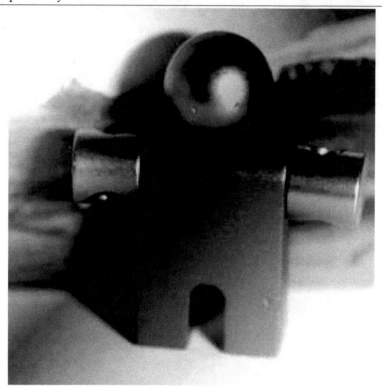

(a) *Mask 1 is used as upper layer with 100% opacity.*

(b) *Mask 2 is used as upper layer with 100% opacity.*

Grain extract mode is supposed to extract the "film grain" from a layer to produce a new layer that is pure grain, but it can also be useful for giving images an embossed appearance. It subtracts the pixel value of the upper layer from that of the lower layer and adds 128.

The equation is:

Equation 8.13 Equation for layer mode Grain extract

$$E = I - M + 128$$

Grain merge There are two more layer modes, but these are available only for painting tools. See Painting Modes for detailed information.

Figure 8.22 Example for layer mode "Grain merge"

(a) *Mask 1 is used as upper layer with 100% opacity.*

(b) *Mask 2 is used as upper layer with 100% opacity.*

Grain merge mode merges a grain layer (possibly one created from the "Grain extract" mode) into the current layer, leaving a grainy version of the original layer. It does just the opposite of "Grain extract". It adds the pixel values of the upper and lower layers together and subtracts 128.

The equation is:

Equation 8.14 Equation for layer mode Grain merge

$$E = I + M - 128$$

Difference

Figure 8.23 Example for layer mode "Difference"

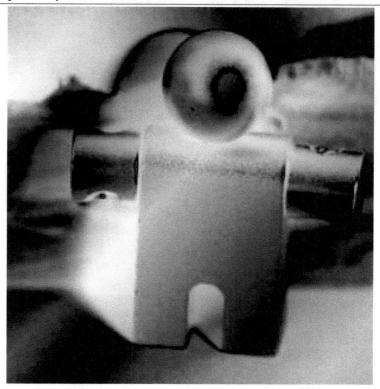

(a) *Mask 1 is used as upper layer with 100% opacity.*

(b) *Mask 2 is used as upper layer with 100% opacity.*

Difference mode subtracts the pixel value of the upper layer from that of the lower layer and then takes the absolute value of the result. No matter what the original two layers look like, the result looks rather odd. You can use it to invert elements of an image.

The equation is:

Equation 8.15 Equation for layer mode Difference

$$E = |I - M|$$

The mode is commutative; the order of the two layers doesn't matter.

Addition

Figure 8.24 Example for layer mode "Addition"

(a) *Mask 1 is used as upper layer with 100% opacity.*

(b) *Mask 2 is used as upper layer with 100% opacity.*

Addition mode is very simple. The pixel values of the upper and lower layers are added to each other. The resulting image is usually lighter. The equation can result in color values greater than

255, so some of the light colors may be set to the maximum value of 255.

The equation is:

Equation 8.16 Equation for layer mode Addition

$$E = \min\big((M + I), 255\big)$$

The mode is commutative; the order of the two layers doesn't matter.

Subtract

Figure 8.25 Example for layer mode "Subtract"

(a) *Mask 1 is used as upper layer with 100% opacity.*

(b) *Mask 2 is used as upper layer with 100% opacity.*

Subtract mode subtracts the pixel values of the upper layer from the pixel values of the lower layer. The resulting image is normally darker. You might get a lot of black or near-black in the resulting image. The equation can result in negative color values, so some of the dark colors may be set to the minimum value of 0.

The equation is:

Equation 8.17 Equation for layer mode Subtraction

$$E = \max\big((I - M), 0\big)$$

Darken only

Figure 8.26 Example for layer mode "Darken only"

(a) *Mask 1 is used as upper layer with 100% opacity.*

(b) *Mask 2 is used as upper layer with 100% opacity.*

Darken only mode compares each component of each pixel in the upper layer with the corresponding one in the lower layer and uses the smaller value in the resulting image. Completely white layers have no effect on the final image and completely black layers result in a black image.

The equation is:

Equation 8.18 Equation for layer mode Darken only

$$E = \min(M, I)$$

The mode is commutative; the order of the two layers doesn't matter.

Lighten only

Figure 8.27 Example for layer mode "Lighten only"

(a) *Mask 1 is used as upper layer with 100% opacity.*

(b) *Mask 2 is used as upper layer with 100% opacity.*

Lighten only mode compares each component of each pixel in the upper layer with the corresponding one in the lower layer and uses the larger value in the resulting image. Completely black layers have no effect on the final image and completely white layers result in a white image.

The equation is:

Equation 8.19 Equation for layer mode Lighten only

$$E = \max(M, I)$$

The mode is commutative; the order of the two layers doesn't matter.

Hue

Figure 8.28 Example for layer mode "Hue"

(a) *Mask 1 is used as upper layer with 100% opacity.*

(b) *Mask 2 is used as upper layer with 100% opacity.*

Hue mode uses the hue of the upper layer and the saturation and value of the lower layer to form the resulting image. However, if the saturation of the upper layer is zero, the hue is taken from the lower layer, too.

Saturation

Figure 8.29 Example for layer mode "Saturation"

(a) *Mask 1 is used as upper layer with 100% opacity.*

(b) *Mask 2 is used as upper layer with 100% opacity.*

Saturation mode uses the saturation of the upper layer and the hue and value of the lower layer to form the resulting image.

Color

Figure 8.30 Example for layer mode "Color"

(a) *Mask 1 is used as upper layer with 100% opacity.*

(b) *Mask 2 is used as upper layer with 100% opacity.*

Color mode uses the hue and saturation of the upper layer and the value of the lower layer to form the resulting image.

Value

Figure 8.31 Example for layer mode "Value"

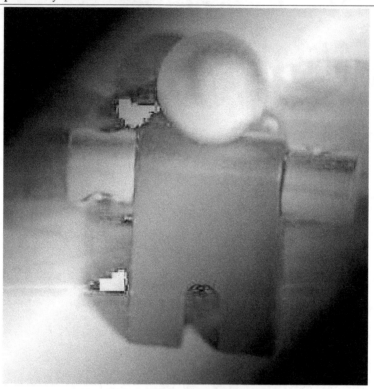

(a) *Mask 1 is used as upper layer with 100% opacity.*

(b) *Mask 2 is used as upper layer with 100% opacity.*

Value mode uses the value of the upper layer and the saturation and hue of the lower layer to form the resulting image. You can use this mode to reveal details in dark and light areas of an image without changing the saturation.

Each layer in an image can have a different layer mode. (Of course, the layer mode of the bottom layer of an image has no effect.) The effects of these layer modes are cumulative. The image shown below has three layers. The top layer consists of Wilber surrounded by transparency and has a layer mode of "Difference". The second layer is solid light blue and has a layer mode of "Addition". The bottom layer is filled with the "Red Cubes" pattern.

Figure 8.32 Multi layer example

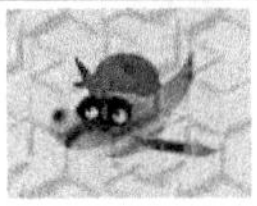

GIMP also has similar modes which are used for the painting tools. These are the same twenty-one modes as the layer modes, plus additionally two modes which are specific to the painting tools. You can set these modes from the Mode menu in the Tools option dialog. In the equations shown above, the layer you are painting on is the "lower layer" and the pixels painted by the tool are the "upper layer". Naturally, you do not need more than one layer in the image to use these modes, since they only operate on the current layer and the selected painting tool.

See Section 14.3.1.3 for a description of the two additional painting modes.

8.3   Creating New Layers

There are several ways to create new layers in an image. Here are the most important ones:

- Selecting Layer → New Layer in the image menu. This brings up a dialog that allows you to set the basic properties of the new layer; see the New Layer dialog section for help with it.

- Selecting Layer → Duplicate Layer in the image menu. This creates a new layer, that is a perfect copy of the currently active layer, just above the active layer.

- When you "cut" or "copy" something, and then paste it using Ctrl-V or Edit → Paste, the result is a "floating selection", which is a sort of temporary layer. Before you can do anything else, you either have to anchor the floating selection to an existing layer, or convert it into a normal layer. If you do the latter, the new layer will be sized just large enough to contain the pasted material.

8.4   Layer Groups

This possibility appeared with GIMP-2.8.

You can group layers that have similarities in a tree-like way. So, the layer list becomes easier to manage.

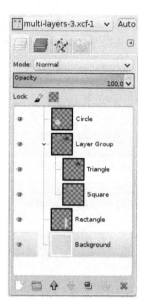

Create a Layer Group You can create a layer group by clicking on the Create a new layer group button at the bottom of the layer dialog,

through Layer → New Layer Group, or through the layer dialog context menu.

This empty layer group appears just above the current layer. It is important to give it an evocative name (double-click or **F2** on the name, or use **Edit Layer Attributes** in the context menu you get by right clicking the Layer dialog, to edit it), else you will get confused when several ones are created.

You can create several layer groups and you can **embbed** them, that is include a layer group in another one.

Adding Layers to a Layer Group You can add *existing layers* to a layer group by click-and-dragging them.

Note

The hand representing the mouse pointer must turn smaller before releasing the mouse button.

A thin horizontal line marks where the layer will be laid down.

To add a *new layer* to the current layer group, click on the Create a new layer at the bottom of the layer dialog, or use the New Layer command in the image menu.

When a layer group is not empty, a small ">" icon appears. By clicking on it, you can fold/unfold the layer list.

You can put layers to be added together to a layer group by making them, them only, visible, and using the "New From Visible " command. All visible layers, outside and inside layer groups, will be added to the active layer group.

Layers that belong to a layer group are slightly indented to the right, allowing you know easily which layers are part of the group.

Raise and Lower Layer Groups You can raise and lower layer groups in the layer dialog as you do with normal layers: click-and-dragging, using arrow up and down keys at the bottom of the layer dialog.

Duplicate a Layer Group You can duplicate a layer group: click on the Create a duplicate of the layer button or right-click and select the **Duplicate Layer** command in the pop up context menu.

Move Layer Groups You can **move a layer group to another image** by click-and-dragging. You can also copy-paste it using Ctrl-C and Ctrl-V: then, you get a floating selection that you must anchor (anchor button at the bottom of the layer dialog).

You can also **move a layer group to the canvas**: this duplicates the group *in* the group. Chain all layers in the duplicated layer group, activate the Move tool, then, in the image, move the layer. That's a way to multiply multi-layer objects in an image.

Delete a Layer Group To delete a layer group, click on the red cross button at the bottom of the layer dialog or right-click and select **Delete layer**.

Embed Layer Groups When a layer group is activated, you can add another group inside it with the "Add New Layer Group" command. There seems to be no limit, excepted memory, to the number of embedded layer groups.

Layer Modes and Groups A layer mode applied to a layer group acts on layers that are in this group only. A layer mode above a layer group acts on all layers underneath, outside and inside the layer groups.

Original image

Figure 8.33 Layer Mode in or out Layer Group

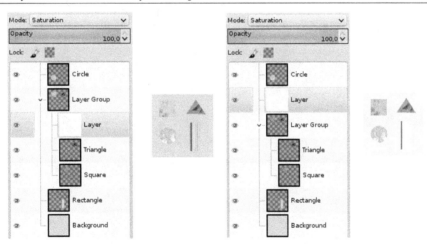

(a) *We added a white layer in the layer group with saturation mode: only square and triangle are grayed out.* (b) *We added a white layer out of the layer group with saturation mode: all layers underneath are grayed out, background layer also.*

Opacity When a layer group is activated, opacity changes are applied to all the layers of the group.

Layer Mask You cannot add a layer mask to a layer group (the corresponding option is grayed out). But, as with normal layers, you can add a layer mask to a layer in the group to mask a part of the layer.

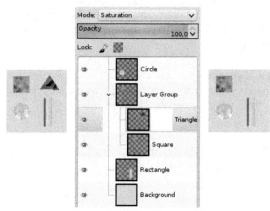

We added a white (Full opacity) layer mask to the triangle layer.

Chapter 9

Text Management

9.1 Text Management

Text is managed with the Text tool. This tool creates a new layer containing the text, above the current layer in the layer dialog, with the size of the text box. Its name is the beginning of the text.

Figure 9.1 Example of a text item

(a) *Example of a text item,* (b) *The layer dialog, with the*
showing the boundary of the text layer above the layer which
text layer. *(Font: Utopia was current.*
Bold)

The Text tool is progressively improved. With GIMP-2.8, you can now edit text directly on canvas. A text tool box has been added which overlays the canvas above the text box.

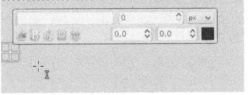

As soon as you click on the canvas with the Text tool, you get a closed text box and a semi-transparent tool box just above.

Text tool options are described in Section 14.6.6.

The default box mode is "Dynamic", and you can start typing text at once. The text box will enlarge gradually. Press **Enter** to add a new line.

You can also **enlarge the text box** by click-and-dragging, as you do with selections. Note that box mode turns to "Fixed". You also have to press **Enter** to add a new line.

To **edit text**, you must, first, select the part you want to edit by click-and-drag, or Shift-arrow key and then use the options of the Section 9.2.

Instead of using the on-canvas text editing, you can use the text editor dialog described in Section 14.6.6.4.

You can **move the text** on the image using the Move tool: you must click on a character, not on the background.

You can get **Unicode characters** with Ctrl-Shift-U plus hexadecimal Unicode code of the desired char. Please see Section 14.6.6.4.

You can **edit the text later**, if the text layer still exists and has not been modified by another tool (see below): make the text layer active in theLayer dialog, select the Text tool and click on the text in the image window.

Managing Text Layer You can operate on a text layer in the same ways as any other layer, but doing so often means giving up the ability to edit the text without losing the results of your work.

To understand some of the idiosyncrasies of text handling, it may help for you to realize that a text layer contains more information than the pixel data that you see: it also contains a representation of the text in a text-editor format. You can see this in the text-editor window that pops up while you are using the Text tool. Every time you alter the text, the image layer is redrawn to reflect your changes.

Now suppose you create a text layer, and then operate on it in some way that does not involve the Text tool: rotate it, for example. Suppose you then come back and try to edit it using the Text tool. As soon as you edit the text, the Text tool will redraw the layer, wiping out the results of the operations you performed in the meantime.

Because this danger is not obvious, the Text tool tries to protect you from it. If you operate on a text layer, and then later try to edit the text, a message pops up, warning you that your alterations will be undone, and giving you three options:

- edit the text anyway;
- cancel;
- create a new text layer with the same text as the existing layer, leaving the existing layer unchanged.

Figure 9.2 Warning lose modifications

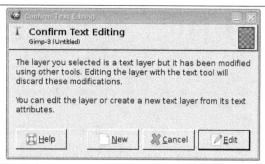

Text Editing Context Menu

Figure 9.3 Text Editing Context Menu

You get this menu by right-clicking on text. It is somewhat different from that of the Text Editor dialog.

- Cut, Copy, Paste, Delete: these options concern a selected text. They remain grayed out as long as no text is selected. "Paste" is activated if the clipboard is full of text.
- Open text file: this command opens a file browser where you can find the wanted text file.
- Clear: this command deletes all the text, selected or not.

- Path from text: this command creates a path from the outlines of the current text. The result is not evident. You have to open the Path dialog and make path visible. Then select the Path tool and click on the text. Every letter is now surrounded with a path component. So you can modify the shape of letters by moving path control points.

This command is similar to Layer → Text to Path.

- Text along path:

This option is enabled only if a path exists. When your text is created, then create or import a path and make it active. If you create your path before the text, the path becomes invisible and you have to make it visible in the Path Dialog.

This command is also available from the "Layer" menu:

Figure 9.4 The Text along Path command among text commands in the Layer menu

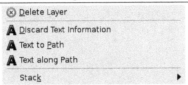

This group of options appears only if a text layer exists.

Click on the Text along Path button. The text is bent along the path. Letters are represented with their outline. Each of them is a component of the new path that appears in the Path dialog. All path options should apply to this new path.

Figure 9.5 "Text along Path" example

- From Left to Right / From Right to Left: fix the writing direction of your language.
- Input Methods: methods are available for some languages. For example, selecting "Inuktitut" transforms your keyboard into an Inuktitut keyboard, temporarily.

9.2 Text Tool Box

Figure 9.6 Text Tool Box

You get this box, which overlays canvas, as soon as you click on canvas with the Text Tool. It allows you to edit text directly on canvas.

Apart from the usual text formatting features like font family, style and size selectors you get numeric control over baseline offset and kerning, as well as the ability to change text color for a selection.

Help pop-ups are self-explanatory.

You can also use Alt-Arrow keys to change baseline offset and kerning.

Important

 These features work on selected text. You get weird effects if no text is selected.

9.2.1 Text Tool Box Context menu

TODO

9.3 Text

9.3.1 Embellishing Text

Figure 9.7 Fancy text

Four fancy text items created using logo scripts: "alien neon", "bovination", "frosty", and "chalk". Default settings were used for everything except font size.

There are many things you can do to vary the appearance of text beyond just rendering it with different fonts or different colors. By converting a text item to a selection or a path, you can fill it, stroke the outlines, transform it, or generally apply the whole panoply of GIMP tools to get interesting effects. As a demonstration of some of the possibilities, try out the "logo" scripts at File → Create → Logos. Each of these scripts allows you to enter some text, and then creates a new image showing a logo constructed out of that text. If you would like to modify one of these scripts, or construct a logo script of your own, the Using Script-Fu and Script-Fu Tutorial sections should help you get started. Of course, you don't need Script-Fu to create these sorts of effects, only to automate them.

9.3.2 Adding Fonts

For the most authoritative and up-to-date information on fonts in GIMP, consult the "Fonts in GIMP 2.0" page [GIMP-FONTS] at the GIMP web site. This section attempts to give you a helpful overview.

GIMP uses the FreeType 2 font engine to render fonts, and a system called Fontconfig to manage them. GIMP will let you use any font in Fontconfig's font path; it will also let you use any font it finds in GIMP's font search path, which is set on the Font Folders page of the Preferences dialog. By default, the font search path includes a system GIMP-fonts folder (which you should not alter, even though it is actually empty), and a `fonts` folder inside your personal GIMP directory. You can add new folders to the font search path if it is more convenient for you.

FreeType 2 is a very powerful and flexible system. By default, it supports the following font file formats:

- TrueType fonts (and collections)

- Type 1 fonts

- CID-keyed Type 1 fonts

- CFF fonts

- OpenType fonts (both TrueType and CFF variants)

- SFNT-based bitmap fonts

- X11 PCF fonts

- Windows FNT fonts

- BDF fonts (including anti-aliased ones)

- PFR fonts

- Type42 fonts (limited support)

You can also add modules to support other types of font files. See FREETYPE 2 [FREETYPE] for more information.

Linux On a Linux system, if the Fontconfig utility is set up as usual, all you need to do to add a new font is to place the file in the directory ~/.fonts. This will make the font available not only to GIMP, but to any other program that uses Fontconfig. If for some reason you want the font to be available to GIMP only, you can place it in the fonts sub-directory of your personal GIMP directory, or some other location in your font search path. Doing either will cause the font to show up the next time you start GIMP. If you want to use it in an already running GIMP, press the *Refresh* 🔄 button in the Fonts dialog.

Windows The easiest way to install a font is to drag the file onto the Fonts directory and let the shell do its magic. Unless you've done something creative, it's probably in its default location of C:\\windows\\fonts or C:\\winnt\\fonts. Sometimes double-clicking on a font will install it as well as display it; sometimes it only displays it. This method will make the font available not only to GIMP, but also to other Windows applications.

Mac OS X There are several ways to install fonts on your system. You can drag-and-drop them to the "Fonts" folder in "Libraries" folder of your "Home Folder". Or you may use Font Book, invoked by double-clicking the font file icon in the Finder. You can see what the font looks like, and click your favorite fonts so that their files are to be installed on the system. These methods will make the fonts available for all applications, not only GIMP. If you want all users can use the fonts, drag-and-drop the fonts to the "Fonts" folder in "Libraries" folder of the Mac OS X Disk, or to the "Computer" folder in the Collection column of Font Book.

To install a Type 1 file, you need both the .pfb and .pfm files. Drag the one that gets an icon into the fonts folder. The other one doesn't strictly need to be in the same directory when you drag the file, since it uses some kind of search algorithm to find it if it's not, but in any case putting it in the same directory does no harm.

In principle, GIMP can use any type of font on Windows that FreeType can handle; however, for fonts that Windows can't handle natively, you should install them by placing the font files in the fonts folder of your personal GIMP directory, or some other location in your font search path. The support Windows has varies by version. All that GIMP runs on support at least TrueType, Windows FON, and Windows FNT. Windows 2000 and later support Type 1 and OpenType. Windows ME supports OpenType and possibly Type 1 (but the most widely used Windows GIMP installer does not officially support Windows ME, although it may work anyway).

> **Note**
>
> GIMP uses Fontconfig to manage fonts on Windows as well as Linux. The instructions above work because Fontconfig by default uses the Windows fonts directory, i. e., the same fonts that Windows uses itself. If for some reason your Fontconfig is set up differently, you will have to figure out where to put fonts so that GIMP can find them: in any case, the `fonts` folder of your personal GIMP directory should work.

9.3.3 Font Problems

Problems with fonts have probably been responsible for more GIMP 2 bug reports than any other single cause, although they have become much less frequent in the most recent releases in the 2.0 series. In most cases they have been caused by malformed font files giving trouble to Fontconfig. If you experience crashes at start-up when GIMP scans your font directories, the best solution is to upgrade to a version of Fontconfig newer than 2.2.0. As a quick workaround you can start gimp with the `--no-fonts` command-line option, but then you will not be able to use the text tool.

Another known problem is that Pango 1.2 cannot load fonts that don't provide an Unicode character mapping. (Pango is the text layout library used by GIMP.) A lot of symbol fonts fall into this category. On some systems, using such a font can cause GIMP to crash. Updating to Pango 1.4 will fix this problem and makes symbol fonts available in GIMP.

A frequent source of confusion occurs on Windows systems, when GIMP encounters a malformed font file and generates an error message: this causes a console window to pop up so that you can see the message. *Do not close that console window. It is harmless, and closing it will shut down GIMP.* When this happens, it often seems to users that GIMP has crashed. It hasn't: closing the console window causes Windows to shut GIMP down. Unfortunately, this annoying situation is caused by an interaction between Windows and the libraries that GIMP links to: it cannot be fixed within GIMP. All you need to do, though, if this happens, is minimize the console window and ignore it.

Chapter 10

Enhancing Photographs

10.1 Working with Digital Camera Photos

10.1.1 Introduction

One of the most common uses of GIMP is to fix digital camera images that for some reason are less than perfect. Maybe the image is overexposed or underexposed; maybe rotated a bit; maybe out of focus: these are all common problems for which GIMP has good tools. The purpose of this chapter is to give you an overview of those tools and the situations in which they are useful. You will not find detailed tutorials here: in most cases it is easier to learn how to use the tools by experimenting with them than by reading about them. (Also, each tool is described more thoroughly in the Help section devoted to it.) You will also not find anything in this chapter about the multitude of "special effects" that you can apply to an image using GIMP. You should be familiar with basic GIMP concepts before reading this chapter, but you certainly don't need to be an expert–if you are, you probably know most of this anyway. And don't hesitate to experiment: GIMP's powerful "undo" system allows you to recover from almost any mistake with a simple Ctrl-Z.

Most commonly the things that you want to do to clean up an imperfect photo are of four types: improving the composition; improving the colors; improving the sharpness; and removing artifacts or other undesirable elements of the image.

10.1.2 Improving Composition

10.1.2.1 Rotating an Image

It is easy, when taking a picture, to hold the camera not quite perfectly vertical, resulting in a picture where things are tilted at an angle. In GIMP, the way to fix this is to use the Rotate tool. Activate this by clicking its icon ![icon] in the Toolbox, or by pressing the Shift-R while inside the image. Make sure the Tool Options are visible, and at the top, make sure for "Transform:" that the left button ("Transform Layer") is selected. If you then click the mouse inside the image and drag it, you will see a grid appear that rotates as you drag. When the grid looks right, click Rotate or press **Enter**, and the image will be rotated.

Now as a matter of fact, it isn't so easy to get things right by this method: you often find that things are better but not quite perfect. One solution is to rotate a bit more, but there is a disadvantage to that approach. Each time you rotate an image, because the rotated pixels don't line up precisely with the original pixels, the image inevitably gets blurred a little bit. For a single rotation, the amount of blurring is quite small, but two rotations cause twice as much blurring as one, and there is no reason to blur things more than you have to. A better alternative is to undo the rotation and then do another, adjusting the angle.

Fortunately, GIMP provides another way of doing it that is considerably easier to use: in the Rotate Tool Options, for the Transform Direction you can select "Backward (Corrective)". When you do this, instead of rotating the grid to compensate for the error, you can rotate it to *line up* with the error. If this seems confusing, try it and you will see that it is quite straightforward.

> **Note**
>
> Since GIMP 2.2, there is an option to preview the results of transformations, instead of just seeing a grid. This makes it easier to get things right on the first try.

After you have rotated an image, there will be unpleasant triangular "holes" at the corners. One way to fix them is to create a background that fills the holes with some unobtrusive or neutral color, but usually a better solution is to crop the image. The greater the rotation, the more cropping is required, so it is best to get the camera aligned as well as possible when you take the picture in the first place.

10.1.2.2 Cropping

When you take a picture with a digital camera, you have some control over what gets included in the image but often not as much as you would like: the result is images that could benefit from trimming. Beyond this, it is often possible to enhance the impact of an image by trimming it so that the most important elements are placed at key points. A rule of thumb, not always to be followed but good to keep in mind, is the "rule of thirds", which says that maximum impact is obtained by placing the center of interest one-third of the way across the image, both widthwise and heightwise.

To crop an image, activate the Crop tool in the Toolbox, or by pressing the "C" key (capitalized) while inside the image. With the tool active, clicking and dragging in the image will sweep out a crop rectangle. It will also pop up a dialog that allows you to adjust the dimensions of the crop region if they aren't quite right. When everything is perfect, hit the Crop button in the dialog.

10.1.3 Improving Colors

10.1.3.1 Automated Tools

In spite of sophisticated exposure-control systems, pictures taken with digital cameras often come out over- or under-exposed, or with color casts due to imperfections in lighting. GIMP gives you a variety of tools to correct colors in an image, ranging to automated tools that run with a simple button-click to highly sophisticated tools that give you many parameters of control. We will start with the simplest first.

GIMP gives you several automated color correction tools. Unfortunately they don't usually give you quite the results you are looking for, but they only take a moment to try out, and if nothing else they often give you an idea of some of the possibilities inherent in the image. Except for "Auto Levels", you can find these tools by following the menu path Colors → Auto in the image menu.

Here they are, with a few words about each:

Normalize This tool (it is really a plug-in) is useful for underexposed images: it adjusts the whole image uniformly until the brightest point is right at the saturation limit, and the darkest point is black. The downside is that the amount of brightening is determined entirely by the lightest and darkest points in the image, so even one single white pixel and/or one single black pixel will make normalization ineffective.

Equalize This is a very powerful adjustment that tries to spread the colors in the image evenly across the range of possible intensities. In some cases the effect is amazing, bringing out contrasts that are very difficult to get in any other way; but more commonly, it just makes the image look weird. Oh well, it only takes a moment to try.

Color Enhance This command increases the saturation range of the colors in the layer, without altering brightness or hue. So this command does not work on grayscale images.

Stretch Contrast This is like "Normalize", except that it operates on the red, green, and blue channels independently. It often has the useful effect of reducing color casts.

Stretch HSV Does the same as Stretch Contrast but works in HSV color space, rather than RGB color space. It preserves the Hue.

White balance This may enhance images with poor white or black by removing little used colors and stretch the remaining range as much as possible.

Auto Levels This is done by activating the Levels tool (Tools → Color Tools → Levels or Colors → Levels in the image menu), and then pressing the Auto button near the center of the dialog. You will see a preview of the result; you must press Okay for it to take effect. Pressing Cancel instead will cause your image to revert to its previous state.

If you can find a point in the image that ought to be perfect white, and a second point that ought to be perfect black, then you can use the Levels tool to do a semi-automatic adjustment that will often do a good job of fixing both brightness and colors throughout the image. First, bring up the Levels tool as previously described. Now, look down near the bottom of the Layers dialog for three buttons with symbols on them that look like eye-droppers (at least, that is what they are supposed to look like). The one on the left, if you mouse over it, shows its function to be "Pick Black Point". Click on this, then click on a point in the image that ought to be black–really truly perfectly black, not just sort of dark–and watch the image change. Next, click on the rightmost of the three buttons ("Pick White Point"), and then click a point in the image that ought to be white, and once more watch the image change. If you are happy with the result, click the Okay button otherwise Cancel.

Those are the automated color adjustments: if you find that none of them quite does the job for you, it is time to try one of the interactive color tools. All of these, except one, can be accessed via Tools->Color Tools in the image menu. After you select a color tool, click on the image (anywhere) to activate it and bring up its dialog.

10.1.3.2 Exposure Problems

The simplest tool to use is the Brightness/Contrast tool. It is also the least powerful, but in many cases it does everything you need. This tool is often useful for images that are overexposed or underexposed; it is not useful for correcting color casts. The tool gives you two sliders to adjust, for "Brightness" and "Contrast". If you have the option "Preview" checked (and almost certainly you should),you will see any adjustments you make reflected in the image. When you are happy with the results, press Okay and they will take effect. If you can't get results that you are happy with, press Cancel and the image will revert to its previous state.

A more sophisticated, and only slightly more difficult, way of correcting exposure problems is to use the Levels tool. The dialog for this tool looks very complicated, but for the basic usage we have in mind here, the only part you need to deal with is the "Input Levels" area, specifically the three triangular sliders that appear below the histogram. We refer you to the Levels Tool Help for instructions; but actually the easiest way to learn how to use it is to experiment by moving the three sliders around, and watching how the image is affected. (Make sure that "Preview" is checked at the bottom of the dialog.)

A very powerful way of correcting exposure problems is to use the *Curves* tool. This tool allows you to click and drag control points on a curve, in order to create a function mapping input brightness levels to output brightness levels. The Curves tool can replicate any effect you can achieve with Brightness/-Contrast or the Levels tool, so it is more powerful than either of them. Once again, we refer you to the Curves Tool Help for detailed instructions, but the easiest way to learn how to use it is by experimenting.

The most powerful approach to adjusting brightness and contrast across an image, for more expert GIMP users, is to create a new layer above the one you are working on, and then in the Layers dialog set the Mode for the upper layer to "Multiply". The new layer then serves as a "gain control" layer for the layer below it, with white yielding maximum gain and black yielding a gain of zero. Thus, by painting on the new layer, you can selectively adjust the gain for each area of the image, giving you very fine control. You should try to paint only with smooth gradients, because sudden changes in gain will give rise to spurious edges in the result. Paint only using shades of gray, not colors, unless you want to produce color shifts in the image.

Actually, "Multiply" is not the only mode that is useful for gain control. In fact, "Multiply" mode can only darken parts of an image, never lighten them, so it is only useful where some parts of an image are overexposed. Using "Divide" mode has the opposite effect: it can brighten areas of an image but not darken them. Here is a trick that is often useful for bringing out the maximum amount of detail across all areas of an image:

1. Duplicate the layer (producing a new layer above it).

2. Desaturate the new layer.

3. Apply a Gaussian blur to the result, with a large radius (100 or more).

4. Set Mode in the Layers dialog to Divide.

5. Control the amount of correction by adjusting opacity in the Layers dialog, or by using Brightness/Contrast, Levels, or Curves tools on the new layer.

6. When you are happy with the result, you can use Merge Down to combine the control layer and the original layer into a single layer.

In addition to "Multiply" and "Divide", you may every so often get useful effects with other layer combination modes, such as "Dodge", "Burn", or "Soft Light". It is all too easy, though, once you start playing with these things, to look away from the computer for a moment and suddenly find that you have just spent an hour twiddling parameters. Be warned: the more options you have, the harder it is to make a decision.

10.1.3.3 Adjusting Hue and Saturation

In our experience, if your image has a color cast---too much red, too much blue, etc---the easiest way to correct it is to use the Levels tool, adjusting levels individually on the red, green, and blue channels. If this doesn't work for you, it might be worth your while to try the Color Balance tool or the Curves tool, but these are much more difficult to use effectively. (They are very good for creating certain types of special effects, though.)

Sometimes it is hard to tell whether you have adjusted colors adequately. A good, objective technique is to find a point in the image that you know should be either white or a shade of gray. Activate the Color Picker tool (the eyedropper symbol in the Toolbox), and click on the aforesaid point: this brings up the Color Picker dialog. If the colors are correctly adjusted, then the red, green, and blue components of the reported color should all be equal; if not, then you should see what sort of adjustment you need to make. This technique, when well used, allows even color-blind people to color-correct an image.

If your image is washed out---which can easily happen when you take pictures in bright light---try the Hue/Saturation tool, which gives you three sliders to manipulate, for Hue, Lightness, and Saturation. Raising the saturation will probably make the image look better. In same cases it is useful to adjust the lightness at the same time. ("Lightness" here is similar to "Brightness" in the Brightness/Contrast tool, except that they are formed from different combinations of the red, green, and blue channels.) The Hue/Saturation tool gives you the option of adjusting restricted subranges of colors (using the buttons at the top of the dialog), but if you want to get natural-looking colors, in most cases you should avoid doing this.

Tip

Even if an image does not seemed washed out, often you can increase its impact by pushing up the saturation a bit. Veterans of the film era sometimes call this trick "Fujifying", after Fujichrome film, which is notorious for producing highly saturated prints.

When you take pictures in low light conditions, in some cases you have the opposite problem: too much saturation. In this case too the Hue/Saturation tool is a good one to use, only by reducing the saturation instead of increasing it.

10.1.4 Adjusting Sharpness

10.1.4.1 Unblurring

If the focus on the camera is not set perfectly, or the camera is moving when the picture is taken, the result is a blurred image. If there is a lot of blurring, you probably won't be able to do much about it with any technique, but if there is only a moderate amount, you should be able to improve the image.

The most generally useful technique for sharpening a fuzzy image is called the Unsharp Mask. In spite of the rather confusing name, which derives from its origins as a technique used by film developers, its result is to make the image sharper, not "unsharp". It is a plug-in, and you can access it as Filters->Enhance->Unsharp Mask in the image menu. There are two parameters, "Radius" and "Amount". The default values often work pretty well, so you should try them first. Increasing either the radius or the amount increases the strength of the effect. Don't get carried away, though: if you make the unsharp mask too strong, it will amplify noise in the image and also give rise to visible artifacts where there are sharp edges.

Tip

Sometimes using Unsharp Mask can cause color distortion where there are strong contrasts in an image. When this happens, you can often get better results by de-composing the image into separate Hue-Saturation-Value (HSV) layers, and running Unsharp Mask on the Value layer only, then recomposing. This works because the human eye has much finer resolution for brightness than for color. See the sections on Decompose and Compose for more information.

Next to "Unsharp Mask" in the Filters menu is another filter called Sharpen, which does similar things. It is a little easier to use but not nearly as effective: our recommendation is that you ignore it and go straight to Unsharp Mask.

In some situations, you may be able to get useful results by selectively sharpening specific parts of an image using the Blur or Sharpen tool from the Toolbox, in "Sharpen" mode. This allows you to increase the sharpness in areas by painting over them with any paintbrush. You should be restrained about this, though, or the results will not look very natural: sharpening increases the apparent sharpness of edges in the image, but also amplifies noise.

10.1.4.2 Reducing Graininess

When you take pictures in low-light conditions or with a very fast exposure time, the camera does not get enough data to make good estimates of the true color at each pixel, and consequently the resulting image looks grainy. You can "smooth out" the graininess by blurring the image, but then you will also lose sharpness. There are a couple of approaches that may give better results. Probably the best, if the graininess is not too bad, is to use the filter called Selective Blur, setting the blurring radius to 1 or 2 pixels. The other approach is to use the Despeckle filter. This has a nice preview, so you can play with the settings and try to find some that give good results. When graininess is really bad, though, it is often very difficult to fix by anything except heroic measures (i.e., retouching with paint tools).

10.1.4.3 Softening

Every so often you have the opposite problem: an image is *too* crisp. The solution is to blur it a bit: fortunately blurring an image is much easier than sharpening it. Since you probably don't want to blur it very much, the simplest method is to use the "Blur" plug-in, accessed via Filters->Blur->Blur from the image menu. This will soften the focus of the image a little bit. If you want more softening, just repeat until you get the result you desire.

10.1.5 Removing Unwanted Objects from an Image

There are two kinds of objects you might want to remove from an image: first, artifacts caused by junk such as dust or hair on the lens; second, things that were really present but impair the quality of the image, such as a telephone wire running across the edge of a beautiful mountain landscape.

10.1.5.1 Despeckling

A good tool for removing dust and other types of lens grunge is the Despeckle filter, accessed as Filters->Enhance->Despeckle from the image menu. Very important: to use this filter effectively, you must begin by making a small selection containing the artifact and a small area around it. The selection must be small enough so that the artifact pixels are statistically distinguishable from the other pixels inside the selection. If you try to run despeckle on the whole image, you will hardly ever get anything useful. Once you have created a reasonable selection, activate Despeckle, and watch the preview as you adjust the parameters. If you are lucky, you will be able to find a setting that removes the junk while minimally affecting the area around it. The more the junk stands out from the area around it, the better your results are likely to be. If it isn't working for you, it might be worthwhile to cancel the filter, create a different selection, and then try again.

If you have more than one artifact in the image, it is necessary to use Despeckle on each individually.

10.1.5.2 Garbage Removal

The most useful method for removing unwanted "clutter" from an image is the Clone   tool, which allows you to paint over one part of an image using pixel data taken from another part (or even from a different image). The trick to using the clone tool effectively is to be able to find a different part of the image that can be used to "copy over" the unwanted part: if the area surrounding the unwanted object is very different from the rest of the image, you won't have much luck. For example, if you have a lovely beach scene, with a nasty human walking across the beach who you would like to teleport away, you will probably be able to find an empty part of the beach that looks similar to the part he is walking across, and use it to clone over him. It is quite astonishing how natural the results can look when this technique works well.

Consult the Clone Tool Help for more detailed instructions. Cloning is as much an art as a science, and the more you practice at it, the better you will get. At first it may seem impossible to produce anything except ugly blotches, but persistence will pay off.

Another tool looking very much as the clone tool, but smarter, is the healing tool which also takes the area around the destination into account when cloning. A typical usage is removal of wrinkles and other minor errors in images.

In some cases you may be able to get good results by simply cutting out the offending object from the image, and then using a plug-in called "Resynthesizer" to fill in the void. This plug-in is not included with the main GIMP distribution, but it can be obtained from the author's web site [PLUGIN-RESYNTH]. As with many things, your mileage may vary.

10.1.5.3 Removing Red-eye

When you take a flash picture of somebody who is looking directly toward the camera, the iris of the eye can bounce the light of the flash back toward the camera in such a way as to make the eye appear bright red: this effect is called "red eye", and looks very bizarre. Many modern cameras have special flash modes that minimize red-eye, but they only work if you use them, and even then they don't always work perfectly. Interestingly, the same effect occurs with animals, but the eyes may show up as other colors, such as green.

From version 2.4, GIMP incorporated a special remove red eye filter. Make a selection with one of the selection tools of the red part of the eye and then choose the "Remove Red Eye" filter. Perhaps you have to fiddle around a bit with the threshold slider to get the right color.

10.1.6 Saving Your Results

10.1.6.1 Files

What file format should you use to save the results of your work, and should you resize it? The answers depend on what you intend to use the image for.

- If you intend to open the image in GIMP again for further work, you should save it in GIMP's native XCF format (i. e., name it something.xcf), because this is the only format that guarantees that none of the information in the image is lost.

- If you intend to print the image on paper, you should avoid shrinking the image, except by cropping it. The reason is that printers are capable of achieving much higher resolutions than video monitors — 600 to 1400 dpi ("dots per inch", the physical density) for typical printers, as compared to 72 to 100 pixels per inch for monitors. A 3000 x 5000-pixel image looks huge on a monitor, but it only comes to about 5 inches by 8 inches on paper at 600 ppi. There is usually no good reason to *expand* the image either: you can't increase the true resolution that way, and it can always be scaled up at the time it is printed. As for the file format, it will usually be fine to use JPEG at a quality level of 75 to 85. In rare cases, where there are large swaths of nearly uniform color, you may need to set the quality level even higher or use a lossless format such as TIFF instead.

- If you intend to display the image on screen or project it with a video projector, bear in mind that the highest screen resolution for most commonly available systems is 1600 x 1200, so there is nothing to gain by keeping the image larger than that. For this purpose, the JPEG format is almost always a good choice.

- If you want to put the image on a web page or send it by email, it is a good idea to make every effort to keep the file size as small as possible. First, scale the image down to the smallest size that makes it possible to see the relevant details (bear in mind that other people may be using different sized monitors and/or different monitor resolution settings). Second, save the image as a JPEG file. In the JPEG save dialog, check the option to "Preview in image window" , and then adjust the Quality slider to the lowest level that gives you acceptable image quality. (You will see in the image the effects of each change.) Make sure that the image is zoomed at 1:1 while you do this, so you are not misled by the effects of zooming.

See the File Formats section for more information.

10.1.6.2   Printing Your Photos

As in most softwares, in GIMP, printing needs to go to main menu File → Print. However it is very useful to keep in mind some elementary concepts to prevent some unpleasant surprises when looking at result, or to cure them if that occurs. You always must remember:

- that image displayed on the screen is in RGB mode and printing will be in CMYK mode; consequently color feature you'll get on printed sheet will not be exactly what you was waiting for. That depends on the used corresponding chart. For the curious ones some adding explanations can be got through a click on these useful Wikipedia links:

    - ICC-Profile [WKPD-ICC]
    - CMYK [WKPD-CMYK]
    - Gamut [WKPD-GAMUT]

- that a screen resolution is roughly within a range from 75 up to 100 dpi; a printer resolution is about 10x higher (or more) than a screen one; printed image size depends on available pixels and resolution; so actual printed size doesn't correspond inevitably to what is displayed on screen nor available sheet size.

Consequently, before any printing it is relevant to go to: Image → Print size and choose here your convenient output size in "print size" box adjusting either sizes or resolution. The symbol shows that the both values are linked. You can dissociate x and y resolution by clicking on that symbol, but it is risky! Probably this possibility is open because printers are built with different x vs. y resolutions. Nevertheless if you unlinked them you can be very surprised! You can try this in special effects.

Last recommendation: think of checking your margins as well as centering. It would be a pity if a too much large margin cuts off some part of your image or if an inappropriate centering damages your work especially if you use a special photo paper.

10.1.6.3   EXIF Data

Modern digital cameras, when you take a picture, add information to the data file about the camera settings and the circumstances under which the picture was taken. This data is included in JPEG or TIFF files in a structured format called EXIF. For JPEG files, GIMP is capable of maintaining EXIF data, if it is built appropriately: it depends on a library called "libexif", which may not be available on all systems. If GIMP is built with EXIF support enabled, then loading a JPEG file with EXIF data, and resaving the resulting image in JPEG format, will cause the EXIF data to be preserved unchanged. This is not, strictly speaking, the right way for an image editor to handle EXIF data, but it is better than simply removing it, which is what earlier versions of GIMP did.

If you would like to see the contents of the EXIF data, you can download from the registry an Exif Browser plug-in [PLUGIN-EXIF]. If you are able to build and install it on your system, you can access it as Filters->Generic->Exif Browser from the image menu. (See Installing New Plug-ins for help.)

Chapter 11

Color Management with GIMP

11.1 Color Management in GIMP

Many devices you use in your design or photography workflow, like digital photo cameras, scanners, displays, printers etc., have their own color reproduction characteristics. If those are not taken into account during opening, editing and saving, harmful adjustments can be done to images. With GIMP you can have reliable output for both Web and print.

Figure 11.1 Image Processing Workflow

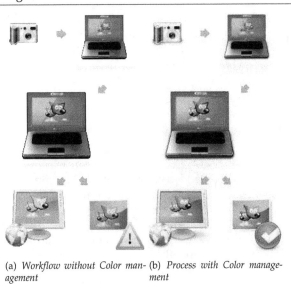

(a) *Workflow without Color man-* (b) *Process with Color manage-*
agement   *ment*

11.1.1 Problems of a non Color Managed Workflow

The basic problem of image manipulation without color management is that you do simply not see what you do. This affects two different areas:

1. There are differences in Colors caused by different color characteristics of different devices like cameras, scanners, displays or printers

2. There are differences in Colors caused by the limitations of the colorspace a specific device is able to handle

The main purpose of color management is to avoid such problems. The approach taken to do so involves the addition of a description of the color characteristic to an image or devices.

These descriptions are called *color profile*. A color profile is basically a look-up table to translate the specific color characteristic of a device to a device-independent color space - the so called working-space.

171

All the image manipulation is then done to images in the working-space. In addition to that the color profile of a device can be used to simulate how colors would look on that device.

The creation of color profiles is most often done by the manufacturer of the devices themselves. To make these profiles usable independent of platform and operating system, the ICC (International Color Consortium) created a standard called ICC-profile that describes how color profiles are stored to files and embedded into images.

11.1.2 Introduction to a Color Managed Workflow

Tip

Most of the parameters and profiles described here can be set in the GIMP preferences. Please see Section 12.1.14 for details.

11.1.2.1 Input

Most digital cameras embed a color profile to individual photo files without user interaction. Digital scanners usually come with a color profile, which they also attach to the scanned images.

Figure 11.2 Applying the ICC-profile

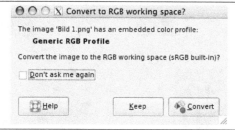

When opening an image with an embedded color profile, GIMP offers to convert the file to the RGB working color space. This is sRGB by default and it is recommended that all work is done in that color space. Should you however decide to keep the embedded color profile, the image will however still be displayed correctly.

In case for some reason a color profile is not embedded in the image and you know (or have a good guess) which one it should be, you can manually assign it to that image.

11.1.2.2 Display

For the best results, you need a color profile for your monitor. If a monitor profile is configured, either system-wide or in the Color Management section of the GIMP Preferences dialog, the image colors will be displayed most accurately.

One of the most important GIMP commands to work with color management is described in Section 16.5.8.

If you do not have a color profile for your monitor, you can create it using hardware calibration and measurement tools. On UNIX systems you will need Argyll Color Management System [ARGYLLCMS] and/or LProf [LPROF] to create color profiles.

11.1.2.2.1 Display Calibration and Profiling For displays there are two steps involved. One is called calibration and the other is called profiling. Also, calibration generally involves two steps. The first involves adjusting external monitor controls such as Contrast, Brightness, Color Temperature, etc, and it is highly dependent on the specific monitor. In addition there are further adjustments that are loaded into the video card memory to bring the monitor as close to a standard state as possible. This information is stored in the monitor profile in the so-called vgct tag. Probably under Windows XP or Mac OS, the operating system loads this information (LUT) in the video card in the process of starting your computer. Under Linux, at present you have to use an external program such as xcalib or dispwin. (If one just does a simple visual calibration using a web site such as that of Norman Koren, one might only use xgamma to load a gamma value.)

The second step, profiling, derives a set of rules which allow GIMP to translate RGB values in the image file into appropriate colors on the screen. This is also stored in the monitor profile. It doesn't change the RGB values in the image, but it does change which values are sent to the video card (which already contains the vgct LUT).

11.1.2.3 Print Simulation

Using GIMP, you can easily get a preview of what your image will look like on paper. Given a color profile for your printer, the display can be switched into Soft Proof mode. In such a simulated printout, colors that cannot be reproduced will optionally be marked with neutral gray color, allowing you to correct such mistakes before sending your images to the printer.

Chapter 12

Enrich my GIMP

12.1 Preferences Dialog

12.1.1 Introduction

Figure 12.1 List of preference pages

The preferences dialog can be accessed from the image menu-bar, through Edit → Preferences. It lets you customize many aspects of the way GIMP works. The following sections detail the settings that you can customize, and what they affect.

All of the Preferences information is stored in a file called gimprc in your personal GIMP directory, so if you are a "power user" who would rather work with a text editor than a graphical interface, you can alter preferences by editing that file. If you do, and you are on a Linux system, then **man gimprc** will give you a lot of technical information about the contents of the file and what they are used for.

175

12.1.2 Environment

Figure 12.2 Environment Preferences

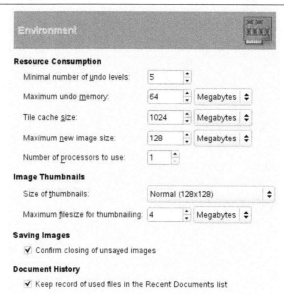

This page lets you customize the amount of system memory allocated for various purposes. It also allows you to disable the confirmation dialogs that appear when you close unsaved images, and to set the size of thumbnail files that GIMP produces.

12.1.2.1 Options

Resource Consumption

Minimal number of undo levels GIMP allows you to undo most actions by maintaining an "Undo History" for each image, for which a certain amount of memory is allocated. Regardless of memory usage, however, GIMP always permits some minimal number of the most recent actions to be undone: this is the number specified here. See Section 3.3 for more information about GIMP's Undo mechanism.

Maximum undo memory This is the amount of undo memory allocated for each image. If the Undo History size exceeds this, the oldest points are deleted, unless this would result in fewer points being present than the minimal number specified above.

Tile cache size This is the amount of system RAM allocated for GIMP image data. If GIMP requires more memory than this, it begins to swap to disk, which may in some circumstances cause a dramatic slowdown. You are given an opportunity to set this number when you install GIMP, but you can alter it here. See How to Set Your Tile Cache for more information.

Maximum new image size This is not a hard constraint: if you try to create a new image larger than the specified size, you are asked to confirm that you really want to do it. This is to prevent you from accidentally creating images much larger than you intend, which can either crash GIMP or cause it to respond verrrrrrrry slowwwwwwwwly.

Number of processors to use Default is one. Your computer may have more than one processor.

Image Thumbnails

Size of thumbnails This options allows you to set the size of the thumbnails shown in the File Open dialog (and also saved for possible use by other programs). The options are "None", "Normal (128x128)", and "Large (256x256)".

Maximum filesize for thumbnailing If an image file is larger than the specified maximum size, GIMP will not generate a thumbnail for it. This options allows you to prevent thumbnailing of extremely large image files from slowing GIMP to a crawl.

Saving Images

Confirm closing of unsaved images Closing an image is not undoable, so by default GIMP asks you to confirm that you really want to do it, whenever it would lead to a loss of unsaved changes. You can disable this if you find it annoying; but then of course you are responsible for remembering what you have and have not saved.

Document history

Keep record of used files in the Recent Documents list When checked, files you have opened will be saved in the Document history. You can access the list of files with the Document history dialog from the image menu-bar : File → Open Recent → Document History.

12.1.3   Interface

Figure 12.3 Assorted Interface Preferences

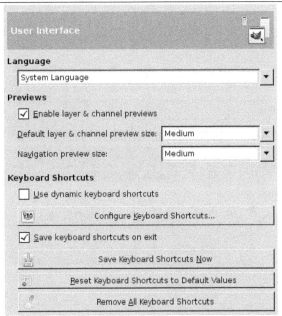

This page lets you customize language, layer/channel previews and keyboard shortcuts.

Options

Language The GIMP's default language is that of your system. You can select another language in the drop-down list. You have to start GIMP again to make this change effective. Please refer to Section 2.1.2.

Previews By default, GIMP shows miniature previews of the contents of layers and channels in several places, including the Layers dialog. If for some reason you would prefer to disable these, you can do it by unchecking Enable layer and channel previews. If you do want previews to be shown, you can customize their sizes using the menus for Default layer and channel preview size and Navigation preview size.

Keyboard Shortcuts Any menu item can be activated by holding down **Alt** and pressing a sequence of keys. Normally, the key associated with each menu entry is shown as an underlined letter in the text, called *accelerator*. If for some reason you would prefer the underlines to go away (maybe because you think they're ugly and you don't use them anyway), then you can make this happen by unchecking Show menu mnemonics.

GIMP can give you the ability to create keyboard shortcuts (key combinations that activate a menu entry) dynamically, by pressing the keys while the pointer hovers over the desired menu entry. However, this capability is disabled by default, because it might lead novice users to accidentally overwrite the standard keyboard shortcuts. If you want to enable it, check Use dynamics keyboard shortcuts here.

Pressing the button for Configure Keyboard Shortcuts brings up the Shortcut Editor, which gives you a graphical interface to select menu items and assign shortcuts to them.

If you change shortcuts, you will probably want your changes to continue to apply in future GIMP sessions. If not, uncheck Save keyboard shortcuts on exit. But remember that you have done this, or you may be frustrated later. If you don't want to save shortcuts on exit every session, you can save the current settings at any time using the Save Keyboard Shortcuts Now button, and they will be applied to future sessions. If you decide that you have made some bad decisions concerning shortcuts, you can reset them to their original state by pressing Reset Saved Keyboard Shortcuts to Default Values.

12.1.4   Theme

Figure 12.4 Theme Preference

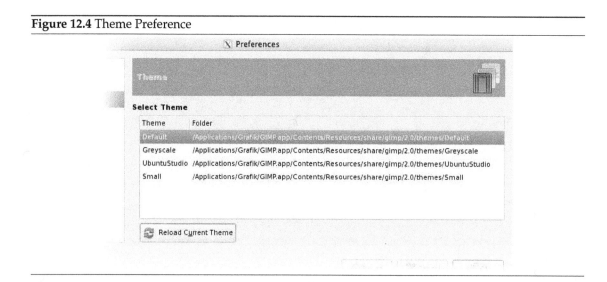

This page lets you select a theme, which determines many aspects of the appearance of the GIMP user interface, including the set of icons used, their sizes, fonts, spacing allowed in dialogs, etc. Two themes are supplied with GIMP: Default, which is probably best for most people, and Small, which may be preferable for those with small or low-resolution monitors. Clicking on a theme in the list causes it to be applied immediately, so it is easy to see the result and change your mind if you don't like it.

You can also use custom themes, either by downloading them from the net, or by copying one of the supplied themes and modifying it. Custom themes should be places in the themes subdirectory of your personal GIMP directory: if they are, they will appear in the list here. Each theme is actually a directory containing ASCII files that you can edit. They are pretty complicated, and the meaning of the contents goes beyond the scope of this documentation, but you should feel free to experiment: in the worst case, if you mess things up completely, you can always revert back to one of the supplied themes.

You cannot edit the supplied themes unless you have administrator permissions, and even if you do, you shouldn't: if you want to customize a theme, make a copy in your personal directory and work on it. If you make a change and would like to see the result "on the fly", you can do so by saving the edited theme file and then pressing Reload Current Theme.

12.1.5   Help System

Figure 12.5 Help System Preferences

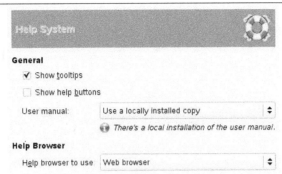

This page lets you customize the behaviour of the GIMP help system.

12.1.5.1   Options

General

Show tool tips Tool tips are small help pop-ups that appear when the pointer hovers for a moment over some element of the interface, such as a button or icon. Sometimes they explain what the element does; sometimes they give you hints about non-obvious ways to use it. If you find them too distracting, you can disable them here by unchecking this option. We recommend that you leave them enabled unless you are a very advanced user.

Show help buttons This option controls whether the help buttons are shown on every tool dialog, which may be used alternatively to invoke the help system.

User manual This drop-down list lets you select between Use a locally installed copy and Use the online version. See Section 16.12.2.

Help Browser

Help browser to use GIMP Help is supplied in the form of HTML files, i. e., web pages. You can view them using either a special help browser that comes with GIMP, or a web browser of your choice. Here you choose which option to use. Because the help pages were carefully checked to make sure they work well with GIMP's browser, whereas other web browsers are somewhat variable in their support of features, the safer option is to use the internal browser; but really any modern web browser should be okay.

> **Note**
>
> Note that the GIMP help browser is not available on all platforms. If it is missing, this option is hidden and the standard web browser will be used to read the help pages.

12.1.6   Tool Options

Figure 12.6 Tool Options Preferences

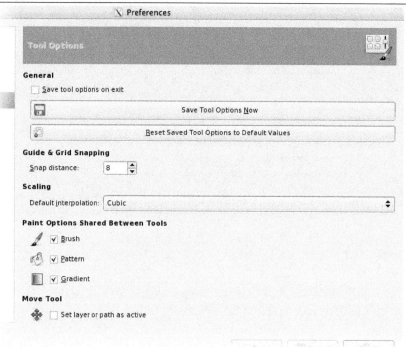

This page lets you customize several aspects of the behavior of tools.

12.1.6.1   Options

General

Save Tool Options On Exit Self explanatory

Save Tool Options Now Self explanatory

Reset Saved Tool Options To Default Values Self explanatory

Guide and Grid Snapping

Snap distance "Snapping" to guides, or to an image grid, means that when a tool is applied by clicking somewhere on the image display, if the clicked point is near enough to a guide or grid, it is shifted exactly onto the guide or grid. Snapping to guides can be toggled using View → Snap to Guides in the image menu; and if the grid is switched on, snapping to it can be toggled using View → Snap to Grid. This preference option determines how close a clicked point must be to a guide or grid in order to be snapped onto it, in pixels.

Scaling

Default interpolation When you scale something, each pixel in the result is calculated by interpolating several pixels in the source. This option determines the default interpolation method: it can always be changed, though, in the Tool Options dialog.

There are four choices:

None This is the fastest method, but it's quite crude: you should only consider using it if your machine is very seriously speed-impaired.

Linear This used to be the default, and is good enough for most purposes.

Cubic This is the best choice (although it can actually look worse than Linear for some types of images), but also the slowest. Since GIMP 2.6, this method is the default.

Sinc (Lanczos3) This method performs a high quality interpolation.

Paint Options Shared Between Tools

Brush, Pattern, Gradient You can decide here whether changing the brush etc for one tool should cause the new item to be used for all tools, or whether each individual tool (pencil, paintbrush, airbrush, etc) should remember the item that was last used for it specifically.

Move tool

Set layer or path as active You can decide here whether changing the current layer or path when using the move tool and without pressing any key.

12.1.7 Toolbox

Figure 12.7 Toolbox Preferences

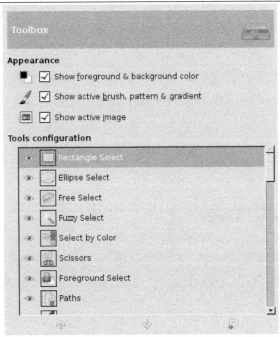

12.1.7.1 Options

Figure 12.8 Default Toolbox appearance

This page lets you customize the appearance of the Toolbox, by deciding whether the three "context information" areas should be shown at the bottom.

Appearance

Show foreground and background color Controls whether the color area on the left (2) appears in the Toolbox.

Show active brush, pattern, and gradient Controls whether the area in the center (3), with the brush, pattern, and gradient icons, appears in the Toolbox.

Show active image Controls whether a preview of the currently active image appears on the right (4).

Tools configuration

In this list, tools with an eye are present in the Toolbox. By default, color tools have no eye: you can add them to the Toolbox by clicking the corresponding checkbox.

You can also sort tools by priority using the arrow up and down buttons at the bottom of the dialog.

This option replaces the Tools Dialog of former GIMP versions.

12.1.8 Default Image Preferences

Figure 12.9 Default New Image Preferences

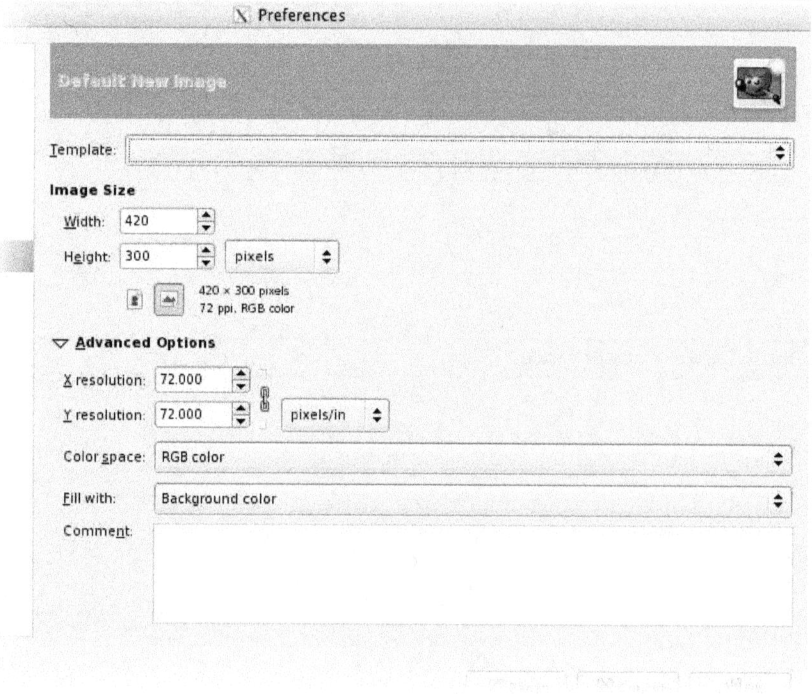

This tab lets you customize the default settings for the New Image dialog. See the New Image Dialog section for an explanation of what each of the values means.

12.1.9   Default Image Grid

Figure 12.10 Default Grid Preferences

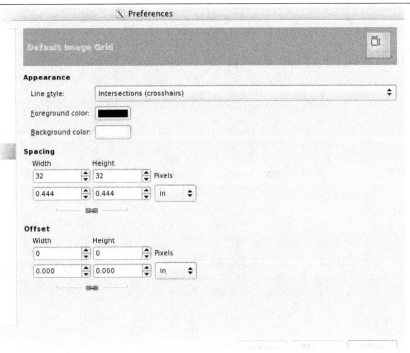

This page lets you customize the default properties of GIMP's grid, which can be toggled on or off using View → Show Grid from the image menu. The settings here match those in the Configure Image Grid dialog, which can be used to reconfigure the grid for an existing image, by choosing Image → Configure Grid from the image menu. See the Configure Grid dialog section for information on the meaning of each of the settings.

12.1.10 Image Windows

Figure 12.11 General Image Window Preference

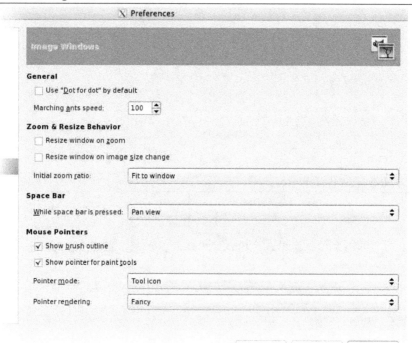

This page lets you customize several aspects of the behaviour of image windows.

12.1.10.1 Options

General

Use "Dot for dot" by default Using "Dot for dot" means that at 1:1 zoom, each pixel is the image is scaled to one pixel on the display. If "Dot for dot" is not used, then the displayed image size is determined by the X and Y resolution of the image. See the Scale Image section for more information.

Marching ants speed When you create a selection, the edge of it is shown as a dashed line with dashes that appear to move, marching slowly along the boundary: they are jokingly called "marching ants". The smaller the value entered here, the faster the ants march (and consequently the more distracting they are!).

Zoom and Resize Behavior

Resize window on zoom If this option is checked, then each time you zoom the image, the image window will automatically resize to follow it. Otherwise, the image window will maintain the same size when you zoom the image.

Resize window on image size change If this option is checked, then each time change the size of the image, by cropping or resizing it, the image window will automatically resize to follow. Otherwise, the image window will maintain the same size.

Initial zoom ratio You can choose either to have images, when they are first opened, scaled so that the whole image fits comfortably on your display, or else shown at 1:1 zoom. If you choose the second option, and the image is too large to fit on your display, then the image window will show only part of it (but you will be able to scroll to other parts).

Space bar

While space bar is pressed

- Pan view (default) or

- Toogle to Move Tool
- No action

Mouse Cursors

Show brush outline If this option is checked, then when you use a paint tool, the outline of the brush will be shown on the image as you move the pointer around. On slow systems, if the brush is very large, this could occasionally cause some lag in GIMP's ability to follow your movements: if so, switching this off might help. Otherwise, you will probably find it quite useful.

Show paint tool cursor If this is checked, a cursor will be shown. This is in addition to the brush outline, if the brush outline is being shown. The type of cursor is determined by the next option.

Cursor mode This option has no effect unless Show paint tool cursor is checked. If it is, you have three choices: Tool icon, which causes a small iconic representation of the currently active tool to be shown beside the cursor; Tool icon with crosshair, which shows the icon as well as a crosshair indicating the center of the cursor; or Crosshair only.

Cursor rendering If you choose "Fancy" here, the cursor is drawn in grayscale. If you choose "Black and White", it is drawn in a simpler way that may speed things up a little bit if you have speed issues.

12.1.11   Image Window Appearance

Figure 12.12 Image Window Appearance Defaults

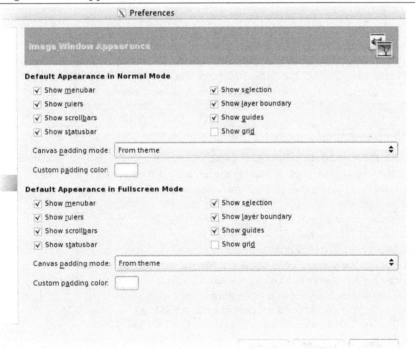

This page lets you customize the default appearance of image windows, for normal mode and for fullscreen mode. All of the settings here can be altered on an image-specific basis using entries in the View menu. See the Image Window section for information on the meaning of the entries.

The only parts that may need further explanation are the ones related to padding. "Padding" is the color shown around the edges of the image, if it does not occupy all of the display area (shown in light gray in all the figures here). You can choose among four colors for the padding color: to use the color specified by the current theme; to use the light or dark colors specified for checks, such as represent transparent parts of the image; or to use a custom color, which can be set using the color button for "Custom padding color".

12.1.12   Image Window Title and Statusbar

Figure 12.13 Image Window Title and Statusbar formats

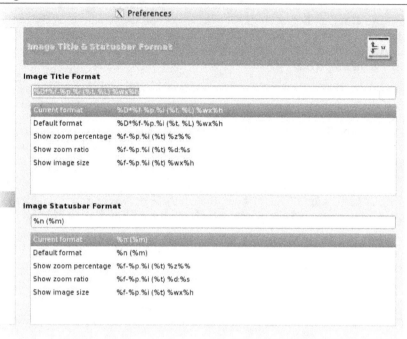

This page lets you customize the text that appears in two places: the title bar of an image, and the status bar. The title bar should appear above the image; however this depends on cooperation from the window manager, so it is not guaranteed to work in all cases. The statusbar appears underneath the image, on the right side. See the Image Window section for more information.

12.1.12.1   Choosing a Format

You can choose among several predesigned formats, or you can create one of your own, by writing a *format string* in the entry area. Here is how to understand a format string: anything you type is shown exactly as you type it, with the exception of *variables*, whose names all begin with "%". Here is a list of the variables you can use:

Variable: %f, *Meaning:* Bare filename of the image, or "Untitled"
Variable: %F, *Meaning:* Full path to file, or "Untitled"
Variable: %p, *Meaning:* Image id number (this is unique)
Variable: %i, *Meaning:* View number, if an image has more than one display
Variable: %t, *Meaning:* Image type (RGB, grayscale, indexed)
Variable: %z, *Meaning:* Zoom factor as a percentage
Variable: %s, *Meaning:* Source scale factor (zoom level = %d/%s)
Variable: %d, *Meaning:* Destination scale factor (zoom level = %d/%s)
Variable: %Dx, *Meaning:* Expands to x if the image is dirty, nothing otherwise
Variable: %Cx, *Meaning:* Expands to x if the image is clean, nothing otherwise
Variable: %l, *Meaning:* The number of layers
Variable: %L, *Meaning:* Number of layers (long form)
Variable: %m, *Meaning:* Memory used by the image
Variable: %n, *Meaning:* Name of the active layer/channel
Variable: %P, *Meaning:* id of the active layer/channel
Variable: %w, *Meaning:* Image width in pixels
Variable: %W, *Meaning:* Image width in real-world units
Variable: %h, *Meaning:* Image height in pixels
Variable: %H, *Meaning:* Image height in real-world units
Variable: %u, *Meaning:* Unit symbol (eg. px for Pixel)

Variable: %U, *Meaning:* Unit abbreviation
Variable: %%, *Meaning:* A literal "%" symbol

12.1.13 Display

Figure 12.14 Display Preferences

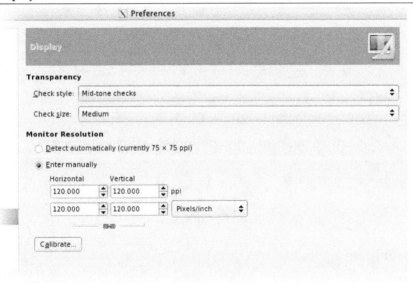

Figure 12.14 Display Preferences

This page lets you customize the way transparent parts of an image are represented, and lets you recalibrate the resolution of your monitor.

12.1.13.1 Options

Transparency

Transparency type By default, GIMP indicates transparency using a checkerboard pattern with mid-tone checks, but you can change this if you want, either to a different type of checkerboard, or to solid black, white, or gray.

Check size Here you can alter the size of the squares in the checkerboard pattern used to indicate transparency.

Figure 12.15 The Calibration dialog

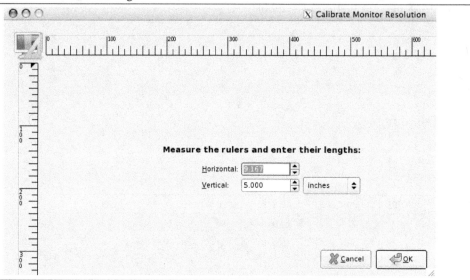

Monitor Resolution Monitor Resolution is the ratio of pixels, horizontally and vertically, to inches. You
   have three ways to proceed here:

- Get Resolution from windowing system. (easiest, probably inaccurate).
- Set Manually
- Push the Calibrate Button.

The Calibrate Dialog My monitor was impressively off when I tried the Calibrate Dialog. The "Calibrate Game" is fun to play. You will need a soft ruler.

12.1.14   Color Management

Figure 12.16 Color Management Preferences

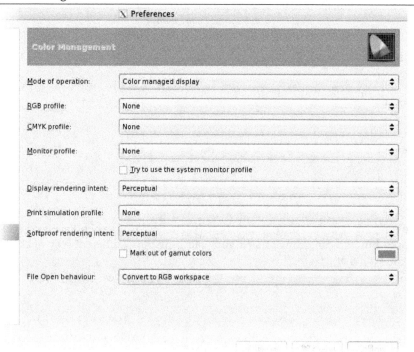

12.1.14.1   Options

This page lets you customize the GIMP color management.

Some of the options let you choose a color profile from a menu. If the desired profile is not in the menu yet, you can add it by clicking on the Select color profile from disk... item.

Tip

Files containing color profiles are easily recognizable by their `.icc` suffix. In addition to that they are usually stored all together in only a few places. If you are running GIMP on Mac OS X, you should try `/Library/ColorSync/Profiles/` and `Library/Printers/[manufacturer]/Profiles`.

Mode of operation Using this option you can decide how the GIMP color management operates. There are three modes you can choose from:

- No color management: choosing this selection shuts down the color management in GIMP completely.

- Color managed display: with this selection you can enable the GIMP color management to provide a fully corrected display of the images according to the given color profile for the display.

- Print simulation: when choosing this selection, you enable the GIMP color management not only to apply the profile for the display, but also the selected printer simulation profile. Doing so, you can preview the color results of a print with that printer.

Note

Please note, that the GIMP color management is used to enhance the display of images and the embedding of profiles to image files only. Especially are the options you choose in this dialog in no way used for printing from within GIMP. This is because the printing is a special task done by a more specialized printing engine that is no part of GIMP.

RGB profile Select the default color profile for working with RGB images.

CMYK profile Select the default color profile for conversion between RGB for the screen work and CMYK for printing.

Monitor profile This option gives you two elements for interaction:

- You should select a display profile for this option. The selected color profile is used to display GIMP on the screen.

- If you activate the Try to use the system monitor profile option, GIMP will use the color profile provided for the displays by the operating systems color management system.

Display rendering intent Rendering intents, as the one you can configure with this option, are ways of dealing with colors that are out-of- *Gamut* colors present in the source space that the destination space is incapable of producing. There are four method rendering intents to choose from:

- Perceptual

- Relative colorimetric

- Saturation

- Absolute colorimetric

A description of the individual methods can be found at *Rendering Intent* .

Print simulation mode You should select a printer profile for this option. The selected color profile is used for the print simulation mode.

Softproof rendering intent This option again provides two different elements for interaction:

- You can use the menu to select the rendering intent for the soft proof. They are the same as already described for the display rendering intent.

- If you enable the Mark out of gamut colors option, all pixels that have a color that is not printable are marked by a special color. Which color is used for this can also be chosen by you. You can do this simply by clicking on the color icon on the right besides the checkbox.

File Open behaviour Using this menu you can determine how GIMP behaves when opening a file that contains an embedded color profile that is not matches the workspace sRGB. You can choose from the following entries:

- Ask what to do: if selected, GIMP will ask every time what to do.

- Keep embedded profile: if you choose this, GIMP will keep the attached profile and not convert the image to the workspace. The image is displayed correctly anyways, because the attached profile will be applied for display.

- Convert to RGB workspace: by choosing this entry GIMP will automatically use the attached color profile to convert the image to the workspace.

Note

For more explanations:

- ICC Profiles are explained in Wikipedia [WKPD-ICC].

- See OpenICC project ([OPENICC]) where GIMP and others great names of free infography contribute to.

 Many profiles to load from the web:

- ICC sRGB Workspace: ICCsRGB [ICCsRGB]

- Microsoft sRGB Workspace: MsRGB [MsRGB]

- Adobe RGB98 Workspace : Adobe RGB (1998) [AdobeRGB]

- ECI (European Color Initiative) Profiles: ECI [ECI]

12.1.15   Input Devices

Figure 12.17 Input devices preferences

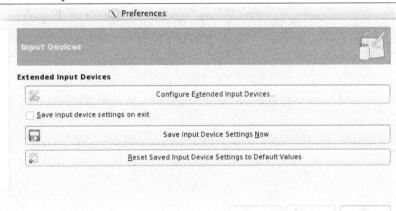

Extended Input Devices

Configure Extended Input Devices This large button allows you to set the devices associated with your computer: tablet, MIDI keyboard... If you have a tablet, you will see a dialog like this:

Figure 12.18 Preferences for a tablet

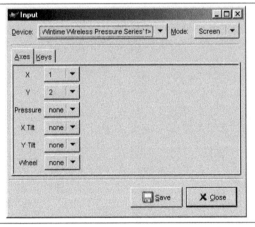

Save input device settings on exit When you check this box, GIMP remembers the tool, color, pattern and brush you were using the last time you quitted.

Save Input Device Settings Now Self explanatory.

Reset Saved Input Device Settings to Default Values Delete your settings and restore default settings.

12.1.16   Input Controllers

Figure 12.19 Input controllers preferences

This dialog has two lists of additional input controllers: Available Controllers on the left, Active Controllers on the right.

A click on an item will highlight it and you can move the controller from one list to the other by clicking on the respective arrow key. When you try to move a controller from the list of active controllers to the available controllers, a dialog pops up and you will have the choice of removing the controller or just disabling it.

When you double click on a (typically active) controller or alternatively click on the Edit button at the bottom of the list, you can configure this controller in a dialog window:

Main Mouse Wheel

Figure 12.20 Main Mouse Wheel

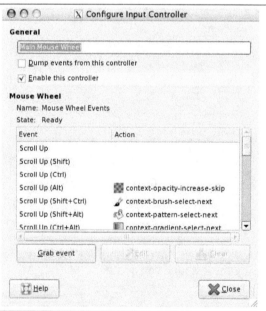

General

Dump events from this controller This option must be checked if you want a print on the stdout of the events generated by the enabled controllers. If you want to see those event you should start GIMP from a terminal or making it to print the stdout to file by the shell redirection. The main use of this option is for debug.

Enable this controller This option must be checked if you want to add a new actions to the mouse wheel.

Mouse Wheel Events In this window with scroll bars you have: on the left, the possible events concerning the mouse wheel, more or less associated with control keys; on the right, the action assigned to the event when it will happen. You have also two buttons, one to Edit the selected event, the other to Cancel the action of the selected event.

Some actions are assigned to events yet. They seem to be examples, as they are not functional.

Select the action allocated to the event After selecting an event, if you click on the Edit button, you open the following dialog:

Figure 12.21 Select Controller Event Action

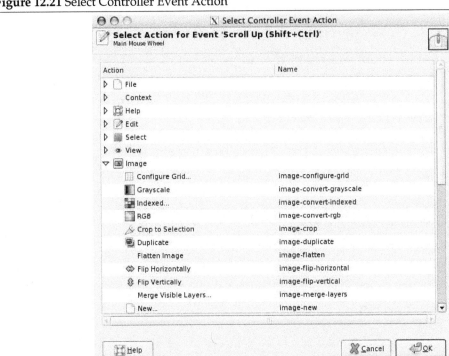

If an action exists yet for this event, the window will open on this action. Else, the window will display the sections that order actions. Click on an action to select it.

Main Keyboard

You can use this dialog in the same way as that of the mouse wheel. Events are related to the arrow keys of the keyboard, combined or not with control keys.

Figure 12.22 Main Keyboard

Note

 You will find an example of these notions in Creating a variable size brush.

12.1.17 Window Management

Figure 12.23 Window Management Preferences

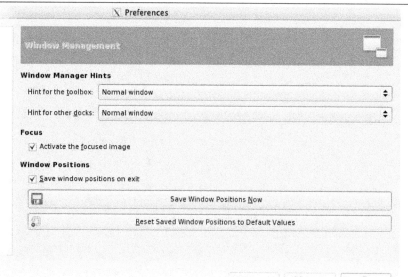

This page lets you customize the way windows are handled in GIMP. You should note that GIMP does not manipulate windows directly, instead it sends requests to the window manager (i. e., to Windows if you are running in Windows; to Metacity if you are running in a standard Gnome setup in Linux; etc). Because there are many window managers, and not all of them are well behaved, it cannot be guaranteed that the functions described here will actually work as described. However, if you are using a modern, standards-compliant window manager, they ought to.

12.1.17.1 Options

Window Manager Hints

Window type hints for the toolbox and the docks The choices you make here determine how the Toolbox, and the docks that hold dialogs, will be treated. You have three possibilities for them:

- If you choose Normal Window, they will be treated like any other windows.
- If you choose Utility Window, the reduce button in the title bar is absent and the docks will remain permanently on your screen.

Figure 12.24 Utility window title bar

(a) *Normal title bar*   (b) *The title bar in a utility window*

- If you choose Keep above, they will be kept in front of every other window at all times.

Note that changes you make here will not take effect until the next time you start GIMP.

Focus

Activate the focused image Normally, when you focus an image window (usually indicated by a change in the color of the frame), it becomes the "active image" for GIMP, and therefore the target for any image-related actions you perform. Some people, though, prefer to set up their window managers such that any window entered by the pointer is automatically focused. If you do this, you may find that it is inconvenient for focused images to automatically become active, and may be happier if you uncheck this option.

Window Positions

Save window positions on exit If this option is checked, the next time you start GIMP, you will see the same set of dialog windows, in the same positions they occupied when you last exited.

Save Window Positions Now This button is only useful if "Save window positions on exit" is unchecked. It allows you to set up your windows they way you like, click the button, and then have them come up in that arrangement each time you start GIMP.

Reset Saved Window Positions to Default Values If you decide that you are unhappy with the arrangement of windows you have saved, and would rather go back to the default arrangement than spend time moving them around, you can do so by pressing this button.

12.1.18 Folders

Figure 12.25 Basic Folder Preferences

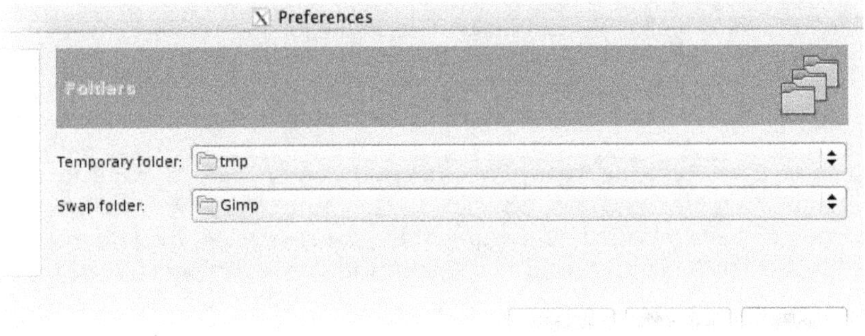

This page allows you to set the locations for two important folders used by GIMP for temporary files. The pages below it allow you to customize the locations searched for resources such as brushes etc.; see Data Folders for a description that applies to them. You can change the folders here by editing the entries, or by pressing the buttons on the right to bring up a file chooser window.

  Folders

Temp folder This folder is used for temporary files: files created for temporary storage of working data, and then deleted within the same GIMP session. It does not require a lot of space or high performance. By default, a subdirectory called `tmp` in your personal GIMP directory is used, but if that disk is very cramped for space, or has serious performance issues, you can change it to a different directory. The directory must exist and be writable by you, or bad things will happen.

Swap folder This is the folder used as a "memory bank" when the total size of images and data open in GIMP exceeds the available RAM. If you work with very large images, or images with many layers, or have many images open at once, GIMP can potentially require hundreds of megabytes of swap space, so available disk space and performance are definitely things to think about for this folder. By default, it is set to your personal GIMP directory, but if you have another disk with more free space, or substantially better performance, you may see a significant benefit from moving your swap folder there. The directory must exist and be writable by you.

12.1.19   Data Folders

Figure 12.26 Preferences: Brush Folders

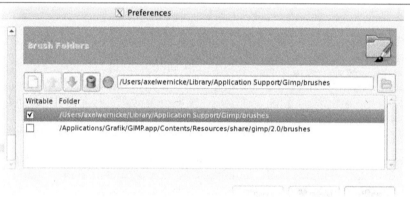

GIMP uses several types of resources – such as brushes, patterns, gradients, etc. – for which a basic set are supplied by GIMP when it is installed, and others can be created or downloaded by the user. For each such resource type, there is a Preference page that allows you to specify the *search path*: the set of directories from which items of the type in question are automatically loaded when GIMP starts. These pages all look very much the same: the page for brushes is shown to the right as an example.

  By default, the search path includes two folders: a *system* folder, where items installed along with GIMP are placed, and a *personal* folder, inside your personal GIMP directory, where items added by you should be placed. The system folder should not be marked as writable, and you should not try to alter its contents. The personal folder must be marked as writable or it is useless, because there is nothing inside it except what you put there.

  You can customize the search path with the buttons at the top of the dialog.

  Options

Select a Folder If you click on one of the folders in the list, it is selected for whatever action comes next.

Add/Replace Folder If you type the name of a folder in the entry space, or navigate to it using the file chooser button 🖹 on the right, and then click the left button, this will replace the selected folder with the one you have specified. If nothing in the list is selected, the folder you specify will be added to the list. If the light-symbol to the left of the text entry area is red instead of green, it means that the folder you have specified does not exist. GIMP will not create it for you, so you should do this immediately.

Move Up/Down If you click on the up-arrow or down-arrow buttons, the selected folder will be changed to the following or preceding one in the list. Since the folders are read in order, using those buttons change the loading precedence of the items located in those folders.

Delete Folder If you click the trash-can button, the selected folder will be deleted from the list. (The folder itself is not affected; it is merely removed from the search path.) Deleting the system folder is probably a bad idea, but nothing prevents you from doing it.

12.2 Grids and Guides

You will probably have it happen many times that you need to place something in an image very precisely, and find that it is not easy to do using a mouse. Often you can get better results by using the arrow keys on the keyboard (which move the affected object one pixel at a time, or 25 pixels if you hold down the **Shift** key), but GIMP also provides you with two other aids to make positioning easier: grids and guides.

Figure 12.27 Image used for examples below

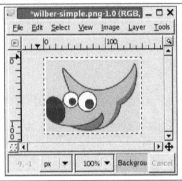

12.2.1 The Image Grid

Figure 12.28 Image with default grid

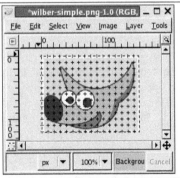

Each image has a grid. It is always present, but by default it is not visible until you activate it by toggling View → Show Grid in the image menu. If you want grids to be present more often than not, you can change the default behavior by checking "Show grid" in the Image Window Appearance page of the Preferences dialog. (Note that there are separate settings for Normal Mode and Fullscreen Mode.)

The default grid appearance, set up when you install GIMP, consists of plus-shaped black crosshairs at the grid line intersections, with grid lines spaced every 10 pixels both vertically and horizontally. You can customize the default grid using the Default Image Grid page of the Preferences dialog. If you only want to change the grid appearance for the current image, you can do so by choosing Image → Configure Grid from the image menu: this brings up the Configure Grid dialog.

Figure 12.29 A different grid style

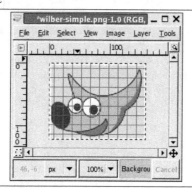

Not only can a grid be helpful for judging distances and spatial relationships, it can also permit you to align things exactly with the grid, if you toggle View → Snap to Grid in the image menu: this causes the pointer to "warp" perfectly to any grid line located within a certain distance. You can customize the snap distance threshold by setting "Snap distance" in the Tool Options page of the Preferences dialog, but most people seem to be happy with the default value of 8 pixels. (Note that it is perfectly possible to snap to the grid even if the grid is not visible. It isn't easy to imagine why you might want to do this, though.)

12.2.2 Guides

Figure 12.30 Image with four guides

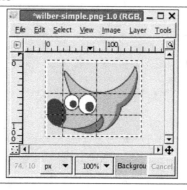

In addition to the image grid, GIMP also gives you a more flexible type of positioning aid: *guides*. These are horizontal or vertical lines you can temporarily display on an image while you are working on it.

To create a guide, simply click on one of the rulers in the image window and pull out a guide, while holding the mouse button pressed. The guide is then displayed as a blue, dashed line, which follows the pointer. As soon as you create a guide, the "Move" tool is activated and the mouse pointer changes to the Move icon.

You can also create a guide with the New Guide command, which allows you to precisely place the guide on the image, the New Guide (by Percent) command, or the New Guides from Selection command.

You can create as many guides as you like, positioned wherever you like. To move a guide after you have created it, activate the Move tool in the Toolbox (or press the **M** key), you can then click and drag a guide. To delete a guide, simply drag it outside the image. Holding down the **Shift** key, you can move everything but a guide, using the guides as an effective alignment aid.

The behavior of the guides depends upon the Move (Affect) mode of the "Move" tool. When *Layer* mode is selected, the mouse pointer turns into a small hand as soon as it gets close to a guide. Then the guide is activated and it turns red, and you can move the guide or delete it by moving it back into the ruler. If *Selection* mode is selected, you can position a guide, but you cannot move it after that.

As with the grid, you can cause the pointer to snap to nearby guides, by toggling View → Snap to Guides in the image menu. If you have a number of guides and they are making it difficult for you to judge the image properly, you can hide them by toggling View → Show Guides. It is suggested that you only do this momentarily, otherwise you may get confused the next time you try to create a guide and don't see anything happening.

If it makes things easier for you, you can change the default behavior for guides in the Image Windows Appearance page of the Preferences dialog. Disabling Show guides is probably a bad idea, though, for the reason just given.

You can remove the guides with the Image → Guides → Remove all Guides command.

Note

 Another use for guides: the Guillotine plugin can use guides to slice an image into a set of sub-images.

12.3 Rendering a Grid

How can you create a grid that is actually part of the image? You can't do this using the image grid: that is only an aid, and is only visible on the monitor or in a screenshot. You can, however, use the Grid plugin to render a grid very similar to the image grid. (Actually, the plugin has substantially more options.)

See also Grid and Guides.

12.4 How to Set Your Tile Cache

During the data processing and manipulation of pictures, GIMP becomes in the need of much main memory. The more is available the better is. GIMP uses the operating system memory available resources as effectively as possible, striving to maintain the work on the pictures fast and comfortable for the user. That Data memory, during the treatment, is organized in buffered blocks of graphic data, which could exist in two different forms of data memory: in the slow not removable disk or in the fast main RAM memory. GIMP uses preferably the RAM, and when it runs short of this memory, it uses the hard disk for the remaining data. These chunks of graphic data are commonly referred to as "tiles" and the entire system is called "tile cache".

A low value for tile cache means that GIMP sends data to the disk very quickly, not making real use of the available RAM, and making the disks work for no real reason. Too high a value for tile cache, and other applications start to have less system resources, forcing them to use swap space, which also makes the disks work too hard; some of them may even terminate or start to malfunction due lack of RAM.

How do you choose a number for the Tile Cache size? Here are some tips to help you decide what value to use, as well as a few tricks:

- The easiest method is to just forget about this and hope the default works. This was a usable method when computers had little RAM, and most people just tried to make small images with GIMP while running one or two other applications at the same time. If you want something easy and only use GIMP to make screenshots and logos, this is probably the best solution.

- If you have a modern computer with plenty of memory–say, 512 MB or more–setting the Tile Cache to half of your RAM will probably give good performance for GIMP in most situations without depriving other applications. Probably even 3/4 of your RAM would be fine.

- Ask someone to do it for you, which in the case of a computer serving multiple users at the same time can be a good idea: that way the administrator and other users do not get mad at you for abusing the machine, nor do you get a badly underperforming GIMP. If it is your machine and only serves a single user at a given time, this could mean money, or drinks, as price for the service.

- Start changing the value a bit each time and check that it goes faster and faster with each increase, but the system does not complain about lack of memory. Be forewarned that sometimes lack of memory shows up suddenly with some applications being killed to make space for the others.

- Do some simple math and calculate a viable value. Maybe you will have to tune it later, but maybe you have to tune it anyway with the other previous methods. At least you know what is happening and can get the best from your computer.

Let's suppose you prefer the last option, and want to get a good value to start with. First, you need to get some data about your computer. This data is the amount of RAM installed in your system, the operating system's swap space available, and a general idea about the speed of the disks that store the operating system's swap and the directory used for GIMP's swap. You do not need to do disk tests, nor check the RPM of the disks, the thing is to see which one seems clearly faster or slower, or whether all are similar. You can change GIMP's swap directory in the Folders page of the Preferences dialog.

The next thing to do is to see how much resources you require for other apps you want to run at the same time than GIMP. So start all your tools and do some work with them, except GIMP of course, and check the usage. You can use applications like free or top, depending in what OS and what environment you use. The numbers you want is the memory left, including file cache. Modern Unix keeps a very small area free, in order to be able to keep large file and buffer caches. Linux's *free* command does the maths for you: check the column that says "free", and the line "-/+ buffers/cache". Note down also the free swap.

Now time for decisions and a bit of simple math. Basically the concept is to decide if you want to base all Tile Cache in RAM, or RAM plus operating system swap:

1. Do you change applications a lot? Or keep working in GIMP for a long time? If you spend a lot of time in GIMP, you can consider free RAM plus free swap as available; if not, you need to go to the following steps. (If you're feeling unsure about it, check the following steps.) If you are sure you switch apps every few minutes, only count the free RAM and just go to the final decision; no more things to check.

2. Does the operating system swap live in the same physical disk as GIMP swap? If so, add RAM and swap. Otherwise go to the next step.

3. Is the disk that holds the OS swap faster or the same speed as the disk that holds the GIMP swap? If slower, take only the free RAM; if faster or similar, add free RAM and swap.

4. You now have a number, be it just the free RAM or the free RAM plus the free OS swap. Reduce it a bit, to be on the safe side, and that is the Tile Cache you could use as a good start.

As you can see, all is about checking the free resources, and decide if the OS swap is worth using or will cause more problems than help.

There are some reasons you want to adjust this value, though. The basic one is changes in your computer usage pattern, or changing hardware. That could mean your assumptions about how you use your computer, or the speed of it, are no longer valid. That would require a reevaluation of the previous steps, which can drive you to a similar value or a completely new value.

Another reason to change the value is because it seems that GIMP runs too slowly, while changing to other applications is fast: this means that GIMP could use more memory without impairing the other applications. On the other hand, if you get complaints from other applications about not having enough memory, then it may benefit you to not let GIMP hog so much of it.

If you decided to use only RAM and GIMP runs slowly, you could try increasing the value a bit, but never to use also all the free swap. If the case is the contrary, using both RAM and swap, and you have problems about lack of resources, then you should decrease the amount of RAM available to GIMP.

Another trick is to put the Swap Dir on a very fast disk, or on a different disk than the one where most of your files reside. Spreading the operating system swap file over multiple disks is also a good way to speed things up, in general. And of course, you might have to buy more RAM or stop using lots of programs at the same time: you can not expect to edit a poster on a computer with 16MB and be fast.

You can also check what memory requirements your images have. The larger the images, and the number of undoes, the more resources you need. This is another way to choose a number, but it is only good if you always work with the same kind of images, and thus the real requirements do not vary. It is also helpful to know if you will require more RAM and/or disk space.

12.5   Creating Shortcuts to Menu Functions

Many functions which are accessible via the image menu have a default keyboard shortcut. You may want to create a new shortcut for a command that you use a lot and doesn't have one or, more rarely, edit an existing shortcut. There are two methods for doing this.

Using dynamic keyboard shortcuts

1. First, you have to activate this capability by checking the Use dynamic keyboard shortcuts option in the Interface item of the Preferences menu. This option is usually not checked, to prevent accidental key presses from creating an unwanted shortcut.

2. While you're doing that, also check the Save keyboard shortcuts on exit option so that your shortcut will be saved.

3. To create a keyboard shortcut, simply place the mouse pointer on a command in the menu: it will then be highlighted. Be careful that the mouse pointer doesn't move and type a sequence of three keys, keeping the keys pressed. You will see this sequence appear on the right of the command.

4. It is best to use the Ctrl-Alt-Key sequence for your custom shortcuts.

Figure 12.31 Configure Keyboard Shortcuts

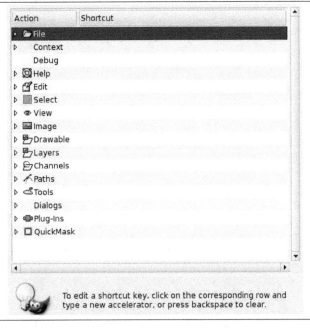

Using the Keyboard Shortcut Editor

1. You get to this Editor by clicking on Configure keyboard shortcuts in the "Interface" item of the Preferences menu.

2. As shown in this dialog, you can select the command you want to create a shortcut for, in the "Action" area. Then you type your key sequence as above. In principle, the Space bar should clear a shortcut. (In practice, it clears it, but doesn't delete it.)

3. This shortcut editor also allows you to *control the tool parameter settings* with the keyboard. At the top of this dialog, you can find a Context menu that takes you to the tool parameters. To make your work easier, tool types are marked with small icons.

Note

Custom Keyboard shortcuts are stored in one of Gimp's hidden directory (`/home/[username]/.gimp-2.8/menurc`) under Linux, and `C:\\Documents and Settings\\[Username]\\.gimp-2.8\\menurc` under Windows XP. It is a simple text file that you can transport from one computer to another.

12.6   Customize Splash-Screen

When you start GIMP, you see the *splash-screen* displaying short status messages while the program is loading all its components.

Of course, you can customize the splash-screen: Create a `splashes` directory in your in your personal GIMP folder (`/home/user_name/.gimp-2.8` on Linux, `C:\\Documents and Settings\ \user_name\\.gimp-2.8\\` on Windows).

Copy your image(s) into this `splashes` directory. On start, GIMP will read this directory and choose one of the images at random.

Tip

 Make sure that your images aren't too small.

Chapter 13

Scripting

13.1 Plugins

13.1.1 Introduction

One of the nicest things about GIMP is how easily its functionality can be extended, by using plugins. GIMP plugins are external programs that run under the control of the main GIMP application and interact with it very closely. Plugins can manipulate images in almost any way that users can. Their advantage is that it is much easier to add a capability to GIMP by writing a small plugin than by modifying the huge mass of complex code that makes up the GIMP core. Many valuable plugins have C source code that only comes to 100-200 lines or so.

Several dozen plugins are included in the main GIMP distribution, and installed automatically along with GIMP. Most of them can be accessed through the Filters menu (in fact, everything in that menu is a plugin), but a number are located in other menus. In many cases you can use one without ever realizing that it is a plugin: for example, the "Normalize" function for automatic color correction is actually a plugin, although there is nothing about the way it works that would tell you this.

In addition to the plugins included with GIMP , many more are available on the net. A large number can be found at the GIMP Plugin Registry [GIMP-REGISTRY], a web site whose purpose is to provide a central repository for plugins. Creators of plugins can upload them there; users in search of plugins for a specific purpose can search the site in a variety of ways.

Anybody in the world can write a GIMP plugin and make it available over the web, either via the Registry or a personal web site, and many very valuable plugins can be obtained in this way some are described elsewhere in the User's Manual. With this freedom from constraint comes a certain degree of risk, though: the fact that anybody can do it means that there is no effective quality control. The plugins distributed with GIMP have all been tested and tuned by the developers, but many that you can download were just hacked together in a few hours and then tossed to the winds. Some plugin creators just don't care about robustness, and even for those who do, their ability to test on a variety of systems in a variety of situations is often quite limited. Basically, when you download a plugin, you are getting something for free, and sometimes you get exactly what you pay for. This is not said in an attempt to discourage you, just to make sure you understand reality.

Warning

 Plugins, being full-fledged executable programs, can do any of the things that any other program can do, including install back-doors on your system or otherwise compromise its security. Don't install a plugin unless it comes from a trusted source.

These caveats apply as much to the Plugin Registry as to any other source of plugins. The Registry is available to any plugin creator who wants to use it: there is no systematic oversight. Obviously if the maintainers became aware that something evil was there, they would remove it. (That hasn't happened yet.) There is, however, for GIMP and its plugins the same warranty as for any other free software: namely, none.

Caution

Plugins have been a feature of GIMP for many versions. However, plugins written
for one version of GIMP can hardly ever be used successfully with other versions.
They need to be ported: sometimes this is easy, sometimes not. Many plugins are
already available in several versions. Bottom line: before trying to install a plugin,
make sure that it is written for your version of GIMP.

13.1.2 Using Plugins

For the most part you can use a plugin like any other GIMP tool, without needing to be aware that it is
a plugin. But there are a few things about plugins that are useful to understand.

One is that plugins are generally not as robust as the GIMP core. When GIMP crashes, it is considered
a very serious thing: it can cost the user a lot of trouble and headache. When a plugin crashes, the consequences are usually not so serious. In most cases you can just continuing working without worrying
about it.

Note

Because plugins are separate programs, they communicate with the GIMP core
in a special way: The GIMP developers call it "talking over a wire". When a plugin
crashes, the communication breaks down, and you will see an error message about
a "wire read error".

Tip

When a plugin crashes, GIMP gives you a very ominous-looking message telling
you that the plugin may have left GIMP in a corrupted state, and you should consider
saving your images and exiting. Strictly speaking, this is quite correct, because
plugins have the power to alter almost anything in GIMP, but for practical purposes,
experience has shown that corruption is actually quite rare, and many users just
continue working and don't worry about it. Our advice is that you simply think about
how much trouble it would cause you if something went wrong, and weigh it against
the odds.

Because of the way plugins communicate with GIMP, they do not have any mechanism for being
informed about changes you make to an image after the plugin has been started. If you start a plugin,
and then alter the image using some other tool, the plugin will often crash, and when it doesn't will
usually give a bogus result. You should avoid running more than one plugin at a time on an image, and
avoid doing anything to the image until the plugin has finished working on it. If you ignore this advice,
not only will you probably screw up the image, you will probably screw up the undo system as well, so
that you won't even be able to recover from your foolishness.

13.1.3 Installing New Plugins

The plugins that are distributed with GIMP don't require any special installation. Plugins that you download yourself do. There are several scenarios, depending on what OS you are using and how the plugin
is structured. In Linux it is usually pretty easy to install a new plugin; in Windows, it is either easy or
very hard. In any case, the two are best considered separately.

13.1.3.1 Linux / Unix-sytem like systems

Most plugins fall into two categories: small ones whose source code is distributed as a single .c file, and larger ones whose source code is distributed as a directory containing multiple files including a `Makefile`.

For a simple one-file plugin, call it `borker.c`, installing it is just a matter of running the command **gimptool-2.0 --install borker.c**. This command compiles the plugin and installs it in your personal plugin directory, `~/gimp-2.4/plugins` unless you have changed it. This will cause it to be loaded automatically the next time you start GIMP. You don't need to be root to do these things; in fact, you shouldn't be. If the plugin fails to compile, well, be creative.

Once you have installed the plugin, how do you activate it? The menu path is determined by the plugin itself, so to answer this you need to either look at the documentation for the plugin (if there is any), or launch the Plugin Description dialog (from Xtns/Plugins Details) search the plug-in by its name and look of the Tree view tab. If you still don't find, finally explore the menus or look at the source code in the Register section -- whichever is easiest.

For more complex plugins, organized as a directory with multiple files, there ought to be a file inside called either `INSTALL` or `README`, with instructions. If not, the best advice is to toss the plugin in the trash and spend your time on something else: any code written with so little concern for the user is likely to be frustrating in myriad ways.

Some plugins (specifically those based on the GIMP Plugin Template) are designed to be installed in the main system GIMP directory, rather than your home directory. For these, you will need to be root to perform the final stage of installation (when issuing the **make install** command).

If you install in your personal plugin directory a plugin that has the same name as one in the system plugin directory, only one can be loaded, and it will be the one in your home directory. You will receive messages telling you this each time you start GIMP. This is probably a situation best avoided.

13.1.3.2 Windows

Windows is a much more problematic environment for building software than Linux. Every decent Linux distribution comes fully supplied with tools for compiling software, and they are all very similar in the way they work, but Windows does not come with such tools. It is possible to set up a good software-building environment in Windows, but it requires either a substantial amount of money or a substantial amount of effort and knowledge.

What this means in relation to GIMP plugins is the following: either you have an environment in which you can build software, or you don't. If you don't, then your best hope is to find a precompiled version of the plugin somewhere (or persuade somebody to compile it for you), in which case you simply need to put it into your personal plugin directory. If you do have an environment in which you can build software (which for present purposes means an environment in which you can build GIMP), then you no doubt already know quite a bit about these things, and just need to follow the Linux instructions.

13.1.3.3 Apple Mac OS X

How you install plugins on OS X mostly depends on how you installed GIMP itself. If you were one of the brave and installed GIMP through one of the package managers like fink [DARWINORTS] or darwinports, [FINK] the plugin installation works exactly the way it is described for the Linux platform already. The only difference is, that a couple of plugins might be even available in the repository of you package manager, so give it a try.

If you on the other hand are one of the Users that preferred to grab a prebuild GIMP package like GIMP.app, you most probably want to stick to that prebuild stuff. So you can try to get a prebuild version of the plugin of you dreams from the author of the plugin, but I'd not want to bet on this. Building your own binaries unfortunately involves installing GIMP through one of the package managers mentioned above.

13.1.4 Writing Plugins

If you want to learn how to write a plugin, you can find plenty of help at the GIMP Developers web site [GIMP-DEV-PLUGIN]. GIMP is a complex program, but the development team has made strenuous efforts to flatten the learning curve for plugin writing: there are good instructions and examples, and the main library that plugins use to interface with GIMP (called "libgimp") has a well-documented API.

Good programmers, learning by modifying existing plugins, are often able to accomplish interesting things after just a couple of days of work.

13.2 Using Script-Fu Scripts

13.2.1 Script-Fu?

Script-Fu is what the Windows world would call "macros" But Script-Fu is more powerful than that. Script-Fu is based on an interpreting language called Scheme, and works by using querying functions to the GIMP database. You can do all kinds of things with Script-Fu, but an ordinary GIMP user will probably use it for automating things that:

- You want to do frequently.

- Are really complicated to do, and hard to remember.

Remember that you can do a whole lot with Script-Fu. The scripts that come with GIMP can be quite useful, but they can also serve as models for learning Script-Fu, or at least as a framework and source of modification when you make your own script. Read the Script-Fu Tutorial in the next section if you want to learn more about how to make scripts.

We will describe some of the most useful scripts in this chapter, but we won't cover them all. There are simply too many scripts. Some of the scripts are also very simple and you will probably not need any documentation to be able to use them.

Script-Fu (a dialect of Scheme) isn't the only scripting language available for GIMP. But Script-Fu is the only scripting language that is installed by default. Other available scripting extensions are Perl and Tcl. You can download and install both extensions at the GIMP Plugin Registry [GIMP-REGISTRY].

13.2.2 Installing Script-Fus

One of the great things about Script-Fu is that you can share your script with all your GIMP friends. There are many scripts that come with GIMP by default, but there are also vast quantities of scripts that are available for download all around the Internet.

1. If you have downloaded a script, copy or move it to your scripts directory. It can be found in the Preferences: Folders → Scripts.

2. Do a refresh by using Filters → Script-Fu → Refresh Scripts from the image menubar. The script will now appear in one of your menus. If you don't find it, look for it under the root file menu filters. If it doesn't appear at all, something was wrong with the script (e.g. it contains syntax errors).

13.2.3 Do's and Don'ts

A common error when you are dealing with Script-Fus is that you simply bring them up and press the OK button. When nothing happens, you probably think that the script is broken or buggy, but there is most likely nothing wrong with it.

13.2.4 Different Kinds Of Script-Fus

There are two kinds of Script-Fus:

Standalone Script-Fus You will find the standalone variants under File → Create → Type of Script in the image menubar (see the figure below).

Figure 13.1 Script-Fus by category

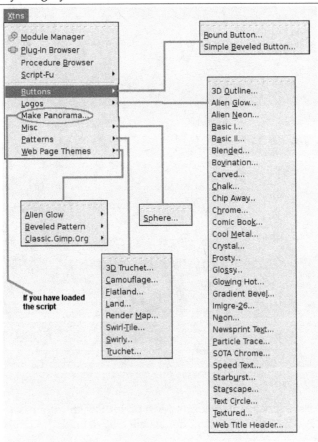

Image-dependent Script-Fus Menus have been reorganized. A new Colors-menu appears. It groups together all scripts that work on colors, for example tools that adjust hue, saturation, lightness..., filters...etc. Filters-menu and Script-Fu-menu are merged in one Filters-menu and it is organized according to new categories. Image-dependent Plug-ins and Script-Fus are now disseminated in the image-menus. For example, Color to Alpha filter is in Colors-menu. At the beginning, it's disconcerting, but you finish to get used to this because it's more logical.

The figure below show where you can find them in the image-menu.

Figure 13.2 Where find Image-dependent scripts

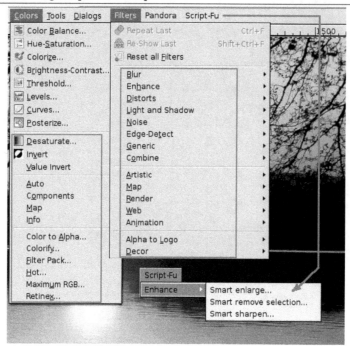

13.2.5   Standalone Scripts

We will not try to describe every script in depth. Most Script-Fus are very easy to understand and use. At the time of this writing, the following types are installed by default:

- Patterns

- Web page themes

- Logos

- Buttons

Patterns You will find all kinds of pattern-generating scripts here. Generally, they are quite useful because you can add many arguments to your own patterns.

We'll take a look at the Land script. In this script you have to set the image/pattern size, and specify what levels of random to use for your land creation. The colors used to generate the land map are taken from the currently selected gradient in the gradient editor. You must also supply values for the level of detail, land and sea height/depth and the scale. Scale refers to the scale of your map, just as in an ordinary road map, 1:10 will be typed as 10.

Web Page Themes Here is clearly a practical use for scripts. By creating a script for making custom text, logos, buttons arrows, etc., for your web site, you will give them all the same style and shape. You will also be saving a lot of time, because you don't have to create every logo, text or button by hand.

Most of the scripts are quite self-explanatory, but here are some hints:

- Leave all strange characters like ' and " intact.

- Make sure that the pattern specified in the script exists.

- Padding refers to the amount of space around your text.

- A high value for bevel width gives the illusion of a higher button.

- If you type TRUE for "Press", the button will look pushed down.

- Choose transparency if you don't want a solid background. If you choose a solid background, make sure it is the same color as the web page background.

Here you will find all kinds of logo-generating scripts. This is nice, but use it with care, as people might recognize your logo as being made by a known GIMP script. You should rather regard it as a base that you can modify to fit your needs. The dialog for making a logo is more or less the same for all such scripts:

Logos   1. In the Text String field, type your logo name, like Frozenriver.

2. In the Font Size text field, type the size of your logo in pixels.

3. In the Font text field, type the name of the font that you want to use for your logo.

4. To choose the color of your logo, just click on the color button. This brings up a color dialog.

5. If you look at the current command field, you can watch the script run.

Make Buttons Under this headline you'll find two scripts that makes rectangular beveled buttons, with or without round corners (Round Button or Simple Beveled Button). They have a dozen parameters or so, and most of them are similar to those in the logo scripts. You can experiment with different settings to come up with a button you like.

13.2.6 Image-Dependent Scripts

Now, scripts and filters that perform operations on an existing image are accessible directly by the appropriate menu. For example, the script New Brush (script-fu-paste-as-brush) is integrated in the Edit image menu (Edit → Paste as... → New Brush), that is more logical.

Furthermore, a new Color menu has been created that regroups together all that concern works on colors, the hue or level color adjustment tools, etc...

Filters menu and Scripts-Fu menu are regrouped in one Filters menu and organised according to new categories. Now if a plugin and a filter works similarly, they are nearby in the menu.

The Scripts-Fu menu only appears if you have loaded additional scripts: for example the gimp-resynthesizer pack corresponding to your Linux distribution (.deb, .rpm, .gz ...).

13.3 A Script-Fu Tutorial

In this training course, we'll introduce you to the fundamentals of Scheme necessary to use Script-Fu, and then build a handy script that you can add to your toolbox of scripts. The script prompts the user for some text, then creates a new image sized perfectly to the text. We will then enhance the script to allow for a buffer of space around the text. We will conclude with a few suggestions for ways to ramp up your knowledge of Script-Fu.

> **Note**
>
> This section as adapted from a tutorial written for the GIMP 1 User Manual by Mike Terry.

13.3.1 Getting Acquainted With Scheme

13.3.1.1 Let's Start Scheme'ing

The first thing to learn is that:

> Every statement in Scheme is surrounded by parentheses ().

The second thing you need to know is that:

> The function name/operator is always the first item in the parentheses, and the rest of the items are parameters to the function.

However, not everything enclosed in parentheses is a function — they can also be items in a list — but we'll get to that later. This notation is referred to as prefix notation, because the function prefixes everything else. If you're familiar with postfix notation, or own a calculator that uses Reverse Polish Notation (such as most HP calculators), you should have no problem adapting to formulating expressions in Scheme.

The third thing to understand is that:

> Mathematical operators are also considered functions, and thus are listed first when writing mathematical expressions.

This follows logically from the prefix notation that we just mentioned.

13.3.1.2 Examples Of Prefix, Infix, And Postfix Notations

Here are some quick examples illustrating the differences between *prefix*, *infix*, and *postfix* notations. We'll add a 1 and 23 together:

- Prefix notation: **+ 1   23** (the way Scheme will want it)

- Infix notation: **1   +   23** (the way we "normally" write it)

- Postfix notation: **1   23   +** (the way many HP calculators will want it)

13.3.1.3 Practicing In Scheme

Now, let's practice what we have just learned. Start up GIMP, if you have not already done so, and choose Filters → Script-Fu → Console. This will start up the Script-Fu Console window, which allows us to work interactively in Scheme. In a matter of moments, the Script-Fu Console will appear:

13.3.1.4 The Script-Fu Console Window

At the bottom of this window is an entry-field ought to be entitled Current Command. Here, we can test out simple Scheme commands interactively. Let's start out easy, and add some numbers:

```
(+  3  5)
```

Typing this in and hitting **Enter** yields the expected answer of 8 in the center window.

Figure 13.3 Use Script-Fu Console.

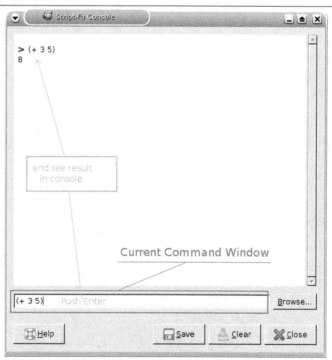

Now, what if we wanted to add more than one number? The "+" function can take two or more arguments, so this is not a problem:

```
(+ 3 5 6)
```

This also yields the expected answer of 14.

So far, so good — we type in a Scheme statement and it's executed immediately in the Script-Fu Console window. Now for a word of caution...

13.3.1.5 Watch Out For Extra Parentheses

If you're like me, you're used to being able to use extra parentheses whenever you want to — like when you're typing a complex mathematical equation and you want to separate the parts by parentheses to make it clearer when you read it. In Scheme, you have to be careful and not insert these extra parentheses incorrectly. For example, say we wanted to add 3 to the result of adding 5 and 6 together:

```
3 + (5 + 6) + 7 = ?
```

Knowing that the + operator can take a list of numbers to add, you might be tempted to convert the above to the following:

```
(+ 3 (5 6) 7)
```

However, this is incorrect — remember, every statement in Scheme starts and ends with parens, so the Scheme interpreter will think that you're trying to call a function named "5" in the second group of parens, rather than summing those numbers before adding them to 3.

The correct way to write the above statement would be:

```
(+ 3 (+ 5 6) 7)
```

13.3.1.6 Make Sure You Have The Proper Spacing, Too

If you are familiar with other programming languages, like C/C++, Perl or Java, you know that you don't need white space around mathematical operators to properly form an expression:

```
3+5, 3 +5, 3+ 5
```

These are all accepted by C/C++, Perl and Java compilers. However, the same is not true for Scheme. You must have a space after a mathematical operator (or any other function name or operator) in Scheme for it to be correctly interpreted by the Scheme interpreter.

Practice a bit with simple mathematical equations in the Script-Fu Console until you're totally comfortable with these initial concepts.

13.3.2 Variables And Functions

Now that we know that every Scheme statement is enclosed in parentheses, and that the function name/-operator is listed first, we need to know how to create and use variables, and how to create and use functions. We'll start with the variables.

13.3.2.1 Declaring Variables

Although there are a couple of different methods for declaring variables, the preferred method is to use the **let*** construct. If you're familiar with other programming languages, this construct is equivalent to defining a list of local variables and a scope in which they're active. As an example, to declare two variables, a and b, initialized to 1 and 2, respectively, you'd write:

```
(let*
    (
        (a 1)
        (b 2)
    )
    (+ a b)
)
```

or, as one line:

```
(let* ( (a 1) (b 2) ) (+ a b) )
```

> **Note**
>
> You'll have to put all of this on one line if you're using the console window. In general, however, you'll want to adopt a similar practice of indentation to help make your scripts more readable. We'll talk a bit more about this in the section on White Space.

This declares two local variables, a and b, initializes them, then prints the sum of the two variables.

13.3.2.2   What Is A Local Variable?

You'll notice that we wrote the summation (+ a b) within the parens of the let* expression, not after it.

This is because the let* statement defines an area in your script in which the declared variables are usable; if you type the **(+ a b)** statement after the **(let* ...)** statement, you'll get an error, because the declared variables are only valid within the context of the let* statement; they are what programmers call local variables.

13.3.2.3   The General Syntax Of let*

The general form of a let* statement is:

```
(let* ( variables )
   expressions )
```

where variables are declared within parens, e.g., **(a 2)**, and expressions are any valid Scheme expressions. Remember that the variables declared here are only valid within the let* statement — they're local variables.

13.3.2.4   White Space

Previously, we mentioned the fact that you'll probably want to use indentation to help clarify and organize your scripts. This is a good policy to adopt, and is not a problem in Scheme — white space is ignored by the Scheme interpreter, and can thus be liberally applied to help clarify and organize the code within a script. However, if you're working in Script-Fu's Console window, you'll have to enter an entire expression on one line; that is, everything between the opening and closing parens of an expression must come on one line in the Script-Fu Console window.

13.3.2.5   Assigning A New Value To A Variable

Once you've initialized a variable, you might need to change its value later on in the script. Use the set! statement to change the variable's value:

```
(let* ( (theNum 10) ) (set! theNum (+ theNum theNum)) )
```

Try to guess what the above statement will do, then go ahead and enter it in the Script-Fu Console window.

> **Note**
>
> The "\" indicates that there is no line break. Ignore it (don't type it in your Script-Fu console and don't hit **Enter**), just continue with the next line.

13.3.2.6 Functions

Now that you've got the hang of variables, let's get to work with some functions. You declare a function with the following syntax:

```
(define
  (
    name
    param-list
  )
  expressions
)
```

where *name* is the name assigned to this function, *param-list* is a space-delimited list of parameter names, and *expressions* is a series of expressions that the function executes when it's called. For example:

```
(define (AddXY inX inY) (+ inX inY) )
```

AddXY is the function's name and inX and inY are the variables. This function takes its two parameters and adds them together.

If you've programmed in other imperative languages (like C/C++, Java, Pascal, etc.), you might notice that a couple of things are absent in this function definition when compared to other programming languages.

- First, notice that the parameters don't have any "types" (that is, we didn't declare them as strings, or integers, etc.). Scheme is a type-less language. This is handy and allows for quicker script writing.

- Second, notice that we don't need to worry about how to "return" the result of our function — the last statement is the value "returned" when calling this function. Type the function into the console, then try something like:

  ```
  (AddXY (AddXY 5 6) 4)
  ```

13.3.3 Lists, Lists And More Lists

We've trained you in variables and functions, and now enter the murky swamps of Scheme's lists.

13.3.3.1 Defining A List

Before we talk more about lists, it is necessary that you know the difference between atomic values and lists.

You've already seen atomic values when we initialized variables in the previous lesson. An atomic value is a single value. So, for example, we can assign the variable "x" the single value of 8 in the following statement:

```
(let* ( (x 8) ) x)
```

(We added the expression x at the end to print out the value assigned to x—normally you won't need to do this. Notice how let* operates just like a function: The value of the last statement is the value returned.)

A variable may also refer to a list of values, rather than a single value. To assign the variable x the list of values 1, 3, 5, we'd type:

```
(let* ( (x '(1 3 5))) x)
```

Try typing both statements into the Script-Fu Console and notice how it replies. When you type the first statement in, it simply replies with the result:

```
8
```

However, when you type in the other statement, it replies with the following result:

```
(1 3 5)
```

When it replies with the value 8 it is informing you that x contains the atomic value 8. However, when it replies with (1 3 5), it is then informing you that x contains not a single value, but a list of values. Notice that there are no commas in our declaration or assignment of the list, nor in the printed result.

The syntax to define a list is:

```
'(a b c)
```

where a, b, and c are literals. We use the apostrophe (') to indicate that what follows in the parentheses is a list of literal values, rather than a function or expression.

An empty list can be defined as such:

```
'()
```

or simply:

```
()
```

Lists can contain atomic values, as well as other lists:

```
(let*
    (
        (x
           '("GIMP" (1 2 3) ("is" ("great" () ) ) )
        )
    )
    x
)
```

Notice that after the first apostrophe, you no longer need to use an apostrophe when defining the inner lists. Go ahead and copy the statement into the Script-Fu Console and see what it returns.

You should notice that the result returned is not a list of single, atomic values; rather, it is a list of a literal ("The GIMP"), the list (1 2 3), etc.

13.3.3.2   How To Think Of Lists

It's useful to think of lists as composed of a "head" and a "tail". The head is the first element of the list, the tail the rest of the list. You'll see why this is important when we discuss how to add to lists and how to access elements in the list.

13.3.3.3   Creating Lists Through Concatenation (The Cons Function)

One of the more common functions you'll encounter is the cons function. It takes a value and places it to its second argument, a list. From the previous section, I suggested that you think of a list as being composed of an element (the head) and the remainder of the list (the tail). This is exactly how cons functions — it adds an element to the head of a list. Thus, you could create a list as follows:

```
(cons 1 '(2 3 4) )
```

The result is the list (1 2 3 4).
You could also create a list with one element:

```
(cons 1 () )
```

You can use previously declared variables in place of any literals, as you would expect.

13.3.3.4   Defining A List Using The `list` Function

To define a list composed of literals or previously declared variables, use the `list` function:

```
(list 5 4 3 a b c)
```

This will compose and return a list containing the values held by the variables a, b and c. For example:

```
(let*   (
              (a 1)
              (b 2)
              (c 3)
          )

          (list 5 4 3 a b c)
  )
```

This code creates the list (5 4 3 1 2 3).

13.3.3.5 Accessing Values In A List

To access the values in a list, use the functions `car` and `cdr`, which return the first element of the list and the rest of the list, respectively. These functions break the list down into the head::tail construct I mentioned earlier.

13.3.3.6 The `car` Function

`car` returns the first element of the list (the head of the list). The list needs to be non-null. Thus, the following returns the first element of the list:

```
(car '("first" 2 "third"))
```

which is:

```
"first"
```

13.3.3.7 The `cdr` function

`cdr` returns the rest of the list after the first element (the tail of the list). If there is only one element in the list, it returns an empty list.

```
(cdr '("first" 2 "third"))
```

returns:

```
(2 "third")
```

whereas the following:

```
(cdr '("one and only"))
```

returns:

```
()
```

13.3.3.8 Accessing Other Elements In A List

OK, great, we can get the first element in a list, as well as the rest of the list, but how do we access the second, third or other elements of a list? There exist several "convenience" functions to access, for example, the head of the head of the tail of a list (`caadr`), the tail of the tail of a list (`cddr`), etc.

The basic naming convention is easy: The a's and d's represent the heads and tails of lists, so

```
(car (cdr (car x ) ) )
```

could be written as:

```
(cadar x)
```

To get some practice with list-accessing functions, try typing in the following (except all on one line if you're using the console); use different variations of `car` and `cdr` to access the different elements of the list:

```
(let* (
       (x   '( (1 2 (3 4 5) 6)   7   8   (9 10) )
       )
      )
      ; place your car/cdr code here
)
```

Try accessing the number 3 in the list using only two function calls. If you can do that, you're on your way to becoming a Script-Fu Master!

Note

 In Scheme, a semicolon (;) marks a comment. It, and anything that follows it on the same line, are ignored by the script interpreter, so you can use this to add comments to jog your memory when you look at the script later.

13.3.4   Your First Script-Fu Script

Do you not need to stop and catch your breath? No? Well then, let's proceed with your fourth lesson — your first Script-Fu Script.

13.3.4.1   Creating A Text Box Script

One of the most common operations I perform in GIMP is creating a box with some text in it for a web page, a logo or whatever. However, you never quite know how big to make the initial image when you start out. You don't know how much space the text will fill with the font and font size you want.

The Script-Fu Master (and student) will quickly realize that this problem can easily be solved and automated with Script-Fu.

We will, therefore, create a script, called Text Box, which creates an image correctly sized to fit snugly around a line of text the user inputs. We'll also let the user choose the font, font size and text color.

13.3.4.2   Editing And Storing Your Scripts

Up until now, we've been working in the Script-Fu Console. Now, however, we're going to switch to editing script text files.

Where you place your scripts is a matter of preference — if you have access to GIMP's default script directory, you can place your scripts there. However, I prefer keeping my personal scripts in my own script directory, to keep them separate from the factory-installed scripts.

In the `.gimp-2.8` directory that GIMP made off of your home directory, you should find a directory called `scripts`. GIMP will automatically look in your `.gimp-2.8` directory for a `scripts` directory, and add the scripts in this directory to the Script-Fu database. You should place your personal scripts here.

13.3.4.3   The Bare Essentials

Every Script-Fu script defines at least one function, which is the script's main function. This is where you do the work.

Every script must also register with the procedural database, so you can access it within GIMP. We'll define the main function first:

```
(define (script-fu-text-box inText inFont inFontSize inTextColor))
```

Here, we've defined a new function called `script-fu-text-box` that takes four parameters, which will later correspond to some text, a font, the font size, and the text's color. The function is currently empty and thus does nothing. So far, so good — nothing new, nothing fancy.

13.3.4.4 Naming Conventions

Scheme's naming conventions seem to prefer lowercase letters with hyphens, which I've followed in the naming of the function. However, I've departed from the convention with the parameters. I like more descriptive names for my parameters and variables, and thus add the "in" prefix to the parameters so I can quickly see that they're values passed into the script, rather than created within it. I use the prefix "the" for variables defined within the script.

It's GIMP convention to name your script functions `script-fu-abc`, because then when they're listed in the procedural database, they'll all show up under script-fu when you're listing the functions. This also helps distinguish them from plug-ins.

13.3.4.5 Registering The Function

Now, let's register the function with GIMP. This is done by calling the function `script-fu-register`. When GIMP reads in a script, it will execute this function, which registers the script with the procedural database. You can place this function call wherever you wish in your script, but I usually place it at the end, after all my other code.

Here's the listing for registering this function (I will explain all its parameters in a minute):

```
(script-fu-register
  "script-fu-text-box"                            ;func name
  "Text Box"                                      ;menu label
  "Creates a simple text box, sized to fit\
    around the user's choice of text,\
    font, font size, and color."                  ;description
  "Michael Terry"                                 ;author
  "copyright 1997, Michael Terry;\
    2009, the GIMP Documentation Team"            ;copyright notice
  "October 27, 1997"                              ;date created
  ""                    ;image type that the script works on
  SF-STRING      "Text"         "Text Box"   ;a string variable
  SF-FONT        "Font"         "Charter"    ;a font variable
  SF-ADJUSTMENT  "Font size"    '(50 1 1000 1 10 0 1)
                                             ;a spin-button
  SF-COLOR       "Color"        '(0 0 0)     ;color variable
)
(script-fu-menu-register "script-fu-text-box" "<Image>/File/Create/Text")
```

If you save these functions in a text file with a `.scm` suffix in your script directory, then choose Filters → Script-Fu → Refresh Scripts, this new script will appear as File → Create → Text → Text Box.

If you invoke this new script, it won't do anything, of course, but you can view the prompts you created when registering the script (more information about what we did is covered next).

Finally, if you invoke the Procedure Browser (Help → Procedure Browser), you'll notice that our script now appears in the database.

13.3.4.6 Steps For Registering The Script

To register our script with GIMP, we call the function `script-fu-register`, fill in the seven required parameters and add our script's own parameters, along with a description and default value for each parameter.

The Required Parameters

- The *name* of the function we defined. This is the function called when our script is invoked (the entry-point into our script). This is necessary because we may define additional functions within the same file, and GIMP needs to know which of these functions to call. In our example, we only defined one function, text-box, which we registered.

- The *location* in the menu where the script will be inserted. The exact location of the script is specified like a path in Unix, with the root of the path being image menu as `<Image>`.[1]

---

[1] Before version 2.6, `<Toolbox>` could be also used, but now the toolbox menu is removed, so don't use it.

If your script does not operate on an existing image (and thus creates a new image, like our Text Box script will), you'll want to insert it in the image window menu, which you can access through the image menu bar, by right-clicking the image window, by clicking the menu button icon at the left-top corner of the image window, or by pressing **F10**.

If your script is intended to work on an image being edited, you'll want to insert it in the image window menu. The rest of the path points to the menu lists, menus and sub-menus. Thus, we registered our Text Box script in the Text menu of the Create menu of the File menu.[2] (File → Create → Text → Text Box).

If you notice, the Text sub-menu in the File/Create menu wasn't there when we began — GIMP automatically creates any menus not already existing.

- A *description* of your script, to be displayed in the Procedure Browser.

- *Your name* (the author of the script).

- *Copyright* information.

- The *date* the script was made, or the last revision of the script.

- The *types* of images the script works on. This may be any of the following: RGB, RGBA, GRAY, GRAYA, INDEXED, INDEXEDA. Or it may be none at all — in our case, we're creating an image, and thus don't need to define the type of image on which we work.

Figure 13.4 The menu of our script.

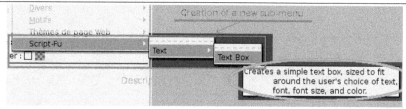

13.3.4.7   Registering The Script's Parameters

Once we have listed the required parameters, we then need to list the parameters that correspond to the parameters our script needs. When we list these params, we give hints as to what their types are. This is for the dialog which pops up when the user selects our script. We also provide a default value.

This section of the registration process has the following format:

Param Type	Description	Example
SF-IMAGE	If your script operates on an open image, this should be the first parameter after the required parameters. GIMP will pass in a reference to the image in this parameter.	3
SF-DRAWABLE	If your script operates on an open image, this should be the second parameter after the SF-IMAGE param. It refers to the active layer. GIMP will pass in a reference to the active layer in this parameter.	17

---

[2] The original, written by Mike, says put the menu entry in the Script-Fu menu of the Xtns menu at the Toolbox, but since version 2.6, the Toolbox menu had been removed and merged with the image window menubar.

Param Type	Description	Example
SF-VALUE	Accepts numbers and strings. Note that quotes must be escaped for default text, so better use SF-STRING.	42
SF-STRING	Accepts strings.	"Some text"
SF-COLOR	Indicates that a color is requested in this parameter.	'(0 102 255)
SF-TOGGLE	A checkbox is displayed, to get a Boolean value.	TRUE or FALSE

13.3.4.8   The Script-Fu parameter API[3]

> **Note**
>
> Beside the above parameter types there are more types for the interactive mode, each of them will create a widget in the control dialog. You will find a list of these parameters with descriptions and examples in the test script `plug-ins/script-fu/scripts/test-sphere.scm` shipped with the GIMP source code.

Param Type	Description
SF-ADJUSTMENT	Creates an adjustment widget in the dialog. SF-ADJUSTMENT "label" '(value lower upper step_inc page_inc digits type) **Widget arguments list** *Element:* "label", *Description:* Text printed before the widget. *Element:* value, *Description:* Value print at the start. *Element:* lower / upper, *Description:* The lower / upper values (range of choice). *Element:* step_inc, *Description:* Increment/decrement value. *Element:* page_inc, *Description:* Increment/decrement value using page key. *Element:* digits, *Description:* Digits after the point (decimal part). *Element:* type, *Description:* One of: SF-SLIDER or 0, SF-SPINNER or 1

---

[3] This section is not part of the original tutorial.

Param Type	Description
SF-COLOR	Creates a color button in the dialog. SF-COLOR "label" '(red green blue) or SF-COLOR "label" "color" **Widget arguments list** *Element:* "label", *Description:* Text printed before the widget. *Element:* '(red green blue), *Description:* List of three values for the red, green and blue components. *Element:* "color", *Description:* Color name in CSS notatation.
SF-FONT	Creates a font-selection widget in the dialog. It returns a fontname as a string. There are two new gimp-text procedures to ease the use of this return parameter: (gimp-text-fontname image drawable x-pos y-pos text border antialias size unit font) (gimp-text-get-extents-fontname text size unit font) where font is the fontname you get. The size specified in the fontname is silently ignored. It is only used in the font-selector. So you are asked to set it to a useful value (24 pixels is a good choice). SF-FONT "label" "fontname" **Widget arguments list** *Element:* "label", *Description:* Text printed before the widget. *Element:* "fontname", *Description:* Name of the default font.
SF-BRUSH	It will create a widget in the control dialog. The widget consists of a preview area (which when pressed will produce a popup preview) and a button with the "..." label. The button will popup a dialog where brushes can be selected and each of the characteristics of the brush can be modified. SF-BRUSH "Brush" '("Circle (03)" 100 44 0) Here the brush dialog will be popped up with a default brush of Circle (03) opacity 100 spacing 44 and paint mode of Normal (value 0). If this selection was unchanged the value passed to the function as a parameter would be '("Circle (03)" 100 44 0).

Param Type	Description
SF-PATTERN	It will create a widget in the control dialog. The widget consists of a preview area (which when pressed will produce a popup preview) and a button with the "..." label. The button will popup a dialog where patterns can be selected. SF-PATTERN "Pattern" "Maple Leaves" The value returned when the script is invoked is a string containing the pattern name. If the above selection was not altered the string would contain "Maple Leaves".
SF-GRADIENT	It will create a widget in the control dialog. The widget consists of a button containing a preview of the selected gradient. If the button is pressed a gradient selection dialog will popup. SF-GRADIENT "Gradient" "Deep Sea" The value returned when the script is invoked is a string containing the gradient name. If the above selection was not altered the string would contain "Deep Sea".
SF-PALETTE	It will create a widget in the control dialog. The widget consists of a button containing the name of the selected palette. If the button is pressed a palette selection dialog will popup. SF-PALETTE "Palette" "Named Colors" The value returned when the script is invoked is a string containing the palette name. If the above selection was not altered the string would contain "Named Colors".
SF-FILENAME	It will create a widget in the control dialog. The widget consists of a button containing the name of a file. If the button is pressed a file selection dialog will popup. SF-FILENAME "label" (string-append "" gimp-data-directory "/scripts/beavis.jpg") The value returned when the script is invoked is a string containing the filename.
SF-DIRNAME	Only useful in interactive mode. Very similar to SF-FILENAME, but the created widget allows to choose a directory instead of a file. SF-DIRNAME "label" "/var/tmp/images" The value returned when the script is invoked is a string containing the dirname.

Param Type	Description
SF-OPTION	It will create a widget in the control dialog. The widget is a combo-box showing the options that are passed as a list. The first option is the default choice. SF-OPTION "label" '("option1" "option2") The value returned when the script is invoked is the number of the chosen option, where the option first is counted as 0.
SF-ENUM	It will create a widget in the control dialog. The widget is a combo-box showing all enum values for the given enum type. This has to be the name of a registered enum, without the "Gimp" prefix. The second parameter speficies the default value, using the enum value's nick. SF-ENUM "Interpolation" '("InterpolationType" "linear") The value returned when the script is invoked corresponds to chosen enum value.

13.3.5 Giving Our Script Some Guts

Let us continue with our training and add some functionality to our script.

13.3.5.1 Creating A New Image

In the previous lesson, we created an empty function and registered it with GIMP. In this lesson, we want to provide functionality to our script — we want to create a new image, add the user's text to it and resize the image to fit the text exactly.

Once you know how to set variables, define functions and access list members, the rest is all downhill — all you need to do is familiarize yourself with the functions available in GIMP's procedural database and call those functions directly. So fire up the Section 16.12.7 and let's get cookin'!

Let's begin by making a new image. We'll create a new variable, theImage, set to the result of calling GIMP's built-in function gimp-image-new.

As you can see from the DB Browser, the function gimp-image-new takes three parameters — the image's width, height and the type of image. Because we'll later resize the image to fit the text, we'll make a 10x10 pixels RGB image. We'll store the image's width and sizes in some variables, too, as we'll refer to and manipulate them later in the script.

```
(define (script-fu-text-box inText inFont inFontSize inTextColor)
(let*
      (
        ; define our local variables
        ; create a new image:
        (theImageWidth  10)
        (theImageHeight 10)
        (theImage (car
                      (gimp-image-new
                       theImageWidth
                       theImageHeight
                       RGB
                      )
                  )
        )
        (theText)        ;a declaration for the text
                         ;we create later
```

Note: We used the value RGB to specify that the image is an RGB image. We could have also used 0, but RGB is more descriptive when we glance at the code.

You should also notice that we took the head of the result of the function call. This may seem strange, because the database explicitly tells us that it returns only one value — the ID of the newly created image. However, all GIMP functions return a list, even if there is only one element in the list, so we need to get the head of the list.

13.3.5.2   Adding A New Layer To The Image

Now that we have an image, we need to add a layer to it. We'll call the `gimp-layer-new` function to create the layer, passing in the ID of the image we just created. (From now on, instead of listing the complete function, we'll only list the lines we're adding to it. You can see the complete script here.) Because we've declared all of the local variables we'll use, we'll also close the parentheses marking the end of our variable declarations:

```
;create a new layer for the image:
    (theLayer
            (car
                    (gimp-layer-new
                     theImage
                     theImageWidth
                     theImageHeight
                     RGB-IMAGE
                     "layer 1"
                     100
                     NORMAL
                    )
            )
    )
) ;end of our local variables
```

Once we have the new layer, we need to add it to the image:

```
(gimp-image-add-layer theImage theLayer 0)
```

Now, just for fun, let's see the fruits of our labors up until this point, and add this line to show the new, empty image:

```
(gimp-display-new theImage)
```

Save your work, select Filters → Script-Fu → Refresh Scripts, run the script and a new image should pop up. It will probably contain garbage (random colors), because we haven't erased it. We'll get to that in a second.

13.3.5.3   Adding The Text

Go ahead and remove the line to display the image (or comment it out with a (;) as the first character of the line).

Before we add text to the image, we need to set the background and foreground colors so that the text appears in the color the user specified. We'll use the gimp-context-set-back/foreground functions:

```
(gimp-context-set-background '(255 255 255) )
(gimp-context-set-foreground inTextColor)
```

With the colors properly set, let's now clean out the garbage currently in the image by filling the drawable with the background color:

```
(gimp-drawable-fill theLayer BACKGROUND-FILL)
```

With the image cleared, we're ready to add some text:

```
(set! theText
            (car
                    (gimp-text-fontname
                     theImage theLayer
                     0 0
                     inText
```

```
                                   0
                                   TRUE
                                   inFontSize PIXELS
                                   "Sans")
                         )
            )
```

Although a long function call, it's fairly straightforward if you go over the parameters while looking at the function's entry in the DB Browser. Basically, we're creating a new text layer and assigning it to the variable `theText`.

Now that we have the text, we can grab its width and height and resize the image and the image's layer to the text's size:

```
(set! theImageWidth   (car (gimp-drawable-width  theText) ) )
(set! theImageHeight  (car (gimp-drawable-height theText) ) )

(gimp-image-resize theImage theImageWidth theImageHeight 0 0)

(gimp-layer-resize theLayer theImageWidth theImageHeight 0 0)
```

If you're like me, you're probably wondering what a drawable is when compared to a layer. The difference between the two is that a drawable is anything that can be drawn into, including layers but also channels, layer masks, the selection, etc; a layer is a more specific version of a drawable. In most cases, the distinction is not important.

With the image ready to go, we can now re-add our display line:

```
(gimp-display-new theImage)
```

Save your work, refresh the database and give your first script a run!

13.3.5.4   Clearing The Dirty Flag

If you try to close the image created without first saving the file, GIMP will ask you if you want to save your work before you close the image. It asks this because the image is marked as dirty, or unsaved. In the case of our script, this is a nuisance for the times when we simply give it a test run and don't add or change anything in the resulting image — that is, our work is easily reproducible in such a simple script, so it makes sense to get rid of this dirty flag.

To do this, we can clear the dirty flag after displaying the image:

```
(gimp-image-clean-all theImage)
```

This will set dirty count to 0, making it appear to be a "clean" image.

Whether to add this line or not is a matter of personal taste. I use it in scripts that produce new images, where the results are trivial, as in this case. If your script is very complicated, or if it works on an existing image, you will probably not want to use this function.

13.3.6   Extending The Text Box Script

13.3.6.1   Handling Undo Correctly

When creating a script, you want to give your users the ability to undo their actions, should they make a mistake. This is easily accomplished by calling the functions `gimp-undo-push-group-start` and `gimp-undo-push-group-end` around the code that manipulates the image. You can think of them as matched statements that let GIMP know when to start and stop recording manipulations on the image, so that those manipulations can later be undone.

If you are creating a new image entirely, it doesn't make sense to use these functions because you're not changing an existing image. However, when you are changing an existing image, you most surely want to use these functions.

Undoing a script works nearly flawlessly when using these functions.

13.3.6.2 Extending The Script A Little More

Now that we have a very handy-dandy script to create text boxes, let's add two features to it:

- Currently, the image is resized to fit exactly around the text — there's no room for anything, like drop shadows or special effects (even though many scripts will automatically resize the image as necessary). Let's add a buffer around the text, and even let the user specify how much buffer to add as a percentage of the size of the resultant text.

- This script could easily be used in other scripts that work with text. Let's extend it so that it returns the image and the layers, so other scripts can call this script and use the image and layers we create.

13.3.6.3 Modifying The Parameters And The Registration Function

To let the user specify the amount of buffer, we'll add a parameter to our function and the registration function:

```
(define (script-fu-text-box inTest inFont inFontSize inTextColor inBufferAmount ←
    )
(let*
      (
        ; define our local variables
        ; create a new image:
        (theImageWidth  10)
        (theImageHeight 10)
        (theImage (car
                    (gimp-image-new
                    theImageWidth
                    theImageHeight
                    RGB
                  )
                )
        )
        (theText)          ;a declaration for the text
                           ;we create later

        (theBuffer)        ; added

        (theLayer
                (car
                    (gimp-layer-new
                    theImage
                    theImageWidth
                    theImageHeight
                    RGB-IMAGE
                    "layer 1"
                    100
                    NORMAL
                  )
                )
        )
      ) ;end of our local variables

  [Code here]
)


(script-fu-register
  "script-fu-text-box"                    ;func name
  "Text Box"                              ;menu label
  "Creates a simple text box, sized to fit\
    around the user's choice of text,\
    font, font size, and color."          ;description
  "Michael Terry"                          ;author
  "copyright 1997, Michael Terry;\
```

```
     2009, the GIMP Documentation Team"        ;copyright notice
  "October 27, 1997"                           ;date created
  ""                    ;image type that the script works on
  SF-STRING     "Text"           "Text Box"    ;a string variable
  SF-FONT       "Font"           "Charter"     ;a font variable
  SF-ADJUSTMENT "Font size"      '(50 1 1000 1 10 0 1)
                                               ;a spin-button
  SF-COLOR      "Color"          '(0 0 0)      ;color variable
  SF-ADJUSTMENT "Buffer amount" '(35 0 100 1 10 1 0)
                                               ;a slider
)
(script-fu-menu-register "script-fu-text-box" "<Image>/Font/Create/Text")
```

13.3.6.4   Adding The New Code

We're going to add code in two places: right before we resize the image, and at the end of the script (to return the new image, the layer and the text).

After we get the text's height and width, we need to resize these values based on the buffer amount specified by the user. We won't do any error checking to make sure it's in the range of 0-100% because it's not life-threatening, and because there's no reason why the user can't enter a value like "200" as the percent of buffer to add.

```
(set! theBuffer (* theImageHeight (/ inBufferAmount 100) ) )

(set! theImageHeight (+ theImageHeight theBuffer theBuffer) )
(set! theImageWidth  (+ theImageWidth  theBuffer theBuffer) )
```

All we're doing here is setting the buffer based on the height of the text, and adding it twice to both the height and width of our new image. (We add it twice to both dimensions because the buffer needs to be added to both sides of the text.)

Now that we have resized the image to allow for a buffer, we need to center the text within the image. This is done by moving it to the (x, y) coordinates of (`theBuffer`, `theBuffer`). I added this line after resizing the layer and the image:

```
(gimp-layer-set-offsets theText theBuffer theBuffer)
```

Go ahead and save your script, and try it out after refreshing the database.

All that is left to do is return our image, the layer, and the text layer. After displaying the image, we add this line:

```
(list theImage theLayer theText)
```

This is the last line of the function, making this list available to other scripts that want to use it. To use our new text box script in another script, we could write something like the following:

```
(set! theResult (script-fu-text-box
                 "Some text"
                 "Charter" "30"
                 '(0 0 0)
                 "35"
                 )
)
(gimp-image-flatten (car theResult))
```

Congratulations, you are on your way to your Black Belt of Script-Fu!

13.3.7   Your script and its working

13.3.7.1   What you write

Below the complete script:

```
(script-fu-register
        "script-fu-text-box"                    ;func name
        "Text Box"                              ;menu label
        "Creates a simple text box, sized to fit\
          around the user's choice of text,\
          font, font size, and color."         ;description
        "Michael Terry"                         ;author
        "copyright 1997, Michael Terry;\
          2009, the GIMP Documentation Team"    ;copyright notice
        "October 27, 1997"                      ;date created
        ""                      ;image type that the script works on
        SF-STRING       "Text"          "Text Box"    ;a string variable
        SF-FONT         "Font"          "Charter"     ;a font variable
        SF-ADJUSTMENT   "Font size"     '(50 1 1000 1 10 0 1)
                                                ;a spin-button
        SF-COLOR        "Color"         '(0 0 0)      ;color variable
        SF-ADJUSTMENT   "Buffer amount" '(35 0 100 1 10 1 0)
                                                ;a slider
)
(script-fu-menu-register "script-fu-text-box" "<Image>/File/Create/Text")
(define (script-fu-text-box inText inFont inFontSize inTextColor inBufferAmount ←
    )
  (let*
    (
      ; define our local variables
      ; create a new image:
      (theImageWidth  10)
      (theImageHeight 10)
      (theImage)
      (theImage
              (car
                  (gimp-image-new
                    theImageWidth
                    theImageHeight
                    RGB
                  )
              )
      )
      (theText)                 ;a declaration for the text
      (theBuffer)               ;create a new layer for the image
      (theLayer
              (car
                  (gimp-layer-new
                    theImage
                    theImageWidth
                    theImageHeight
                    RGB-IMAGE
                    "layer 1"
                    100
                    NORMAL
                  )
              )
      )
    ) ;end of our local variables
    (gimp-image-add-layer theImage theLayer 0)
    (gimp-context-set-background '(255 255 255) )
    (gimp-context-set-foreground inTextColor)
    (gimp-drawable-fill theLayer BACKGROUND-FILL)
    (set! theText
              (car
                  (gimp-text-fontname
                    theImage theLayer
                    0 0
```

```
                           inText
                           0
                           TRUE
                           inFontSize PIXELS
                           "Sans")
                   )
        )
    (set! theImageWidth   (car (gimp-drawable-width  theText) ) )
    (set! theImageHeight  (car (gimp-drawable-height theText) ) )
    (set! theBuffer (* theImageHeight (/ inBufferAmount 100) ) )
    (set! theImageHeight (+ theImageHeight theBuffer theBuffer) )
    (set! theImageWidth  (+ theImageWidth  theBuffer theBuffer) )
    (gimp-image-resize theImage theImageWidth theImageHeight 0 0)
    (gimp-layer-resize theLayer theImageWidth theImageHeight 0 0)
    (gimp-layer-set-offsets theText theBuffer theBuffer)
    (gimp-display-new theImage)
    (list theImage theLayer theText)
    )
)
```

13.3.7.2 What you obtain

Figure 13.5 And the result on the screen.

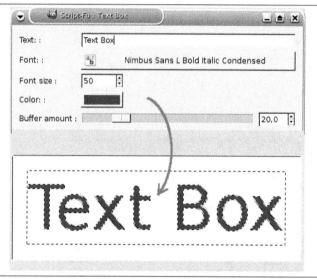

Part III

Function Reference

Chapter 14

Tools

14.1 The Toolbox

14.1.1 Introduction

GIMP provides a comprehensive toolbox in order to quickly perform basic tasks such as making selections or drawing paths. The many tools contained within GIMP's toolbox are discussed in detail here.

(In case you're curious, in GIMP lingo a "tool" is a way of acting on an image that requires access to its display, either to let you indicate what you want to do by moving the pointer around inside the display, or to show you interactively the results of changes that you have made. But if you want to think of a tool as a saw, and an image as a piece of wood, it probably won't do you a great deal of harm.)

Note

 See Main Windows: The Toolbox for an overview of the toolbox and its components.

GIMP has a diverse assortment of tools that let you perform a large variety of tasks. The tools can be thought of as falling into five categories:

- *Selection tools*, which specify or modify the portion of the image that will be affected by subsequent actions;

- *Paint tools*, which alter the colors in some part of the image;

- *Transform tools*, which alter the geometry of the image;

- *Color tools*, which alter the distribution of colors across the entire image;

- *Other tools*, which don't fall into the other four categories.

231

14.1.2   Tool Icons

Figure 14.1 The Tool Icons in the Toolbox

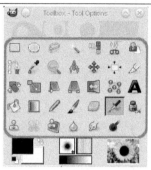

Most tools can be activated by clicking on an icon in the Toolbox. By default, some tools are accessible only via the menus (namely the Color tools are accessible only either as Colors or as Tools → Colors). Every tool, in fact, can be activated from the *Tools* menu; also, every tool can be activated from the keyboard using an accelerator key.

In the default setup, created when GIMP is first installed, not all tools show icons in the Toolbox: the Color tools are omitted. You can customize the set of tools that are shown in the Toolbox through Edit → Preferences → Toolbox. There are two reasons you might want to do this: first, if you only rarely use a tool, it might be easier to find the tools you want if the distracting icon is removed; second, if you use the Color tools a lot, you might find it convenient to have icons for them easily available. In any case, regardless of the Toolbox, you can always access any tool at any time using the Tools menu from an image menubar.

The shape of the cursor changes when it is inside an image, to one that indicates which tool is active (if in Preferences you have set Image Windows → Mouse Pointers → Pointer mode → Tool icon).

14.1.3   Color and Indicator Area

Figure 14.2 Color and Indicator Area in the Toolbox

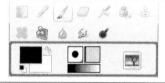

14.1.3.1   Color Area

Figure 14.3 Active Colors in the Toolbox

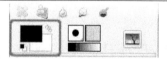

Color area This area shows GIMP's basic palette, consisting of two colors, the Foreground and Background, used for painting, filling, and many other operations. Clicking on either of the color displays brings up a Color Editor dialog, which permits you to change it.

Default colors Clicking on this small symbol resets the Foreground and Background colors to black and white, respectively. Pressing the **D** key has the same effect.

Swap FG/BG colors Clicking on the small curved line with two arrowheads causes the Foreground and Background colors to be swapped. Pressing the **X** key has the same effect.

> **Tip**
>
> You can click-and-drag one of these colors directly into a layer: it will fill the whole layer.

14.1.3.2 Tools Indicator Area

Figure 14.4 Active Brush, Pattern and Gradient in the Toolbox

This part of the Toolbox shows the currently selected brush, pattern, and gradient. Clicking on any of them brings up a dialog that allows you to change it.

14.1.3.3 Active Image Area

Figure 14.5 Active Image in the Toolbox

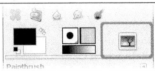

A thumbnail of the active image can be displayed in this area if the "Display Active Image" option is checked in Preferences/Toolbox. If you click on this thumbnail, the "Images" dialog is opened, useful if you have many images on your screen. You can also click and drag this thumbnail to an enabled XDS[1] file manager to directly save the corresponding image.

---

[1] See [XDS].

14.1.4 Tool Options

Figure 14.6 Tool Options Dialog

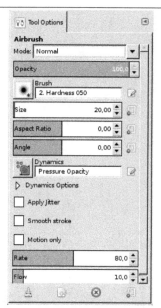

The Tool Options dialog of the Airbrush tool.

If you have things set up like most people do, activating a tool causes its Tool Options dialog to appear below the Toolbox. If you don't have things set up this way, you probably should: it is very difficult to use tools effectively without being able to manipulate their options.

> **Tip**
>
> The Tool Options appear beneath the Toolbox in the default setup. If you lose it somehow, you can get it back by creating a new Tool Options dialog using Windows → Dockable Dialogs → Tool Options and then docking it below the Toolbox. See the section on Dialogs and Docking if you need help.

Each tool has its own specific set of options. The choices you make for them are kept throughout the session, until you change them. In fact, the tool options are maintained from session to session. The persistence of tool options across sessions can sometimes be an annoying nuisance: a tool behaves very strangely, and you can't figure out why until you remember that you were using some unusual option the last time you worked with it, two weeks ago.

At the bottom of the Tool Options dialog, four buttons appear:

 Save Options to This button allows you to save the settings for the current tool, so that you can restore them later. It brings up the Section 15.5.1 allowing you to give a name for the new preset. When you Restore options, only saved presets for the active tool are shown, so you need not worry about including the name of the tool when you assign a name here.

Restore Options This button allows you to restore a previously saved preset of options for the active tool. If no presets have ever been saved for the active tool, the button will be insensitive. Otherwise, clicking it will bring up a menu showing the names of all saved option sets: choosing a menu entry will apply those settings.

Delete Options This button allows you to delete a previously saved set of options for the active tool. If no option-sets have ever been saved for the active tool, the button will simply repeat the tool name. Otherwise, clicking it will bring up a menu showing the names of all saved presets: the selected preset will be deleted.

 Reset Options   This button resets the options for the active tool to their default values.

New sliders   Option sliders have changed with GIMP-2.8: it is not visible, but the slider area is now divided into upper and lower parts.

Figure 14.7 The new sliders of tool options dialogs

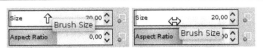

(a) *The upwards arrow pointer* (b) *The horizontal two-way ar-*
in the top half of the slider area   row pointer in the lower half of
the slider area

- **In the top half of the slider area:** Clicking with the up arrow pointer sets slider to a value that depends on the position of the pointer (no reference, imprecise). Clicking and dragging the up arrow pointer sets the value by large amounts.

- **In the lower half of the slider area:** Clicking with the two-way arrow pointer has no effect. Clicking and dragging the two-way arrow pointer sets the value by small amounts.

Once you have set the value approximately, you can tune it precisely using the two small arrow buttons at the right of the slider.

The value area in the slider area works as a text editor: there, you can edit the value or enter a new value directly.

For some options, you can drag the pointer outside the tool dialog. For example with the size slider, whose maximum value is 10,000, you can drag the mouse pointer up to the right side of your screen.

14.2   Selection Tools

Figure 14.8 The Selection tools

14.2.1   Common Features

Selection tools are designed to select regions from the active layer so you can work on them without affecting the unselected areas. Each tool has its own individual properties, but the selection tools also share a number of options and features in common. These common features are described here; the variations are explained in the following sections for each tool specifically. If you need help with what a "selection" is in GIMP, and how it works, see Selection.

There are seven selection tools:

- the Rectangle Select;

- the Ellipse Select;

- **the** Free Select (the Lasso);

- **the** Select Contiguous Regions (the Magic Wand);

- **the** Select by Color;

- **the** Select Shapes from Image (Intelligent Scissors) **and**

- **the** Foreground Select.

In some ways the Path tool can also be thought of as a selection tool: any closed path can be converted into a selection. It also can do a great deal more, though, and does not share the same set of options with the other selection tools.

14.2.1.1 Key modifiers (Defaults)

The behavior of selection tools is modified if you hold down the **Ctrl**, **Shift**, and/or **Alt** keys while you use them.

Note

 Advanced users find the modifier keys very valuable, but novice users often find them confusing. Fortunately, it is possible for most purposes to use the Mode buttons (described below) instead of modifier keys.

Ctrl When creating a selection, holding down the **Ctrl** key can have two different actions according to the way you use it:

- Holding down the key *while drawing* the selection toggles the "Expand from center" option.
- If you hold down the **Ctrl** key *before drawing a selection*, this new selection switches to the Subtract mode. So, this new selection will be subtracted from an existing one as soon as you release the click, as far as they have common pixels.

Alt Holding **Alt** will allow movement of the current selection (only its frame, not its content). If the whole image is moved instead of the selection only, try Shift-Alt. Note that the **Alt** key is sometimes intercepted by the windowing system (meaning that GIMP never knows that it was pressed), so this may not work for everybody.

Shift When creating a selection, holding down the **Shift** key can have two different actions according to the way you use it:

- If you hold down the key *before clicking* to start the selection, this selection will be in *Addition* mode as long as you press the key.
- If you hold down the **Shift** key *after clicking* to start the selection, the effect will depend on the tool you are using: for example, the selection will be a square with the Rectangle Select tool.

Ctrl-Shift Using Ctrl-Shift together can do a variety of things, depending on which tool is used. Common to all selection tools is that the selection mode will be switched to intersection, so that after the operation is finished, the selection will consist of the intersection of the region traced out with the pre-existing selection. It is an exercise for the reader to play with the various combinations available when performing selections while holding Ctrl-Shift and releasing either both or either prior to releasing the mouse button.

Key modifiers to move selections Ctrl-Alt-Click-and-drag and Shift-Alt-Click-and-drag are used to move selections. See Section 7.2.1.

Space bar Pressing the **Space Bar** while using a selection tool transforms this tool into the Navigation cross as long as you press the bar, allowing you to pan around the image instead of using the scrollbars when your image is bigger than the canvas. This is the default option: in Preferences/Image Windows, you can toggle the Space bar to the Move tool.

14.2.1.2 Options

Here we describe the tool options that apply to all selection tools: options that apply only to some tools, or that affect each tool differently, are described in the sections devoted to the individual tools. The current settings for these options can be seen in the Tool Options dialog, which you should always have visible when you are using tools. To make the interface consistent, the same options are presented for all selection tools, even though some of them don't have any effect for some of the tools.

Figure 14.9 Common options of selection tools

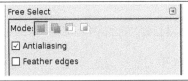

Mode This determines the way that the selection you create is combined with any pre-existing selection. Note that the functions performed by these buttons can be duplicated using modifier keys, as described above. For the most part, advanced users use the modifier keys; novice users find the mode buttons easier.

Replace mode will cause any existing selection to be destroyed or replaced when the new selection is created.

Add mode will cause the new selection to be added to any existing selection regions.

Subtract mode will remove the new selection area from any existing selection regions.

Intersection mode will make a new selection from the area where the existing selection region and the new selection region overlap.

Antialiasing This option only affects some selection tools: it causes the boundary of the selection to be drawn more smoothly.

Feather Edges This options allows the boundary of the selection to be blurred, so that points near the boundary are only partially selected. For further information regarding feathering, see the glossary entry Feathering.

14.2.2 Rectangle Selection

Figure 14.10 Rectangle Select icon in the Toolbox

The Rectangle Selection tool is designed to select rectangular regions of the active layer: it is the most basic of the selection tools, but very commonly used. For information on selections and how they are used in GIMP see Selections; for information on features common to all selection tools see Selection Tools.

This tool is also used for rendering a rectangle on an image. To render a filled rectangle, create a rectangular selection, and then fill it using the Bucket Fill tool. To create a rectangular outline, the simplest and most flexible approach is to create a rectangular selection and then stroke it.

14.2.2.1 Activating the tool

You can access the Selection Tool in different ways:

- from the image menu bar Tools → Selection Tools → Rectangle Select,

- by clicking on the tool icon in the ToolBox,

- by using the keyboard shortcut **R**.

14.2.2.2 Key modifiers

> **Note**
>
> See Selection Tools for help with modifier keys that affect all these tools in the same way. Only effects options that are specific to this tool are explained here.

Ctrl Pressing the **Ctrl** key after starting your selection, and holding it down until you are finished, causes your starting point to be used as the center of the selected rectangle, instead of a corner. Note that if you press the **Ctrl** key *before* starting to make the selection, the resulting selection will be subtracted from the existing selection. The cursor becomes

Shift If you press the **Shift** key *before* starting the selection, the resulting selection will be added to the existing one. The cursor becomes

Pressing the **Shift** key *after* starting your selection, toggles the Fixed option, and holding it down until you are finished, will constrain the selection to a square, if it is your first selection. Later, with the default Aspect Ratio , your selection will respect the aspect ratio of the previous selection.

Ctrl-Shift Pressing both keys after starting your selection combines the two effects, giving you a square selection centered on your starting point. Note that pressing these keys before starting your selection intersects the resulting selection with the existing one and the pointer change shape accordingly :

14.2.2.3 Tool manipulation

Figure 14.11 Example of Rectangle Selection.

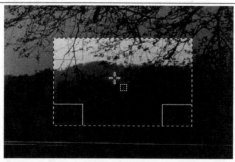

When this tool is selected the mouse pointer is displayed like this: as soon as it is over the image. A drag and drop allows to get a rectangular (or square) shape. When the mouse button is relaxed, a dotted line ("marching ants") outlines the selection. It's not necessary to adjust the selection with care; you can resize it easily later.

When the pointer is moving on the canvas, the pointer and selection aspects change:

- outside the selection it looks like previously; this allows to design a new selection but will erase the existing one if this isn't combined with an action on the relevant key to add or subtract another selection as described in the previous paragraph.

- within selection peripheral parts, the mouse pointer changes into various shapes when overflying rectangular sensitive and clearly marked areas. These *handles* allow you to resize the selection. In selection corners the pointer changes into a shape according to the context; for instance in the low right corner it becomes: . So, by click-and-dragging these areas, you can magnify or shrink the selection size. Over median selection parts, lateral, low or up, pointer is changed into appropriate shapes according to the context. For instance, when the mouse pointer is over the median right side, the pointer looks like: . So you can click-and-drag to magnify or to shrink the selection size by moving the chosen boundary.

- inside selection central area the mouse pointer looks like usual for object manipulation, i.e.: . So you can move the whole selection by a click-and-drag.

Moreover, if you have not unchecked the Highlight option, your work will be easier because what is out the selection will be darkest than what is in the selection, and then the selection seems highlighted.

> **Tip**
>
> If you use moving keys you can move the selection or modify its size by one pixel step. If you use it in combination with **Shift** you can move it by a 25 pixel step.

Figure 14.12 Sensitive selection areas

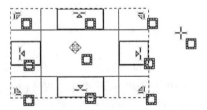

Display of all possible pointers in function of their localization with respect to the selection area.

After creating and modifying the selection, you will have to exit this editing mode (and commit any changes). You can do this with a single click inside the selection or by pressing the **Enter** key. Or you can just use a non-selection tool and, for example, fill or paint the selection.

14.2.2.4   Tool Options

Figure 14.13 Tool Options for the Rectangle Select tool

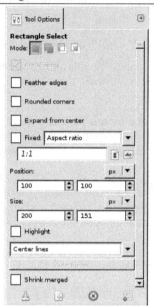

Normally, tool options are displayed in a window attached under the Toolbox as soon as you activate a tool. If they are not, you can access them from the image menu bar through Windows → Dockable Windows → Tool Options which opens the option window of the selected tool.

Note

 See Selection Tools for help with options that are common to all these tools. Only options that are specific to this tool are explained here.

Mode; Antialiasing; Feather edges   Common select options.

Rounded corners   If you enable this option, a slider appears. You can use this to adjust the radius that is used to round the corners of the selection.

Expand from center   If you enable this option, the point the selection is started by pressing the mouse button is used as center of the selected area.

Fixed   This menu allows you the option of constraining the shape of the rectangle in different ways.

>   **Aspect ratio**   This option allows you to design and resize the selection while keeping the aspect ratio fixed and written within the relevant box. By default the ratio is 1:1 (so we have a square) but it can be changed. With the two little landscape and picture icons, you can invert this ratio.
>
>   **Width**   With this choice you can fix the width of the selection.
>
>   **Height**   With this choice you can fix the height of the selection.
>
>   **Size**   With this choice you can fix the width and height of the selection.

Position   These two text fields contain the current horizontal and vertical coordinates of the upper left corner of the selection. You can use these fields to adjust the selection position precisely.

Size   These two text fields contain the current width and height of the the selection. You can use these fields to adjust the selection size precisely.

Highlight If you enable this option, the selected area is emphasized by a surrounding mask to make visual selection much easier.

Guides With this menu you can select the type of guides that is shown within the selection to make the creation of a selection easier, respecting *Photo composition rules*.

Six options are available:

- No Guides
- Center lines
- Rule of thirds
- Rule of fifths
- Golden sections
- Diagonal lines

Auto Shrink Selection The Auto Shrink Selection check-box will make your next selection automatically shrink to the nearest rectangular shape available on the image layer. The algorithm for finding the best rectangle to shrink to is "intelligent", which in this case means that it sometimes does surprisingly sophisticated things, and sometimes does surprisingly strange things. In any case, if the region that you want to select has a solid-colored surround, auto-shrinking will always pick it out correctly. Note that the resulting selection does not need to have the same shape as the one you sweep out.

Shrink merged If Sample Merged is also enabled, then Auto Shrink will use the pixel information from the visible display of the image, rather than just from the active layer. For further information regarding Sample Merge, see the glossary entry Sample Merge.

14.2.3 Ellipse Selection

Figure 14.14 Ellipse Select icon in the Toolbox

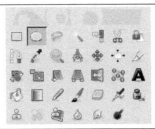

The Ellipse Selection tool is designed to select circular and elliptical regions from an image, with high-quality anti-aliasing if you want it. For information on selections and how they are used in GIMP see Selections; for information on features common to all selection tools see Selection Tools.

This tool is also used for rendering a circle or ellipse on an image. To render a filled ellipse, create an elliptical selection, and then fill it using the Bucket Fill tool. To create an elliptical outline, the simplest and most flexible approach is to create an elliptical selection and then stroke it. However, the quality of anti-aliasing with this approach is rather crude. A higher quality outline can be obtained by creating two elliptical selections with different sizes, subtracting the inner one from the outer one; however this is not always easy to get right. The command Select → Border... makes it easy.

14.2.3.1 Activating the tool

You can access the Ellipse Selection Tool in different ways:

- From the image menu bar Tools → Selection Tools → Ellipse Select;

- By clicking on the tool icon ⬭ in the ToolBox,

- By using the keyboard shortcut **E**.

14.2.3.2   Key modifiers

> Note
>
> See Selection Tools for help with modifier keys that affect all these tools in the same way. Only effects options that are specific to this tool are explained here.

Ctrl Pressing the key after starting your selection, and holding it down until you are finished, causes your starting point to be used as the center of the selected ellipse, instead of a corner of the rectangle that may contain it. Note that if you press the **Ctrl** key *before* starting to make the selection, the resulting selection will be subtracted from the existing selection.

Shift Pressing the **Shift** key after starting your selection, and holding it down until you are finished, constrains the selection to be a circle. Note that if you press the **Shift** key *before* starting to make the selection, the resulting selection will be added to the existing selection.

Ctrl-Shift Pressing both keys combines the two effects, giving you a circular selection centered on your starting point.

14.2.3.3   Tool handling

Figure 14.15 Example of Ellipse Selection.

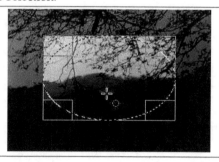

When this tool is selected the mouse pointer comes with a circle icon as soon as it is over the image. A drag-and-drop allows you to get an ellipse (or a circle) within a rectangular box. When the mouse button is relaxed, a dotted line ("marching ants") outlines the elliptic selection. It's not necessary to adjust the selection with care; you can resize it easily later.

When the pointer is moving on the canvas, the pointer and selection aspects change. You can change the size of the selection by using handles. See Tool handling within the rectangular chapter.

14.2.3.4   Options

Figure 14.16 Tool Options for the Ellipse Select tool

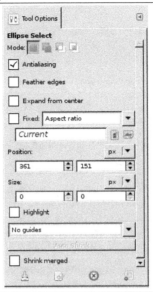

Normally, tool options are displayed in a window attached under the Toolbox as soon as you activate a tool. If they are not, you can access them from the image menu bar through Windows → Dockable Windows → Tool Options which opens the option window of the selected tool.

> **Note**
>
> See Selection Tools for help with options that are common to all these tools. Only options that are specific to this tool are explained here.

Modes; Antialiasing; Feather edges Common select options.

All other options All these options work exactly the same way, they were described for the rectangular selection already. See for Section 14.2.2.4 details.

14.2.4   Free Selection (Lasso)

Figure 14.17 Free Selection icon in the Toolbox

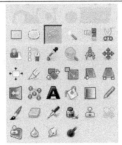

The Free Selection tool, or Lasso, lets you create a selection by drawing it free-hand with the pointer, while holding down the left mouse button (or, for a stylus, pressing it against the tablet). When you release the mouse button, the selection is closed by connecting the current pointer location to the start location with a straight line. You can go outside the edge of the image display and come back in if you want to. The Lasso is often a good tool to use for "roughing in" a selection; it is not so good for precise definition. Experienced users find that it is often convenient to begin with the lasso tool, but then switch to QuickMask mode for detail work.

For information on selections and how they are used in GIMP see Selections. For information on features common to all selection tools see Selection Tools.

Note

The Free Selection tool is much easier to use with a tablet than with a mouse.

A new possibility came up with GIMP-2.6: the polygonal selection. Instead of click-and-dragging to draw a free hand selection, you can click only. This creates an anchor point. Then moving the mouse pointer draws a line with a new anchor point that you can move as long as you don't click again (the mouse pointer comes with the moving cross). Clicking again anchors this point and creates a segment. By pressing the **Ctrl** keyboard key while moving the mouse pointer contrains moving angles to 15°.

So, you can mix free hand segments and polygonal segments.

Figure 14.18 Mixing free hand segments and polygonal segments

14.2.4.1   Activating the tool

You can access the Lasso Tool in different ways:

- From the image menu bar Tools → Selection Tools → Free Select,

- by clicking on the tool icon in the ToolBox,

- by using the keyboard shortcut **F**.

14.2.4.2   Key modifiers

The Free Select tool does not have any special key modifiers, only the ones that affect all selection tools in the same way. See Selection Tools for help with these.

14.2.4.3   Tool handling

To move the selection, see Moving selections.

Figure 14.19 Rough selection with the Free Selection tool.

14.2.4.4 Options

Figure 14.20 Tool Options for the Lasso tool

Normally, tool options are displayed in a window attached under the Toolbox as soon as you activate a tool. If they are not, you can access them from the image menu bar through Windows → Dockable Windows → Tool Options which opens the option window of the selected tool.

The Free Select tool has no special tool options, only the ones that affect all selection tools in the same way. See Selection Tools for help with these.

14.2.5 Fuzzy selection (Magic wand)

Figure 14.21 Magic Wand tool icon in the Toolbox

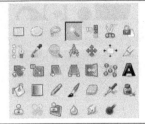

The Fuzzy Select (Magic Wand) tool is designed to select areas of the current layer or image based on color similarity.

When using this tool, it is very important to pick the right starting point. If you select the wrong spot, you might get something very different from what you want, or even the opposite.

The Wand is a good tool for selecting objects with sharp edges. It is fun to use, so beginners often start out using it a lot. You will probably find, however, that the more you use it, the more frustrated you become with the difficulty of selecting exactly what you want, no more, no less. More experienced users find that the Path and Color Select tools are often more efficient, and use the Wand less. Still, it is useful for selecting an area within a contour, or touching up imperfect selections. It often works very well for selecting a solid-colored (or nearly solid-colored) background area.

Note that as the selected area expands outward from the center, it does not only propagate to pixels that touch each other: it is capable of jumping over small gaps, depending on Threshold option. To increase/decrease Threshold, during the use of Fuzzy Selection, after the first button-press, dragging the pointer downward (or to the right) or upward (or to the left).

14.2.5.1 Activating the tool

You can access the Magic Wand Tool in different ways:

- From the image menu bar Tools → Selection Tools → Fuzzy Select,

- by clicking on the tool icon ✎ in the ToolBox,

- by using the keyboard shortcut **U**.

14.2.5.2 Key modifiers (Defaults)

The Fuzzy Select tool does not have any special key modifiers, only the ones that affect all selection tools in the same way. See Section 14.2.1 for help with these.

14.2.5.3 Tool handling

Figure 14.22 Using Magic Wand tool: selected pixels are contiguous

It starts selecting when you click at a spot in the image, and expands outwards like water flooding low-lying areas, selecting contiguous pixels whose colors are similar to the starting pixel. You can control the threshold of similarity by dragging the mouse downward or to the right: the farther you drag it, the larger you get the selected region. And you can reduce the selection by dragging upwards or to the left.

To move the selection see Moving selections.

14.2.5.4   Options

Figure 14.23 Tool Options for the Magic Wand tool

Normally, tool options are displayed in a window attached under the Toolbox as soon as you activate a tool. If they are not, you can access them from the image menu bar through Windows → Dockable Windows → Tool Options which opens the option window of the selected tool.

Note

See Selection Tools for help with options that are common to all these tools. Only options that are specific to this tool are explained here.

Mode; Antialiasing; Feather edges   Common select options.

Finding Similar Colors   These options affect the way the Magic Wand expands the selection out from the initial point.

    Select Transparent Areas   This option gives the Magic Wand the ability to select areas that are completely transparent. If this option is not checked, transparent areas will never be included in the selection.

    Sample Merged   This option becomes relevant when you have several layers in your image, and the active layer is either semi-transparent or is set to another Layer Mode than Normal. If this is the case, the colors present in the layer will be different from the colors in the composite image. If the "Sample Merged" option is unchecked, the wand will only react to the color in the active layer when it creates a selection. If it is checked it will react to the composite color of all visible layers. For further information, see the glossary entry Sample Merged.

    Threshold   This slider determines the range of colors that will be selected at the moment you click the pointer on the initial point, before dragging it: the higher the threshold, the larger the resulting selection. After the first button-press, dragging the pointer downward or to the right will increase the size of the selection; dragging upward or to the left will decrease it. Thus, you have the same set of possibilities regardless of the Threshold setting: what differs is the amount of dragging you have to do to get the result you want.

    Selection by   With this option you can choose which component of the image GIMP shall use to calculate the similarity.

        The components you can choose from are Red, Green, Blue, Hue, Saturation and Value.

14.2.6   Select By Color

Figure 14.24 Select by Color tool icon in the Toolbox

The Select by Color tool is designed to select areas of an image based on color similarity. It works a lot like the Fuzzy Select tool ("Magic Wand"). The main difference between them is that the Magic Wand selects *contiguous* regions, with all parts connected to the starting point by paths containing no large gaps; while the Select by Color tool selects all pixels that are sufficiently similar in color to the pixel you click on, regardless of where they are located.

14.2.6.1   Activating the tool

You can access the Select by Color Tool in different ways:

- From the image menu bar Tools → Selection Tools → By Color Select,

- by clicking on the tool icon in the ToolBox,

- by using the keyboard shortcut Shift -O.

14.2.6.2   Key modifiers (Defaults)

The select by color tool does not have any special key modifiers, only the ones that affect all selection tools in the same way. See Selection Tools for help with these.

14.2.6.3   Handling tool

Figure 14.25 Using Select by Color tool: selected pixels are not only contiguous

As with fuzzy tool, the selection starts as soon as you click and the reference is the first clicked pixel. If you click and drag, you can change the threshold by the same way as with the fuzzy tool.

To move the selection see Moving selections.

14.2.6.4   Options

Figure 14.26 Tool Options for the Select by Color tool

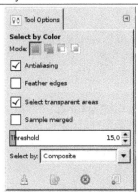

Normally, tool options are displayed in a window attached under the Toolbox as soon as you activate a tool. If they are not, you can access them from the image menu bar through Windows → Dockable Windows → Tool Options which opens the option window of the selected tool.

Note

 See Selection Tools for help with options that are common to all these tools. Only options that are specific to this tool are explained here.

Mode; Antialiasing; Feather edges   Common select options.

Similar colors   All these options work exactly the same way, they were described for the fuzzy selection already. See for Section 14.2.5.4 details.

14.2.7   Intelligent Scissors

Figure 14.27 Intelligent Scissors tool icon in the Toolbox

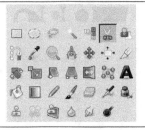

The Intelligent Scissors tool is an interesting piece of equipment: it has some features in common with the Lasso, some features in common with the Path tool, and some features all its own. It is useful when you are trying to select a region defined by strong color-changes at the edges. To use the Scissors, you click to create a set of "control nodes", also referred to as anchors or control points, at the edges of the region you are trying to select. The tool produces a continuous curve passing through these control nodes, following any high-contrast edges it can find. If you are lucky, the path that the tool finds will correspond to the contour you are trying to select.

Unfortunately, there seem to be some problems with the edge-following logic for this tool, with the result that the selections it creates tend to be pretty crude in a lot of cases. A good way to clean them up is to switch to QuickMask mode, and use paint tools to paint in the problematic parts. On the whole, most people find the Path tool to be more useful than the Scissors, because, even though it does not have the intelligent edge-finding capability, the paths it produces persist until you delete them, and can be altered at any time.

14.2.7.1   Activating the tool

You can access the Intelligent Scissors Tool in different ways:

- From the image menu bar Tools → Selection Tools → Intelligent Scissors,

- by clicking on the tool icon ✂ in the ToolBox,

- by using the keyboard shortcut **I**.

14.2.7.2   Key modifiers

The default behavior of the **Shift**, **Ctrl**, and **Alt** keys is described in Section 14.2.1.1 for all selection tools.

There is, however, one key modifier that has a special behavior if you use it while editing a selection, that is *after* you have added the first node:

Shift   By default, the *auto-edge snap feature* is enabled: whenever you click and drag the mouse pointer, the Scissors tool finds the point of the maximal gradient (where the color change is maximal) for placing a new control node or moving an existing node.

Holding down this key while clicking and dragging disables this feature, and the control node will be placed at the position of the mouse pointer.

14.2.7.3   Tool handling

Figure 14.28 Using Intelligent Scissors

Each time you left-click with the mouse, you create a new control point, which is connected to the last control point by a curve that tries to follow edges in the image. To finish, click on the first point (the cursor changes to indicate when you are in the right spot). You can adjust the curve by dragging the control nodes, or by clicking to create new control nodes. When you are satisfied, click anywhere inside the curve to convert it into a selection.

As said above when you click with this tool you drop points. The selection boundary is driven by these control points. During creation you can move each one by clicking and dragging, except the first and the last one. The selection is closed when you are clicking the last point over the first one. When the selection is closed the pointer shape changes according to its position: inside 🔲, on the boundary

, and outside . You can adjust the selection creating new points by clicking on the boundary or by moving each control points (merged first and last point). The selection is validated when you click inside.

You have to notice that you can get only one selection; if you create a second selection, the first one is erased when you validate the second one.

> **Warning**
>
> Be sure not to click inside the curve until you are completely done adjusting it. Once you have converted it into a selection, undoing takes you back to zero, and you will have to start constructing the curve again from scratch if you need to change it. Also be sure not to switch to a different tool, or again all of your carefully created control nodes will be lost. (But you still can transform your selection into a path and work it with the Path tool.)

To move the selection, see Moving selections.

14.2.7.4   Options

Figure 14.29 Tool Options for the Intelligent Scissors

Normally, tool options are displayed in a window attached under the Toolbox as soon as you activate a tool. If they are not, you can access them from the image menu bar through Windows → Dockable Windows → Tool Options which opens the option window of the selected tool.

Modes; Antialiasing; Feather edges

> **Note**
>
> See Selection Tools for help with options that are common to all these tools. Only options that are specific to this tool are explained here.

Interactive boundary If this option is enabled, dragging a control node during placement will indicate the path that will be taken by the selection boundary. If it is not enabled, the node will be shown connected to the previous node by a straight line while you are dragging it around, and you won't see the resulting path until you release the pointer button. On slow systems, if your control nodes are far apart, this may give a bit of a speed-up.

14.2.8 Foreground Select

Figure 14.30 The "Foreground Select" tool in the Toolbox

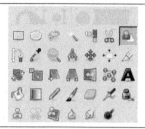

This tool lets you extract the foreground from the active layer or from a selection. It is based on the SIOX method (Simple Interactive Object Extraction). You can visit its Web page at [SIOX].

14.2.8.1 Directions for use

The creation of a selection with this tool works in a couple of steps:

1. *Roughly select the foreground* you want to extract. When you select this tool, the mouse pointer goes with the lasso icon. It actually works like the Fuzzy Select tool. Select as little as possible from the background.

   As soon as you release the mouse button, the non selected part of the image is covered with a dark blue mask. If the selection is not closed, its ends will be linked automatically together by a straight line. The mouse pointer goes now with the Paint-brush icon for the next step.

Figure 14.31 The foreground is roughly selected

2. *Draw a line through the foreground*: using the paintbrush, whose size can be changed in options, draw a continuous line in the selected foreground going over colors which will be kept for the extraction. The color used to draw the line is of no importance; not using the same color as foreground is better. Be careful not painting background pixels.

Figure 14.32 The line drawn on the foreground

In this example, it is important that the line goes over the yellow capitulum of the flower.

3. When you release the mouse button, all non-selected areas are in dark:

Figure 14.33 The area which will be selected

4. You still have to press the **Enter** key to get the wanted selection:

Figure 14.34 Foreground is selected

Note

 Until you press **Enter**, you can't undo this selection by Ctrl-Z nor by Select → None, and the Undo History is not concerned. To delete this selection, you must select another tool.

14.2.8.2 Activating the Tool

You can activate the Foreground Select tool in two ways:

- by clicking on the tool icon ![icon] in the Toolbox,

- through Tools → Selection Tools → Foreground Select in the image menu.

- This tool has no shortcut, but you can set one using Edit → Preferences → Interface → Configure Keyboard Shortcuts → Tools → Foreground Select

14.2.8.3 Key modifiers (Defaults)

Ctrl By pressing the **Ctrl** key, you can switching between foreground and background selection painting.

14.2.8.4   Options

Figure 14.35 "Foreground Select" tool options

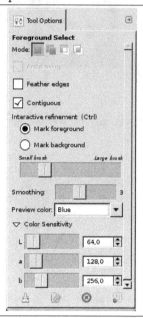

Normally, tool options are displayed in a window attached under the Toolbox as soon as you activate a tool. If they are not, you can access them from the image menu bar through Windows → Dockable Windows → Tool Options which opens the option window of the selected tool.

Mode; Antialiasing; Feather edges

> **Note**
>
> See Selection Tools for help with options that are common to all these tools. Only options that are specific to this tool are explained here.

Contiguous If this option is enabled, only the area contiguous to the stroke will be selected. Otherwise all the areas with same colors will be selected.

Figure 14.36 "Contiguous" option effect

(a) *Two separated ar-* (b) *The Contiguous* (c) *The   Contiguous*
eas with the same color. *option is checked: only* *option is not checked:*
On the left, only the left *the area close to the* *both areas, although*
area is marked. *painted line is selected.* *they are separated, are*
selected.

Interactive refinement Here are some options to work more precisely on your selection:

   Mark foreground default option. The foreground color of the Toolbox is used to paint. Colors covered by the painted line will be used for extraction.

Mark background You can access this option either by clicking on the radio button or, more simply, by pressing the **Ctrl** key. The mouse pointer goes with a small eraser icon. The used color is the background color of Toolbox. The pixels of the selection which have the same color as the "erased" pixels will NOT be extracted.

Small brush / Large brush This slider lets you adapt the size of the brush used to paint the line. A small brush fits well thin details.

Smoothing Smaller values give a more accurate selection border but may introduce holes in the selection.

Preview color You can select between Red, Green and Blue to mask the image background.

Color Sensitivity This option uses the L*a*b color model. If your image contains many pixels of the same color in different tones, you can increase the sensibility of the selection for this color.

14.3 Paint Tools

Figure 14.37 The Paint Tools (Tools menu)

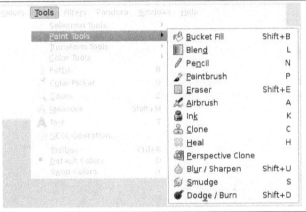

14.3.1 Common Features

The GIMP Toolbox includes thirteen "paint tools", all grouped together at the bottom (in the default arrangement).

Figure 14.38 The Paint Tools (Tools Box)

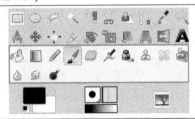

The feature they all have in common is that all of them are used by moving the pointer across the image display, creating brush-strokes. Four of them

- the Pencil,

- the Paintbrush,

- the Airbrush and

- the Ink tool

behave like the intuitive notion of "painting" with a brush. Pencil, Paintbrush, and Airbrush are called "basic painting tools" or brush tools.

The other tools use a brush to modify an image in some way rather than paint on it:

- the Bucket Fill fills with color or pattern;

- the Gradient fills with gradients;

- the Eraser erases;

- the Clone tool copies from a pattern, or image;

- the Perspective Clone tool copies into a changed perspective;

- the Heal tool corrects small defects;

- the Convolve tool blurs or sharpens;

- the Smudge tool smears;

- and the Dodge/Burn tool lightens or darkens.

The advantages of using GIMP with a tablet instead of a mouse probably show up more clearly for brush tools than anywhere else: the gain in fine control is invaluable. These tools also have special "Pressure sensitivity" options that are only usable with a tablet.

In addition to the more common "hands-on" method, it is possible to apply paint tools in an automated way, by creating a selection or path and then "stroking" it. You can choose to stroke with any of the paint tools, including nonstandard ones such as the Eraser, Smudge tool, etc., and any options you set for the tool will be applied. See the section on Stroking for more information.

14.3.1.1 Key modifiers

Ctrl Holding down the **Ctrl** key has a special effect on every paint tool. For the Pencil, Paintbrush, Airbrush, Ink, and Eraser, it switches them into "color picker" mode, so that clicking on an image pixel causes GIMP's foreground to be set to the active layer's color at that point (or, for the Eraser, GIMP's background color). For the Clone tool, the **Ctrl** key switches it into a mode where clicking sets the reference point for copying. For the Convolve tool, the **Ctrl** key switches between blur and sharpen modes; for the Dodge/Burn tool, it switches between dodging and burning.

Shift Holding down the **Shift** key has the same effect on most paint tools: it places the tool into *straight line* mode. To create a straight line with any of the paint tools, first click on the starting point, *then* press the **Shift** key. As long as you hold it down, you will see a thin line connecting the previously clicked point with the current pointer location. If you click again, while continuing to hold down the **Shift** key, a straight line will be rendered. You can continue this process to create a series of connected line segments.

Ctrl-Shift Holding down both keys puts the tool into *constrained straight line* mode. This is similar to the effect of the **Shift** key alone, except that the orientation of the line is constrained to the nearest multiple of 15 degrees. Use this if you want to create perfect horizontal, vertical, or diagonal lines.

14.3.1.2 Tool Options

Figure 14.39 Tool options shared by paint tools

Many tool options are shared by several paint tools: these are described here. Options that apply only to one specific tool, or to a small number of tools, are described in the sections devoted to those tools.

Mode The Mode drop-down list provides a selection of paint application modes. As with the opacity, the easiest way to understand what the Mode setting does is to imagine that the paint is actually applied to a layer above the layer you are working on, with the layer combination mode in the Layers dialog set to the selected mode. You can obtain a great variety of special effects in this way. The Mode option is only usable for tools that can be thought of as adding color to the image: the Pencil, Paintbrush, Airbrush, Ink, and Clone tools. For the other paint tools, the option appears for the sake of consistency but is always grayed out. A list of modes can be found in Section 8.2.

In this list, some modes are particular and are described below.

Opacity The Opacity slider sets the transparency level for the brush operation. To understand how it works, imagine that instead of altering the active layer, the tool creates a transparent layer above the active layer and acts on that layer. Changing Opacity in the Tool Options has the same effect that changing opacity in the Layers dialog would have in the latter situation. It controls the "strength" of all paint tools, not just those that paint on the active layer. In the case of the Eraser, this can come across as a bit confusing: it works out that the higher the "opacity" is, the more transparency you get.

Brush The brush determines how much of the image is affected by the tool, and how it is affected, when you trace out a brushstroke with the pointer. GIMP allows you to use several different types of brushes, which are described in the Brushes section. The same brush choices are available for all paint tools except the Ink tool, which uses a unique type of procedurally generated brush. The colors of a brush only come into play for tools where they are meaningful: the Pencil, Paintbrush, and Airbrush tools. For the other paint tools, only the intensity distribution of a brush is relevant.

Size This option lets you to modify precisely the size of the brush. You can use the arrow keys to vary by ±0.01 or the Page-Up and Page-Down keys to vary by ±1.00. You can obtain the same result if you have correctly set your mouse-wheel in the Preferences. See How to vary the size of a brush

---

14.3. PAINT TOOLS

Aspect Ratio This determines the ratio between the height and the width of the brush. The slider is scaled from -20.00 to 20.00 with the default value set to 0.00. A negative value from 0.00 to -20 will narrow the height of the brush while a positive value between 0.00 and 20.00 indicates the narrowing rate of the width of the brush.

Angle This option makes the brush turn round its center. This is visible if the brush is not circular or made from a rotated figure.

Dynamics

Figure 14.40 The Brush Dynamics in the Tool Options Dialog

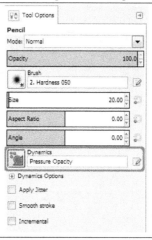

Brush dynamics let you map different brush parameters to several input dynamics. They are mostly used with graphic tablets, but some of them are also usable with a mouse.

You can read more about dynamics in Dynamics

When stroking paths and selections using a paint tool there is a an option to select "Emulate brush dynamics". That means that when you stoke, brush pressure and velocity are varying along the length of the stroke. Pressure starts with zero, ramps up to full pressure and then ramps down again to no pressure. Velocity starts from zero and ramps up to full speed by the end of the stroke.

Dynamics Options These options are described in Dynamics Options

Apply Jitter You know "spacing" in brush strokes: strokes are made of successive brush marks which, when they are very near, seem to draw a continuous line. Here, instead of being aligned brush marks are scattered over a distance you can set with the Amount slider.

Figure 14.41 "Jitter" example

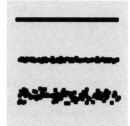

From top to bottom: without jitter, jitter = 1, jitter = 4.

Jitter is also available in the Paint Dynamic Editor where you can connect jitter to the behavior of the brush.

Smooth Stroke This option doesn't affect the rendering of the brush stroke but its "shape". It takes away the wobbles of the line you are drawing. It makes drawing with a mouse easier.

When this option is checked, two setting areas appear, Quality and Weight. You can change the default values to adapt them to your skill.

High weight values rigidifies the brush stroke.

Figure 14.42 "Smooth Stroke" example

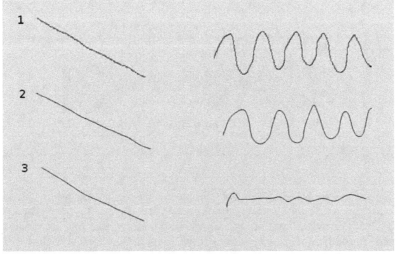

Trying to draw a straight line and a sine curve with the mouse. 1 : option unchecked 2 : default values 3 : maximum values

Incremental The incremental check-box does not seems to work as everyone expect. If it is deactivated (the default value) the maximum effect of a single stroke is determined by the opacity set in the opacity slider. If the opacity is set to less than 100, moving the brush over the same spot will increase the opacity if the brush is lifted in the meantime. Painting over with the same stroke has no such effect. If Incremental is active the brush will paint with full opacity independent of the slider's setting. This option is available for all paint tools except those which have a "rate" control, which automatically implies an incremental effect. See also Section 8.2.

14.3.1.3 Paint Mode Examples

The following examples demonstrate some of GIMP's paint modes:

Dissolve

Figure 14.43 Dissolve mode example

Two brush-strokes made with the Airbrush, using the same fuzzy circular brush. Left: Normal mode. Right: Dissolve mode.

For any paint tool with opacity less than 100%, this very useful mode doesn't draw transparency but determines the probability of applying paint. This gives nice patterns of dots to paint-strokes or filling.

Figure 14.44 Painting in Dissolve mode

This image has only the background layer and no Alpha channel. The background color is sky blue. Three strokes with Pencil and various opacities: 100%, 50%, 25%. Foreground color pixels are scattered along brushstroke.

Behind

Figure 14.45 Example for layer mode "Behind"

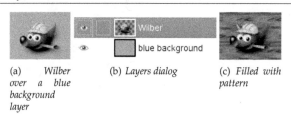

(a)   Wilber
over   a   blue
background
layer

(b) *Layers dialog*

(c) *Filled with
pattern*

This mode applies paint only to transparent areas of the layer: the lower the opacity, the more paint is applied. Thus, painting opaque areas has no effect; painting transparent areas has the same effect as normal mode. The result is always an increase in opacity. Of course none of this is meaningful for layers that lack an alpha channel.

In the above example image, Wilber is on the top layer, surrounded by transparency. The lower layer is solid light blue. The Bucket Fill tool was used, with the Fill Whole Selection option checked and the entire layer was selected. A pattern was used to paint with the Bucket Fill tool.

The next image (below) has two layers. The upper layer is active. Three brushtrokes with pencil, red color at 100%, 50%, 25%: only transparent or semi-transparent pixels of the layer are painted.

Figure 14.46 Painting in "Behind" mode

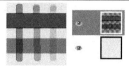

Painting with 100%, 50%, 25% transparency (from left to right)

Color Erase

Figure 14.47 Example for layer mode "Color erase"

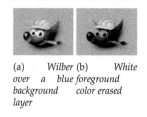

(a)   Wilber
over   a   blue
background
layer

(b)   White
foreground
color erased

This mode erases the foreground color, replacing it with partial transparency. It acts like the Color to Alpha filter, applied to the area under the brushstroke. Note that this only works on layers that possess an alpha channel; otherwise, this mode is identical to Normal.

In the above example image, the color of the Bucket Fill tool was white, so white parts of Wilber were erased and the blue background shows through.

This image below has only one layer, the background layer. Background color is sky blue. Three brushtrokes with pencil:

1. With the exact color of the blue area: only this blue color is erased.

2. With the exact color of the red area. Only this red color is erased, whatever its transparency. Erased areas are made transparent.

3. With the sky blue color of the layer background: only this color is erased.

Figure 14.48 Painting in "Color Erase" mode

Painted with 1. blue; 2. red; 3. background color

14.3.1.4 Further Information

Advanced users may be interested to know that paint tools actually operate at a sub-pixel level, in order to avoid producing jagged-looking results. One consequence of this is that even if you work with a hard-edged brush, such as one of the Circle brushes, pixels on the edge of the brushstroke will only be partially affected. If you need to have all-or-nothing effects (which may be necessary for getting a good selection, or for cutting and pasting, or for operating pixel-by-pixel at a high zoom level), use the Pencil tool, which makes all brushes perfectly hard and disables sub-pixel anti-aliasing.

14.3.2 Dynamics

The dynamics apply a more "real feeling" to the brush by connecting one or more of the brush parameters to the way of using the brush. You may for instance let the width of the pencil vary according to the speed of the stylus or the mouse, make the color saturation depending on the stylus pressure, make the color changing as the direction of the brush changes on the canvas, and so on. You may choose among several presets or define your own. The dynamics are created to be used together with drawing tablets, but some are available using the mouse.

The dynamics will make some of the behaviors of the drawing tools act more like the physical ("real") tools.

Figure 14.49 Dynamics in Tool Options

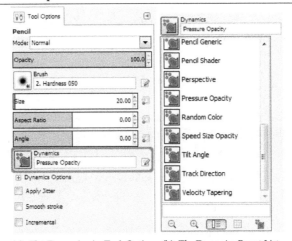

(a) *The Dynamics in Tool Options* (b) *The Dynamics Preset List Dialog*

The Dynamics area in the Tool Option dialog shows from left to right, the button to open the list containing the available dynamic presets, a field displaying the name of the current preset, and rightmost the edit button. Click on the  button to open the dialog window displaying the available dynamics presets and select another preset.

14.3.2.1 The Paint Dynamics Selection Dialog

Figure 14.50 The Paint Dynamics Selection Dialog

The Paint Dynamics dialog window can be opened

- from the image-menu: Windows → Dockable Dialogs → Paint Dynamics,

- or by clicking on the Open the dynamics selection button in the list of dynamics presets.

The Paint Dynamics dialog is a dockable dialog; please see the section Section 3.2.3 for help on manipulating it.

From this dialog you can select from all the available presets, just as from the list of dynamics presets. In addition there are five buttons:

- Edit dynamics: Click on this to edit the selected dynamics.

- Create a new dynamics: Do just that.

- Duplicate this dynamics: Make a copy of the selected dynamics.

- Delete this dynamics: Delete the selected dynamics.

- Refresh dynamics: Update the dynamics list.

14.3.2.2   Editing Paint Dynamics

Figure 14.51 Editing Paint Dynamics

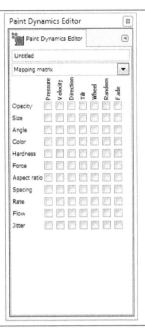

The Paint Dynamics Editor can be called from:

- the edit button in the Tool Options dialog,

- the Paint Dynamics selection dialog by clicking either the Edit Dynamics button or the Create a New Dynamics button.

You select the desired behaviors by clicking in the small squares. Clicking a second time will unselect the marking.

Note

Pre-installed dynamics are grayed out meaning you are not allowed to change the settings. To edit the options you have to work on a copy made from one of the pre-installed dynamics or create a new dynamics.

14.3.2.3   The Paint Dynamics Matrix

The main part of the edit dialog is a table where you can decide which brush parameters should be affected by the way you use the stylus or the mouse. You can enable as many parameters and parameter combinations you want, but usually the fewer the better.

Each column in the table represents a stylus or mouse action except the random and the fade functions. All functions works with graphic tablet. Some of the functions are also available using the mouse. These functions are marked in the tables. The descriptions are using the default settings of all functions

- Pressure: It allows you to decide which aspects of the tool's action will be affected by pressing the stylus against the tablet.

- Velocity: (mouse) This is the speed of the brush.

- Direction: (mouse) This is the moving direction of the brush.

- Tilt: The behavior of the function depends on the tilting of the stylus.

- Wheel: The output depends on the rotation of the stylus or the setting of the wheel on the airbrush pen.

- Random: (mouse) The selected option will change at random.

- Fade: (mouse) The selected option will be faded in or out depending on the settings of the fade options in the Dynamic Options menu of the Tools Option dialog.

Each row shows a brush parameter and seven check-boxes, one for each action. You connect the parameters to the actions by clicking the appropriate boxes. Clicking on a selected box will unselect the connection.

Opacity Pressure: Press harder to make the drawing less transparent.

Velocity: (mouse) The opacity decreases as the speed of the stylus increases.

Direction: (mouse) The opacity depends on the direction of the stylus or the mouse. The effect seems to have a touch of randomness built in.

Tilt: The opacity depends on the tilt of the stylus.

Wheel: TO DO

Random: (mouse) The opacity changes at random in the interval set by the opacity slider in the Tool Options dialog.

Fade: (mouse) Starting with full transparency and ending with the opacity set by the opacity slider in the Tool Options dialog.

Size Pressure: Press harder to make the brush wider.

Velocity: (mouse) Increasing speed decreases the width of the brush.

Direction: (mouse) The size of the brush depends on the moving direction of the stylus or the mouse. The effect seems to have a touch of randomness built in.

Tilt: The size of the brush depends on the tilt of the stylus.

Wheel: TODO

Random: (mouse) The size of the brush changes at random up to the size set in the brush size slider in the Tool Options dialog.

Fade: (mouse) Fades from a narrow brush to the size set by the brush size slider in the Tools Options dialog.

Angle TO DO

Color By default the color is picked from the foreground color in the toolbox. However, if the color is activated in the dynamics editor, the color is instead collected from the active gradient.

Velocity: (mouse) At slow speeds the color is collected from the right side of the gradient. As the speed increase the color is picked more and more from the left side of the gradient.

Direction: (mouse) The direction determine where on the gradient the color is picked from. The effect seems to work a bit on random.

Random: (mouse) The color is picked at random from the gradient.

Fade: (mouse) The start color is collected from the left side of the gradient and then more and more from the right side during the stroke. The behavior of the fading is set in the Fade Options in the Tool Options Dialog.

Hardness The hardness option is useful only for fuzzy brushes.

Velocity: (mouse) At slow speed the brush is hard and become more fuzzy as the speed increase.

Random: (mouse) The fussiness of the brush varies at random.

Fade:(mouse) The brush become less fuzzy during the stroke. The behavior of the fading is set in the Fade Options in the Tool Options Dialog.

Force TO DO

Aspect Ratio The Aspect Ratio Slider in the Tool Options Dialog must be set to other values than the default value of 0.00 to activate the dynamics. If the aspect ratio slider is set to a negative value the width of the brush will vary while the height of the brush is constant. If the slider is set to a positive value only the height of the brush will vary.

Velocity: (mouse) The aspect ratio of the brush (width / height) varies with the speed of the brush.

Direction: (mouse) The aspect ratio of the brush varies with the moving direction of the brush. The effect seems to have a touch of randomness built in.

Random: (mouse) The aspect ratio of the brush varies at random.

Fade: (mouse) If the Aspect Ratio Slider is set to a positive value the brush will fade from full height at the start of the stroke to the height set by the aspect ratio slider. If the slider is set to a negative value the brush fades from full width to the width set by the aspect ratio slider. The behavior of the fading is set in the Fade Options in the Tool Options Dialog.

Spacing Spacing is the distance between the marks set by the brush when drawing lines. With this option set the spacing is affected by how the stylus or mouse is used.

Velocity: (mouse) The spacing between the footprints of the brush increases with increasing speed.

Direction: (mouse) The spacing varies with the moving direction of the brush. The effect seems to have a touch of randomness built in.

Random: (mouse) The spacing varies at random.

Fade: (mouse) Starting with a wide spacing and gradually make the spacing narrower. The behavior of the fading is set in the Fade Options in the Tool Options Dialog.

Rate This option applies to the Airbrush, Convolve tool, and Smudge tool, all of which have time-based effects.

The actions of these tools are more or less quick. The amount of Rate depends on the setting of the Rate slider in the Tool Options dialog.

Flow Significant only for the Airbrush: more or less paint is delivered. The amount of flow depends on the setting of the Flow slider in the Tool Options dialog.

Jitter Normally the brush draws a line by printing the brush marks close together. Adding jitter means that the brush prints are scattered along the line. The amount of scattering depends on the setting of the jitter slider in the Tool Options dialog window.

Pressure: At low pressure the brush prints are spread according to the value set in the jitter amount slider. As the pressure increases the scattering amount decreases.

Velocity: (mouse) At slow speed the brush prints are spread according to the value set in the jitter amount slider. As the speed increase the scattering amount decrease.

Direction: (mouse) The jitter effect depends on the direction of the brush. The effect seems to have a touch of randomness built in.

Random: (mouse)The jitter varies at random.

Fade: (mouse) Starting with no jitter and ending with the amount of jitter set in the jitter amount slider. The behavior of the fading is set in the fade options in the Tool Options dialog.

14.3.2.4 Customizing the Dynamics

Figure 14.52 Customizing the Dynamics

If the current options do not suits you, you may fine-tune the settings from the Paint Dynamics Editor. Click on the down arrow to open the drop down menu and then select what option to change.

Figure 14.53 The Fine Tuning Curve

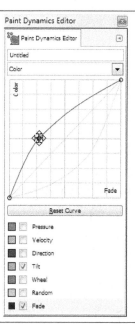

Click on one of the options to open the customizing dialog. The upper part of the dialog contains a curve where you can adjust the behaviour of the chosen parameters selected in the lower part of the dialog. You can drag the curve by pointing on it with the mouse pointer, holding down the left mouse button and the move the curve wherever you want inside the diagram.

14.3.2.5   Dynamics Examples

Figure 14.54 Dynamics Options

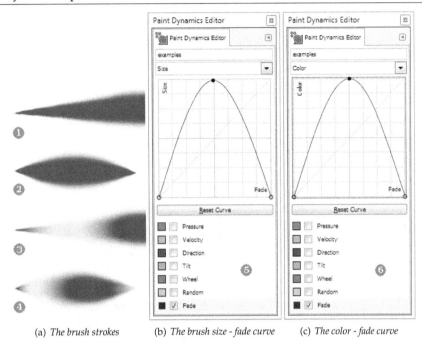

(a) *The brush strokes*   (b) *The brush size - fade curve*   (c) *The color - fade curve*

The examples shown are very brief, but will perhaps give you an idea of how to use this functions. Feel free to try other combinations. In these examples the foreground color is set to blue (#0000ff) and the background color to yellow (#ffff00). Fading: 200 pixels. Paintbrush size: 72. All other settings are the default values except for those values changed

- Example 1 shows the result when the brush size is connected to the fading. Default options. The brush size starts as zero and increase to the size set in the brush size slider in the Tools Options Dialog.

- In example 2 the brush size is still connected to the fade tool, but the fade curve is set as in image 5. The brush size starts at zero, fades up to full size and then fades down to zero again.

    The full fade length is set along the x-axis from left to right. The y-axis determines the size of the brush. At the bottom the brush size is zero, and at the top of the diagram the brush is set to the full size according to the size set in the slider in the Brush Options Dialog. Study the example and the curve to see the relationship.

- In example 3 the brush size is disconnected from the fade tool. The color is connected with the fade option with the curve set as in image 6. At the start of the drawing the color is picked from the left side of the gradient, then gradually more from the right side of the gradient and then finally fading back to the left side again.

    As usual the x-axis is the total fade length. When the curve is near the bottom of the diagram the color is picked from the left side of the gradient. With the curve at the top of the diagram the color is picked from the right side of the gradient.

- The last example shows a combination of these two settings. Both the size of the brush and the color are connected to the fading function with the curves set as in image 5 and 6.

14.3.2.6 Dynamics Options

Figure 14.55 Dynamics Options

Many of the dynamics behaviors also depends on the settings of the Dynamics Options in the Tool Options dialog and vice versa. For example the fading will not work if it is not applied in the Dynamics section.

Fade Options This slider determines the length of the fading. What will actually happen depends on the setting of the Dynamic. If set to act on the color for example, the color will be taken from the current gradient starting from the left side of the gradient and moving toward the right side of the gradient.

The Fade Options has a drop down list determining how the fading is repeated.

Figure 14.56 Illustration of the effects of the three gradient-repeat options, for the Abstract 2 gradient.

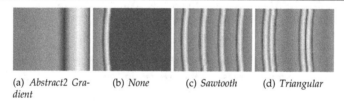

(a) *Abstract2 Gra-*   (b) *None*   (c) *Sawtooth*   (d) *Triangular*
dient

This option determines what happens if a brush stroke extends farther than the Length specified by the slider. There are three possibilities:

- None means that the color from the end of the gradient will be used throughout the remainder of the stroke;

- Sawtooth wave means that the gradient will be restarted from the beginning, which will often produce a color discontinuity;

- Triangular wave means that the gradient will be traversed in reverse, afterwards bouncing back and forth until the end of the brush stroke.

Color Options Here you can choose the gradient to use as color source when using the brush with the color option set. Click on the box showing the gradient to change to another one from the gradient list.

If no color option is selected in the currently used dynamics, the brush will use the foreground color set in the toolbox.

14.3.3 Brush Tools (Pencil, Paintbrush, Airbrush)

Figure 14.57 Painting example

Three strokes painted with the same round fuzzy brush (outline shown in upper left), using the Pencil (left), Paintbrush (middle), and Airbrush (right).

The tools in this group are GIMP's basic painting tools, and they have enough features in common to be worth discussing together in this section. Features common to all paint tools are described in the Common Features section. Features specific to an individual tool are described in the section devoted to that tool.

The Pencil is the crudest of the tools in this group: it makes hard, non-anti-aliased brushstrokes. The Paintbrush is intermediate: it is probably the most commonly used of the group. The Airbrush is the most flexible and controllable. This flexibility also makes it a bit more difficult to use than the Paintbrush, however.

All of these tools share the same brushes, and the same options for choosing colors, either from the basic palette or from a gradient. All are capable of painting in a wide variety of modes.

14.3.3.1 Key modifiers

Ctrl Holding down the **Ctrl** key changes each of these tools to a Color Picker: clicking on any pixel of any layer sets the foreground color (as displayed in the Toolbox Color Area) to the color of the pixel.

Shift This key places these tools into straight line mode. Holding **Shift** while clicking Button 1 will generate a straight line. Consecutive clicks will continue drawing straight lines that originate from the end of the last line.

14.3.4 Bucket Fill

Figure 14.58 Toolbox Fill

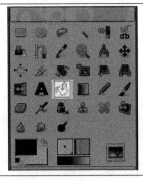

This tool fills a selection with the current foreground color. If you **Ctrl**+click and use the Bucket tool, it will use the background color instead. Depending on how the tool options are set, the Bucket Fill tool will either fill the entire selection, or only parts whose colors are similar to the point you click on. The tool options also affect the way transparency is handled.

The amount of fill depends on what Fill Threshold you have specified. The fill threshold determines how far the fill will spread (similar to the way in which the magic wand works). The fill starts at the point where you click and spreads outward until the color or alpha value becomes "too different".

When you fill objects in a transparent layer (such as letters in a text layer) with a different color than before, you may find that a border of the old color still surrounds the objects. This is due to a low fill-threshold in the Bucket Fill options dialog. With a low threshold, the bucket tool won't fill semi-transparent pixels, and they will stand out against the fill because they have kept their original color.

If you want to fill areas that are totally transparent, you have to make sure that the "Lock" option (in the Layers dialog) is unchecked. If this option is checked, only the non-transparent parts of the layer will be filled.

14.3.4.1 Activating the tool

- You can find the Bucket Fill tool from the image-menu through: Tools → Paint Tools → Bucket Fill

- You can also call it by clicking the tool icon: 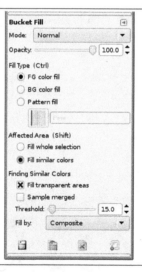 in the toolbox.

- or by pressing the Shift-B keys.

14.3.4.2 Key modifiers (Defaults)

- **Ctrl** toggles the use of BG Color Fill or FG Color Fill on the fly.

- **Shift** toggles the use of Fill Similar Color or Fill Whole Selection on the fly.

14.3.4.3 Options

Figure 14.59 "Bucket Fill" tool options

Normally, tool options are displayed in a window attached under the Toolbox as soon as you activate a tool. If they are not, you can access them from the image menu bar through Windows → Dockable Windows → Tool Options which opens the option window of the selected tool.

Mode; Opacity See Paint Tools for help with options that are common to all these tools. Only options that are specific to the Bucket Fill tool are explained here.

Fill Type GIMP provides three fill types:

   FG Color Fill sets the fill color to the currently selected foreground color.

   BG Color Fill sets the fill color to the currently selected background color.

Pattern Fill sets the fill color to the currently selected pattern. You can select the pattern to use in a drop down list.

This drop-down list allows the user to select one of many fill patterns to use on the next fill operation. The manner in which the list is presented is controlled by the four buttons at the bottom of the selector.

Affected Area

Fill whole selection This option makes GIMP fill a pre-existent selection or the whole image. A quicker approach to do the same thing could be to click and drag the foreground, background or pattern color, leaving it onto the selection.

Fill similar colors This is the default setting: the tool fills the area with a color near the pixel onto you have clicked. The color similarity is defined by a brightness threshold, that you can set by a value or by a cursor position.

Finding Similar Colors Under this section you can find two options:

Fill Transparent Areas The option Fill Transparent Areas offers the possibility of filling areas with low opacity.

Sample Merged The option Sample Merged toggles the sampling from all layers. If Sample Merged is active, fills can be made on a lower layer, while the color information used for threshold checking is located further up. Simply select the lower level and ensure that a layer above is visible for color weighting.

Threshold The Threshold slider sets the level at which color weights are measured for fill boundaries. A higher setting will fill more of a multi colored image and conversely, a lower setting will fill less area.

Fill by With this option you can choose which component of the image GIMP shall use to calculate the similarity and to determine the borders of filling.

The components you can choose from are Composite, Red, Green, Blue, Hue, Saturation and Value.

This option is not easy to understand. You have chosen, for example, the Red channel. When you click on any pixel, the tool searches for contiguous pixels similar for *the red channel* to the clicked pixel, according to the set threshold. Here is an example:

Original image: three strips with gradients of pure colors. Red (255;0;0), Green (0;255;0), Blue (0;0;255). We are going to use the Bucket-fill tool with the magenta color and a Threshold set to 15.

Image 1: Fill By = Composite. We successively clicked in the three color strips. Every strip is filled according to the threshold.

Image 2: Fill By = Red. We clicked in the red strip. The tool searches for contiguous pixels which have a similar value in the red channel, according to the set threshold. Only a narrow area corresponds to these standards. In the green and the blue strip, the value of pixels in the red channel is 0, very much different from the red channel value of the clicked pixel: the color doesn't spread to them.

Image 3: Fill By = Red. We clicked in the green strip. There, the value of the clicked pixel in the red channel is 0. All pixels in the green and the blue strips have the same red channel value (0): they are all painted.

Figure 14.60 Example for "Fill By"

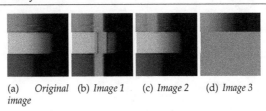

(a)   *Original*   (b) *Image 1*   (c) *Image 2*   (d) *Image 3*
image

14.3.4.4   Fill a feathered selection

By clicking repeatedly in a selection with feathered edges, you progressively fill the feathered border:

Figure 14.61 Example for "Fill a feathered Selection"

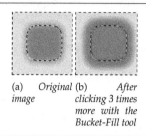

(a)   Original (b)   After
image   clicking 3 times
                 more with the
                 Bucket-Fill tool

14.3.5   Blend

Figure 14.62 The Blend tool in Toolbox

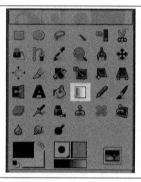

This tool fills the selected area with a gradient blend of the foreground and background colors by default, but there are many options. To make a blend, drag the cursor in the direction you want the gradient to go, and release the mouse button when you feel you have the right position and size of your blend. The softness of the blend depends on how far you drag the cursor. The shorter the drag distance, the sharper it will be.

There are an astonishing number of things you can do with this tool, and the possibilities may seem a bit overwhelming at first. The two most important options you have are the Gradient and the Shape. Clicking the Gradient button in the tool options brings up a Gradient Select window, allowing you to choose from among a variety of gradients supplied with GIMP; you can also construct and save custom gradients. Further information about gradients can be found in Section 7.10 and Section 15.3.4.

For Shape, there are 11 options: Linear, Bilinear, Radial, Square, Conical (symmetric), Conical (asymmetric), Shaped (angular), Shaped (spherical), Shaped (dimpled), Spiral (clockwise), and Spiral (counterclockwise); these are described in detail below. The Shaped options are the most interesting: they cause the gradient to follow the shape of the selection boundary, no matter how twisty it is. Unlike the other shapes, Shaped gradients are not affected by the length or direction of the line you draw: for them as well as every other type of gradient you are required to click inside the selection and move the mouse, but a Shaped appears the same no matter where you click or how you move.

Tip

   Check out the Difference option in the Mode menu, where doing the same thing (even with full opacity) will result in fantastic swirling patterns, changing and adding every time you drag the cursor.

14.3.5.1 Activating the Tool

There are different possibilities to activate the tool:

- From the image-menu: Tools → Paint Tools → Blend.

- By clicking the tool icon  .

- By clicking on the **L** keyboard shortcut.

14.3.5.2 Key modifiers (Defaults)

Ctrl **Ctrl** is used to create straight lines that are constrained to 15 degree absolute angles.

14.3.5.3 Options

Figure 14.63 "Blend" tool options

Normally, tool options are displayed in a window attached under the Toolbox as soon as you activate a tool. If they are not, you can access them from the image menu bar through Windows → Dockable Windows → Tool Options which opens the option window of the selected tool.

Mode; Opacity See the Common Paint Tool Options for a description of tool options that apply to many or all paint tools.

Gradient A variety of gradient patterns can be selected from the drop-down list. The tool causes a shading pattern that transitions from foreground to background color or introducing others colors, in the direction the user determines by drawing a line in the image. For the purposes of drawing the gradient, the Reverse ⬌ check-box reverse the gradient direction with the effect, for instance, of swapping the foreground and background colors.

Offset The Offset value permits to increase the "slope" of the gradient. It determines how far from the clicked starting point the gradient will begin. Shaped forms are not affected by this option.

Figure 14.64 "Blend" tool: Offset example

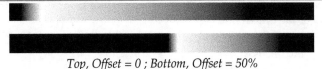

Top, Offset = 0 ; Bottom, Offset = 50%

Shape The GIMP provides 11 shapes, which can be selected from the drop-down list. Details on each of the shapes are given below.

Figure 14.65 Examples of gradient shapes

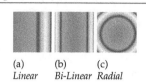

(a)   (b)   (c)
Linear   Bi-Linear Radial

Linear This gradient begins with the foreground color at the starting point of the drawn line and transitions linearly to the background color at the ending point.

Bi-Linear This shape proceeds in both directions from the starting point, for a distance determined by the length of the drawn line. It is useful, for example, for giving the appearance of a cylinder.

Radial This gradient gives a circle, with foreground color at the center and background color outside the circle. It gives the appearance of a sphere without directional lighting.

Square; Shaped

Figure 14.66 Square-shaped gradient examples

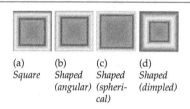

(a)   (b)   (c)   (d)
Square   Shaped   Shaped   Shaped
           (angular) (spheri-   (dimpled)
                      cal)

There are four shapes that are some variant on a square: Square, Shaped (angular), Shaped (spherical), and Shaped (dimpled). They all put the foreground color at the center of a square, whose center is at the start of the drawn line, and whose half-diagonal is the length of the drawn line. The four options provide a variety in the manner in which the gradient is calculated; experimentation is the best means of seeing the differences.

Conical (symmetric); Conical (asymmetric)

Figure 14.67 Conical gradient examples

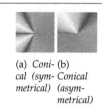

(a) Coni- (b)
cal (sym- Conical
metrical) (asym-
          metrical)

The Conical (symmetrical) shape gives the sensation of looking down at the tip of a cone, which appears to be illuminated with the background color from a direction determined by the direction of the drawn line.

Conical (asymmetric) is similar to Conical (symmetric) except that the "cone" appears to have a ridge where the line is drawn.

Spiral (clockwise); Spiral (counterclockwise)

Figure 14.68 Spiral gradient examples

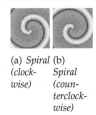

(a) *Spiral* (b)
(clock- *Spiral*
wise) *(coun-*
terclock-
wise)

The Spiral shape provide spirals whose repeat width is determined by the length of the drawn line.

Repeat There are two repeat modes: Sawtooth Wave and Triangular Wave. The Sawtooth pattern is achieved by beginning with the foreground, transitioning to the background, then starting over with the foreground. The Triangular starts with the foreground, transitions to the background, then transitions back to the foreground.

Dithering Dithering is fully explained in the Glossary

Adaptive Supersampling This a more sophisticated means of smoothing the "jagged" effect of a sharp transition of color along a slanted or curved line. Only tests can allow you to choose.

14.3.6 Pencil

Figure 14.69 Pencil tool

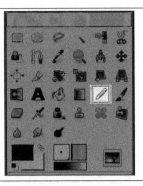

The Pencil tool is used to draw free hand lines with a hard edge. The pencil and paintbrush are similar tools. The main difference between the two tools is that although both use the same type of brush, the pencil tool will not produce fuzzy edges, even with a very fuzzy brush. It does not even do anti-aliasing.

Why would you want to work with such a crude tool? Perhaps the most important usage is when working with very small images, such as icons, where you operate at a high zoom level and need to get every pixel exactly right. With the pencil tool, you can be confident that every pixel within the brush outline will be changed in exactly the way you expect.

Tip

 If you want to draw straight lines with the Pencil (or any of several other paint tools), click at the starting point, then hold down **Shift** and click at the ending point.

14.3.6.1 Activating the Tool

- The Pencil Tool can be called from the image-menu: Tools → Paint Tools → Pencil

- The Tool can also be called by clicking the tool icon:

- or by clicking on the **N** keyboard shortcut.

14.3.6.2 Key modifiers (Defaults)

Ctrl This key changes the pencil to a Color Picker.

Shift This key places the pencil tool into straight line mode. Holding **Shift** while clicking Button 1 will generate a straight line. Consecutive clicks will continue drawing straight lines that originate from the end of the last line.

14.3.6.3 Options

Figure 14.70 "Pencil" Tool options

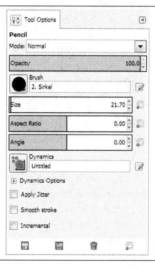

Normally, tool options are displayed in a window attached under the Toolbox as soon as you activate a tool. If they are not, you can access them from the image menu bar through Windows → Dockable Windows → Tool Options which opens the option window of the selected tool.

Mode; Opacity; Brush; Dynamics; Dynamics Options; Apply Jitter; Smooth Stroke; Incremental See the Common Paint Tool Options for a description of tool options that apply to many or all paint tools.

14.3.7 Paintbrush

Figure 14.71 Paintbrush

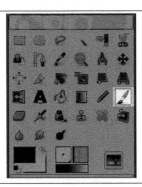

The paintbrush tool paints fuzzy brush strokes. All strokes are rendered using the current brush.

14.3.7.1 Activating the Tool

- You can call the Paintbrush Tool in the following order, from the image-menu: Tools → Paint Tools → Paintbrush.

- The Tool can also be called by clicking the tool icon:

- or by using the **P** keyboard shortcut.

14.3.7.2 Key modifiers (Defaults)

Ctrl This key changes the paintbrush to a Color Picker.

Shift This key places the paintbrush into straight line mode. Holding **Shift** while clicking Button 1 will generate a straight line. Consecutive clicks will continue drawing straight lines that originate from the end of the last line.

14.3.7.3 Options

Figure 14.72 Paintbrush tool options

Normally, tool options are displayed in a window attached under the Toolbox as soon as you activate a tool. If they are not, you can access them from the image menu bar through Windows → Dockable Windows → Tool Options which opens the option window of the selected tool.

Mode; Opacity; Brush; Dynamics; Dynamics Options; Apply Jitter; Smoot Stroke; Incremental: See the Common Paint Tool Options for a description of tool options that apply to many or all paint tools.

14.3.8 Eraser

Figure 14.73 Eraser tool icon in the Toolbox

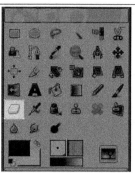

The Eraser is used to remove areas of color from the current layer or from a selection of this layer. If the Eraser is used on something that does not support transparency (a selection mask channel, a layer mask, or the Background layer if it lacks an alpha channel), then erasing will show the background color, as displayed in the Color Area of the Toolbox (in case of a mask, the selection will be modified). Otherwise, erasing will produce either partial or full transparency, depending on the settings for the tool options. You can learn more on how to add an alpha channel to a layer in Section 16.7.33.

Figure 14.74 Eraser and Alpha channel

(a) *The Background Color* (b) *The image has is White. The image has no an Alpha channel. Alpha channel. The Eraser The Eraser shows (Opacity 100%) shows the transparency. BG color.*

If you need to erase some group of pixels completely, leaving no trace behind of their previous contents, you should check the "Hard edge" box in the Tool Options. Otherwise, sub-pixel brush placement will cause partial erasure at the edges of the brush-stroke, even if you use a hard-edged brush.

> **Tip**
>
> If you use GIMP with a tablet, you may find it convenient to treat the reverse end of the stylus as an eraser. To make this work, all you need to do is click the reverse end on the Eraser tool in the Toolbox. Because each end of the stylus is treated as a separate input device, and each input device has its own separate tool assignment, the reverse end will then continue to function as an Eraser as long as you don't select a different tool with it.

14.3.8.1 Activating the tool

You can activate this tool in several ways:

- From the image menu through Tools → Paint Tools → Eraser;

- from the Toolbox by clicking on the tool icon ▱ ;

- or from the keyboard using the shortcut Shift-E.

14.3.8.2 Key modifiers

See the Section 14.3.1 for a description of key modifiers that have the same effect on all paint tools.

Ctrl For the Eraser, holding down the **Ctrl** key puts it into "color picker" mode, so that it selects the color of any pixel it is clicked on. Unlike other brush tools, however, the Eraser sets the *background* color rather than the foreground color. This is more useful, because on drawables that don't support transparency, erasing replaces the erased areas with the current background color.

Alt For the Eraser, holding down the **Alt** key switches it into "anti-erase" mode, as described below in the Tool Options section. Note that on some systems, the **Alt** key is trapped by the Window Manager. If this happens to you, you may be able to use Alt-Shift instead.

14.3.8.3 Tool Options

Figure 14.75 Tool Options for the Eraser tool

Normally, tool options are displayed in a window attached under the Toolbox as soon as you activate a tool. If they are not, you can access them from the image menu bar through Windows → Dockable Windows → Tool Options which opens the option window of the selected tool.

Brush; Size; Brush Dynamics; Dynamic Options; Apply Jitter; Incremental See the Common Paint Tool Options for a description of tool options that apply to many or all paint tools.

Opacity The Opacity slider, in spite of its name, in this tool determines the "strength" of the tool. Thus, when you erase on a layer with an alpha channel, the higher the opacity you use, the more transparency you get!

Hard Edge This option avoids partial erasure at the edges of the brush-stroke. See above.

Anti Erase The Anti Erase option of the Erase tool can un-erase areas of an image, even if they are completely transparent. This feature only works when used on layers with an alpha channel. In addition to the check-button in the Tool Options, it can also be activated on-the-fly by holding down the **Alt** key (or, if the **Alt** key is trapped by the Window Manager, by holding down Alt-Shift).

Note

 To understand how anti-erasing is possible, you should realize that erasing (or cutting, for that matter) only affects the alpha channel, not the RGB channels that contain the image data. Even if the result is completely transparent, the RGB data is still there, you simply can't see it. Anti-erasing increases the alpha value so that you can see the RGB data once again.

Tip

 You can use the Eraser tool to change the shape of a floating selection. By erasing, you can trim the edges of the selection.

14.3.9 Airbrush

Figure 14.76 The Airbrush tool in Toolbox

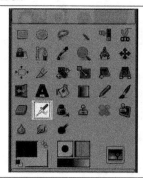

The Airbrush tool emulates a traditional airbrush. This tool is suitable for painting soft areas of color.

14.3.9.1 Activating the Tool

You can activate the Airbrush tool in several ways :

- From the image-menu, through : Tools → PaintTools → Airbrush

- By clicking on the tool icon: 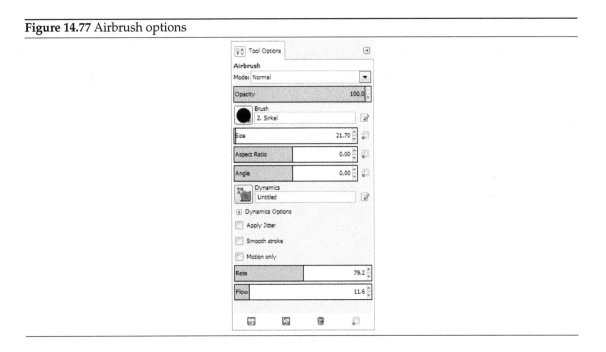 in the Toolbox,

- By using the **A** keyboard shortcut.

14.3.9.2   Key modifiers (Defaults)

Ctrl   **Ctrl** changes the airbrush to a Color Picker.

Shift   **Shift** places the airbrush into straight line mode. Holding **Shift** while clicking Button 1 will generate a straight line. Consecutive clicks will continue drawing straight lines that originate from the end of the last line.

14.3.9.3   Options

Figure 14.77 Airbrush options

Normally, tool options are displayed in a window attached under the Toolbox as soon as you activate a tool. If they are not, you can access them from the image menu bar through Windows → Dockable Windows → Tool Options which opens the option window of the selected tool.

Mode; Opacity; Brush; Size; Dynamics; Dynamic Options; Fade Options; Color Options; Apply Jitter
    See the Common Paint Tool Options for a description of tool options that apply to many or all paint tools.

Rate The Rate slider adjusts the speed of color application that the airbrush paints. A higher setting will produce darker brush strokes in a shorter amount of time.

Flow This slider controls the amount of color that the airbrush paints. A higher setting here will result in darker strokes.

14.3.10   Ink

Figure 14.78 The "Ink" tool in Toolbox

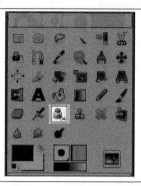

The Ink tool uses a simulation of an ink pen with a controllable nib to paint solid brush strokes with an antialiased edge. The size, shape and angle of the nib can be set to determine how the strokes will be rendered.

14.3.10.1   Activating the Tool

You can find the Ink tool in several ways :

- In the image-menu through: Tools → Paint Tools → Ink.

- By clicking on the tool icon: ![icon] in Toolbox,

- or by using the **K** keyboard shortcut.

14.3.10.2   Key modifiers (Defaults)

Ctrl   This key changes the nib to a Color Picker.

14.3.10.3   Options

Figure 14.79 Ink Tool options

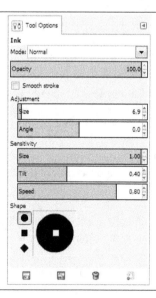

Normally, tool options are displayed in a window attached under the Toolbox as soon as you activate a tool. If they are not, you can access them from the image menu bar through Windows → Dockable Windows → Tool Options which opens the option window of the selected tool.

Mode; Opacity See the Common Paint Tool Options for a description of tool options that apply to many or all paint tools.

Adjustment

> **Size** Controls the apparent width of the pen's nib with values that ranges from 0 (very thin) to 20 (very thick).

> **Angle** This controls the apparent angle of the pen's nib relative to horizontal.

Sensitivity

> **Size** This controls the size of the nib, from minimum to maximum. Note that a size of 0 does not result in a nib of size zero, but rather a nib of minimum size.

> **Tilt** Controls the apparent tilt of the nib relative to horizontal. This control and the Angle control described above are interrelated. Experimentation is the best means of learning how to use them.

> **Speed** This controls the effective size of the nib as a function of drawing speed. That is, as with a physical pen, the faster you draw, the narrower the line.

Type and Shape

> **Type** There are three nib shapes to choose from: circle, square, and diamond.

> **Shape** The geometry of the nib type can be adjusted by holding button 1 of the mouse on the small square at the center of the Shape icon and moving it around.

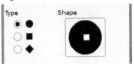

14.3.11   Clone

Figure 14.80 Clone tool icon in the Toolbox

The Clone tool uses the current brush to copy from an image or pattern. It has many uses: one of the most important is to repair problem areas in digital photos, by "painting over" them with pixel data from other areas. This technique takes a while to learn, but in the hands of a skilled user it is very powerful. Another important use is to draw patterned lines or curves: see Patterns for examples.

If you want to clone from an image, instead of a pattern, you must tell GIMP which image you want to copy from. You do this by holding down the **Ctrl** key and clicking in the desired source image. Until you have set the source in this way, you will not be able to paint with the Clone tool: the tool cursor tells you this by showing ⊘.

If you clone from a pattern, the pattern is *tiled*; that is, when the point you are copying from moves past one of the edges, it jumps to the opposite edge and continues, as though the pattern were repeated side-by-side, indefinitely. When you clone from an image this does not happen: if you go beyond the edges of the source, the Clone tool stops producing any changes.

You can clone from any drawable (that is, any layer, layer mask, or channel) to any other drawable. You can even clone to or from the selection mask, by switching to QuickMask mode. If this means copying colors that the target does not support (for example, cloning from an RGB layer to an Indexed layer or a layer mask), then the colors will be converted to the closest possible approximations.

14.3.11.1   Activating the tool

You can activate this tool in several ways:

- From the image menu through Tools → Paint Tools → Clone.

- By clicking on the tool icon  in Toolbox.

- By pressing the **C** keyboard shortcut.

14.3.11.2   Key modifiers (default)

See the Paint tools key modifiers for a description of key modifiers that have the same effect on all paint tools.

Ctrl   The **Ctrl** key is used to select the source, if you are cloning from an image: it has no effect if you are cloning from a pattern. You can clone from any layer of any image, by clicking on the image display, with the **Ctrl** key held down, while the layer is active (as shown in the Layers dialog). If Alignment is set to None, Aligned, or **Fixed** in tool options, then the point you click on becomes the origin for cloning: the image data at that point will be used when you first begin painting with the Clone tool. In source-selection mode, the cursor changes to a reticle cross symbol.

14.3.11.3   Options

Figure 14.81 Tool Options for the Clone tool

Normally, tool options are displayed in a window attached under the Toolbox as soon as you activate a tool. If they are not, you can access them from the image menu bar through Windows → Dockable Windows → Tool Options which opens the option window of the selected tool.

Mode; Opacity; Brush; Dynamics; Dynamics Options; Fade Options; Apply Jitter; Smooth Stroke; Hard Edge
See the Common Paint Tool Options for a description of tool options that apply to many or all paint tools.

Source The choice you make here determines whether data will be copied from the pattern shown above, or from one of the images you have open.

Image If you choose Image source, you must tell GIMP which layer to use as the source, by **Ctrl**-clicking on it, before you can paint with the tool.

If you check Sample merged it's what you "see" (color made with all the layers of a multi-layer image) that's cloned. If it's unchecked, only the selected layer is cloned. For more information see the glossary entry Sample Merge.

Pattern Clicking on the pattern symbol brings up the Patterns dialog, which you can use to select the pattern to paint with. This option is only relevant if you are cloning from a Pattern source.

Alignment The Alignment mode defines the relation between the brush position and the source position.

In the following examples, we will use a source image where the sample to be cloned will be taken, and a destination image where the sample will be cloned (it could be a layer in the source image)

Figure 14.82 Original images for clone alignment

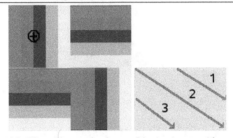

(a) *We will use the largest brush with the Pencil tool. The solid source is represented here with a ringed cross.* (b) *An image with a background only. We shall draw three cloning strokes successively.*

None In this mode, each brushstroke is treated separately. For each stroke, the point where you first click is copied from the source origin; there is no relationship between one brush stroke and another. In non-aligned mode, different brush strokes will usually clash if they intersect each other.

Example below: At every new brush stroke, the source goes back to its first position. The same sample is always cloned.

Figure 14.83 "None" clone alignment

Aligned In this mode, the first click you make when painting sets the offset between the source origin and the cloned result, and all subsequent brushstrokes use the same offset. Thus, you can use as many brushstrokes as you like, and they will all mesh smoothly with one another.

If you want to change the offset, select a new source origin by clicking with the **Ctrl** key pressed.

In the example below, at every new brush stroke, the source keeps the same offset it had with the previous brush stroke. So, there is no cloning offset for the first brush stroke. Here, for

---

the following strokes, the source ends up out of the source image canvas; hence the truncated aspect.

Figure 14.84 "Aligned" clone alignment

Registered The "Registered" mode is different from the other alignment modes. When you copy from an image, a **Ctrl**-click will register a source layer. Then painting in a target layer will clone each corresponding pixel (pixel with the same offset) from the source layer. This is useful when you want to clone parts of an image from one layer to another layer within the same image. (But remember that you can also clone from one image to another image.)

At every brush stroke, the source adopts the position of the mouse pointer in the destination layer. In the following example, the destination layer is smaller than the source layer; so, there is no truncated aspect.

Figure 14.85 "Registered" clone alignment

Fixed Using this mode you will paint with the source origin, unlike the modes None or Aligned even when drawing a line. The source will not be moved.

See that the source remains fixed. The same small sample is reproduced identically in a tightened way:

Figure 14.86 "Fixed" clone alignment

14.3.11.4 Further Information

Transparency The effects of the Clone tool on transparency are a bit complicated. You cannot clone transparency: if you try to clone from a transparent source, nothing happens to the target. If you clone from a partially transparent source, the effect is weighted by the opacity of the source. So, assuming 100% opacity and a hard brush:

- Cloning translucent black onto white produces gray.
- Cloning translucent black onto black produces black.
- Cloning translucent white onto white produces white.
- Cloning translucent white onto black produces gray.

Cloning can never increase transparency, but, unless "keep transparency" is turned on for the layer, it can reduce it. Cloning an opaque area onto a translucent area produces an opaque result; cloning a translucent area onto another translucent area causes an increase in opacity.

"Filter" brushes There are a few non-obvious ways to use the Clone tool to obtain powerful effects. One thing you can do is to create "Filter brushes", that is, create the effect of applying a filter with a brush. To do this, duplicate the layer you want to work on, and apply the filter to the copy. Then activate the Clone tool, setting Source to "Image source" and Alignment to "Registered". **Ctrl**-click on the filtered layer to set it as the source, and paint on the original layer: you will then in effect be painting the filtered image data onto the original layer.

History brush You can use a similar approach to imitate Photoshop's "History brush", which allows you to selectively undo or redo changes using a brush. To do this, start by duplicating the image; then, in the original, go back to the desired state in the image's history, either by undoing or by using the Undo History dialog. (This must be done in the original, not the copy, because duplicating an image does not duplicate the Undo history.) Now activate the Clone tool, setting Source to "Image source" and Alignment to "Registered". **Ctrl**-click on a layer from one image, and paint on the corresponding layer from the other image. Depending on how you do it, this gives you either an "undo brush" or a "redo brush".

14.3.12 Heal

Figure 14.87 The "Heal tool" in the Toolbox

This tool was once described as "The healing brush looks like a smart clone tool on steroids". And indeed the Healing Tool is a close relative to the Clone Tool, but it is more smart to remove small failures in images. A typical usage is the removal of wrinkles in photographs. To do so, pixels are not simply copied from source to destination, but the area around the destination is taken into account before cloning is applied. The algorithm used for this, is described in a scientific paper by Todor Georgiev [GEORGIEV01].

To use it, first choose a brush with a size adapted to the defect. Then **Ctrl**-click on the area you want to reproduce. Release the **Ctrl** key and drag the sample to the defect. Click. If the defect is slight, not very different from its surrounding, it will be corrected as soon. Else, you can correct it with repeated clicks, but with a risk of daubing

14.3.12.1 Activating the Tool

There are different possibilities to activate the tool:

- From the image-menu: Tools → Paint tools → Heal,

- or by clicking the tool icon: ![icon] in the Toolbox,

- or by clicking on the **H** keyboard shortcut.

14.3.12.2 Key modifiers (Defaults)

Ctrl The **Ctrl** key is used to select the source. You can heal from any layer of any image, by clicking on the image display, with the **Ctrl** key held down, while the layer is active (as shown in the Layers dialog). If Alignment is set to "Non-aligned" or "Aligned" in Tool Options, then the point you click on becomes the origin for healing: the image data at that point will be used when you first begin painting with the Heal tool. In source-selection mode, the cursor changes to a crosshair-symbol.

Shift Once the source is set, if you press this key, you will see a thin line connecting the previously clicked point with the current pointer location. If you click again, while going on holding the **Shift** key down, the tool will "heal" along this line.

14.3.12.3 Options

Figure 14.88 Heal Tool options

Normally, tool options are displayed in a window attached under the Toolbox as soon as you activate a tool. If they are not, you can access them from the image menu bar through Windows → Dockable Windows → Tool Options which opens the option window of the selected tool.

Mode; Opacity; Brush; Dynamics; Dynamics Options; Apply Jitter; Smoot Stroke; Hard Edge See the Common Paint Tool Options for a description of tool options that apply to many or all paint tools.

Sample merged If you enable this option, healing is not calculated only from the values of the active layer, but from all visible layers.

Alignment This option is described in Clone tool.

14.3.12.4 Healing is not cloning

Although the Heal tool has common features with the Clone tool on using, the result is quite different.

Figure 14.89 Comparing "Clone" and "Heal"

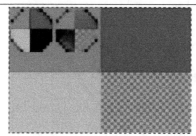

Two black spots in the red area. Zoom x800. The source is where the four colors meet. Cloning on the left spot. Healing on the right spot.

14.3.13   Perspective Clone

Figure 14.90 The "Perspective Clone" tool in the Toolbox

This tool allows you to clone according to the perspective you want. First, set the wanted vanishing lines in the same way as with the Perspective tool. Then copy the source area in the same way as with the Clone tool.

14.3.13.1   Activating the Tool

There are different possibilities to activate the tool:

- From the image-menu: Tools → Paint tools → Perspective Clone.

- The Tool can also be called by clicking the tool icon: in the Toolbox.

14.3.13.2   Key modifiers (Defaults)

Ctrl   **Ctrl**-click allows you to select a new clone source.

Shift   When the source is set and you press this key, you will see a thin line connecting the previously clicked point with the current pointer location. If you click again, while continuing to hold down the **Shift** key, the tool will clone along this line. Particularly useful when cloning from a pattern.

14.3.13.3 Options

Figure 14.91 Perspective Clone tool options

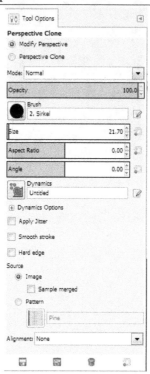

Normally, tool options are displayed in a window attached under the Toolbox as soon as you activate a tool. If they are not, you can access them from the image menu bar through Windows → Dockable Windows → Tool Options which opens the option window of the selected tool.

Operating mode When using this tool you first have to choose Modify Perspective. This works like the tool perspective. Then you choose Perspective Clone and use this in the same way as the Clone tool.

Mode; Opacity; Brush; Dynamics; Dynamics Options; Fade Options; Apply Jitter; Smooth Stroke; Hard Edge
See the Common Paint Tool Options for a description of tool options that apply to many or all paint tools.

Source, Alignment This are the same as in the tool Clone.

14.3.13.4 Example

Figure 14.92 "Perspective Clone" example

(a) *The "Modify Perspective Plane" is checked. Vanishing lines have been placed.* (b) *The "Perspective Clone" option is checked. The white rectangle has been cloned. You see it goes smaller going away.*

14.3.14 Blur/Sharpen

Figure 14.93 Blur/Sharpen tool icon in the Toolbox

The Blur/Sharpen tool uses the current brush to locally blur or sharpen your image. Blurring with it can be useful if some element of your image stands out too much, and you would like to soften it. If you want to blur a whole layer, or a large part of one, you will probably be better off using one of the Blur Filters. The direction of a brushstroke has no effect: if you want directional blurring, use the Smudge tool.

In "Sharpen" mode, the tool works by increasing the contrast where the brush is applied. A little bit of this may be useful, but over-application will produce noise. Some of the Enhancement Filters, particularly the Unsharp Mask, do a much cleaner job of sharpening areas of a layer.

Tip

You can create a more sophisticated sharpening brush using the Clone tool. To do this, start by duplicating the layer you want to work on, and run a sharpening filter, such as Unsharp Mask, on the copy. Then activate the Clone tool, and in its Tool Options set Source to "Image source" and Alignment to "Registered". Set the Opacity to a modest value, such as 10. Then **Ctrl**-click on the copy to make it the source image. If you now paint on the original layer, you will mix together, where the brush is applied, the sharpened version with the unsharpened version.

Both blurring and sharpening work incrementally: moving the brush repeatedly over an area will increase the effect with each additional pass. The Rate control allows you to determine how quickly the modifications accumulate. The Opacity control, however, can be used to limit the amount of blurring that can be produced by a single brushstroke, regardless of how many passes are made with it.

14.3.14.1 Activating the Tool

There are different possibilities to activate the tool:

- From the image-menu: Tools → Paint tools → Blur/Sharpen.

- The Tool can also be called by clicking the tool icon: in the Toolbox.

- By using the keyboard shortcut Shift-U.

14.3.14.2 Key modifiers (Defaults)

See the Paint Tools' Common Features for a description of key modifiers that have the same effect on all paint tools.

Ctrl Holding down the **Ctrl** key toggles between Blur and Sharpen modes; it reverses the setting shown in the Tool Options.

14.3.14.3 Options

Figure 14.94 Tool Options for the Blur/Sharpen tool

Normally, tool options are displayed in a window attached under the Toolbox as soon as you activate a tool. If they are not, you can access them from the image menu bar through Windows → Dockable Windows → Tool Options which opens the option window of the selected tool.

Opacity; Brush; Dynamics; Dynamics Options; Apply Jitter; Hard Edges See the Common Paint Tool Options for a description of tool options that apply to many or all paint tools.

Convolve Type *Blur* mode causes each pixel affected by the brush to be blended with neighboring pixels, thereby increasing the similarity of pixels inside the brushstroke area. *Sharpen* mode causes each pixel to become more different from its neighbors than it previously was: it increases contrast inside the brushstroke area. Too much Sharpen ends in an ugly flocculation aspect. Whatever setting you choose here, you can reverse it on-the-fly by holding down the **Ctrl** key.

"Convolve" refers to a mathematical method using matrices.

Rate The Rate slider sets the strength of the Blur/Sharpen effect.

14.3.15 Smudge

Figure 14.95 Smudge tool

The Smudge tool uses the current brush to smudge colors on the active layer or a selection. It takes color in passing and uses it to mix it to the next colors it meets, on a distance you can set.

14.3.15.1 Activating the Tool

You can find the Smudge tool in various ways :

- through Tools → Paint Tools → Smudge. in the image menu,

- by clicking on the tool icon:  in Toolbox,

- or by pressing the **S** key on keyboard.

14.3.15.2 Key modifiers (Defaults)

Shift The **Shift** key places the smudge tool into straight line mode. Holding **Shift** while clicking Button1 will smudge in a straight line. Consecutive clicks will continue smudging in straight lines that originate from the end of the last line.

Ctrl Using **Ctrl** with **Shift**, you can constrain the angle between two successive lines to vary by steps of 15°.

14.3.15.3 Options

Figure 14.96 The Smudge tool in Toolbox

Normally, tool options are displayed in a window attached under the Toolbox as soon as you activate a tool. If they are not, you can access them from the image menu bar through Windows → Dockable Windows → Tool Options which opens the option window of the selected tool.

Opacity; Brush; Dynamics; Dynamics Options; Fade Options; Apply Jitter; Hard Edge; Rate See the Common Paint Tool Options for a description of tool options that apply to many or all paint tools.

14.3.16 Dodge/Burn

Figure 14.97 Dodge tool

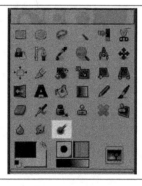

The Dodge or Burn tool uses the current brush to lighten or darken the colors in your image. The mode will determine which type of pixels are affected.

14.3.16.1 Activating the Tool

There are different possibilities to activate the tool:

- From the image-menu: Tools → Paint Tools → Dodge / Burn.

- The Tool can also be called by clicking the tool icon: ,

- or by using the Shift-D keyboard shortcut.

14.3.16.2   Key modifiers (Defaults)

Ctrl Toggle between dodge or burn types. The type will remain switched until **Ctrl** is released.

Shift **Shift** places the Dodge or Burn tool into straight line mode. Holding **Shift** while clicking Button1 will Dodge or Burn in a straight line. Consecutive clicks will continue Dodge or Burn in straight lines that originate from the end of the last line.

14.3.16.3   Options

Figure 14.98 "Dodge/Burn" tool options

Normally, tool options are displayed in a window attached under the Toolbox as soon as you activate a tool. If they are not, you can access them from the image menu bar through Windows → Dockable Windows → Tool Options which opens the option window of the selected tool.

Opacity; Brush; Dynamics; Dynamics Options; Apply Jitter; Hard Edge See the Common Paint Tool Options for a description of tool options that apply to many or all paint tools.

Type The dodge effect lightens colors.

The burn effect darkens colors.

Range There are three modes:

- Shadows restricts the effect to darkest pixels.

- Midtones restricts the effect to pixels of average tone.

- Highlights restricts the effect to lightest pixels.

Exposure Exposure defines how much the tool effect will be strong, as a more or less exposed photograph. Default slider is 50 but can vary from 0 to 100.

14.4 Transform Tools

Figure 14.99 An overview of the transform tools

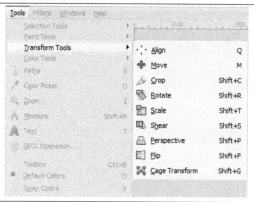

14.4.1 Common Features

Inside the Transformation tool dialog, you will find eight tools to modify the presentation of the image or the presentation of an element of the image, selection, layer or path. Each transform tool has an Option dialog and an Information dialog to set parameters.

14.4.1.1 Tool Options

Figure 14.100 Common options of transform tools

Some options are shared by several transform tools. We will describe them here. More specific options will be described with their tool.

Transform GIMP offers you three buttons which let you select which image element the transform tool will work on.

Note

Remember that the Transform option persists when you quit the tool.

- When you activate the first button 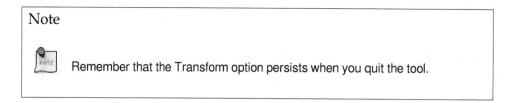 the tool works on the active layer. If no selection exists in this layer, the whole layer will be transformed.

- When you activate the second button the tool works on the selection contour only (the whole layer contour if no selection).

- When you activate the third button,  the tool works on the path only.

Direction This option sets which way or direction a layer is transformed:

The "Normal (Forward)" mode will transform the image or layer as one might expect. You just use the handles to perform the transformation you want. If you use a grid (see below), the image or layer is transformed according to the shape and position you put the grid into.

"Corrective (Backward)" inverts the direction. Primarily used with the Rotation tool to repair digital images that have some geometric errors (a horizon not horizontal, a wall not vertical...). See Section 14.4.5.

Interpolation This drop-down list lets you choose the method and thus the quality of the transformation:

None The color of each pixel is copied from its closest neighboring pixel in the original image. This often results in aliasing (the "stair-step" effect) and a coarse image, but it is the fastest method. Sometimes this method is called "Nearest Neighbor".

Linear The color of each pixel is computed as the average color of the four closest pixels in the original image. This gives a satisfactory result for most images and is a good compromise between speed and quality. Sometimes this method is called "Bilinear".

Cubic The color of each pixel is computed as the average color of the eight closest pixels in the original image. This usually gives a good result, but it naturally takes more time. Sometimes this method is called "Bicubic".

Sinc (Lanczos3) The Lanczos3 method uses the Sinc mathematical function and performs a high quality interpolation. This is usually the best method but if you are not satisfied with the result, you may give "Cubic" a try.

You can set the default interpolation method in the Tools Options Preferences dialog.

Clipping After transformation, the image can be bigger. This option will clip the transformed image to the original image size.

You can choose between several ways to clip:

Adjust

Figure 14.101 Original image for examples

(a) *Original image* (b) *Rotation applied with* (c) *Rotation applied with*
"Adjust" *"Adjust" and canvas enlarged to layer size*

With Adjust: the layer is enlarged to contain all the rotated layer. The new layer border is visible; the whole layer becomes visible by using the Image → Fit Canvas to Layers command.

Clip

Figure 14.102 Example for Clip

Clip

With Clip: all what exceeds image limits is deleted.

Crop to result

Figure 14.103 Example for Crop to result

(a) *Rotation 45° (b) The crop limit is marked with red. No trans-*
with Crop to result parent area is included.

If this option is selected, the image is cropped so that the transparent area, created by the transform operation in corners, will not be included in the resulting image.

Crop with aspect

Figure 14.104 Example for Crop with aspect

(a) *Original image*   (b) *Rotation -22°*   (c) *The rotated image*

This option works like the one described before, but makes sure, that the aspect ratio is maintained.

If this is marked, which is the default setting, the transformed image will be visible on top of the original image or layer. There will also be a slider with which you may select the preview opacity.

Preview Guides This is a drop down list where you select the type of guide lines which suits your transforming. All the guides uses a frame to mark the image's outline in addition to the lines used by the different selections.

No guides As the name tells you, there are no guides used.

Center lines Uses one vertical line and one horizontal line crossing each other in the center of the image or layer.

Rule of thirds Divides the transforming area in nine equal parts by adding two horizontal lines and two vertical lines equally spaced. According to this rule the most interesting parts of the image should be placed at the intersection points.

Rule of fifths Just as the "Rules of thirds" but divides the area in five by five parts.

Golden sections Also called "The Golden Ratio". This divides the transforming area in nine parts using a mathematical formula proportioning the parts to each others and to the area to be transformed.

Diagonal lines Divide the transforming area using diagonally lines.

Number of lines Puts a rectangular grid with equal numbers of vertically and horizontally lines. The number of lines is set in the slider popping up when this guide is selected.

Line spacing Puts a rectangular grid on the transforming area using the spacing between the lines set in the slider.

14.4.1.2 Transforming Paths

If you for some reason want to transform paths, it is possible to do this using the transform tools.

Figure 14.105 Rotating paths

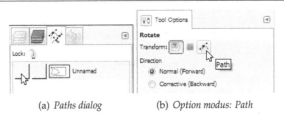

(a) *Paths dialog*   (b) *Option modus: Path*

When the path is drawn go to the path dialog and click on the first field before the path outline in the dialog window to get the eye icon visible. Then choose the transformation tool and in the upper part of the option dialog click on the path icon to tell the tool to act on the path.

Do the transformation the usual way and confirm it when finished. It could be a good idea to set the Guides to "No guides" to get the path more recognizable.

When the transformation is finished, choose the path tool and click on the changed path to activate it again for further working on it.

14.4.2 Align

Figure 14.106 The Align tool in the toolbox

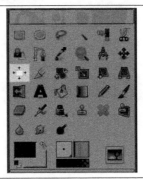

The Align tool is useful to align the image layers with various image objects. When this tool is selected, the mouse pointer turns to a small hand. By clicking on an element of a layer in the image, you choose the layer which will be moved (with **Shift** + click, you can choose several layers to be aligned); this focalised layer has small squares in corners. Various buttons in the dialog allow you to select how the layer will be moved. And you can select the image object (other layer, selection, path...) the selected layer will be aligned on. This object is called *target*.

14.4.2.1 Activating the Tool

You can activate the Align tool in several ways :

- From the image-menu, through: Tools → Transform Tools → Align,

- by clicking on the tool icon: in the toolbox,

- by using the **Q** keyboard shortcut.

14.4.2.2 Key modifiers (Defaults)

Shift You can select several layers by holding **Shift** when clicking the layers.

> **Tip**
>
> Sometimes it's easier to choose multiple layers using rubber-banding: click somewhere outside an imaginary rectangular region covering the layers you want to choose. Then drag out that region by moving the pointer, and release the mouse button. Now every layer, which is completely inside the dragged rectangle, is selected.
>
> Note that now there is no target "first item" the selected layers can be aligned on.

14.4.2.3 Tool Options

Figure 14.107 Tool Options for the Align tool

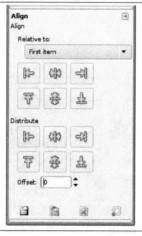

Normally, tool options are displayed in a window attached under the Toolbox as soon as you activate a tool. If they are not, you can access them from the image menu bar through Windows → Dockable Windows → Tool Options which opens the option window of the selected tool.

Align

Relative to: This is the target - the image object the selected layer will be aligned on.

- First item: the first selected item when selecting multiple layers holding the **Shift** key. Note that there is no "first item" when you select multiple layers using rubber-banding.
- Image: the image is used as a target.
- Selection: the minimal rectangular region covering the active selection.
- Active layer:
- Active Channel:
- Active Path:

⬅ ⬌ ➡ ⬆ ⬍ ⬇ These buttons become active when a layer is selected. When you click on one of these buttons, you align the selected layer with left edge, horizontal middle, right edge, top edge, vertical middle, or bottom of the target.

Distribute

⬅ ⬌ ➡ ⬆ ⬍ ⬇ These options seem to differ from the "Related to " options only by the possibility to set an offset. This offset is the distance which will separate the selected layer(s) from the target once the alignment is performed. It can be positive or negative and is expressed in pixel. Distribute add this offset to the left edges, horizontal centers, right edges, top edges, vertical centers, or bottoms of targets.

Offset This entry controls the amount of displacement that could be given to the desired alignment effect (in pixel) regarding the target. The default value is 0; it can be positive or negative.

14.4.2.4 Example for the "Align" command

Figure 14.108 Base image

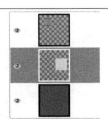

This image has three layers with different sizes and a rectangular selection. The yellow layer is active.

Figure 14.109 Red layer selected

Click on red: the red layer is selected, with a small square in every corner.

Figure 14.110 Red layer aligned

We chose "Selection" as a target and we clicked on the ➡ button (Related to). The red layer alignes with the right side of the selection.

Figure 14.111 Distribute with offset

We set Offset to -5, we chose "Active layer" as a target and we clicked on the ⬦ button (Distribution). The layer is aligned 5 pixels before the right side of the yellow active layer.

Figure 14.112 Align using rubber-band box

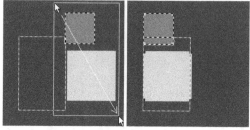

(a) *We clicked left from and above the red layer, and dragged out a region covering the red and the yellow layer by moving the pointer towards the bottom right corner.*
(b) *Again, Selection is the target. After a click on the ⬦ button, both layers aligne with the left side of the selection.*

14.4.3   Move

Figure 14.113 The Move tool in Toolbox

The Move Tool is used to move layers, selections, paths or guides. It works also on texts.

14.4.3.1   Activating the Tool

You can access the Move Tool in different ways:

- From the image menu bar Tools → Transform Tools → Move,

- By clicking the tool icon: ✥ .

- By using the keyboard shortcut **M**.

- The Move tool is automatically activated when you create a guide.

> **Note**
>
>
> Holding down the **space** bar changes the active tool to Move temporarily.
> The Move tool remains active as long as the space bar is held down. The
> original tool is reactivated after releasing the space bar. This behaviour exists
> only if the Switch to Move tool option is enabled in Edit → Preferences →
> Image Windows → Space Bar.

14.4.3.2 Options

Figure 14.114 Move Tool options

Normally, tool options are displayed in a window attached under the Toolbox as soon as you activate
a tool. If they are not, you can access them from the image menu bar through Windows → Dockable
Windows → Tool Options which opens the option window of the selected tool.

Move

> **Note**
>
>
> These options are described in Transform tools common options.

Keep in mind that your Move choice persists after quitting the tool.

Tool toggle (Shift) If Move is on "Layer"

> **Pick a layer or guide** On an image with several layers, the mouse pointer turns to a crosshair when
> it goes over an element belonging to the current layer. Then you can click-and-drag it. If the
> mouse pointer has a small hand shape (showing that you do *not* pick an element of the active
> layer), you will move a non-active layer instead (it becomes the active layer while moving).
>
> If a guide exists on your image, it will turn to red when the mouse pointer goes over. Then it
> is activated and you can move it.
>
> **Move the active layer** Only the current layer will be moved. This may be useful if you want to
> move a layer with transparent areas, where you can easily pick the wrong layer.

If Move is on "Selection"

The selection's outline will be moved (see Section 7.2.1).

If Move is on "Path"

Pick a path That's the default option. The mouse pointer turns to a small hand when it goes over a visible path. Then you can move this path by click-and-dragging it (it will be the active path while moving).

Move the active path Only the current path will be moved. You can change the current path in the Path Dialog.

14.4.3.3 Summary of Move tool actions

Moving a selection The Move tool allows to move the selection outline only. If the Move Mode is "Layer", you must hold down Ctrl-Alt keys.

If the Move Mode is Selection, you can click-and-drag any point in canvas to move the selection outline. You can also use the arrow keys to move selections precisely. Then, holding down the **Shift** key moves then by increments of 25 pixels.

When you move a selection with the Move tool, the center of the selection is marked with a small cross. This cross and selection boundaries snap to guides or grid if the View → Snap to Guides (or Grid) option is checked: this makes aligning selections easier.

See Moving selections for other possibilities.

Moving a layer The Move Mode must be "Layer". Then you can choose between Move the Active Layer and, if you have one or more layers, Point to Layer (or Guide).

Moving Grouped Layers If layers are grouped (with the little chain symbol) they will all move, regardless of which layer is currently active.

Moving a guide When you pull a guide from a ruler, the Move tool is automatically activated. That's not the case after using another tool, and you have to activate it by yourself. When the mouse pointer goes over a guide, this guide turns to red and you can click-and-drag to move it.

Moving a path The Path Tool dialog has its own moving function: see Section 14.6.2. But you can also use the Move Tool. The Move Mode must be set to "Path". Note that the path becomes invisible; make it visible in the Path Dialog. You can choose the path to be moved or move the active path.

Moving a text Every text has its own layer and can be moved as layers. See Section 14.6.6.

14.4.4 Crop

Figure 14.115 Crop tool

The Crop Tool is used to crop or clip an image. It works on all the layers of the image, visible and invisible. This tool is often used to remove borders, or to eliminate unwanted areas to provide you with a more focused working area. It is also useful if you need a specific image size that does not match the original dimensions of your image.

Just like the selection tools, the new crop tool has been enhanced with the v2.4 release. The resize handles actually resize the crop rectangle instead of providing both resize and move functionality. The tool behaves more naturally and consistently with other GIMP tools. To move, simply drag the rectangle clicking within the area. Resizing is possible in one or two axes at the same time dragging the handle-bars on the sides and corners. The outside area can be darkened with a nice passepartout effect to better get the idea of how the final crop will look like. To validate cropping, click inside the crop rectangle or press the **Enter** key.

When the mouse becomes the moving cross-hair, you can use the keyboard arrow keys to move the crop rectangle. Holding the **Shift** key down allows to move by increments of 25 pixels.

You can use Guides to position the crop area. Make sure that the View → Snap to Guides option is checked.

Note

You can see the aspect ratio in the status bar:

124, 75   px ↕   100 % ▾ ✎ Rectangle: 79 × 48 (1,65:1)

14.4.4.1 Activating the Tool

You can activate this tool in different ways:

- From the image menu bar Tools → Transform tools → Crop,

- by clicking the tool icon: ✎ in the ToolBox,

- by using the keyboard shortcut Shift-C.

14.4.4.2 Key modifiers (Defaults)

When you maintain click on the crop rectangle, handles disappear and

- holding down the **Ctrl** key toggles to the Extend from Center option,

- holding down the **Shift** key toggles to the Fixed option, which makes some dimensions fixed.

14.4.4.3 Tool Options

Figure 14.116 Tool Options for the "Crop" tool

Normally, tool options are displayed in a window attached under the Toolbox as soon as you activate a tool. If they are not, you can access them from the image menu bar through Windows → Dockable Windows → Tool Options which opens the option window of the selected tool.

Current Layer Only This option will make crop affect only the active layer.

Allow Growing This option allows the crop or resize to take place outside the image (or layer), and even the canvas. So, you can give the size you want to the resulting image. Transparency will be used if there is no material to crop.

Figure 14.117 Example for "Allow Growing"

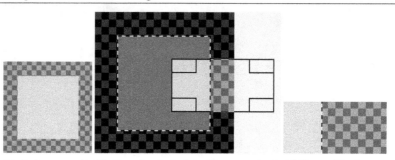

(a) *An image on a big* (b) *The option is checked. The crop rectangle* (c) *The resulting image.*
canvas   *extends outside the canvas.*

Expand from Center When this option is checked, the crop rectangle expands from the first pixel you clicked taken for center. You can toggle this option with **Ctrl** while drawing the crop rectangle.

Fixed You can also access this option by holding down the **Ctrl** key while drawing the crop rectangle. This option offers you several to make drawing the crop rectangle respect fixed dimensions, or their ratio:

- Aspect ratio: That's the default possibility. Width and Height keep the same ratio they have in the original image, when drawing the crop rectangle.

- Width / Height: Only Width or Height will remain fixed. The value of this dimension can be set in the text box below; it defaults to 100 pixels.

- Size: Both Width and Height will be fixed. Their values can be set in the text box below, in the form "150x100" for example. The crop rectangle will adopt this values as soon as you click the image. On the right, two buttons let you choose a Landscape (widthwise) or Portrait (upright) format for the crop rectangle.

Position These two text boxes show the position (horizontal on the left, vertical on the right) of the upper left corner of the crop rectangle in real time and you can change it manually too. It is stated in pixels, but you can change the unit thanks to the drop-down list of the px button. The coordinate origin is the upper left corner of the canvas (not of the image).

Size These two text boxes show the size (horizontal on the left, vertical on the right) of the crop-rectangle in real time and you can change it manually too. It is stated in pixels, but you can change the unit thanks to the drop-down list of the px button.

Highlight This option toggles the dark outside area intended for highlighting the crop rectangle.

Guides All kinds of guides are described in Section 14.2.2

Autoshrink The Auto Shrink button will attempt to locate a border, in the active layer, from which to draw dimensions from. This option only works well with isolated objects contrasting sharply with background.

Figure 14.118 Example for "Autoshrink"

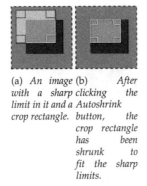

(a) An image (b)   After
with a sharp clicking   the
limit in it and a Autoshrink
crop rectangle. button,   the
                 crop   rectangle
                 has   been
                 shrunk   to
                 fit the sharp
                 limits.

Shrink Merged This option works the same, with Auto Shrink or not. It uses the pixel information from all *visible* layers, rather than just from the active layer.

14.4.5 Rotate

Figure 14.119 The Rotate tool in Toolbox

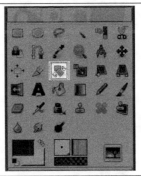

14.4.5.1 Overview

This tool is used to rotate the active layer, a selection or a path. When you click on the image or the selection with this tool a *Rotation Information* dialog is opened. There, you can set the rotation axis, marked with a point, and the rotation angle. You can do the same by dragging the mouse pointer on the image or the rotation point.

14.4.5.2 Activating the Tool

You can access the Selection Tool in different ways:

- from the image menu bar Tools → Transform Tools → Rotate,

- by clicking the tool icon: ![icon] in the Toolbox,

- by using the Shift-R key combination.

14.4.5.3 Key modifiers (Defaults)

Ctrl Holding **Ctrl** will constrain the rotation angle to 15 degrees increments.

14.4.5.4   Options

Figure 14.120 Rotation tool options

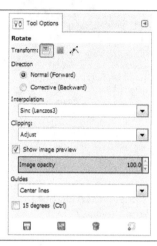

Normally, tool options are displayed in a window attached under the Toolbox as soon as you activate a tool. If they are not, you can access them from the image menu bar through Windows → Dockable Windows → Tool Options which opens the option window of the selected tool.

Transform; Direction, Interpolation; Clipping; Preview; Guides

Note

These options are described in Transform tools common options.

Transform Direction   The Transform Direction sets which way or direction a layer is rotated. The Normal mode will rotate the layer as one might expect. If a layer is rotated 10 degrees to the right, then the layer will be rendered as such. This behaviour is contrary to Corrective rotation.

Corrective Rotation is primarily used to repair digital images that are not straight. If the image is 13 degrees askew then you need not try to rotate by that angle. By using Corrective Rotation you can rotate visually and line up the layer with the image. Because the transformation is reversed, or performed backwards, the image will be rotated with sufficient angle to correct the error.

Constraints   15 Degrees (Ctrl) will constrain the rotation to angles divisible by 15 degrees.

14.4.5.5   The Rotation Information window

Figure 14.121 The Rotation Information dialog window

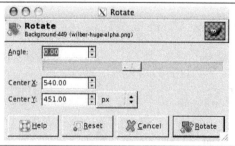

Angle   Here you can set the rotation angle, from -180° to +180°, i.e. 360°.

Center X/Y This option allows you to set the position of the rotation center, represented by a cross surrounded by a circle in the image. A click-and-drag on this point also allows you to move this center even outside the image. Default unit of measurement is pixel, but you can change it by using the drop-down list.

Figure 14.122 The rotating center

The layer rotated around the rotating center outside the image

---

Note

 You can also rotate layers with Layer → Transform → Arbitrary Rotation...

14.4.6   Scale

Figure 14.123 The Scale tool in Toolbox

14.4.6.1   Overview

The Scale Tool is used to scale layers, selections or paths (the Object).

When you click on image with the tool the Scaling Information dialog box is opened, allowing to change separately Width and Height. At the same time a Preview (possibly with a grid or an outline) is superimposed on the object and handles appear on corners and borders that you can click and drag to change dimensions. A small circle appears at center of the Preview allowing to move this preview.

14.4.6.2   Activating the Tool

You can access the Scale Tool in different ways:

- from the image menu bar Tools → Transform Tools → Scale,

- by clicking the tool icon: [icon] in the Toolbox,

- by using the Shift-T key combination.

14.4.6.3   Key modifiers (Defaults)

Ctrl   Holding the **Ctrl** key down will toggle the Keep Aspect option.

14.4.6.4   Tool Options

Figure 14.124 Tool options for the Scale tool

Normally, tool options are displayed in a window attached under the Toolbox as soon as you activate a tool. If they are not, you can access them from the image menu bar through Windows → Dockable Windows → Tool Options which opens the option window of the selected tool.

Transform; Interpolation; Direction; Clipping; Preview; Guides

Note

These options are described in Transform tools common options.

Note

The Transform mode works on the active layer only. To work on all layers of the image, use Scale Image.

Keep Aspect (Ctrl)   When you move a corner of the selection frame, this option will constrain the scale such as the Height/Width ratio of the layer will remain constant. Note that this doesn't work with border handles. Note also that it toggles the linking chain in the dialog.

14.4.6.5 The Scaling Information dialog window

Figure 14.125 The Scaling Information dialog window

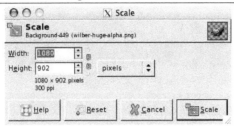

Width/Height Here, you can set Width and Height you want to give to the object. The default unit of measurement is pixel. You can change it by using the drop-down list. These values are also automatically changed when you drag handles in the image. If the associated linking chain is broken, you can change Width and Height separately.

14.4.7 Shear

Figure 14.126 The Shear tool in Toolbox

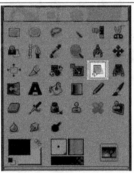

Shear tool is used to shift one part of an image, a layer, a selection or a path to a direction and the other part to the opposite direction. For instance, a horizontal shearing will shift the upper part to the right and the lower part to the left. A rectangle becomes a diamond. This is not a rotation: the image is distorted. To use this tool after selecting, click on the image or the selection: a grid is possibly surperimposed and the Shearing Information dialog is opened. By dragging the mouse pointer on the image you distort the image, horizontally or vertically according to the direction given to the pointer. When you are satisfied, click on the Shear button in the info dialog to validate.

Figure 14.127 Shear example

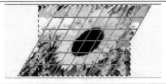

Note

    You can't shear both ways at the same time, you have to use the shear tool twice on end.

14.4.7.1 Activating the Tool

You can access the Shear Tool in different ways:

- from the image menu bar Tools → Transform Tools → Shear,

- by clicking on the tool icon:  in Toolbox,

- by using the Shift-S key combination.

14.4.7.2 Options

Figure 14.128 Shear tool options

Normally, tool options are displayed in a window attached under the Toolbox as soon as you activate a tool. If they are not, you can access them from the image menu bar through Windows → Dockable Windows → Tool Options which opens the option window of the selected tool.

Transform Direction; Interpolation; Clippping; Preview; Guides

> **Note**
>
>  These options are described in Transform tools common options.

14.4.7.3 Shearing Information

Figure 14.129 Shearing Information window

Shear magnitude X Here, you can set the horizontal shearing amplitude. A positive value produces a clock-wise tilt. A negative value gives a counter-clock-wise tilt. The unit used by shearing are half-pixels.

Shear magnitude Y As above, in the vertical direction.

14.4.8 Perspective

Figure 14.130 Perspective tool

The Perspective Tool is used to change the "perspective" of the active layer content, of a selection content or of a path. When you click on the image, according to the Preview type you have selected, a rectangular frame or a grid pops up around the selection (or around the whole layer if there is no selection), with a handle on each of the four corners. By moving these handles by click-and-drag, you can modify the perspective. At the same time, a "Transformation information" pops up, which lets you valid the transformation. At the center of the element, a circle lets you move the element by click-and-drag.

Note

 This tool is not actually a perspective tool, as it doesn't impose perspective rules. It is better described as a distort tool.

14.4.8.1 Activating the Tool

You can access the Perspective tool in different ways:

- From the image menu bar Tools/ Transform Tools Perspective,

- By clicking the tool icon: in Toolbox,

- By using the Shift-P key combination.

14.4.8.2   Options

Figure 14.131 "Perspective" tool options

Normally, tool options are displayed in a window attached under the Toolbox as soon as you activate a tool. If they are not, you can access them from the image menu bar through Windows → Dockable Windows → Tool Options which opens the option window of the selected tool.

Transform; Interpolation; Direction; Clipping; Preview; Guides

Note

These options are described in Transform tools common options.

14.4.8.3   The information window for perspective transformation

Figure 14.132 The information window of the "Perspective" tool

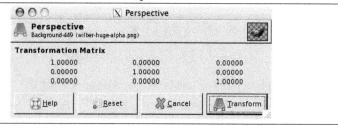

Matrix The information window shows a mathematical representation of the perspective transformation. You can find more information about transformation matrices on Wikipedia.

14.4.9   Flip

Figure 14.133 Flip tool

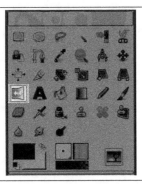

The Flip tool provides the ability to flip layers or selections either horizontally or vertically. When a selection is flipped, a new layer with a Floating Selection is created. You can use this tool to create reflections.

14.4.9.1   Activating the Tool

You can access the Flip Tool in different ways:

- From the image menu bar Tools/ Transform Tools Flip,

- By clicking the tool icon: in Toolbox,

- by using the Shift-F key combination.

14.4.9.2   Key modifiers (Defaults)

Ctrl **Ctrl** lets you change the modes between horizontal and vertical flipping.

14.4.9.3   Options

Figure 14.134 "Flip Tool" Options

Normally, tool options are displayed in a window attached under the Toolbox as soon as you activate a tool. If they are not, you can access them from the image menu bar through Windows → Dockable Windows → Tool Options which opens the option window of the selected tool.

Affect

> **Note**
>
> 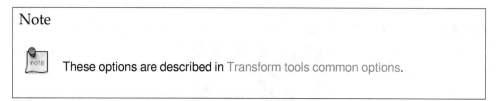 These options are described in Transform tools common options.

Flip Type The Tool Toggle settings control flipping in either a Horizontal or Vertical direction. This toggle can also be switched using a key modifier.

14.4.10 The Cage Tool

Figure 14.135 The Cage Tool in the Toolbox

The Cage tool is a special transforming tool allowing you to select the transforming area by setting anchor points by free hand drawing similar to the way you do it with the Free Selection (Lasso) tool. The tool adds nothing to the image until you confirm the transformation by pressing the **Enter** key.

14.4.10.1 Activating the Tool

You can activate the Cage tool in several ways:

- From the image-menu, through: Tools → Transform Tools → Cage Transform

- by clicking on the tool icon: in the toolbox

- or by using the **Shift G** keyboard shortcut.

14.4.10.2 Tool Options

Figure 14.136 Cage Tool options

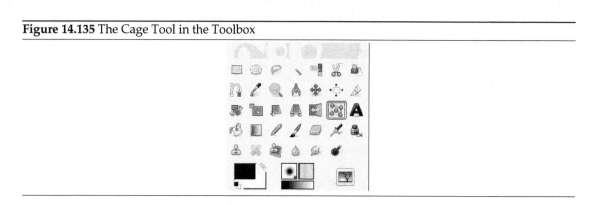

Normally, tool options are displayed in a window attached under the Toolbox as soon as you activate a tool. If they are not, you can access them from the image menu bar through Windows → Dockable Windows → Tool Options which opens the option window of the selected tool.

Create or adjust the cage When activating the Cage Tool this option is selected. You can now click in the image to make anchor points around the desired area. If you need to add anchor points at a later stage, you click on this option.

Deform the cage to deform the image GIMP switch to this option automatically when the cage outline is finished. Now you are able to drag the anchor points around in the image and even outside it to transform the picture. The transforming starts when you release the mouse button.

You can activate more than one anchor point by holding down the **Shift** key while clicking on the points. You can also select more points by holding down the mouse button while drawing a rectangle around the desired points.

Fill the original position of the cage with a plain color If the transforming action results in empty areas these areas will be filled with color if this option is checked. It looks like the color is picked from the start pixel of the cage line.

14.4.10.3 Example for the "Cage" tool

Figure 14.137 Cage Tool example

(a) *The cage area selected*   (b) *Transformed*

When clicking on the cage icon in the toolbox the cage option is set to "Create or adjust the cage". You are now able to draw a cage outline in the image by successively clicking around the area you want to transform. Click on the starting point to finish the selection. GIMP will then do some mathematics and activate the "Deform the cage to deform the image" to allow you to drag the points on the line to deform the cage and the image.

The selected point(s) turns to a square. Drag the points around in the image to transform it. The transforming will occur every time you release the press on the mouse button. The transforming may take some time so be patient especially when working with large images.

If you desire to add more points to the line you have to select the "Create or adjust the cage" in the tool options dialog. Put the points on the line and switch back to the "Deform the cage to deform the image" to transform the image or layer.

When the work is done, press the **Enter** key to confirm it.

14.5 Color Tools

14.5.1 Overview

Figure 14.138 The Color tools in the Tools menu

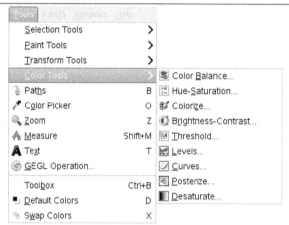

Access to the Color tools through the "classical" Tools menu.

Figure 14.139 The Color tools in the Colors menu

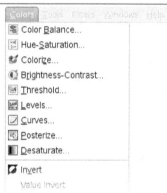

Access through the Colors menu is easier and faster.

With the Color tools you can manipulate image colors in several ways:

- Modify the color balance: Section 14.5.2

- Adjust hue, saturation and lightness levels: Section 14.5.3

- Render into a greyscale image seen through a colored glass: Section 14.5.4

- Adjust brightness and contrast levels: Section 14.5.5

- Transform into a black and white image depending on pixel value: Section 14.5.6

- Change the intensity range in a channel: Section 14.5.7

- Change color, brightness, contrast or transparency in a sophisticated way: Section 14.5.8

- Reduce the number of colors: Section 14.5.9

- Convert all colors to corresponding shades of gray: Section 14.5.10

14.5.1.1   Color Tool Presets

Except Desaturate and Posterize, color tools have *presets*: saved tool settings that you can retrieve later.

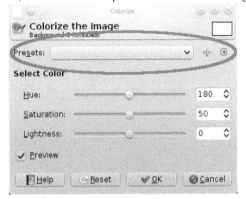

Three elements:

- **Presets**: this drop-down list shows you the existing presets. *Every time you change tool settings, a new preset is automatically saved, with date and hour;* you must be aware of that, to preserve your computer memory.

- **The cross**: clicking on this cross opens a window where you can save current settings under the name you want.

- **The small triangle**: clicking on this triangle opens a small menu:

Three options:

- Import settings from file

- Export settings to file

- Manage settings

14.5.2   Color Balance

The color balance tool modifies the color balance of the active selection or layer. Changes are not drastic. This tool is suitable to correct predominant colors in digital photos.

14.5.2.1 Activating the Tool

You can get to the Color balance tool in several ways :

- In the image-menu through: Tools → Color Tools → Color Balance, or Colors → Color Balance,

- by clicking the tool icon: in Toolbox, provided that you have installed color tools in Toolbox. For this, please refer to Section 12.1.7.

14.5.2.2 Options

Figure 14.140 Color Balance options

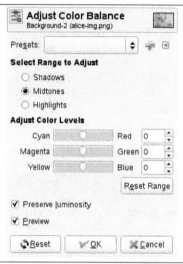

Presets You can save the color settings of your image by clicking the Add settings to favourites button

The □ button opens a menu:

Figure 14.141 Preset Menu

which lets you Import Settings from File or Export Settings to File, and gives you access to the Manage Save Settings dialog:

Figure 14.142 Manage saved Settings Dialog

Select range to adjust Selecting one of these options will restrict the range of colors which are changed with the sliders or input boxes for Shadows (darkest pixels), Midtones (medium pixels) and Highlights (brightest pixels).

Adjust color levels Sliders and range from the three RGB colors to their complementary colors (CMY). The zero position corresponds to the current level value of pixels in the original image. You can change the pixel color either towards Red or Cyan, Green or Magenta, Blue or Yellow.

Reset Range This button sets color levels of the selected range back to the zero position (original values).

Preserve Luminosity This option ensures that brightness of the active layer or selection is maintained. The Value of brightest pixels is not changed.

Preview The Preview checkbox toggles dynamic image updating. If this option is on, any change made to the RGB levels are immediately seen on the active selection or layer.

14.5.3   Hue-Saturation

The Hue-Saturation tool is used to adjust hue, saturation and lightness levels on a range of color weights for the selected area or active layer.

14.5.3.1   Activating the Tool

You can get to the Hue-Saturation tool in two ways :

- In the image-menu through: Tools → Color Tools → Hue-Saturation, or Colors → Hue-Saturation

- By clicking the tool icon: 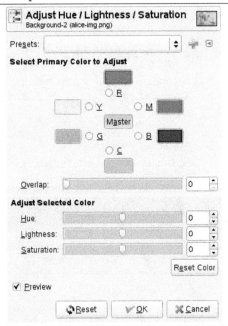 in Toolbox, provided that you have installed color tools in Toolbox. For this, please refer to Section 12.1.7.

14.5.3.2   Options

Figure 14.143 Hue-Saturation tool options

Presets You can save the color settings of your image by clicking the Add settings to favourites button

The  button opens a menu:

Figure 14.144 Preset Menu

> Import Settings from File...
> Export Settings to File...
> Manage Settings...

which lets you Import Settings from File or Export Settings to File, and gives you access to the Manage Save Settings dialog:

Figure 14.145 Manage saved Settings Dialog

Select Primary Color to Adjust You can choose, between six, the three primary colors (Red, Green and Blue) and the three complementary colors (Cyan, Magenta and Yellow), the color to be modified. They are arranged according to the color circle. When hue increases, hue goes counter-clockwise. When it decreases, it goes clockwise. If you click on the Master button, all colors will be concerned with changes. GIMP standard is to set Red as 0. Note that this colors refer to color ranges and not to color channels.

Hue changes are shown in color swatches and the result is visible in the image if the "Preview" option is enabled.

Overlap This slider lets you set how much color ranges will overlap. This effect is very subtle and works on very next colors only:

Figure 14.146 Example for the "Overlap" option

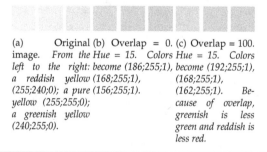

(a)   Original (b) Overlap = 0. (c) Overlap = 100.
image.   From the Hue = 15. Colors Hue = 15. Colors
left to the right: become (186;255;1), become (192;255;1),
a reddish yellow (168;255;1),   (168;255;1),
(255;240;0); a pure (156;255;1).   (162;255;1).   Be-
yellow (255;255;0);   cause of overlap,
a greenish yellow   greenish is less
(240;255;0).   green and reddish is
                                       less red.

Adjust Selected Color

- Hue: The slider and the input box allow you to select a hue in the color circle (-180, 180).

- Lightness: The slider and the input box allow you to select a value (luminosity): -100, 100.

Note

Lightness changes here concern a color range, while they concern a color tone with Curves and Levels tools, which work on color channels. If you change the Yellow lightness with Hue-Saturation, all yellow pixels will be changed, while only dark, bright or medium pixels luminosity will be changed with Curves or Levels tools.

- Saturation: The slider and the input box allow you to select a saturation: -100, 100.

The Initialize Color button deletes changes to hue, lightness and saturation of the selected color.

Preview The Preview button makes all changes dynamically so that they can be viewed straight away.

14.5.4 Colorize

The Colorize tool renders the active layer or selection into a greyscale image seen through a colored glass. You can use it to give a "Sepia" effect to your image. See *Color model* for Hue, Saturation, Luminosity.

14.5.4.1 Activating tool

You can get to the Colorize tool in two ways:

- In the image-menu through: Tools → Color Tools → Colorize or Colors → Colorize,

- or by clicking the tool icon: in Toolbox, provided that you have installed color tools in Toolbox. For this, please refer to Section 12.1.7.

14.5.4.2 Options

Figure 14.147 Colorize options

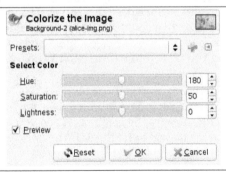

Presets You can save the color settings of your image by clicking the Add settings to favourites button

The  button opens a menu:

Figure 14.148 Preset Menu

Import Settings from File...
Export Settings to File...
Manage Settings...

which lets you Import Settings from File or Export Settings to File, and gives you access to the Manage Save Settings dialog:

Figure 14.149 Manage saved Settings Dialog

Select Color

- Hue: The slider and the numeric text box allow you to select a hue in the HSV color circle (0 - 360).

- Saturation: The slider and the input box allows you to select a saturation: 0 through 100.

- Lightness : The slider and the text box allow you to select a value: -100 (dark) through 100 (light).

Preview The Preview button makes all changes dynamically so that they can be viewed immediately.

14.5.5   Brightness-Contrast

The Brightness-Contrast tool adjusts the brightness and contrast levels for the active layer or selection. This tool is easy to use, but relatively unsophisticated. The Levels and Curve tools allow you to make the same types of adjustments, but also give you the ability to treat bright colors differently from darker colors. Generally speaking, the BC tool is great for doing a "quick and dirty" adjustment in a few seconds, but if the image is important and you want it to look as good as possible, you will use one of the other tools.

In GIMP 2.4, a new way of operating this tool has been added: by clicking the mouse inside the image, and dragging while keeping the left mouse button down. Moving the mouse vertically changes the brightness; moving horizontally changes the contrast. When you are satisfied with the result, you can either press the OK button on the dialog, or hit the **Return** key on your keyboard.

14.5.5.1   Activating the Tool

You can get to the Brightness-Contrast tool in two ways:

- In the image-menu through: Tools → Color Tools → Brightness-Contrast or Colors → Brightness-Contrast,

- by clicking the tool icon: ⬤ in Toolbox, provided that you have installed color tools in Toolbox. For this, please refer to Section 12.1.7.

14.5.5.2 Options

Figure 14.150 Brightness-Contrast options dialog

Presets You can save the color settings of your image by clicking the Add settings to favourites button

The  button opens a menu:

Figure 14.151 Preset Menu

which lets you Import Settings from File or Export Settings to File, and gives you access to the Manage Save Settings dialog:

Figure 14.152 Manage saved Settings Dialog

Brightness This slider sets a negative (to darken) or positive (to brighten) value for the brightness, decreasing or increasing bright tones.

Contrast This slider sets a negative (to decrease) or positive (to increase) value for the contrast.

Edit these settings as Levels To make your work easier, this button lets you turn to the Levels tool with the same settings.

Preview The Preview check-box makes all changes to the brightness and contrast dynamically so that the new level settings can be viewed immediately.

14.5.6 Threshold

The Threshold tool transforms the current layer or the selection into a black and white image, where white pixels represent the pixels of the image whose Value is in the threshold range, and black pixels represent pixels with Value out of the threshold range.

You can use it to enhance a black and white image (a scanned text for example) or to create selection masks.

Note

 As this tool creates a black and white image, the anti-aliasing of the original image disappears. If this poses a problem, rather use the Levels tool.

14.5.6.1 Activating the Tool

There are different possibilities to activate the tool:

- You can access this tool from the image menu through Tools → Color Tools → Threshold,,

- or through Colors → Threshold,

- or by clicking on the icon in Toolbox if this tool has been installed in it. For this, please refer to Section 12.1.7.

14.5.6.2 Options

Figure 14.153 Threshold tool options

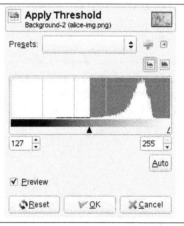

Presets You can save the color settings of your image by clicking the Add settings to favourites button

The button opens a menu:

Figure 14.154 Preset Menu

which lets you Import Settings from File or Export Settings to File, and gives you access to the Manage Save Settings dialog:

Figure 14.155 Manage saved Settings Dialog

Threshold range The Threshold tool provides a visual graph, a histogram, of the intensity value of the active layer or selection. You can set the threshold range either using the input boxes or clicking button 1 and dragging on the graph. It allows you to select a part of the image with some intensity from a background with another intensity. Pixels inside the range will be white, and the others will be black. Adjust the range to get the selection you want in white on black background.

Preview The Preview toggle allows dynamic updating of the active layer or selection while changes are made to the intensity level.

14.5.6.3 Using Threshold and Quick Mask to create a selection mask

That's not always the case, but an element you want to extract from an image can stand out well against the background. In this case, you can use the Threshold tool to select this element as a whole. Grokking the GIMP described a method based on a channel mask, but now, using the Quick mask is easier.

1. First start decomposing you image into its RGB and HSV components by using the Decompose filter. A new grey-scaled image is created and the components are displayed as layers in the Layer Dialog. These layers come with a thumbnail but it is too small for an easy study. You can, of course, increase the size of this preview with the dialog menu (the small triangular button), but playing with the "eyes" is more simple to display the wanted layer in the decompose image. Select the layer that isolates the element the best.

Figure 14.156 The original image, the decompose image and its Layer Dialog

2. Call the Threshold tool from the decompose image. By moving the black cursor, fit threshold to isolate the best the element you want to extract. This will probably not be perfect: we will enhance the result with the selection mask we are going to create.

Warning

 Make sure you have selected the right layer when you call the Threshold tool: when it is opened, you can't change to another layer.

Figure 14.157 The selected layer after threshold fit

We got the best outline for our flower. There are several red objects which we must remove.

3. Make sure the image displaying the selected layer is active and copy it to the clipboard with Ctrl-C.

4. Now, make the original image active. Click on the Quick Mask button at the bottom-left corner of the image window: the image gets covered with a red (default) translucent mask. This red color does not suit well to our image with much red: go to the Channel Dialog, activate the "Quick mask" channel and change this color with the Edit Channel Attributes. Come back to the original image. Press Ctrl-V to paste the previously copied layer.

Figure 14.158 The mask

5. Voilà. Your selection mask is ready: you can improve the selection as usually. When the selection is ready, disable the Quick mask by clicking again on its button: you will see the marching ants around the selection.

Figure 14.159 The result

CHAPTER 14. TOOLS
14.5. COLOR TOOLS

We used the Zoom to work at a pixel level, the Lasso to remove large unwanted areas, the pencil (to get hard limits), black paint to remove selected areas, white paint to add selected areas, especially for stem.

14.5.7 Levels

The Level tool provides features similar to the Histogram dialog but can also change the intensity range of the active layer or selection in every channel. This tool is used to make an image lighter or darker, to change contrast or to correct a predominant color cast.

14.5.7.1 Activating the Tool

You can get to this tools in several ways:

- In the image menu through Tools → Color Tools → Levels.

- In the image menu through Colors → Levels.

- By clicking on the tool icon ![icon] in the toolbox if this tool has been installed there. For this, please refer to Section 12.1.7.

14.5.7.2 Options

Figure 14.160 Level tool options

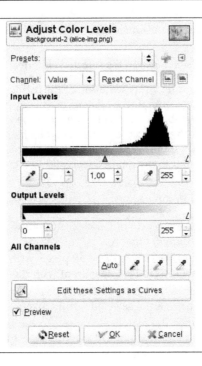

Presets You can save the color settings of your image by clicking the Add settings to favourites button

The 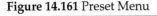 button opens a menu:

Figure 14.161 Preset Menu

329

which lets you Import Settings from File or Export Settings to File, and gives you access to the Manage Save Settings dialog:

Figure 14.162 Manage saved Settings Dialog

Channel You can select the specific channel which will be modified by the tool:

- Value makes changes to the value of all RGB channels in the image: the image becomes darker or lighter.
- Red, Green and Blue work on a particular color channel: the image gets more or less color. Remember that adding or removing a color result in removing or adding the complementary color
- Alpha works on semi-transparent layers or selections: here, dark means more transparency, and white is fully opaque. Your image must have an Alpha Channel, otherwise this option is disabled.
- Initialize channel cancels changes to the selected channel.

Input Levels The main area is a graphic representation of the active layer or selection dark (Shadows), mid and light (Highlight)tones content (the Histogram). They are on abscissa from level 0 (black) to level 255 (white). Pixel number for a level is on ordinate axis. The curve surface represents all the pixels of the image for the selected channel. A well balanced image is an image with levels (tones) distributed all over the whole range. An image with a blue predominant color, for example, will produce a histogram shifted to the left in Green and Red channels, signified by green and red lacking on highlights.

Level ranges can be modified in three ways:

- Three triangles as sliders: one black for dark tones (Shadows), one grey for midtones (Gamma), one white for light (Highlights) tones.
  The black slider determines the *black point* : all pixels with this value or less will be black (no color with a color channel selected / transparent with the Alpha channel selected).
  The white slider determines the *white point* : all pixels with this value or higher, will be white (fully colored with a color channel selected / fully opaque with the Alpha channel selected).
  The gray slider determines the *mid point*. Going to the left, to the black, makes the image lighter (more colored / more opaque) . Going to the right, to the white, makes the image darker (less colored / more transparent).
- Two eye-droppers: when you click them, the mouse pointer becomes an eye-dropper. Then clicking on the image determines the black or the white point according to the chosen eye-dropper. Use the left, dark one to determine the black-point; use the right, white one to determine the white point.
- Three numeric text boxes to enter values directly.

Input Levels are used to lighten highlights (bright tones), darken shadows (dark tones), change the balance of bright and dark tones. Move sliders to the left to increase lightness (increase the chosen color / increase opacity). Move the sliders to the right to lessen lightness (lessen the chosen color / lessen opacity).

Examples for Input Levels

The original image is a gray-scaled image with three stripes: Shadows (64), Mid Tones (127), Highlights (192). The histogram shows three peaks, one for each of the three tones.

Original image

1. The Value channel is selected. The black slider (Shadows) has been moved up to the Shadows peak. The 64 value became 0 and the Shadows stripe became black (0). The Gamma (mid tones) slider is automatically moved to the middle of the tone range. Mid tones are made darker to 84 and Highlights to 171.

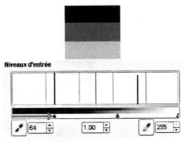

Black slider has been moved

2. The white slider (highlights) has been moved up to the highlight peak. The 192 value became 255 and the highlight stripe became white. The Gamma (mid tones) slider is automatically moved to the middle of the tone range. Mid tones are made lighter to 169 and Shadows to 84.

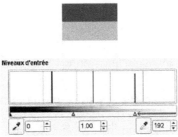

White slider has been moved

Output Levels Output levels allows manual selection of a constrained output level range. There are also numeric text boxes with arrow-heads located here that can be used to interactively change the Output Levels.

Output levels force the tone range to fit the new limits you have set.

- Working with Value: values are compressed and look more alike; so contrast is reduced. Shadows are made lighter: new details can show up but contrast is less; a compromise is necessary. Highlights are made darker.

- Working with Color channels: if you the use the green channel for example and set the output levels between 100 and 140, all pixels with some green, even a low value, will have their green channel value shifted between 100 and 140.

- Working with Alpha channel: all Alpha values will be shifted to the range you have set.

Example for Output Levels

1. The original image is a RGB gradient from black (0;0;0) to white (255;255;255). Output Levels has no histogram; here, we used Windows → Dockable Dialogs → Histogram.

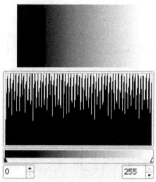

Original image (a gradient)

2. Value channel selected. The black slider has been moved to 63 and the white slider to 189. The Histogram shows the compression of pixels. No pixel is less than 63, and no pixel is more than 189. In the image, Shadows are lighter and Highlights are darker: contrast is reduced.

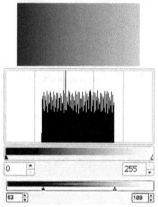

Black slider has been moved

All Channels Auto: Performs an automatic setting of the levels.

> **Three eyedroppers , , .** These three buttons respectively represent a white, a gray and a black eye-dropper. When you click one of these buttons, the mouse pointer takes the form of the eye-dropper it represents. Then, when clicking the image, the clicked pixel determines the *white point* , the *black point* or the *mid point* according to the eye-dropper you chose. Works on all channels, even if a particular channel is selected.

Figure 14.163 Example for Levels eye-droppers

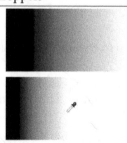

Above is original gradient from black to white. Below is the result after clicking with the white eye-dropper: all pixels with a value higher than that of the clicked pixel turned to white.

Edit these settings as Curves To make your work easier, this button lets you turn to the Curves tool with the same settings.

Preview The Preview button makes all changes to the levels dynamically so that the new level settings can be viewed straight away.

14.5.7.3 Tool Options dialog

Figure 14.164 "Levels" tool options

Although this tool is not present in the Toolbox by default (please refer to Section 12.1.7 if you want to add it), nevertheless it has a Tool Option Dialog under the Toolbox. These options are described here:

Histogram Scale These two options have the same action as the Logarithmic 📷 and Linear 📷 buttons in the Levels dialog.

Sample Average This slider sets the "radius" of the color-picking area. This area appears as a more or less enlarged square when you maintain the click on a pixel.

14.5.7.4 Actual practice

Figure 14.165 A very under-exposed image

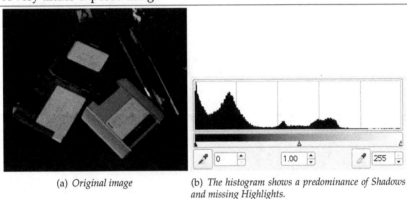

(a) *Original image*

(b) *The histogram shows a predominance of Shadows and missing Highlights.*

Figure 14.166 Setting the white point

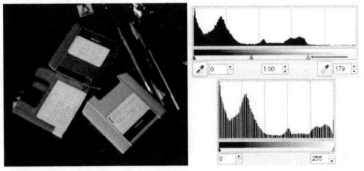

(a) *The white slider has been moved to the start of well marked Highlights. The image lightens up.*

(b) *The resulting histogram (down) shows Highlights now, but Shadows are still predominant.*

Figure 14.167 Setting the balance between Shadows and Highlights

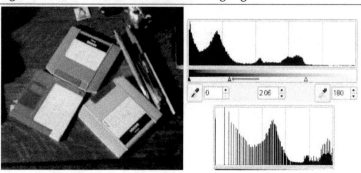

(a) *The mid slider has been moved to the left. This results in reducing the proportion of Shadows and increasing the proportion of Highlights.* (b) *The resulting histogram (down) confirms the reduction of Shadows.*

14.5.8 Curves

The Curves tool is the most sophisticated tool for changing the color, brightness, contrast or transparency of the active layer or a selection. While the Levels tool allows you to work on Shadows and Highlights, the Curves tool allows you to work on any tonal range. It works on RGB images.

14.5.8.1 Activating the Tool

You can get to this tool in several ways:

- In the image menu through Tools → Color Tools → Curves or Colors → Curves.

- By clicking on the tool icon ![icon] in Toolbox, if this tool has been installed there. For this, please refer to Section 12.1.7.

14.5.8.2 "Adjust Color Curves" options

Figure 14.168 The "Adjust Color Curves" dialog

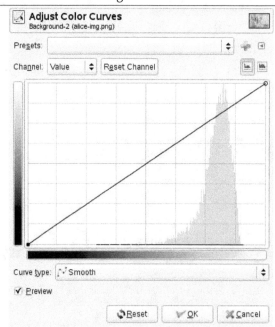

Presets You can save the color settings of your image by clicking the Add settings to favourites button

The  button opens a menu:

Figure 14.169 Preset Menu

which lets you Import Settings from File or Export Settings to File, and gives you access to the Manage Save Settings dialog:

Figure 14.170 Manage saved Settings Dialog

Channel There are five options:

Value The curve represents the Value, i.e. the brightness of pixels as you can see them in the composite image.

Red; Green; Blue The curve represents the quantity of color in each of the three RGB channels. Here, *dark* means *little* of the color. *Light* means *a lot* of the color.

Alpha The curve represents the opacity of the pixels. *Dark* means *very transparent*. *Light* means *very opaque*. Your image or active layer must have an Alpha channel for this option to be enabled.

Reset Channel This button deletes all changes made to the selected channel and returns to default values.

Linear and Logarithmic buttons These buttons allow to choose the Linear or Logarithmic type of the histogram. You can also use the same options in Tool Options dialog. This grayed out histogram is not displayed by default.

Main Editing Area

- *The horizontal gradient*: it represents the input tonal scale. It, too, ranges from 0 (black) to 255 (white), from Shadows to Highlights. When you adjust the curve, it splits up into two parts; the upper part then represents the *tonal balance* of the layer or selection.

- *The vertical gradient*: it represents the destination, the output tonal scale. It ranges from 0 (black) to 255 (white), from Shadows to Highlights.

- *The chart*: the curve is drawn on a grid and goes from the bottom left corner to the top right corner. The pointer x/y position is permanently displayed in the top left part of the grid. By default, this curve is straight, because every input level corresponds to the same ouput tone. GIMP automatically places an anchor at both ends of the curve, for black (0) and white (255).

  If you click on the curve, a new *anchor* is created. When the mouse pointer goes over an anchor, it takes the form of a small hand. You can click-and-drag the anchor to bend the curve. If you click outside of the curve, an anchor is also created, and the curve includes it automatically.

Unactive anchors are black. The active anchor is white. You can activate an anchor by clicking on it. You can also swap the anchor activation by using the Left and Right arrow keys of your keyboard. You can move the anchor vertically with the Up and Down arrow keys. This allows you to fine tune the anchor position. Holding the **Shift** down lets you move it by increments of 15 pixels.

Two anchors define a *curve segment* which represents a tonal range in the layer. You can click-and-drag this segment (this creates a new anchor). Of course, you can't drag it beyond the end anchors.

To delete all anchors (apart from both ends), click on the Reset Channel button. To delete only one anchor, move beyond any adjacent anchor on horizontal axis.

Meanwhile, on the canvas, the mouse pointer has the form of an eye-dropper. If you click on a pixel, a vertical line appears on the chart, positioned to the source value of this pixel in the selected channel. If you **Shift**-click, you create an anchor in the selected channel. If you **Ctrl**-click, you create an anchor in all channels, possibly including the Alpha channel. You can also **Shift**-drag and **Ctrl**-drag: this will move the vertical line and the anchor will show up when releasing the mouse left button.

The histogram of the active layer or selection for the selected channel is represented grayed out in the chart. It's only a reference.

Curve type

    Smooth This the default mode. It constrains the curve type to a smooth line with tension. It provides a more realistic render than the following.

    Free Hand With this mode, you can draw a broken line that you can smooth by clicking the Curve Type button again.

Preview The Preview button makes all changes to the levels dynamically so that the new level settings can be viewed immediately.

    Tool Options dialog

Although this tool is not present in the Toolbox by default (For this, please refer to Section 12.1.7 if you want to add it), nevertheless it has a Tool Option Dialog under the Toolbox. These options are described here:

Histogram Scale These two options have the same action as the Logarithmic ▨ and Linear ▨ buttons in the Curves dialog.

Sample Average This slider sets the "radius" of the color-picking area. This area appears as a more or less enlarged square when you maintain the click on a pixel. Here, the eye-dropper is used to locate a pixel: radius = 1 seems the best.

14.5.8.3   Using the "Curves" tool

14.5.8.3.1   Summary and basic shapes We create anchors and segments on the curve and we move them to shape the curve. This curve maps "input" tones of the active layer or selection to "output" tones.

    14.5.8.3.1.1   How the Curves tool works Moving the anchor of a pixel upwards makes this pixel brighter.

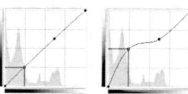

Moving the anchor upwards

    14.5.8.3.1.2   Making the curve more horizontal Making the curve more horizontal forces all the input tonal range to occupy a shrunk output tonal range.

The histogram shows the compression of pixels into the output range. Darkest and brightest pixels disappeared: contrast decreases.

Figure 14.171 Making the curve more horizontal

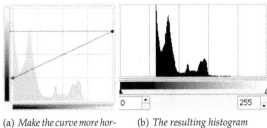

(a) *Make the curve more hor-*   (b) *The resulting histogram*
izontal

14.5.8.3.1.3   Making the curve more vertical   Moving the upper end point to the left and the lower end point to the right is the same as moving the white slider to the left and the black slider to the right in the Levels tool: all pixels whose value is more than the white point (the flat part of the curve) are made white (more colored / more opaque according to the selected channel). All pixels whose value is less than the black point (the lower flattened curve) are made black (black / completely transparent). Pixels corresponding to points of the curve that have moved up are made lighter. Pixels corresponding to points of the curve that have moved down are made darker (green arrows). All these pixels will be extended to the whole output tonal range.

The histogram shows the extension of values, from black (0) to White (255): contrast is increased. Since the Value channel is selected, changes affect all color channels and colors increase.

Figure 14.172 Making the curve more vertical

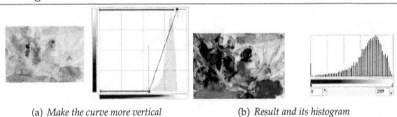

(a) *Make the curve more vertical*   (b) *Result and its histogram*

14.5.8.3.2   Practical cases

14.5.8.3.2.1   Invert colors

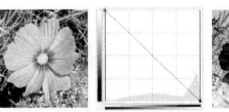

Inverted curve

Black is made White (fully colored / fully opaque). White is made black (black, fully transparent). All pixels adopt the complementary color. Why that? Because subtracting the channel values from 255 gives the complementary color. For example: 19;197;248 a sky blue gives 255-19; 255-197; 255-248 = 236;58;7, a bright red.

14.5.8.3.2.2 Enhance contrast

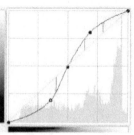

Contrast enhanced

Contrast is increased in mid tones because the curve is steeper there. Highlights and Shadows are increased but contrast is slightly less in these areas because the curve is flatter.

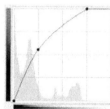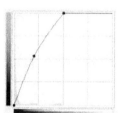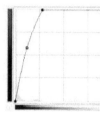

14.5.8.3.2.3 Working on color channels

For every channel, we moved the white point horizontally to the left, to the first Highlights. This lightens Highlights up. Then we shaped the curve to lighten Mid tons and Shadows while keeping black.

The original image and the result

14.5.9 Posterize

This tool is designed to intelligently weigh the pixel colors of the selection or active layer and reduce the number of colors while maintaining a semblance of the original image characteristics.

14.5.9.1 Activating the Tool

You can get to this tool in several ways:

- In the image menu through Tools → Color Tools → Posterize or Colors → Posterize.

- By clicking on the tool icon in Toolbox, if this tool has been installed there. For this, please refer to Section 12.1.7.

14.5.9.2 Options

Figure 14.173 Posterize tool options

Posterize Levels This slider and the input boxes with arrow-heads allow you to set the number of levels (2-256) in each RGB channel that the tool will use to describe the active layer. The total number of colors is the combination of these levels. A level to 3 will give $2^3 = 8$ colors.

Preview The Preview check-box makes all changes dynamically so that they can be viewed straight away.

14.5.9.3 Example

Figure 14.174 Example for the "Posterize" tool

Image posterized in 4 levels. The histogram shows the 4 levels and 10 colors, counting black and white also.

14.5.10 Desaturate

By using the Desaturate command, you can convert all of the colors on the active layer to corresponding shades of gray. This differs from converting the image to grayscale in two respects. First, it only operates on the active layer and second, the colors on the layer are still RGB values with three components. This means that you can paint on the layer, or individual parts of it, using color at a later time.

> **Note**
>
> This command only works on layers of RGB images. If the image is in Grayscale or Indexed mode, it can do nothing.

14.5.10.1 Activating the Command

You can get to this tools in several ways:

- In the image menu through Tools → Color Tools → Desaturate or Colors → Desaturate,

- by clicking on the tool icon ▮ in Toolbox, if this tool has been installed there. For this, please refer to Section 12.1.7.

14.5.10.2 Options

Figure 14.175 The "Desaturate" option dialog

Three options are available:
  Choose shade of gray based on

Lightness The graylevel will be calculated as

$$\text{Lightness} = \tfrac{1}{2} \times (\max(R,G,B) + \min(R,G,B))$$

Luminosity The graylevel will be calculated as

$$\text{Luminosity} = 0.21 \times R + 0.72 \times G + 0.07 \times B$$

Average The graylevel will be calculated as

$$\text{Average Brightness} = (R + G + B) \div 3$$

Figure 14.176 Comparing the three options

(a) *Original image* (b) *"Lightness"* (c) *"Luminosity" ap-* (d) *"Average" applied.*
                      applied   *plied.*

14.6 Other

14.6.1 Overview

Figure 14.177 Other Tools in the Tools Menu

"Other" tools are simply those tools which don't belong to any main group of tools. You will find here, for example, the important and powerful Path tool as well as useful helper tools like the Color Picker:

- Section 14.6.2

- Section 14.6.3

- Section 14.6.4

- Section 14.6.5

- Section 14.6.6

- Section 14.6.7

14.6.2 Paths

Figure 14.178 Paths tool

The Paths tool allows to create complex selections called Bézier Curves, a bit like Lasso but with all the adaptability of vectorial curves. You can edit your curve, you can paint with your curve, or even save, import, and export the curve. You can also use paths to create geometrical figures. Paths have their own dialog box: Dialog.

14.6.2.1 Activating the Tool

You can get this tool in several ways:

- In the image menu through Tools → Paths,

- By clicking the tool icon: in Toolbox,

- or by using the **B** keyboard shortcut.

14.6.2.2 Key modifiers (Defaults)

> **Note**
>
> Help messages pop up at the bottom of the image window to help you about all these keys.

Shift This key has several functions depending on context. See Options for more details.

Ctrl ; Alt Three modes are available to work with the Paths tool: Design,Edit and Move. **Ctrl** key toggles between Design and Edit. **Alt** (or Ctrl-Alt) key toggles between Design and Move.

14.6.2.3 Options

Figure 14.179 "Path" tool options

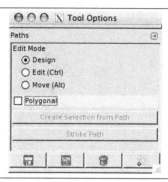

Normally, tool options are displayed in a window attached under the Toolbox as soon as you activate a tool. If they are not, you can access them from the image menu bar through Windows → Dockable Windows → Tool Options which opens the option window of the selected tool.

Design Mode By default, this tool is in Design mode. You draw the path by clicking successively. You can move control points by clicking on them and dragging them. Between control points are segments.

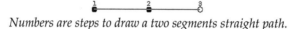

Numbers are steps to draw a two segments straight path.

Curved segments are easily built by dragging a segment or a new node. Blue arrows indicate curve. Two little handles appear that you can drag to bend the curve.

Tip

To quickly close the curve, press **Ctrl** key and click on the initial control point. In previous versions, clicking inside a closed path converted it into Selection.

Now, you can use the Create selection from path button or ▓ the *Path to Selection* button in the Path Dialog.

Tip

When you have two handles, they work symmetrically by default. Release the pressure on the mouse button to move handles individually. The **Shift** key will force the handles to be symmetrical again.

Several functions are available with this mode:

Add a new node: If the active node (a small empty circle after clicking on a node) is at the end of the path, the mouse pointer is a '+' sign and a new node is created, linked to the previous one by a segment. If the active node is on the path, the pointer is a square and you can create a new component to the path. This new component is independent from the other, but belongs to the path as you can see on the Path dialog. Pressing **Shift** forces the creation of a new component.

Move one or several nodes: On a node, the mouse pointer becomes a 4-arrows cross. You can click and drag it. You can select several nodes by **Shift** and click and move them by click and drag. Pressing Ctrl-Alt allows to move all the path, as a selection.

Modify handles: You have to Edit a node before. A handle appears. Drag it to bend the curve. Pressing **Shift** toggles to symmetric handles.

Modify segment: When the mouse pointer goes over a segment, it turns to a 4-arrows cross. Click-and-drag it to bend the segment. As soon as you move, handles appear at both ends of the segment. Pressing **Shift** key toggles to symmetric handles.

Edit Mode Edit performs functions which are not available in Design mode. With this mode, you can work only on the existing path. Outside, the pointer is a small crossed circle (on the whole image if there is no path!) and you can do nothing.

Add a segment between two nodes: Click on a node at one end of the path to activate it. The pointer is like a union symbol. Click on an other node to link both nodes. This is useful when you have to link unclosed components.

Remove a segment from a path: While pressing Shift-Ctrl key combination, point to a segment. Pointer turns to -. Click to delete the segment.

Add a node to a path: point to a segment. Pointer turns to +. Click where you want to place the new control point.

Remove a node: While pressing Shift-Ctrl key combination, point to a node. Pointer turns to -. Click to delete the node.

Add a handle to a node: Point to a node. Pointer turns to small hand. Drag the node: handle appears. Pressing **Shift** toggles to symmetric handles.

Remove a handle from a node: While pressing Shift-Ctrl key combination, point to a handle. The pointer doesn't turn to the expected - and remains a hand. Click to delete the handle.

Caution

 No warning before removing a node, a segment or a handle.

Move Mode Move mode allows to move one or all components of a path. Simply click on the path and drag it.

If you have several components, only the selected one is moved. If you click and drag outside the path, all components are moved. Pressing **Shift** key toggles to move all components also.

Polygonal With this option, segments are linear only. Handles are not available and segments are not bent when moving them.

Create selection from path This button allows creation of a selection that is based on the path in its present state. This selection is marked with the usual "marching ants". Note that the path is still present: current tool is still path tool and you can modify this path without modifying the selection that has become independent. If you change tool, the path becomes invisible, but it persists in Path Dialog and you can re-activate it.

If the path is not closed, GIMP will close it with a straight line.

As the help pop-up tells, pressing **Shift** when clicking on the button will add the new selection to an eventually pre-existent. Pressing the **Ctrl** will subtract the selection from the pre-existent and the Shift-Ctrl key combination will intersect the two selections.

Stroke path In previous versions, you could access to this command only by the Edit sub-menu in the Image Menu. Now you can access to it also via this button. See Section 16.3.18 and Section 7.5.

See the Pathconcept.

14.6.3 Color Picker

Figure 14.180 The Color Picker in the toolbox (eye dropper icon)

The Color Picker Tool is used to select a color on any image opened on your screen. By clicking a point on an image, you can change the active color to that which is located under the pointer. By default, the tool works on the active layer, but the Sample Merge option lets you grab the color as it is in the image, resulting of the combination of all layers. *Only colors in visible layers are used.* An Info window opens when you click on the image.

14.6.3.1 Activating the Tool

You can get to this tool in several ways :

- In the image menu through Tools → Color Picker.,

- by clicking the tool icon in Toolbox,

- by pressing the **O** keyboard shortcut,

- by pressing the **Ctrl** key while using a paint tool. The Color-picker dialog is not opened during this operation and the tool remains unchanged after releasing the key. Nevertheless, you can get information by using the Pointer window.

14.6.3.2 Key modifiers (Defaults)

Ctrl If the pick mode is set to Set foreground color, then pressing the **Ctrl** key switches the tool into the Set background color mode. If the pick mode is set to Set background color then the key switches the mode to Set foreground color. When the pick mode is Pick only, the key doesn't do anything.

Shift By pressing the **Shift** key, the Color Picker Information window is opened when you click on a pixel.

> **Note**
>
> The Pointer Information gives you the same information permanently. But be warned, it defaults to Sample merged.

14.6.3.3   Options

Figure 14.181 Color Picker Options

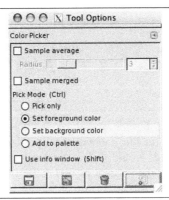

Normally, tool options are displayed in a window attached under the Toolbox as soon as you activate a tool. If they are not, you can access them from the image menu bar through Windows → Dockable Windows → Tool Options which opens the option window of the selected tool.

Sample Merged The Sample Merged check-box when enabled will take color information as a composite from all the visible layers. Further information regarding Sample Merge is available in the glossary entry, Sample Merge.

Sample Average The Radius slider adjusts the size of the square area that is used to determine an average color for the final selection. When you keep clicking the layer, the mouse pointer shows the size of the square or radius.

Pick Mode

    Pick Only The color of the selected pixel will be shown in an Information Dialog, but not otherwise used.

    Set Foreground Color The Foreground color, as shown in the Toolbox Color Area, will be set to the color of the pixel you click on.

    Set Background Color The Background color, as shown in the Toolbox Color Area, will be set to the color of the pixel you click on.

    Add to Palette When this option box is checked, the picked color is sent to the active color palette. See Palette Editor.

Use info window When this option is checked, the information window is opened automatically. The **Shift** key allows you to toggle this possibility temporarily.

Figure 14.182 Color Picker Info Window

14.6.4 Zoom

Figure 14.183 The "Zoom" tool in Toolbox

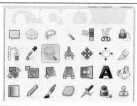

The Zoom Tool is used to change the zoom level of your working image. If you only click on the image, the zoom is applied to the whole image. But you can also click-and-drag the mouse pointer to create a zoom rectangle. Then, the action of this rectangle is better understood if the "Allow window resizing" option is unchecked: you can see that the content of this rectangle will be enlarged or reduced so that its biggest dimension fit the corresponding dimension of the image window (if the biggest dimension of the rectangle is width, then it will fit the width of the image window).

14.6.4.1 Activating the Tool

- You can get to the Zoom Tool from the image-menu through : Tools → Zoom,

- or by clicking the tool icon: in Toolbox.

14.6.4.2 Key modifiers (Defaults)

Ctrl Holding **Ctrl** when clicking on a point of your image will change the zoom direction from zooming in to zooming out.

Ctrl-Mouse wheel Spinning the mouse wheel, while pressing **Ctrl**, varies the zoom level.

14.6.4.3 Options

Figure 14.184 Zoom tool options

Auto-resize window This option will allow the canvas to be resized if the zoom level dictates it.

Tool Toggle The two available tool toggles are used for changing the zoom direction between zooming in and zooming out.

14.6.4.4 Zoom menu

Using the Zoom tool is not the only way to zoom an image. The Zoom menu provides access to several functions for changing the image magnification level. For example, you can easily choose an exact magnification level from this menu.

14.6.5   Measure

Figure 14.185 Measure tool

The Measure Tool is used to gain knowledge about pixel distances in your working image. By clicking and holding the mouse button, you can determine the angle and number of pixels between the point of click and where the mouse pointer is located. The information is displayed on the status bar or can also be displayed in the Info Window.

When you pass the mouse pointer over the end point it turns to a move pointer. Then if you click you can resume the measure.

14.6.5.1   Status Bar

Information is displayed in the status bar, at the bottom of the Image window:

- Distance between the original point and the mouse pointer, in pixels.

- Angle, in every quadrant, from 0° to 90°.

- Pointer coordinates relative to the original point.

14.6.5.2   Activating the Tool

- You can get to the Measure Tool from the image-menu through: Tools → Measure,

- or by clicking the tool icon: in Toolbox.

14.6.5.3   Key modifiers (Defaults)

Shift Holding down the **Shift** allows to start a new measure from the pointed point without deleting the previous measure. Angle is measured from the previous line and not from the default horizontal. The mouse pointer goes with a "+" sign. So, you can *measure any angle* on the image.

Ctrl Holding down the **Ctrl** key puts the tool into constrained straight line mode. The orientation of the line is constrained to the nearest multiple of 15 degrees.

Ctrl key pressed and click on an end point creates a horizontal guide. The mouse pointer goes with the icon.

Alt **Alt** key and click on an end point creates a vertical guide. The mouse pointer goes with the icon.

Ctrl-Alt This key combination and click on a measure line allows to move the measure.

Ctrl-Alt key combination and click on an end point creates a vertical and a horizontal guides.

14.6.5.4   Options

Figure 14.186 "Measure" tool options

Use Info Window This option will display an Info Window dialog that details the measure tool results. The results are more complete on the status bar.

14.6.5.5   Measuring surfaces

You can't measure surfaces directly, but you can use the Histogram that gives you the number of pixels in a selection.

14.6.6   Text

Figure 14.187 The Text tool in Toolbox

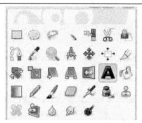

The Text tool places text into an image. With GIMP-2.8, you can write your text directly on the canvas. No Text Editor is needed anymore (although you can still use it if you want by checking the Use editor option in the Tool Options dialog. A text toolbar has been added which allows you to edit text in different ways but you can still go on using the *Text Option dialog*, to change the font, color and size of your text, and justify it, interactively. Right clicking on the frame opens a context menu that allows you to copy, cut, paste, load a text...

As soon as you type your text, it appears on the canvas in a rectangular frame. If you draw the rectangular frame first, the text is automatically adapted to the frame size. You can enlarge this frame as you do with rectangular selections.

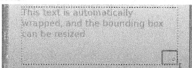

To move the text on canvas, you have to select the Move tool and click on a character to drag the frame and its text.

14.6.6.1   Activating the Tool

You can access this tool in several ways:

- In the image menu through Tools → Text,

- by clicking the tool icon  in Toolbox,

- or by using the **T** keyboard shortcut.

14.6.6.2 Options

Figure 14.188 Text tool options

Normally, tool options are displayed in a window attached under the Toolbox as soon as you activate a tool. If they are not, you can access them from the image menu bar through Windows → Dockable Windows → Tool Options which opens the option window of the selected tool.

Font Click on the fonts button A to open the font selector of this tool, which offers you a list of installed X fonts.

At the bottom of the font selector you find some icons which act as buttons for:

- resizing the font previews,

- selecting *list view* or *grid view*,

- opening the font dialog.

Choose a font from the installed fonts. When you select a font it is interactively applied to your text.

> **Tip**
>
> You can use the scroll wheel of your pointing device (usually your mouse) on the fonts button in order to quickly change the font of your text (move the pointer on the fonts button, and don't click, just use the wheel button).

Size This control sets the size of the font in any of several selectable units.

Use editor Use an external editor window for text editing instead of direct-on-canvas editing.

Antialiasing Antialiasing will render the text with much smoother edges and curves. This is achieved by slight blurring and merging of the edges. This option can radically improve the visual appearance of the rendered typeface. Caution should be exercised when using antialiasing on images that are not in RGB color space.

Hinting Uses the index of adjustment of the font to modify characters in order to produce clear letters in small font sizes.

Color Color of the text that will be drawn next. Defaults to black. Selectable from the color picker dialog box that opens when the current color sample is clicked.

> ### Tip
>
> You can also click-and-drag the color from the Toolbox color area onto the text.

Justify Causes the text to be justified according to any of four rules selectable from the associated icons.

Indent Controls the indent spacing from the left margin, for the first line.

Line Spacing Controls the spacing between successive lines of text. This setting is interactive: it appears at the same time in image text. The number is not the space between lines itself, but how many pixels must be added to or subtracted from this space (the value can be negative).

Letter Spacing Controls the spacing between letters. Also in this case the number is not the space itself between letters, but how many pixels must be added to or subtracted from this space (the value can be negative).

Box Concerns the text box. The associated drop down list offers two options:

Dynamic: default option. The size of the text box increases as you type. Text may go out of the image. You have to press the **Enter** key to add a new line. The indent option indents all lines. If you increase the box size, the option turns to "Fixed".

Fixed: you must enlarge the text box first. Else, usual shortcuts are active! The text is limited by the right side of the box and continues on next line. This is not true new line: you must press the **Enter** key to add a real new line. The text may go out the lower border of the image. The indent option works on the first line only.

14.6.6.3   The Text tool context menu

You get this menu by right clicking in a text frame with handles.

- Cut, Copy, Paste, Delete: these options concern a selected text. They remain grayed out as long as no text is selected. "Paste" is activated if the clipboard is full of text.

- Open text file: this command opens a file browser where you can find the wanted text file.

- Clear: this command deletes all the text, selected or not.

- Path from text: this command creates a path from the outlines of the current text. The result is not evident. You have to open the Path dialog and make path visible. Then select the Path tool and click on the text. Every letter is now surrounded with a path component. So you can modify the shape of letters by moving path control points.

  This command is similar to Layer → Text to Path.

- Text along path:

  This option is enabled only if a path exists. When your text is created, then create or import a path and make it active. If you create your path before the text, the path becomes invisible and you have to make it visible in the Path Dialog.

  This command is also available from the "Layer" menu:

Figure 14.189 The Text along Path command among text commands in the Layer menu

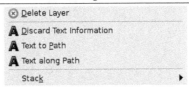

This group of options appears only if a layer text exists.

If you want to use a text that already exists, make it active in the Layer dialog, select the Text tool and click on the text in the image window.

Click on the Text along Path button. The text is bent along the path. Letters are represented with their outline. Each of them is a component of the new path that appears in the Path dialog. All path options should apply to this new path.

Figure 14.190 "Text along Path" example

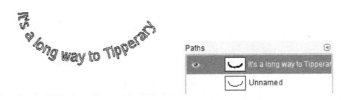

- From Left to Right / From Right to Left: fix the writing direction of your language.

14.6.6.4 Text Editor

Figure 14.191 The Text Editor

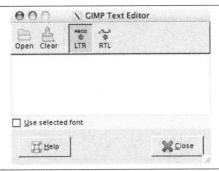

With GIMP-2.8, this text editor is available only if the Use editor option is checked. It persists probably because all its functions are not transferred to the direct-on-canvas mode, for instance the Unicode characters.

You can correct the text you are writing and you can change the text font with the Font Editor.

As soon as you start writing, a Text layer is created in the Layer Dialog. On an image with such a layer (the image you are working on, or a .xcf image), you can resume text editing by activating this text layer then clicking on it (double click). Of course, you can apply to this text layer the same functions you use with other layers.

To add another text to your image click on a non-text layer: a new Text Editor will appear and a new text layer will be created. To pass from a text to another one activate the corresponding text layer and click on it to activate the editor.

You can get Unicode characters with Ctrl-Shift-U plus hexadecimal Unicode code of the desired char, for example:

Figure 14.192 Entering Unicode characters

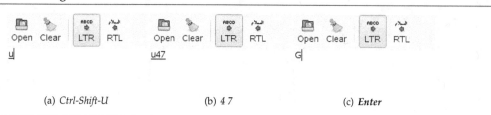

      (a) *Ctrl-Shift-U*   (b) *4 7*   (c) *Enter*

Of course this feature is more useful for entering special (even exotic) characters, provided that the required glyphs for these characters are supplied by the selected font — only few fonts support Klingon. ;-)

Unicode 0x47 ("G"), 0x2665, 0x0271, 0x03C0

The Text Editor options

Load Text from file Text can be loaded from a text file by clicking the folder icon in the text editor. All the text in the file is loaded.

Clear all text Clicking this icon clears the editor and the associated text on the image.

From left to right This option causes text to be entered from left to right, as is the case with most Western languages and may Eastern languages.

From right to left This option allows text to be entered from right to left, as is the case with some Eastern languages, such as Arabic (illustrated in the icon).

Use selected font Default doesn't use the font you have selected in the Options dialog. If you want to use it, check this option.

> **Note**
>
>  See also Section 9.3.

14.6.7 GEGL Operation

Figure 14.193 GEGL Operation tool

GEGL ("Generic Graphical Library") is a graph based image processing library designed to handle various image processing tasks needed in GIMP.

The GEGL Operation tool has been added in GIMP 2.6 and was originally meant as an useful experimental tool for GIMP developers. The GEGL Operation tool enables applying GEGL operations to the image and gives on-canvas previews of the results.

Warning

GEGL is in a very early phase and still under construction.

The GEGL Operation tool is *experimental*.

14.6.7.1 Activating the Tool

You can get to this tool only from the image menu: Tools → GEGL Operation.

Tip

In addition to this tool for performing special GEGL operations you can configure GIMP to use GEGL for all color operations.

14.6.7.2 Options

Figure 14.194 GEGL Operation tool options

GEGL Operation tool with no operation selected.

Operation Click on this button to select the operation you want to apply to the active selection or, if there is no selection, to the active layer.

Some of these operations are very basic operations like "color" which fills the active selection or layer with the specified color, while operations like "fractal-explorer" produce fairly complex patterns — just like a rendering filter.

Remember that this is an experimental tool, so some operations may not work or even crash GIMP. As a consquence, it doesn't make sense to describe the operations here as long as the GEGL Operation tool is experimental

Operation Settings The operation settings depend on the selected Operation:

Figure 14.195 "Operation Settings" example

GEGL operation "Gaussian Blur" selected.

If the options of the selected GEGL operation are not self-explanatory (guess what's the purpose of the "color" operation's "Color" option) you can look for a corresponding non-GEGL tool. For example, the Fractal Explorer filter may have the same or similar options as the "fractal-explorer" operation.

Or you can make use of the nice realtime preview feature and just experiment with different settings.

Preview If this options is checked, as it is by default, you will get an on-canvas preview of the selected operation as soon as the operation in finished. You will have to press the OK button to actually apply the operation to the image.

The tool buttons

Reset Pressing this button resets the operation settings the to their defaults.

Cancel Clicking on this button aborts the GEGL operation tool and leaves your image untouched. This is equivalent to close the dialog window using the usual Close button provided by your window manager.

OK You have to press this button to apply the selected operation to the image. Then the dialog window will be closed.

Chapter 15

Dialogs

15.1 Dialog Introduction

Dialogs are the most common means of setting options and controls in the GIMP. The most important dialogs are explained in this section.

15.2 Image Structure Related Dialogs

The following dialogs let you control and manipulate image structures, such as layers, channels, or paths.

15.2.1 Layers Dialog

Figure 15.1 Layers Dialog

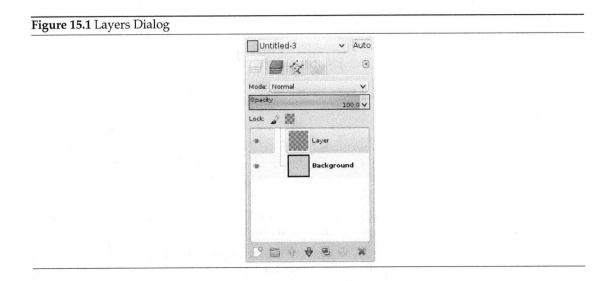

The "Layers" dialog is the main interface to edit, modify and manage your layers. You can think of layers as a stack of slides or clothes on your body. Using layers, you can construct an image of several conceptual parts, each of which can be manipulated without affecting any other part of the image. Layers are stacked on top of each other. The bottom layer is the background of the image, and the components in the foreground of the image come above it.

Figure 15.2 An image with layers

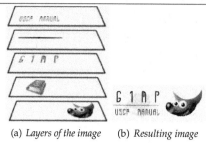

(a) *Layers of the image*   (b) *Resulting image*

15.2.1.1 Activating the dialog

The "Layers" dialog is a dockable dialog; see the section Section 3.2.3 for help on manipulating it. You can access it:

- from the image menu: Windows → Dockable Dialogs → Layers;

- from the Tab menu in any dockable dialog by clicking on ◀ and selecting Add Tab → Layers,

- from the (default) shortcut: Ctrl-L.

In the Windows menu, there is a list of detached windows which exists only if at least one dialog remains open. In this case, you can raise the "Layers" dialog from the image-menu: Windows → Layers.

15.2.1.2 Using the Layer dialog

Overview Every layer appears in the dialog in the form of a thumbnail. When an image has multiple layers as components, they appear as a list. The upper layer in the list is the first one visible, and the lowest layer the last visible, the background. Above the list one can find characteristics related individually to each layer. Under the list one can find management buttons for the layer list. A right-click in a layer thumbnail opens the Layer context menu.

Layer attributes Every layer is shown in the list along with its attributes:

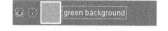

   Layer visibility In front of the thumbnail is an icon showing an eye. By clicking on the eye, you toggle whether the layer is visible or not. (**Shift**-clicking on the eye causes all *other* to be hidden.)

   Chain layers Another icon, showing a chain, allows you to group layers for operations on more than one layer at a time (for example with the Move tool).

   Layer thumbnail The layer content is represented in a thumbnail. Maintaining left-click for a second on this thumbnail makes it larger. When the layer is active, the thumbnail has a white border. The border is black if the layer is inactive. When the layer has a mask, the inactive element takes a black border.

   Layer name The main attribute is the name of the layer. You can edit this by a double-click on the name of the layer. You can also use the "Edit Layer Attributes" dialog you get by double-clicking on the thumbnail (or the mask), or through right-click on the layer and select "Edit Layer Attributes...".

> **Note**
>
>
> In the case of an animation layer (GIF or MNG), the name of the layer can be used to specify certain parameters : Layer_name (delay in ms) (combination mode), for example Frame-1 (100 ms) (replace). The delay sets the time during which the layer is visible in the animation. The combination mode sets whether you combine the layer with the previous layer or replace it: the two modes are (combine) or (replace).

Layers characteristics Above the layer list, it is possible to specify some properties for the active layer. The active layer is the one highlighted in blue. The properties are: "Layer mode", "Opacity", "Lock pixels" and "Lock Alpha channel".

Mode The layer mode determines how the layer interacts with the other layers. From the combo box you can access all the modes provided by GIMP. The layer modes are fully detailed in Section 8.2.

Opacity By moving the slider you give more or less opacity to the layer. With a 0 opacity value, the layer is transparent and completely invisible. Don't confuse this with a Layer Mask, which sets the transparency pixel by pixel.

Lock You have two possibilities:

- **Lock pixels**: when this option is checked, you can't modify layer pixels. This may be necessary to protect them from unwanted changes.
- **Lock alpha channel**: if you check this option the transparent areas of the layer will be kept, even if you have checked the Fill transparent areas option for the Bucket fill tool.

Figure 15.3 Example for Locking Alpha Channel

(a) *The active layer has three horizontal, opaque, green stripes on a transparent back-ground. We paint a vertical red stripe. "Lock" unchecked: Opaque and transparent areas of the active layer are painted with red.*

(b) *"Lock" checked: Only opaque areas of the active layer are painted with red. Trans-parent areas are preserved.*

> **Tip**
>
>
> If a layer name in the Layer Dialog is in bold, then this layer has no Alpha channel.

Layer management Under the layer list a set of buttons allows you to perform some basic operations on the layer list.

New layer Here you can create a new layer. A dialog is opened where you can enter the Layer name, perhaps change the default Height and Width, and choose the Layer fill type that will be the new layer's background.

Raise layer Here you can move the layer up a level in the list. Press the **Shift** key to move the layer to the top of the list.

Lower layer Here you can move the layer down a level in the list. Press the **Shift** key to move the layer to the bottom of the list.

Tip

To move a layer at the bottom of the list, it may first be necessary to add a transparency channel (also called Alpha channel) to the Background layer. To do this, right click on the Background layer and select Add Alpha channel from the menu.

Duplicate layer Here you can create a copy of the active layer. Name of new layer is suffixed with a number.

Anchor layer When the active layer is a temporary layer (also called floating selection) shown by this icon , this button anchors it to the previous active layer.

Delete layer Here you can delete the active layer.

More layer functions Other functions about *layer size* are available in the Layer Drop down menu you get by right clicking on the Layer Dialog. You can find them also in the Layer sub-menu of the image menu.

You will find *merging layers functions* in the Image menu.

Clicking-and-dragging layers Click and hold on layer thumbnail: it enlarges and you can move it by dragging the mouse.

- So you can put this layer down *somewhere else in the layer list*.

- You can also *put the layer down into Toolbox*: a new image is created that contains this layer only.

- Finally, you can *put the layer down into another image*: this layer will be added to the layer list, above existing layers.

15.2.1.3   Layer masks

Figure 15.4 "Add mask" dialog

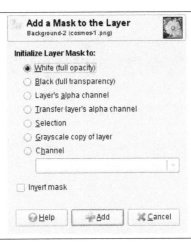

Overview   A transparency mask can be added to each layer, it's called Layer mask. A layer mask has the same size and same number of pixels as the layer to which it is attached. Every pixel of the mask can then be coupled with a pixel at the same location in the layer. The mask is a set of pixels in gray-tone on a value scale from 0 to 255. The pixels with a value 0 are black and give a full transparency to the coupled pixel in the layer. The pixels with a value 255 are white and give a full opacity to the coupled pixel in the layer.

To create a layer mask start with a right click on the layer to call the context menu and select Add layer mask in the menu. A dialog appears where you can initialize the content of the mask:

- White (full opacity): the mask is white in the Layer Dialog. So, all pixels of the layer are visible in the image window since painting the mask with white makes layer pixels fully visible. You will paint with black to make layer pixels transparent.

- Black (full transparency): the mask is black in the Layer Dialog. So, the layer is fully transparent since painting the mask with black makes layer pixels transparent. Painting with white will remove the mask and make layer pixels visible.

- Layer's alpha channel: the mask is initialized according to the content of layer Alpha channel. If the layer still contains transparency it's copied in the mask.

- Transfer layer's alpha channel: Does the same thing as the previous option, except that it also resets the layer's alpha channel to full opacity.

- Selection : the mask is initialized according to pixel values found in the selection.

- Grayscale copy of layer: the mask is initialized according to pixel values of the layer.

- Channel: The layer mask is initialized with a selection mask you have created before, stored in the Channel dialog.

- Invert mask : This checkbox allows you to invert : black turns to white and white turns to black.

When the mask is created it appears as a thumbnail right to the layer thumbnail. By clicking alternatively on the layer and mask thumbnail you can enable one or other. The active item has a white border (which is not well visible around a white mask). That's an important point. Always keep the Layers Dialog prominently when working with masks, because you can't see, looking at the canvas, which of the layer or the mask is active.

Pressing **Alt** (or Ctrl-Alt and click on the layer mask thumbnail) is equivalent to the Show Layer Mask command : the layer mask border turns to green. If you press **Ctrl** the border is red and the result is equivalent to the Disable Layer Mask command. To return to normal view redo last operation. These options are for greater convenience in your work.

Layer Mask example

Figure 15.5 A layer with layer mask

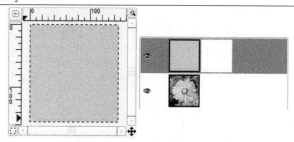

This image has a background layer with a flower and another blue one, fully opaque. A white layer mask has been added to the blue layer. In the image window, the blue layer remains visible because a white mask makes layer pixels visible.

Figure 15.6 Painting the layer mask

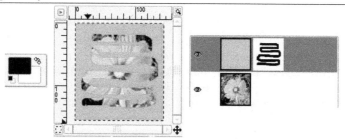

The layer mask is active. You paint with black color, which makes the layer transparent: the underlying layer becomes visible.

15.2.2 Channels Dialog

Figure 15.7 The Channels dialog

The Channels dialog is the main interface to edit, modify and manage your channels. Channels have a double usage. This is why the dialog is divided into two parts: the first part for color channels and the second part for selection masks.

    Color channels apply to the image and not to a specific layer. Basically, three primary colors are necessary to render all the wide range of natural colors. As other digital software, GIMP uses Red, Green, and Blue as primary colors. The first and primary channels display the Red, Green, and Blue values of each pixel in your image. Next to the channel name is a thumbnail displaying a grayscale representation of each channel, where white is 100% and black is 0% of the primary color. Alternatively, if your image is not a colored but a Grayscale image, there is only one primary channel called Gray. For an Indexed image with a fixed number of known colors there is also only one primary channel called Indexed. Then there is a optional channel called Alpha. This channel displays transparency values of each pixel in your image (See Alpha Channel in Glossary). In front of this channel is a thumbnail displaying a grayscale representation of the transparency where white is opaque and visible, and black is transparent and invisible. If you create your image without transparency then the Alpha channel is not present, but you can add it from the Layers dialog menu. Also, if you have more than one layer in your image, GIMP automatically creates an Alpha channel.

Note

 GIMP doesn't support CMYK or YUV color models.

Figure 15.8 Representation of an image with channels

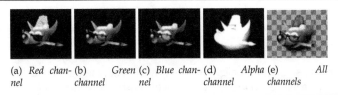

(a) *Red chan-* (b)   *Green* (c) *Blue chan-* (d)   *Alpha* (e)   *All*
nel   *channel*   *nel*   *channel*   *channels*

The right image is decomposed in three color channels (red, green, and blue) and the Alpha channel for transparency. On the right image the transparency is displayed as a gray checkerboard. In the color channel white is always white because all the colors are present and black is black. The red hat is visible in the red channel but quite invisible in the other channels. This is the same for plain green and blue which are visible only in their own channels and invisible in others.

15.2.2.1 Activating the Dialog

The "Channels" dialog is a dockable dialog; see Section 3.2.3 for help on manipulating it.
    You can access it:

- from an image menu: Windows → Dockable Dialogs → Channels;

- from the Tab menu in any dockable dialog by clicking on [icon] and selecting Add Tab → Channels.

In the Windows menu, there is a list of detached windows which exists only if at least one dialog remains open. In this case, you can raise the "Channels" dialog from the image-menu: Windows → Channels.

15.2.2.2 Using the Channel dialog

15.2.2.2.1 Overview The top channels are the color channels and the optional Alpha channel. They are always organized in the same order and they cannot be erased. Selection masks are described below and displayed as a list in the dialog. Every channel appears in the list with its attributes, including a thumbnail and its name. A right-click in a channel list entry opens the channel context menu.

15.2.2.2.2 Channel attributes Every channel is shown in the list with its own attributes, which are very similar to the layer attributes:

Channel visibility By default every channel and thus every color value is visible. This is indicated by an "open eye" icon. Clicking on the eye-symbol (or the space if the channel is not visible) will toggle the visibility of the channel.

Chain channels The channels representing selection masks (the new channels in the lower part of the channel list) may be grouped using the button with the "chain" symbol. Then these channels are all affected in the same way by operations applied to any one of them.

Primary color channels (the default channels in the upper part of the channel list) may be grouped too. By default, all color channels (and the alpha channel) are selected, their list entries are highlighted. Operations will be performed on all channels. By clicking on a channel list entry you can deactivate this channel. Operations like colorizing a layer will then be applied to the selected ("grouped") channels only. Clicking again on the list entry will activate the channel.

Thumbnail A small preview-icon represents the effect of the channel. On a selection mask, this preview can be enlarged by holding click down on it.

Channel name The name of the channel, which must be unique within the image. Double-clicking on the name of a selection mask channel will allow you to edit it. The names of the primary channels (Red, Green, Blue, Alpha) can not be changed.

Caution

Activated channels appear highlighted (generally) in blue in the dialog. If you click on a channel in the list you toggle activation of the corresponding channel. Disabling a color channel red, blue, or green has severe consequences. For instance if you disable the blue channel, all pixels from now on added to the image will not have blue component, and so a white pixel will have the yellow complementary color.

15.2.2.2.3 Managing channels Under the channel list is a set of buttons allowing you to perform some basic operations on channel list.

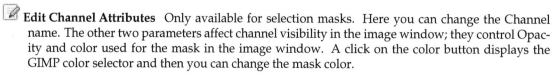 **Edit Channel Attributes** Only available for selection masks. Here you can change the Channel name. The other two parameters affect channel visibility in the image window; they control Opacity and color used for the mask in the image window. A click on the color button displays the GIMP color selector and then you can change the mask color.

New Channel You can create here a new channel. The displayed dialog lets you set Opacity and mask color used in the image to represent the selection. (If you use the New Channel button in Channel Menu, you can create this new channel with the options previously used by pressing the **Shift** key when clicking). This new channel is a channel mask (a selection mask) applied over the image. See Selection Mask

Raise Channel Only available for selection masks: you can here put the channel up a level in the list. Press **Shift** key to move channel to top of the list.

Lower Channel You can here put the channel down a level in the list. Press the **Shift** key to move the channel to bottom of the list.

Duplicate Channel You can create here a copy of the active channel. Name of new channel is suffixed with a number.

Tip

 You can also duplicate a color channel or the Alpha channel. It's an easy way to keep a copy of them and to use them later as a selection in an image.

Channel to Selection   Here you can transform the channel to become a selection. By default the selection derived from a channel replaces any previous active selection. It's possible to change this by clicking on control keys.

- **Shift**: the selection derived from a channel is added to the previous active selection. The final selection is merged from both.

- **Ctrl**: the final selection is the subtraction of selection derived from a channel from the previously active one.

- Shift-Ctrl: the final selection is the intersection of selection derived from a channel with the previously active one. Only common parts are kept.

Delete Channel   Only available for selection masks: you can here delete the active channel.

Figure 15.9 Channel Context Menu

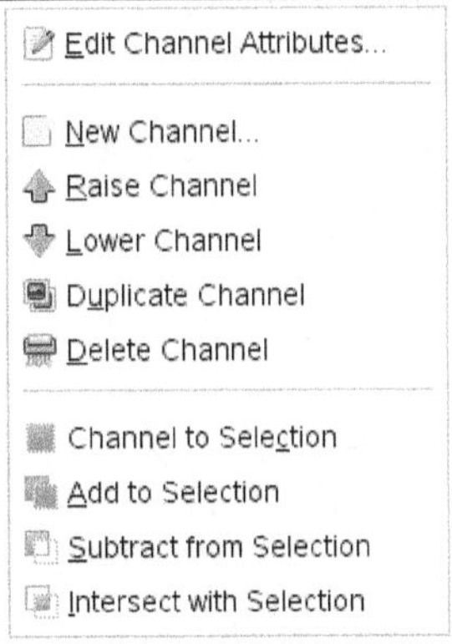

15.2.2.2.4   Channels Context Menu

Overview   You can get the channel context menu by right clicking on a channel thumbnail. This menu gives the same operations on channels as those available from dialog buttons. The only difference concerns transformation to selection operations, each of them having its own entry in the menu.

Edit Channel Attributes, New Channel, Raise Channel, Lower Channel, Duplicate Channel, Delete Channel
See Managing channels.

Channel to Selection   Selection derived from channel replaces any previous active selection.

Add to Selection   Selection derived from channel is added to previous active selection. Final selection is merging of both.

Subtract from Selection   Final selection is subtraction of selection derived from a channel from previous active selection.

Intersect with Selection   Final selection is intersection of selection derived from a channel with the previous active selection. Only common parts are kept.

15.2.2.3   Selection masks

Figure 15.10 A selection composed out of channels.

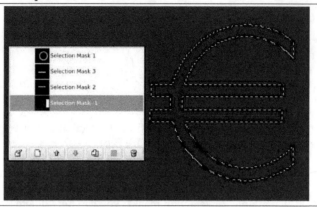

Channels can be used to save and restore your selections. In the channel dialog you can see a thumbnail representing the selection. Selection Masks are a graphical way to build selections into a gray level channel where white pixels are selected and black pixels are not selected. Therefore gray pixels are partially selected. You can think of them as feathering the selection, a smooth transition between selected and not selected. This is important to avoid the ugly pixelization effect when you fill the selection or when you erase its content after isolating a subject from background.

Creating Selection Masks   There are several ways to initialize a selection mask.

- From the image window menu Select → Save to Channel if there is an active selection.

- In the image window the bottom-left button creates a Quick Mask; the content will be initialized with the active selection.

- From the channel dialog, when you click on the New channel button or from the context menu. When created, this Selection mask appears in the Channel dialog, named "Selection maskcopy" with a queuing number. You can change this by using the context menu that you get by right-clicking on the channel.

15.2.2.3.1   Using Selection Masks   Once the channel is initialized, selected (highlighted in blue), visible (eye-icon in the dialog), and displayed as you want (color and opacity attributes), you can start to work with all the paint tools. The colors used are important. If you paint with some color other than white, grey, or black, the color Value (luminosity) will be used to define a gray (medium, light, or dark).

When your mask is painted, you can transform it to a selection by clicking on the ▓ button (Channel to Selection) or from the context menu.

You can work in selection masks not only with the paint tool but also with other tools. For instance, you can use the selection tools to fill areas uniformly with gradients or patterns. By adding many selection masks in your list you can easily compose very complex selections. One can say that a selection mask is to a selection as a layer is to an image.

Caution

 As long as a selection mask is activated you are working in the mask and not in the image. To work in the image you have to deactivate all selection masks. Don't forget also to stop displaying masks in the image by removing the eye icon. Check also that all RGB and Alpha channels are activated and displayed in the image.

15.2.2.4   Quick Mask

Figure 15.11 Dialog Quick Mask

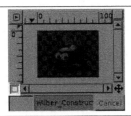

A Quick Mask is a Selection Mask intended to be used temporarily to paint a selection. Temporarily means that, unlike a normal selection mask, it will be deleted from the channel list after its transformation to selection. The selection tools sometimes show their limits when they have to be used for doing complex drawing selection, as progressive. In this case, using the QuickMask is a good idea which can give very good results.

15.2.2.4.1   Activating the dialog   The QuickMask can be activated in different ways:

- From the image menu: Select → Toggle QuickMask.

- By clicking the left-bottom button showed in red on the screenshot.

- By using the Shift-Q shortcut.

15.2.2.4.2   Creating a Quick Mask   To initialize a Quick Mask, click the bottom-left button in the image window. If a selection was active in your image, then its content appears unchanged while the border is covered with a translucent red color. If no selection was active then all the image is covered with a translucent red color. Another click on the bottom-left button will deactivate the quick mask.

From the channel dialog you can double click on the name or the thumbnail to edit the QMask attributes. Then you can change the Opacity and its filling color. At every moment you can hide the mask by clicking on the eye icon ⬤ in front of the QMask.

The mask is coded in gray tones, so you must use white or gray to decrease the area limited by the mask and black to increase it. The area painted in light or dark gray will be transition areas for the selection like feathering. When your mask is ready, click again on the bottom-left button in the image window and the quick mask will be removed from the channel list and converted to a selection.

Quick mask's purpose is to paint a selection and its transitions with the paint tools without worrying about managing selection masks. It's a good way to isolate a subject in a picture because once the selection is made you only have to remove its content (or inverse if the subject is in the selection).

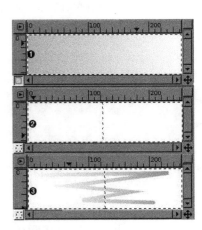

15.2.2.4.3   Using Quick Mask with a gradient

Description

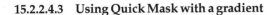

1. Screenshot of the image window with activated QuickMask. As long as the Quickmask is activated, all operations are done on it. A gradient from black (left) to white (right) has been applied to the mask.

2. The QuickMask is now disabled. The selection occupies the right half part of the image (marching ants) because the limit of the selection is at the middle of the gradient.

3. A stroke is now added during the enabled selection. Weird! The gradient, although not visible, remains active all over the image, in selected and non selected areas!

After the QuickMask Button is pressed, the command generates a temporary 8-bit (0-255) channel, on which the progressive selection work is stored. If a selection is already present the mask is initialized with the content of the selection. Once QuickMask has been activated, the image is covered by a red semi-transparent veil. This one represents the non-selected pixels. Any paint tool can be used to create the selection on the QuickMask. They should use only grayscale color, conforming the channel properties, white enabling to define the future selected place. The selection will be displayed as soon as the QuickMask will be toggled but its temporary channel will not be available anymore.

Tip

 To save in a channel the selection done with the Quickmask select in the image menu Select/Save to Channel

---

15.2.2.4.4 Usage

1. Open an image or begin a new document.

2. Activate the Quickmask using the left-bottom button in the image window. If a selection is present the mask is initialized with the content of the selection.

3. Choose a drawing tool and use it with grayscale colors on the QuickMask.

4. Deactivate the Quickmask using the left-bottom button in the image window.

15.2.3 Paths Dialog

Please see Section 7.5 if you don't know what a path is.

Figure 15.12 The "Paths" dialog

The "Paths" dialog is used to manage paths, allowing you to create or delete them, save them, convert them to and from selections, etc.

15.2.3.1 Activating the dialog

The "Paths" dialog is a dockable dialog; see the section Section 3.2.3 for help on manipulating it.
You can access it:

- from the image menu: Windows → Dockable Dialogs → Paths.

- from the Tab menu in any dockable dialog by clicking on ◀ and selecting Add Tab → Paths,

In the Windows menu, there is a list of detached windows which exists only if at least one dialog remains open. In this case, you can raise the "Paths" dialog from the image-menu: Windows → Paths.

15.2.3.2 Using the Paths dialog

Each path belongs to one image: paths are components of images just like layers. The Paths dialog shows you a list of all paths belonging to the currently active image: switching images causes the dialog to show a different list of paths. If the Paths dialog is embedded in a "Layers, Channels, and Paths" dock, you can see the name of the active image in the Image Menu at the top of the dock. (Otherwise, you can add an Image Menu to the dock by choosing "Show Image Menu" from the Tab menu.)
If you are familiar with the Layers dialog, you have a head start, because the Paths dialog is in several ways similar. It shows a list of all paths that exist in the image, with four items for each path:

Path visibility An "open eye" icon if the path is visible, or a blank space if it is not. "Visible" means that a trace of the path is drawn on the image display. The path is not actually shown in the image pixel data unless it has been stroked or otherwise rendered. Clicking in the eye-symbol-space toggles the visibility of the path.

Chain paths A "chain" symbol is shown to the right of the eye-symbol-space if the path is transform-locked, or a blank space if it is not. "Transform-locked" means that it forms part of a set of elements (layers, channels, etc) that are all affected in the same way by transformations (scaling, rotation, etc) applied to any one of them. Clicking in the chain-symbol-space toggles the transform-lock status of the path.

Preview image A small preview-icon showing a sketch of the path. If you click on the icon and drag it into an image, this will create a copy of the path in that image.

Path Name The name of the path, which must be unique within the image. Double-clicking on the name will allow you to edit it. If the name you create already exists, a number will be appended (e.g., "#1") to make it unique.

If the list is non-empty, at any given moment one of the members is the image's *active path*, which will be the subject of any operations you perform using the dialog menu or the buttons at the bottom: the active path is shown highlighted in the list. Clicking on any of the entries will make it the active path.
Right-clicking on any entry in the list brings up the Paths Menu. You can also access the Paths Menu from the dialog Tab menu.

15.2.3.3 Buttons

The buttons at the bottom of the Paths dialog all correspond to entries in the Paths menu (accessed by right-clicking on a path list entry), but some of them have extra options obtainable by holding down modifier keys while you press the button.

New Path See New Path. Holding down the **Shift** key brings up a dialog that allows you to assign a name to the new (empty) path.

Raise Path See Raise Path.

Lower Path See Lower Path.

Duplicate Path See Duplicate Path.

Path to Selection Converts the path into a selection; see Path to Selection for a full explanation. You can use modifier keys to set the way the new selection interacts with the existing selection:

Modifiers: None, *Action:* Replace existing selection
Modifiers: **Shift** , *Action:* Add to selection
Modifiers: **Ctrl** , *Action:* Subtract from selection
Modifiers: Shift-Ctrl , *Action:* Intersect with selection.

Selection to Path Holding down the **Shift** key brings up the Advanced Options dialog, which probably is only useful to GIMP developers.

Paint along the path See Stroke Path.

Delete Path Delete Path deletes the current selected path.

15.2.3.4   The "Paths" context menu

Figure 15.13 The "Paths" context menu

The Paths menu can be brought up by right-clicking on a path entry in the list in the Paths dialog, or by choosing the top entry ("Paths Menu") from the Paths dialog Tab menu. This menu gives you access to most of the operations that affect paths.

Path Tool Path Tool is an alternative way to activate the Path tool, used for creating and manipulating paths. It can also be activated from the Toolbox, or by using the keyboard shortcut **B** (for *Bézier*).

Edit Path Attributes Edit Path Attributes brings up a small dialog that allows you to change the name of the path. You can also do this by double-clicking on the name in the list in the Paths dialog.

New Path New Pathcreates a new path, adds it to the list in the Paths dialog, and makes it the active path for the image. It brings up a dialog that allows you to give a name to the path. The new path is created with no anchor points, so you will need to use the Path tool to give it some before you can use it for anything.

Raise Path Raise Path moves the path one slot higher in the list in the Paths dialog. The position of a path in the list has no functional significance, so this is simply a convenience to help you keep things organized.

Lower Path Lower Pathmoves the path one slot lower in the list in the Paths dialog. The position of a path in the list has no functional significance, so this is simply a convenience to help you keep things organized.

Duplicate Path "Duplicate Path" creates a copy of the active path, assigns it a unique name, adds it to the list in the Paths dialog, and makes it the active path for the image. The copy will be visible only if the original path was visible.

Delete Path Delete Path deletes the current selected path.

Merge Visible Paths Merge Visible Paths takes all the paths in the image that are visible (that is, all that show "open eye" symbols in the Paths dialog), and turns them into components of a single path. This may be convenient if you want to stroke them all in the same way, etc.

Path to Selection; Add to Selection; Subtract from Selection; Intersect with Selection These commands all convert the active path into a selection, and then combine it with the existing selection in the specified ways. ("Path to Selection" discards the existing selection and replaces it with one formed from the path.) If necessary, any unclosed components of the path are closed by connecting the last anchor point to the first anchor point with a straight line. The "marching ants" for the resulting selection should closely follow the path, but don't expect the correspondence to be perfect.

Selection to Path This operation can be accessed in several ways:

- From an image menubar, as Select → To Path
- From the Paths dialog menu, as Selection to Path.
- From the Selection to Path button at the bottom of the Paths dialog.

Selection to Path creates a new path from the image's selection. In most cases the resulting path will closely follow the "marching ants" of the selection, but the correspondence will not usually be perfect.

Converting a two-dimensional selection mask into a one-dimensional path involves some rather tricky algorithms: you can alter the way it is done using the Advanced Options, which are accessed by holding down the **Shift** key while pressing the Selection to Path button at the bottom of the Paths dialog. This brings up the Advanced Options dialog, which allows you to set 20 different options and variables, all with cryptic names. The Advanced Options are really intended for developers only, and help with them goes beyond the scope of this documentation. Generally speaking, Selection to Path will do what you expect it to, and you don't need to worry about how it is done (unless you want to).

Stroke Path This operation can be accessed in several ways:

- From an image menubar, as Edit → Stroke Path
- From the Paths dialog menu, as Stroke Path.
- From the Paint along the path button at the bottom of the Paths dialog.
- From the Stroke Path button in the Tool Options for the Path tool.

"Stroke Path" renders the active path on the active layer of the image, permitting a wide variety of line styles and stroking options. See the section on Stroking for more information.

Copy Path Copy Path copies the active path to the Paths Clipboard, enabling you to paste it into a different image.

Tip

You can also copy and paste a path by dragging its icon from the Paths dialog into the target image's display.

Note

 When you copy a path to an image, it is not visible. You have to make it visible in the Path dialog.

Paste Path Paste Path creates a new path from the contents of the Path Clipboard, adds it to the list in the Paths dialog, and makes it the active path for the image. If no path has previously been copied into the clipboard, the menu entry will be insensitive.

Import Path Import Path creates a new path from an SVG file: it pops up a file chooser dialog that allows you to navigate to the file. See the Paths section for information on SVG files and how they relate to GIMP paths.

Export Path Export Path allows you to save a path to a file: it pops up a file save dialog that allows you to specify the file name and location. You can later add this path to any GIMP image using the Import Path command. The format used for saving paths is SVG: this means that vector-graphics programs such as Sodipodi or Inkscape will also be able to import the paths you save. See the Paths section for more information on SVG files and how they relate to GIMP paths.

15.2.4   Colormap Dialog

Figure 15.14 An indexed image with 6 colors and its Colormap dialog

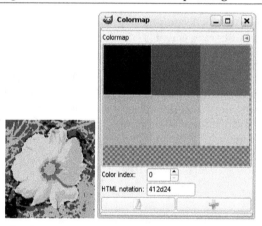

The Colormap (Indexed Palette is a better name) dialog allows you to edit the colormap of an indexed image. (If the mode of the active image is RGB or Grayscale instead of Indexed, the dialog is empty and unusable.) This is a dockable dialog; see the section on Dialogs and Docking for help on manipulating it.

15.2.4.1   Activating the dialog

The "Colormap" dialog is a dockable dialog; see the section Section 3.2.3 for help on manipulating it. You can access it:

- from the image menu: Windows → Dockable Dialogs → Colormap;

- from the Tab menu in any dockable dialog by clicking on ◀ and selecting Add Tab → Colormap.

In the Windows menu, there is a list of detached windows which exists only if at least one dialog remains open. In this case, you can raise the "Colormap" dialog from the image-menu: Windows → Colormap.

15.2.4.2   Colormaps and Indexed Images

In an Indexed image, instead of being assigned a color directly (as happens in RGB and Grayscale images), colors are assigned to pixels by an indirect method, using a look-up table called a *colormap*.

To determine the color that should be shown for that pixel, GIMP looks up the index in the image's colormap. Each indexed image has its own private colormap. In GIMP, the maximum number of entries in a colormap is 256. For a maximum-sized colormap, each index from 0 to 255 is assigned an arbitrary RGB color. There are no rules restricting the colors that can be assigned to an index or the order they appear in: any index can be assigned any color.

It is important to realize that the colors in the colormap are the *only colors available* for an indexed image (that is, unless you add new colors to the colormap). This has a major effect on many GIMP operations: for example, in a pattern fill, GIMP will usually not be able to find exactly the right colors in the colormap, so it will approximate them by using the nearest color available. This is sometimes referred to as Quantization. If the colormap is too limited or poorly chosen, this can easily produce very poor image quality.

The Colormap dialog allows you to alter the colormap for an image, either by creating new entries, or by changing the colors for the existing entries. If you change the color associated with a given index, you will see the changes reflected throughout the image, as a color shift for all pixels that are assigned that index. The entries are numbered with 0 in the upper left corner, 1 to its right, etc.

15.2.4.3   Using the Colormap dialog

Here are the operations you can perform using this dialog:

Click on a color entry This sets GIMP's foreground color to the color you click on, as shown in the Toolbox color area. As a result, this color will be used for the next painting operation you do.

Ctrl-click on a color entry This sets GIMP's background color to the color you **Ctrl**-click on, as shown in the Toolbox color area.

Double-click on a color entry This sets GIMP's foreground color to the color you click on, and also brings up a Color Editor that allows you to change that colormap entry to a new color.

Color index You can select a different colormap entry by typing its index here, or clicking the spinbutton to the right.

HTML-Notation This area shows a hex-code representation (such as is used in HTML) for the color assigned to the currently selected colormap entry. You can edit the color here, instead of using a Color Editor, if you want to. See HTML notation

Edit color This button (in the lower left corner of the dialog) brings up a Color Editor that allows you to change the color for the currently selected colormap entry. The effect is similar to double-clicking on the entry, except that it does not set GIMP's foreground color.

✛ **Add color** This button (in the lower right corner of the dialog) allows you to add new colors to the colormap. If you click on the button, the current foreground color, as shown in the Toolbox, will be tacked on to the end of the colormap. If instead you hold down **Ctrl** and click, the background color from the Toolbox will be added. (If the colormap contains 256 entries, it is full, and trying to add more will have no effect.)

Tip

If you make a mistake, you can undo it by focusing the pointer in the image whose colormap you have changed, and then pressing Ctrl-Z or choosing Edit → Undo in the image menu.

> **Note**
>
>
> This dialog provides the most commonly used methods for altering the colormap for an indexed image. The color tools, such as Brightness/Contrast, Hue/Saturation, etc, do not operate on indexed images. There are a few plug-ins that do so, including the "Normalize", "VColor Enhance", and "Stretch Contrast" operations, and it is possible to create others as well.

> **Note**
>
>
> If you paint an indexed image with a color which is not in the Colormap, GIMP will use the most similar color of the Colormap.

15.2.4.4   The Colormap context menu

Right-clicking on a color in the Colormap selects this color and opens a pop-up submenu:

Figure 15.15 The Colormap context menu

Edit color This command opens a color selector which allows you to modify the color.

Add Color from FG This command is enabled only if the indexed palette contains less than 256 colors. The background color of the Toolbox is appended to the color map.

Add Color from BG This command is enabled only if the indexed palette contains less than 256 colors. The background color of the Toolbox is appended to the color list.

Rearrange Colormap Rearrange Colormap: This command is described in Section 16.8.19.

15.2.5   Histogram dialog

Figure 15.16 The Histogram dialog

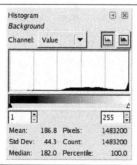

The Histogram dialog shows you information about the statistical distribution of color values in the active layer or selection. This information is often useful when you are trying to *color balance* an image.

However, the Histogram dialog is purely informational: nothing you do with it will cause any change to the image. If you want to perform a histogram-based color correction, use the Levels tool.

15.2.5.1 Activating the dialog

The "Histogram" dialog is a dockable dialog; see the section Section 3.2.3 for help on manipulating it. You can access it:

- from the image menu: Windows → Dockable Dialogs → Histogram.

- from the Tab menu in any dockable dialog by clicking on and selecting Add Tab → Histogram,

- from the image menu: Colors → Info → Histogram.

In the Windows menu, there is a list of detached windows which exists only if at least one dialog remains open. In this case, you can raise the "Histogram" dialog from the image-menu: Windows → Histogram.

15.2.5.2 About Histograms

In GIMP, each layer of an image can be decomposed into one or more color channels: for an RGB image, into R, G, and B channels; for a grayscale image, into a single Value channel. Layers that support transparency have an additional channel, the alpha channel. Each channel supports a range of intensity levels from 0 to 255 (integer valued). Thus, a black pixel is encoded by 0 on all color channels; a white pixel by 255 on all color channels. A transparent pixel is encoded by 0 on the alpha channel; an opaque pixel by 255.

For RGB images, it is convenient to define a Value "pseudochannel". This is not a real color channel: it does not reflect any information stored directly in the image. Instead, the Value at a pixel is given by the equation $V = \max(R, G, B)$. Essentially, the Value is what you would get at that pixel if you converted the image to Grayscale mode.

For more information on channels, please consult the Section 5.1.

15.2.5.3 Using the Histogram dialog

The active layer name is shown at the top of the dialog.

Channel

Figure 15.17 Channel options for an RGB layer with alpha channel

---

This allows you to select which channel to use. The possibilities depend on the layer type of the active layer. Here are the entries you might see, and what they mean:

Value For RGB and Grayscale images, this shows the distribution of brightness values across the layer. For a grayscale image, these are read directly from the image data. For an RGB image, they are taken from the Value pseudochannel.

For an indexed image, the "Value" channel actually shows the distribution of frequencies for each colormap index: thus, it is a "pseudocolor" histogram rather than a true color histogram.

Red, Green, Blue These only appear for layers from RGB images. They show the distribution of intensity levels for the Red, Green, or Blue channels respectively.

Alpha This shows the distribution of opacity levels. If the layer is completely transparent (alpha = 0) or completely opaque (alpha = 255), the histogram will consist of a single bar on the left or right edge.

RGB

Figure 15.18 Combined histograms of R, G, and B channels.

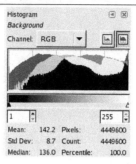

This entry, only available for RGB layers, shows the R, G, and B histograms superimposed, so that you can see all of the color distribution information in a single view.

Linear  **/ Logarithmic** **buttons**

Figure 15.19 The histogram shown at the top, changed to logarithmic mode.

These buttons determine whether the histogram will be displayed using a linear or logarithmic Y axis. For images taken from photographs, the linear mode is most commonly useful. For images that contain substantial areas of constant color, though, a linear histogram will often be dominated by a single bar, and a logarithmic histogram will often be more useful.

Range Setting

Figure 15.20 Dialog aspect after range fixing.

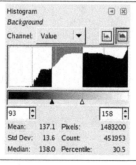

You can restrict the analysis, for the statistics shown at the bottom of the dialog, to a limited range of values if you wish. You can set the range in one of three ways:

- Click and drag the pointer across the histogram display area, from the lowest level to the highest level of the range you want.
- Click and drag the black or white triangles on the slider below the histogram.

- Use the spinbutton entries below the slider (left entry: bottom of range; right entry: top of range).

Statistics At the bottom of the dialog some basic statistics are shown describing the distribution of channel values, restricted to the selected range:

- Mean : the mean value of the interval in the selected channel.

- Std Dev : Standard deviation. Gives an idea about how homogeneous the distribution of values in the interval is.

- Median : For example, the value of the fiftieth peak in a 100 peaks interval.

- Pixels : The number of pixels in the active layer or selection.

- Count : The number of pixels in a peak (when you click on the histogram) or in the interval.

- Percentile : The ratio between the number of pixels in the interval and the total number of pixels in the active layer or selection.

15.2.6   Navigation Dialog

Figure 15.21 Navigation Dialog

The Navigation dialog is designed to offer easy movement around the active image if the zoom is set higher than what the image window can display. If this is the case, there is an inversely colored rectangle that shows the location of the current view area in respect to the image.

To change the viewing region:

- Click and drag the rectangular area.

- Use **Shift** and mouse-wheel to move horizontally, **Alt** and mouse-wheel to move vertically. The mouse pointer must be on the rectangular area in the shape of a grabbing hand.

15.2.6.1   Activating the dialog

The "Navigation" dialog is a dockable dialog; see the section Section 3.2.3 for help on manipulating it. You can access it:

- from the image menu: Windows → Dockable Dialogs → Navigation;

- from the Tab menu in any dockable dialog by clicking on [⊲] and selecting Add Tab → Navigation,

- from the image-menu: View → Navigation window.

- You can access more quickly to it (but without the zoom functions) by clicking on the icon at the right bottom corner of the image window:

15.2.6.2   Using the Navigation Dialog

The slider It allows easy zoom level control, more precise than with the Zoom command. This slider can also be moved using the mouse wheel when the mouse pointer is on the slider, or **Ctrl** and mouse wheel when the mouse pointer is on the rectangular area.

The buttons *Zoom Out* 🔍 *Zoom In* 🔍 and *Zoom 1:1* 🔍 are self explanatory.

Adjust the zoom ratio so that the image becomes fully visible The zoom ratio is adjusted so that the whole image becomes visible in the window as it is.

Adjust the zoom ratio so that the window is used optimally The image size and the zoom are adjusted so that the image is fully displayed with the lesser zoom.

Reduce the image window to the size of the image display Restore the image window to the size which allows the image to be fully displayed with the zoom unchanged. This command is also as menu entry available. See Section 16.5.5 for the details.

15.2.7   Undo History Dialog

Figure 15.22 The Undo History dialog

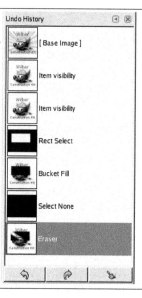

This dialog shows you a list of the actions you have most recently performed on an image, with a small sketch that attempts to illustrate the changes produced by each. You can revert the image to any point in its Undo History simply by clicking on the right entry in the list. For more information on GIMP's Undo mechanism and how it works, see the section on Undoing.

15.2.7.1   Activating the dialog

The "Undo History" dialog is a dockable dialog; see the section Section 3.2.3 for help on manipulating it.

You can access it:

- from the image menu: Windows → Dockable Dialogs → Undo History.

- from the Tab menu in any dockable dialog by clicking on ◀ and selecting Add Tab → Undo History.

15.2.7.2   Using the Undo History dialog

The most basic thing you can do is to select a point in the Undo History by clicking on it in the list. You can go back and forth between states in this way as much as you please, without losing any information or consuming any resources. In most cases, the changes are very fast.

Tip

 Ctrl-F opens a search field. See View as List; View as Grid

At the bottom of the dialog are three buttons:

Undo   This button has the same effect as choosing Edit → Undo from the menu, or pressing Ctrl-Z; it reverts the image to the next state back in the undo history.

Redo   This button has the same effect as choosing Edit → Redo from the menu, or pressing Ctrl-Y; it advances the image to the next state forward in the Undo History.

Clear Undo History   This button removes all contents from the undo history except the current state. If you press it, you are asked to confirm that you really want to do this. The only reason for doing it would be if you are very constrained for memory.

Note

 In a tab, this dialog is represented by

Note

 You can set the number of undo levels in Preferences/Environment.

15.3   Image-content Related Dialogs

15.3.1   FG/BG Color Dialog

Figure 15.23 The FG/BG Color dialog

The Color dialog lets you manage and pick up new colors. You can use it into five different modes: GIMP, CMYK, Triangle, Watercolor and Scales. It has an interesting eyedropper to pick up a color anywhere on your screen.

The dialog called from the FG/BG area in the toolbox is a bit different compared to the one called from the image menu:

- the sliders are permanently visible instead of selected from the scale menu,

- twelve buttons show the last used colors. You may choose a color by clicking on one of these buttons or add the current FG or BG color to this history list.

This dialog works either on the foreground or the background color.

15.3.1.1   Activating the Dialog

The "Colors" dialog is a dockable dialog; see the section Section 3.2.3 for help on manipulating it.
You can access it:

- from an image menu: Windows → Dockable Dialogs → Colors;

- from the Tab menu in any dockable dialog by clicking on ◁ and selecting Add Tab → Colors,

- from the toolbox: click on the current Foreground or Background color.

In the Windows menu, there is a list of detached windows which exists only if at least one dialog remains open. In this case, you can raise the "Colors" dialog from the image-menu: Windows → Colors.

15.3.1.2   Using the "FG/BG color" dialog

GIMP Selector With the GIMP Color Selector, you select a color by clicking on a one-dimensional strip located at the right edge, and then in a two-dimensional area located on the left. The one-dimensional strip can encode any of the color parameters H, S, V, R, G, or B, as determined by which of the adjoining buttons is pressed. The two-dimensional area then encodes the two complementary color parameters.

CMYK

Figure 15.24 CMYK

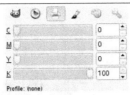

You get to this selector by clicking on the printer icon. The CMYK view gives you the possibility to manage colors from the CMYK color model.

Triangle

Figure 15.25 The triangle selector

This selector uses the *HSV* color model. Click in the *chromatic circle* and drag the mouse pointer to select the Hue. Click-and-drag in the *triangle* to vary intuitively Saturation (vertically) and Value (horizontally).

Watercolor

Figure 15.26 Watercolor Color Selector

This color selector is symbolized by a brush. The function mode of this selector is a little different from that of models presented so far. The principle consists in changing the current foreground color by clicking in the rectangular palette. If the current foreground color is for example white, then it turns to reddish by clicking in the red color area. Repeated clicking strengthens the effect. With the slider, which is right apart from the color palette, you can set the color quantity per every mouse click. The higher the sliding control is, the more color is taken up per click.

Palette

Figure 15.27 Palette Color Selector

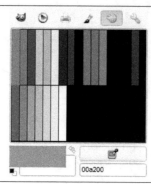

This color selector brings up a list of the colors of the current palette in the Palettes dialog. You can set GIMP's foreground or background colors by clicking on colors in the colors display. You can also use the arrow keys to move within the list of colors.

Scales

Figure 15.28 The Scales selector

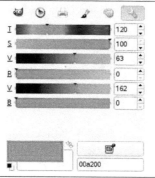

This selector displays a global view of R, G, B channels and H, S, V values, placed in sliders.

Color picker The color picker has a completely different behavior, than the color picker tool. Instead of picking the colors from the active image, you're able to pick colors from the entire screen.

HTML Notation See HTML notation. You can also use the CSS keywords; enter the first letter of a color to get a list of colors with their keyword :

Figure 15.29 CSS keywords example

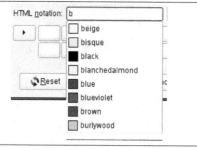

Right-clicking in the HTML Notation text box opens a context menu that allows you to edit your notation, particularly to paste a complex notation you have copied elsewhere. This menu leads to various Input Methods that allow you to use foreign characters, and to the possibility to Insert Unicode Control Characters. This is a vast field, beyond this help. Please see [UNICODE].

Figure 15.30 The HTML Notation context menu

Right up you find a symbol, consisting of two arrows, with which you can exchange the foreground and background color. At the bottom left of the dialog, just below the foreground color block, you find a switching surface with two small, one black and the other white, partially overlapping squares. If you click on these, the front and background color are put back to black and white respectively.

15.3.2   Brushes Dialog

Figure 15.31 The Brushes dialog

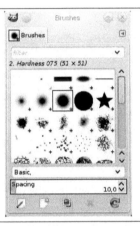

The "Brushes" dialog is used to select a brush, for use with painting tools: see the Brushes section for basic information on brushes and how they are used in GIMP. The dialog also gives you access to several functions for manipulating brushes. You can select a brush by clicking on it in the list: it will then be shown in the Brush/Pattern/Gradient area of the Toolbox. GIMP comes now with 56 brushes, different from each other, because the size, the ratio and the angle of every brush can be set in the tool options dialog. You can also create custom brushes using the Brush Editor, or by saving images in a special brush file format.

15.3.2.1   Activating the Dialog

The "Brushes" dialog is a dockable dialog; see the section Section 3.2.3 for help on manipulating it.
    You can access it:

- from the Toolbox, by clicking on the brush symbol in Brush/Pattern/Gradient area.

- From an image menu: Windows → Dockable Dialogs → Brushes;

- from the Tab menu in any dockable dialog by clicking on 🔳 and selecting Add Tab → Brushes.

- from the Tool Options dialog for any of the paint tools, by clicking on the Brush icon button, you get a popup with similar functionality that permits you to quickly choose a brush from the list; if you click on the button present on the right bottom of the popup, you open the real brush dialog.

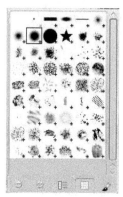

The simplified "Brushes" dialog

This window has five buttons, clearly explained by help pop-ups:

- Smaller previews
- Larger previews
- View as list
- View as Grid
- Open the brush selection dialog

Note that, depending on your Preferences, a brush selected with the popup may only apply to the currently active tool, not to other paint tools. See the Tool Option Preferences section for more information.

15.3.2.2 Using the "Brushes" dialog

15.3.2.2.1 Grid/List mode   In the Tab menu, you can choose between View as Grid and View as List. In Grid mode, the brush shapes are laid out in a rectangular array, making it easy to see many at once and find the one you are looking for. In List mode, the shapes are lined up in a list, with the names beside them.

In the Tab menu, the option Preview Size allows you to adapt the size of brush previews to your liking.

Figure 15.32 Grid/List view

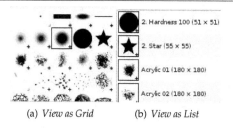

(a) *View as Grid*   (b) *View as List*

Grid mode At the top of the dialog appears the name of the currently selected brush, and its size in pixels.

In the center a grid view of all available brushes appears, with the currently selected one outlined.

List mode For the most part, the dialog works the same way in List mode as in Grid mode, with one exception:

If you double-click on the *name* of a brush, you will be able to edit it. Note, however, that you are only allowed to change the names of brushes that you have created or installed yourself, not the ones that come pre-installed with GIMP. If you try to rename a pre-installed brush, you will be able to edit the name, but as soon as you hit return or click somewhere else, the name will revert to its original value. It is a general rule that you cannot alter the resources that GIMP pre-installs for you: brushes, patterns, gradients, etc; only ones that you create yourself.

Figure 15.33 The "Brushes" dialog

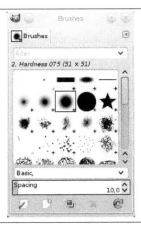

15.3.2.2.2 Brush previews When you click on a brush preview, it becomes the current brush and it gets selected in the brush area of Toolbox and the Brush option of painting tools. When you double-click on a brush preview, you will activate the Brush Editor. You can also click on buttons at the bottom of the dialog to perform various actions.

Meaning of the small symbols at the bottom right corner of every brush preview:

- A blue corner is for brushes in normal size. You can duplicate them.

- A small cross means that the brush preview is in a reduced size. You can get it in normal size by maintaining left click on it.

- A red corner is for animated brushes. If you maintain left click on the thumbnail, the animation is played.

15.3.2.2.3 Tagging You can use tags to reorganize the brushes display. See Section 15.3.6.

15.3.2.2.4 Buttons at the bottom At the bottom of the dialog you find a slider and some buttons:

Spacing This slider lets you set the distance between consecutive brush marks when you trace out a brushstroke with the mouse pointer. Spacing is a percentage of the brush width.

Edit Brush This activates the Brush Editor. Pressing the button will open the Editor for any brush. It only works, however, for parametric brushes: for any other type, the Editor will show you the brush but not allow you to do anything with it.

New Brush This creates a new parametric brush, initializes it with a small fuzzy round shape, and opens the Brush Editor so that you can modify it. The new brush is automatically saved in your personal brushes folder.

Duplicate Brush This button is only enabled if the currently selected brush is a parametric brush. If so, the brush is duplicated, and the Brush Editor is opened so that you can modify the copy. The result is automatically saved in your personal brushes folder.

Delete Brush This option is active for parametric brushes only. This removes all traces of the brush, both from the dialog and the folder where its file is stored, if you have permission to do so. It asks for confirmation before doing anything.

Refresh Brushes If you add brushes to your personal brushes folder or any other folder in your brush search path, by some means other than the Brush Editor, this button causes the list to be reloaded, so that the new entries will be available in the dialog.

The functions performed by these buttons can also be accessed from the dialog pop-up menu, activated by right-clicking anywhere in the brush grid/list, or by choosing the top item, Brushes menu, from the dialog Tab menu.

Figure 15.34 The "Brushes" context menu

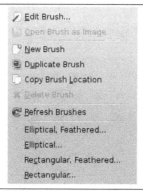

15.3.2.2.5 The "Brushes" context menu Right clicking on a brush preview opens a context menu. This menu has now some options which let you create elliptical and rectangular brushes. These brushes can be feathered, but they are not parametric brushes.

The other commands of this submenu are described with the Buttons, except for Copy Brush Location which allows to copy brush path into clipboard. By using the File → Open Location, command, you can open the brush as a new image.

15.3.2.3 Brush Editor

Figure 15.35 The "Brushes" Editor dialog

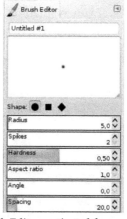

The Brush Editor, activated for a new brush.

The Brush Editor allows you to view the brush parameters of a brush supplied by GIMP, and you can't change them. You can also create a custom brush: click on the New Brush button to activate the functions of the brush editor; you can select a geometrical shape, a circle, a square or a diamond. This editor has several elements:

The dialog bar: As with all dialog windows, a click on the small triangle prompts a menu allowing you to set the aspect of the Brush Editor.

The title bar: To give a name to your brush.

The preview area: Brush changes appear in real time in this preview.

Settings:

Shape A circle, a square and a diamond are available. You will modify them by using the following options:

Radius Distance between brush center and edge, in the width direction. A square with a 10 pixels radius will have a 20 pixels side. A diamond with a 5 pixels radius will have a 10 pixels width.

Spikes This parameter is useful only for square and diamond. With a square, increasing spikes results in a polygon. With a diamond, you get a star.

Hardness This parameter controls the feathering of the brush border. Value = 1.00 gives a brush with a sharp border (0.00-1.00).

Aspect ratio This parameter controls the brush Width/Height ratio. A diamond with a 5 pixels radius and an Aspect Ratio = 2, will be flattened with a 10 pixels width and a 5 pixels height (1.0-20.0).

Angle This angle is the angle between the brush width direction, which is normally horizontal, and the horizontal direction, counter-clock-wise. When this value increases, the brush width turns counter-clock-wise (0° to 180°).

Spacing When the brush draws a line, it actually stamps the brush icon repeatedly. If brush stamps are very close, you get the impression of a solid line: you get that with Spacing = 1. (1.00 to 200.0).

15.3.2.4 The Clipboard Brush

When you use the Copy or Cut command on an image or a selection of it, a copy appears as a new brush in the upper left corner of the "Brushes" dialog. This brush will persist until you use the Copy command again. It disappears when you close GIMP.

Figure 15.36 A new "Clipboard Brush"

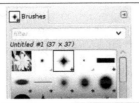

Note

 You can save this clipboard brush by using the Edit → Paste as → New brush as soon as it appears in the "Brushes" dialog. (See Section 16.3.11.3.)

15.3.3 Patterns Dialog

In GIMP, a *pattern* is a small image used to fill areas by placing copies of side by side. See the Patterns section for basic information on patterns and how they can be created and used.

You can use them with the Bucket Fill and Clone tools and the Fill with pattern command.

The "Patterns" dialog is used to select a pattern, by clicking on it in a list or grid view: the selected pattern will then be shown in the Brush/Pattern/Gradient area of the Toolbox. A few dozen more or less randomly chosen patterns are supplied with GIMP, and you can easily add new patterns of your own.

15.3.3.1 Activating the dialog

The "Patterns" dialog is a dockable dialog; see the section Section 3.2.3 for help on manipulating it.

You can access it:

- From the Toolbox, by clicking on the pattern symbol in the Brush/Pattern/Gradient area.

- from the image menu: Windows → Dockable Dialogs → Patterns;

- from the Tab menu in any dockable dialog by clicking on ◁ and selecting Add Tab → Patterns.

- From the Tool Options dialog of the Clone tool and the Bucket Fill tool, by clicking on the pattern source button, you get a pop-up with similar functionality that permits you to quickly choose a pattern from the list; if you clic on the Bucket Fill button present on the right bottom of the pop-up, you open the real pattern dialog. Note that, depending on your Preferences, a pattern selected with the pop-up may only apply to the currently active tool, not to other paint tools. See the Tool Option Preferences section for more information.

15.3.3.2 Using the pattern dialog

Grid/List modes In the Tab menu, you can choose between View as Grid and View as List. In Grid mode, the patterns are laid out in a rectangular array, making it easy to see many at once and find the one you are looking for. In List mode, the patterns are lined up in a list, with the names beside them.

Tip

Independent of the real size of a pattern all patterns are shown the same size in the dialog. So for larger patterns this means that you see only a small portion of the pattern in the dialog at all - no matter whether you view the dialog in the list or the grid view. To see the full pattern you simply click on the pattern *and hold the mouse button* for a second.

Note

In the Tab menu, the option Preview Size allows you to adapt the size of pattern previews to your liking.

Figure 15.37 The Patterns dialog

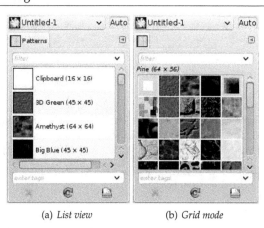

(a) *List view*   (b) *Grid mode*

Using the Patterns dialog (Grid mode) At the top appears the name of the currently selected patterns, and its dimensions in pixels.

In the center appears a grid view of all available patterns, with the currently selected one outlined. Clicking on one of them sets it as GIMP's current pattern, and causes it to appear in the Brush/Pattern/Gradient area of the Toolbox.

Using the Patterns dialog (List view) In this view, instead of a grid, you see a list of patterns, each labeled with its name and size. Clicking on a row in the list sets that pattern as GIMP's current pattern, just as it does in the grid view.

If you *double-click* on the name of a pattern, you will be able to edit the name. Note that you are only allowed to rename patterns that you have added yourself, not the ones that are supplied with GIMP. If you edit a name that you don't have permission to change, as soon as you hit return or move to a different control, the name will revert back to its previous value.

Everything else in the List view works the same way as it does in the Grid view.

Delete Pattern Pressing this button removes the pattern from the list and causes the file representing it to be deleted from disk. Note that you cannot remove any of the patterns that are supplied with GIMP and installed in the system `patterns` directory; you can only remove patterns that you have added to folders where you have write permission.

Refresh Patterns Pressing this button causes GIMP to rescan the folders in your pattern search path, adding any newly discovered patterns to the list. This button is useful if you add new patterns to a folder, and want to make them available without having to restart GIMP.

Open pattern as image If you click on this button, the current pattern is opened in a new image window. So, you can edit it. But if you try to save it with the `.pat`, even with a new name, you will bang into a "Denied permission " problem because this image file is "root". But this is possible under Windows, less protected.

15.3.3.3 Tagging

You can use tags to reorganize the patterns display. See Section 15.3.6.

15.3.3.4 The Pattern context menu

You get it by right-clicking on the "Patterns" dialog. The commands of this menu are described with Buttons, except for Copy Location which allows to copy the path to pattern into clipboard.

15.3.3.5 The Clipboard pattern

When you use the Copy or Cut command, a copy appears as a new pattern in the upper left corner of the Patterns dialog. This brush will persist until you use the Copy (or Cut) command again. It will disappear when you close GIMP.

Figure 15.38 A new "Clipboard Pattern"

Note

 You can save this clipboard pattern by using the Edit → Paste as → New pattern as soon as it appears in the Patterns dialog.

15.3.4   Gradients Dialog

Figure 15.39 The screenshot illustrates the Gradients dialog

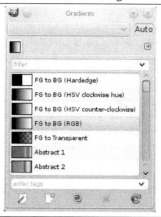

The "Gradients" dialog offers a gradient palette which is used to select a gradient — a set of colors arranged in a linear scale — for use with the Blend tool and numerous other operations. It also gives you access to several functions for manipulating gradients. You can select a gradient by clicking on it in the list: it will then be shown in the Brush/Pattern/Gradient area of the Toolbox. A few dozen nice gradients come pre-installed with GIMP. You can create more using the Gradient Editor. General information about gradients and how they are used in GIMP can be found in the Gradients section.

The first five gradients are particular: they reproduce the gradient between Foreground and background colors of toolbox in different ways.

- FG to BG (Hardedge): only black and white with a sharp limit.

- FG to BG (HSV clock-wise/counter-clockwise Hue): all hues in the color circle between the Foreground and the background color, clockwise or counter-clockwise.

- FG to BG (RGB): default gradient, between the Foreground and the background colors of the Toolbox, in the RGB mode.

- FG to Transparent: only uses one color (the Foreground color) from complete opacity to complete transparency. This gradient is very useful when you work with softly blended collages or fog effects.

15.3.4.1   Activating the Dialog

The "Gradients" dialog is a dockable dialog; see the section Section 3.2.3 for help on manipulating it. You can access it:

- from an image menu: Windows → Dockable Dialogs → Gradients;

- from the Tab menu in any dockable dialog by clicking on [◄] and selecting Add Tab → Gradients,

- from the Toolbox, by clicking on the current gradient in the Brush/Pattern/Gradient area,

- From the image by using the Ctrl-G shortcut.

In the Windows menu, there is a list of detached windows which exists only if at least one dialog remains open. In this case, you can raise the "Gradients" dialog from the image-menu: Windows → Gradients.

15.3.4.2 Using the "Gradients" dialog

The most basic, and most commonly used, operation with the dialog is simply to click on one of the gradients in the scrollable list, in order to make it GIMP's current gradient, which will then be used by any operation that involves a gradient.

If you *double-click* on a gradient, you open the Gradient Editor where you will be able to edit its name. Note, however, that you are only allowed to change the names of gradients that you have created yourself, not the ones that come pre-installed with GIMP. If you try to rename a pre-installed gradient, you will be able to edit the name, but as soon as you hit return or click somewhere else, the name will revert to its original value. It is a general rule that you cannot alter the resources that GIMP pre-installs for you: brushes, patterns, gradients, etc; only ones that you create yourself.

Grid/List modes In the Tab menu, you can choose between View as Grid and View as List. In Grid mode, the gradients are laid out in a rectangular array. They look quite dazzling when viewed this way, but it is not very easy to pick the one you want, because of visual interference from the neighboring ones. In List mode, the more usable default, the gradients are lined up vertically, with each row showing its name.

In the Tab menu, the option Preview Size allows you to adapt the size of gradient previews to your liking.

The buttons at the bottom of the dialog allow you to operate on gradients in several ways:

Edit Gradient This button activates the Gradient Editor.

New Gradient This creates a new gradient, initialized as a simple grayscale, and activates the Gradient Editor so that you can alter it. Gradients that you create are automatically saved in the `gradients` folder of your personal GIMP directory, from which they are automatically loaded when GIMP starts. (You can change this folder, or add new ones, using the Preferences dialog.)

Duplicate Gradient This creates a copy of the currently selected gradient. You will be able to edit the copy even if you cannot edit the original.

Delete Gradient This removes all traces of the gradient, if you have permission to do so. It asks for confirmation before doing anything.

Refresh Gradients If you add gradients to your personal `gradients` folder by some means other than this dialog, this button causes the list to be reloaded, so that the new entries will be available.

The functions performed by these buttons can also be accessed from the dialog pop-up menu, activated by right-clicking anywhere in the gradient list, or via Gradient Menu in the Tab menu:

Figure 15.40 The Gradients Menu

The gradient menu also gives you some additional functions:

Save as POV-Ray... This allows you to save the gradient in the format used by the POV-Ray 3D ray-tracing program.

Copy Gradient Location This command allows you to copy the gradient file location to the clipboard. You can then use it in a text editor.

Custom Gradient... This command creates a sample image filled with the selected gradient. You can select width and height of the image as well as the gradient direction in the dialog window.

Save as CSS The CSS (Cascading Style Sheets) language is used to format the display of HTML and XML files, for instance background color, font size... and background gradient. The "CSS Save" plugin is a CSS3 linear gradient generator that allows you to save a CSS3 code snippet, containing the gradient data for a given GIMP gradient. This code snippet is a text file: you can copy-paste it to the stylesheet related to your HTML file, to get a gradient background on opening the HTML file in Firefox, Chrome or Safari web navigators. This CSS3 code snippet can also be used as a gradient in SVG files.

Here is an example of code snippet, got using the Blue Green gradient:

A CSS snippet created with Save as CSS

```
background-image: linear-gradient(top, rgb(0,123,255) 0%, rgb ↩
    (72,226,255) 56%,
      rgb(0,255,161) 100%);
background-image: -moz-linear-gradient(center top, rgb(0,123,255)  ↩
    0%,rgb(72,
      226,255) 56%,rgb(0,255,
      161) 100%);
background-image: -webkit-gradient(linear, left top, left bottom,
        color-stop(0.000, rgb(0,123,255)),color-stop(0.566, rgb ↩
          (72,226,255)),
      color-stop(1.000, rgb(0,255,161)));
```

15.3.4.2.1 Tagging You can use tags to reorganize the gradients display. See Section 15.3.6.

15.3.4.3 The Gradient Editor

Figure 15.41 The gradient editor

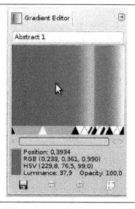

The Gradient Editor allows you to edit the colors in a gradient. It can only be used on gradients you have created yourself (or on a copy of a system gradient), not on system gradients that come pre-installed with GIMP. This is a sophisticated tool that may take a bit of effort to understand. The concept behind it is that a gradient can be decomposed into a series of adjoining *segments*, with each segment consisting of a smooth transition from the color on the left edge to the color on the right edge. The Gradient Editor allows you to pack together any number of segments, with any colors you want for the left and right edges of each segment, and with several options for the shape of the transition from left to right.

15.3.4.3.1 How to Activate the Gradient Editor You can activate the Gradient Editor in several ways:

- by double-clicking on the gradient stripe in the Gradient dialog,

- from the context menu you get by right clicking on the selected gradient name,

- by clicking on the Edit gradient ✎ button in the Gradient Dialog,

- from the Gradient Menu you get by clicking on ◀ in the Gradient Dialog.

15.3.4.3.2   Display

Name In the name area, you have the tab menu button (the small triangle).

The Gradient Preview Window Below the name, you see the current result of your work if the Instant update option is checked; else, changes will appear only when you release the mouse button.

If you simply move the mouse pointer on this display, it works somewhat as a color-picker. Values of the pointed pixel are displayed in a rather odd way. *Position* is a number given to 3 decimal places, from 0.000 on the left to 1.000 on the right of the whole gradient. *RGB, HSV, Intensity and Opacity* are also a ratio...

If you click-n-drag on display, then only position and RGB data are displayed. But they are passed on to the Foreground color in the Toolbox and to the four first gradients of the list (by pressing the **Ctrl** key, the Color is sent to the Background color of the Toolbox).

Range Selection/Control Sliders Below the gradient display, you see a set of black and white triangles lined up in row which allow you to adjust endpoints and midpoints in the gradient preview. A *segment* is the space between two consecutive *black* triangles. Inside each segment is a white triangle, which is used to "warp" the colors in the segment, in the same way that the middle slider in the Levels tool warps the colors there. You can select a segment by clicking between the two black triangles that define it. It turns from white to blue. You can select a range of segments by shift-clicking on them. The selected range always consists of a set of *consecutive* segments, so if you skip over any when shift-clicking, they will be included automatically. If "Instant update" is checked, the display is updated immediately after any slider movement; if it is unchecked, updates only occur when you release the mouse button.

You can move sliders, segments and selections. If you simply *click-n-drag a slider*, you only move the corresponding transition. By *click-n-drag on a segment* you can move this segment up to the next triangle. By *Shift+click-n-drag on a segment/selection*, you can move this segment/selection and compress/ dilate next segments.

Scrollbar Below the sliders is a scrollbar. This only comes into play if you zoom in using the buttons at the bottom.

Feedback Area Below, a color swatch shows the color pointed by the mouse cursor. Informations about this color and helpful hints or feedback messages may appear here.

Buttons At the bottom of the dialog appear five buttons:

> **Save** Clicking this button causes the gradient, in its current state, to be saved in your personal `gradients` folder, so that it will automatically be loaded the next time you start GIMP.

> **Revert** Clicking this button undoes all of your editing. (However, at the time this is being written, this function is not yet implemented.)

> **Zoom Out** Clicking this button shrinks the gradient display horizontally.

> **Zoom In** Clicking this button expands the gradient display horizontally. You can then use the scrollbar to pan the display left or right.

> **Zoom All** Clicking this button resizes the display horizontally so that it fits precisely into the window.

Figure 15.42 The Gradient Editor pop-up menu

15.3.4.3.3 The Gradient Editor pop-up Menu

You can access the Gradient Editor menu either by right-clicking on the gradient display, or by choosing the top item in the dialog's tab menu. The menu allows you to edit endpoint's color (set the left and right edge colors for each segment), blend colors, select a color model and edit segments. This editor works only with custom gradients or a copy of a system gradient.

The following commands can be found in the menu:

Editing endpoint's color

Left/Right color type This command opens a submenu:

Figure 15.43 The Left/Right color type sub-menu

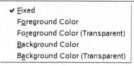

This submenu allows you to select the endpoint color from the toolbox foreground and background colors. Whenever you change the foreground or background color, this endpoint color may be changed as well. The alternative is to select a Fixed endpoint color.

Left [Right] Endpoint's Color These options allow you to choose a color for the respective endpoint using a Color Editor.

> **Note**
>
> This command is related to the previous one and becomes inactive if you have selected any other value than Fixed for the corresponding Left [Right] Color Type.

Figure 15.44 The "Load Color From" submenu

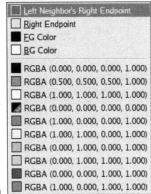

Load Left [Right] Color From

These options give you a number of alternative ways of assigning colors to the endpoints. From the submenu you can choose (assuming we're dealing with the left endpoint):

Left Neighbor's Right Endpoint This choice will cause the color of the right endpoint of the segment neighboring on the left to be assigned to the left endpoint of the selected range.

Right Endpoint This choice will cause the color of the right endpoint of the selected range to be assigned to the left endpoint.

FG/BG color This choice causes GIMP's current foreground or background color, as shown in the Toolbox, to be assigned to the endpoint. Note that changing foreground or background color later will not change the endpoint's color.

RGBA slots At the bottom of the menu are 10 "memory slots". You can assign colors to them using the "Save" menu option described below. If you choose one of the slots, the color in it will be assigned to the endpoint.

Save Left [Right] Color To These options cause the color of the endpoint in question to be assigned to the "memory slot" selected from the submenu.

Click and drag colors You can also click and drag a color from the toolbox FG-BG colors or from a palette

- to an endpoint (a black triangle), to set left [right] colors,
- to the gradient display area, to add a new endpoint with this color on both sides.

Blending and coloring functions for segment

Figure 15.45 The Blending Function submenu

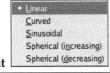

Blending Function for Segment

This option determines the course of the transition from one endpoint of the range (segment or selection) to the other, by fitting the specified type of function to the endpoints and midpoint of the range:

Linear Default option. Color varies linearly from one endpoint of the range to the other.

Curved Gradient varies more quickly on ends of the range than on its middle.

Sinusoidal The opposite of the curved type. Gradients varies more quickly on center of the range than on its ends.

Spherical (increasing) Gradient varies more quickly on the left of the range than on its right.

Spherical (decreasing) Gradient varies more quickly on the right than on the left.

Figure 15.46 The Coloring Type submenu

Coloring Type for Segment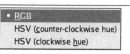

This option gives you additional control of the type of transition from one endpoint to the other: as a line either in RGB space or in HSV space.

Modifying segments

Flip Segment This option does a right-to-left flip of the selected range (segment or selection), flipping all colors and endpoint locations.

Replicate Segment This option splits the selected range (segment or selection) into two parts, each of which is a perfect compressed copy of the original range.

Split Segment at Midpoint This option splits each segment in the selected range in into two segments, splitting at the location of the white triangle.

Split Segment Uniformly This option is similar to the previous one, but it splits each segment halfway between the endpoints, instead of at the white triangle.

Delete Segment This option deletes all segments in the selected range, (segment or selection) replacing them with a single black triangle at the center, and enlarging the segments on both sides to fill the void.

Re-center Segment's midpoint This option moves the white triangle for each segment in the selected range to a point halfway between the neighboring black triangles.

Re-distribute Handles in Segment This option causes the black and white triangles in the selected range to be shifted so that the distances from one to the next are all equal.

Blending colors
These options are available only if more than one segment are selected.

Blend Endpoints' Colors This option causes the colors at interior endpoints in the range to be averaged, so that the transition from each segment to the next is smooth.

Blend Endpoints' Opacity This option does the same thing as the previous option, but with opacity instead of color.

Caution

 There is no "undo" available within the Gradient Editor, so be careful!

15.3.4.3.4 Using example for the Gradient Editor All these options can seem somewhat boring. Here is an example to clear ideas:

1. Open the Gradient Dialog. Click the New Gradient ⬜ . The Gradient Editor is opened and shows a gradient from black to white.

Figure 15.47 New gradient

2. Right click in this new gradient and click the Split Segment Uniformly. Fix the number of segments you want.

Figure 15.48 Gradient with three segments

*Every segment is limited with two black triangular sliders. Click a segment to activate it. By pressing the **Shift** key, you can select several contiguous segments.*

3. In the context menu you get by right-clicking in the gradient, set Left Endpoint Color and Right Endpoint Color for the selected segment or segment group.

Figure 15.49 First segment colored

Red has been chosen for left endpoint and yellow for the right enpoint.

4. Go on the same way for other segments. Then use the Blending functions for segment to achieve various effects.

15.3.5   Palettes Dialog

A *palette* is a set of discrete colors, in no particular order. See the Palettes section for basic information on palettes and how they can be created and used.

The "Palettes" dialog is used to select a palette, by clicking on it in a list or grid view. A few dozen more or less randomly chosen palettes are supplied with GIMP, and you can easily add new palettes of your own. The "Palettes" dialog also give you access to several operations for creating new palettes or manipulating the ones that already exist.

Note

 The "Palettes" dialog is not the same thing as the Index Palette dialog, which is used to manipulate the colormaps of indexed images.

15.3.5.1   Activating the dialog

The "Palettes" dialog is a dockable dialog; see the section Section 3.2.3 for help on manipulating it.
 You can access it:

- from the image menu: Windows → Dockable Dialogs → Palettes;

- from the Tab menu in any dockable dialog by clicking on ◀ and selecting Add Tab → Palettes.

15.3.5.2   Using the Palettes dialog

Clicking on a palette in the dialog selects this palette and brings up the Palette Editor, which allows you to set GIMP's foreground or background colors by clicking on colors in the palette display. You can also use the arrow keys to select a palette.

Double-clicking on a palette *name* (in List View mode) lets you to edit the name. Note that you are only allowed to change the names of palettes that you have added yourself, not those that are supplied with GIMP. If you edit a name that you are not allowed to change, it will revert back to its previous value as soon as you hit return or move the pointer focus elsewhere.

Grid/List modes

Figure 15.50 The "Palettes" dialog

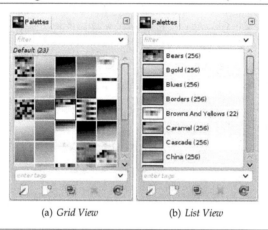

(a) *Grid View*   (b) *List View*

In the Tab menu, you can choose between View as Grid and View as List. In Grid mode, the palettes are laid out in a spectacular rectangular array, making it easy to see many at once and find the one you are looking for. In List mode (the default), the palettes are lined up in a list, with the names beside them.

The option Preview Size allows you to adapt the size of color cell previews to your liking.

Tagging   You can use tags to reorganize the palettes display. See Section 15.3.6.

The buttons of the Palettes Dialog
Below the palettes view, at the bottom of the dialog window, there are several buttons:

Edit Palette   This button brings up the Section 15.3.5.4.

New Palette   For more information on this button please refer to New Palette.

Duplicate Palette   For more information on this button please refer to Duplicate Palette.

Delete Palette   For more information on this button please refer to Delete Palette.

Refresh Palettes   For more information on this button please refer to Refresh Palettes.

15.3.5.3 The "Palettes" pop-menu

Figure 15.51 The "Palettes" pop-menu

The "Palettes" pop-menu can be accessed by right-clicking in the Palettes dialog, or by choosing the top item from the dialog Tab menu ().

> **Note**
>
> Some of the listed pop-menu entries are installation dependend and need the Python language interpreter to be installed. This includes at the time of writing: Offset Palette..., Palette to gradient, Palette to Repeating Gradient and Sort Palette....

Edit Palette "Edit Palette" is an alternative way of activating the Palette Editor: it can also be activated by double-clicking on a palette in the Palettes dialog, or by pressing the "Edit Palette" button at the bottom of the dialog.

New Palette "New Palette" creates a new, untitled palette, initially containing no color entries, and pops up the Palette Editor so that you can add colors to the palette. The result will automatically be saved in your personal `palettes` folder when you quit GIMP, so it will be available from the Palettes dialog in future sessions.

Import Palette

Figure 15.52 The Import Palette dialog

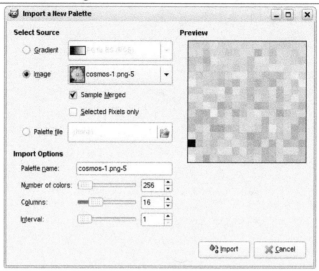

"Import Palette" allows you to create a new palette from the colors in a gradient, an image or a palette file. Choosing it brings up the "Import Palette" dialog, which gives you the following options:

> **Note**
>
> Former versions of GIMP had a "Save palette" command. It no longer exists. To save the palette of an image, indexed or not, you must *import* it in fact from the image.

Select Source You can import a palette either from any of GIMP's gradients (choosing one from the adjoining menu), or from any of the currently open images (chosen from the adjoining menu). Since GIMP 2.2, you can also import a RIFF palette file (with extension `.pal`), of the type used by several Microsoft Windows applications.

Two options concerning image as source, available for RGB images only:

- Sample merged: When this option is checked, colors are picked from all visible layers. If unchecked, pixels are picked from the active layer only, even though not visible.
- Selected pixels only: As the name says, pixels are picked from the selected area only, in the active layer or all visible layers according to the status of the previous option.

Palette name You can give a name to the new palette here. If the name you choose is already used by an existing palette, a unique name will be formed by appending a number (e. g., "#1").

Number of colors Here you specify the number of colors in the palette. The default is 256, chosen for three reasons: (1) every gradient contains 256 distinct colors; (2) GIF files can use a maximum of 256 colors; (3) GIMP indexed images can contain a maximum of 256 distinct colors. You can use any number you like here, though: GIMP will try to create a palette by spacing the specified number of colors even across the color range of the gradient or image.

Columns Here you specify the number of columns for the palette. This only affects the way the palette is displayed, and has no effect on the way the palette is used.

Interval Even setting "Number of colors" to maximum, the number of colors can't exceed 10000 in the palette. RGB images have much more colors. Interval should allow to group similar colors around an average and so get a better palette. This problem doesn't exist with 256 colors indexed images: Interval to 1 allows picking 256 colors (this option is grayed out with more than 256 colors indexed palettes too).

The imported palette will be added to the Palettes dialog, and automatically saved in your personal `palettes` folder when you quit GIMP, so it will be available in future sessions.

Duplicate Palette Duplicate Palette creates a new palette by copying the palette that is currently selected, and brings up a Palette Editor so that you can alter the palette. The result will automatically be saved in your personal `palettes` folder when you quit GIMP, so it will be available from the Palettes dialog in future sessions.

Merge Palettes Currently this operation is not implemented, and the menu entry will always be insensitive.

Copy Palette Location This command allows you to copy the palette file location to clipboard. You can then paste it in a text editor.

Delete Palette Delete Palette removes the palette from the "Palettes "dialog, and deletes the disk file in which it is stored. Before it acts, it asks you confirm that you really want to do these things. Note that you cannot remove any of the palettes that are supplied with GIMP, only palettes you have added yourself.

Refresh Palettes Refresh Palettes rescans all of the folders in your palette search path, and adds any newly discovered palettes to the list in the Palettes dialog. This may be useful if you obtain palette files from some external source, copy them into one of your palettes folders, and want to make them available during the current session.

Offset Palette... This command opens a dialog window:

Figure 15.53 The "Offset Palette"dialog

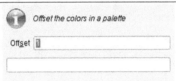

This command takes the last color of the palette and puts it at the first place. The Offset parameter lets you set how many times this action must be performed.

With negative "Offsets" colors are put from the first position to the end of the colors list.

Figure 15.54 "Offset Palette" examples

From top to bottom: original palette, Offset = 1, Offset = 2.

Palette to gradient With this command, all the colors of the palette are used to form the current gradient which is saved in the Gradient Dialog. The created gradient is build with segments just as much as the number of colors on the given palette.

Palette to Repeating Gradient This command creates a repeating gradient, using all the colors of the palette. This gradient appears in the Gradient Dialog and becomes the current gradient. The gradient is created with segments one more than the number of colors on the given palette. The left side color at the leftmost segment will be the same color on the right side at the rightmost segment.

Figure 15.55 "Palette to repeating gradient" examples

Top: palette. Bottom: the gradient created with the command.

Sort Palette... This command opens a dialog window which allows you to sort the colors of the palette according to certain criterions:

Figure 15.56 The "Sort Palette"dialog

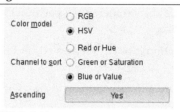

- Color model: you can choose between *RGB* and *HSV*

- Channel to sort: you can choose between the three RGB channels if the RGB model is selected, or the three HSV channels if the HSV channel is selected.

- Ascending (default is Yes): values are sorted from the lower to the upper. By clicking on this Yes you can toggle to No and values will be sorted in descending order.

15.3.5.4   Palette Editor

Figure 15.57 The Palette Editor

The Palette Editor is used mainly for two purposes: first, for setting GIMP's foreground or background colors (as shown in the Color Area of the Toolbox) to selected colors from the palette; second, for modifying the palette. You can activate the Palette Editor for any palette in the Palettes dialog, but you can only modify palettes that you have created yourself, not the palettes that are supplied when you install GIMP. (You can, however, duplicate any palette and then edit the newly created copy.) If you modify a palette, the results of your work will automatically be saved when you exit from GIMP.

15.3.5.4.1   How to Activate the Palette Editor   The Palette Editor is only accessible from the Palettes dialog: you can activate it by double-clicking on a palette, or by pressing the 🖉 "Edit Palette" button at the bottom, or by choosing "Edit Palette" from the "Palettes" Menu.

The Palette Editor is a dockable dialog; see the section on Dialogs and Docking for help on manipulating it.

15.3.5.4.2   Using the Palette Editor   If you click on a color box in the palette display, GIMP's foreground color will be set to the selected color: you can see this in the Color Area of the Toolbox. If you hold down the **Ctrl** key while clicking, GIMP's background color will be set to the selected color.

If the palette is a custom palette, double-clicking on a color not only sets the foreground, it also brings up a color editor that allows you to modify the selected palette entry.

Right-clicking in the palette display area brings up the Palette Editor menu. It's functions are mainly the same as those of the buttons at the bottom of the dialog.

Below the palette display area, at the left, appears a text entry area that shows the name of the selected color (or "Untitled " if it does not have one). This information has no functional significance, and is present only to serve you as a memory aid.

To the right of the name entry is a spinbutton that allows you to set the number of columns used to display the palette. This only affects the display, not how the palette works. If the value is set to 0, a default will be used.

At the bottom of the dialog are a set of buttons, which mostly match the entries in the Palette Editor menu, accessible by right-clicking in the palette display area. Here are the buttons:

Save This button causes the palette to be saved in your personal `palettes` folder. It would be saved automatically when GIMP exits in any case, but you might want to use this button if you are concerned that GIMP might crash in the meantime.

Revert This operation has not yet been implemented.

Edit Color Pops up a color editor allowing you to alter the color. If the palette is one you aren't allowed to alter, this button will be insensitive. See below

New Color from FG For more information on this button please refer to below.

Delete Color For more information on this button please refer to below.

Zoom Out For more information on this button please refer to below.

Zoom In For more information on this button please refer to below.

Zoom All For more information on this button please refer to below.

15.3.5.5   The Palette Editor pop-menu

Figure 15.58 The Palette Editor pop-menu

The Palette Editor Menu can be accessed by right-clicking on the palette display in the Palette Editor, or by choosing the top entry from the dialog Tab menu. The operations in it can also be executed using the buttons at the bottom of the Palette Editor dialog.

Edit Color "Edit Color" brings up a color editor that allows you to modify the color of the selected palette entry. If the palette is one that you are not allowed to edit (that is, one supplied by GIMP when it is installed), then the menu entry will beinsensitive.

New Color from FG; New Color from BG These commands each create a new palette entry, using either GIMP's current foreground color (as shown in the Color Area of the Toolbox), or the current background color.

Delete Color "Delete Color" removes the selected color entry from the palette. If the palette is one that you are not allowed to edit, then the menu entry will be insensitive.

Zoom Out "Zoom Out" reduces the vertical scale of the entries in the palette display.

Zoom In "Zoom In" increases the vertical scale of the entries in the palette display.

Zoom All "Zoom All" adjusts the vertical size of the entries in the palette display so that the entire palette fits into the display area.

Edit Active Palette When this option is checked (default), you can edit another palette by clicking on it in the "Palettes" dialog.

15.3.6 Tagging

In Brushes, Gradients, Patterns and Palettes dialogs and some other dockable dialogs, you can define tags and then, you can reorganize items according to chosen tags only.

You have two input fields:

Figure 15.59 Tagging

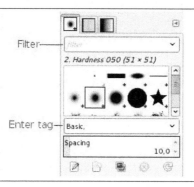

- "Filter" field: There, you can enter a tag previously defined or select a tag in the pop list you get by clicking on the arrow head at the right end of the field. Brushes, gradients, patterns, or palettes are filtered and only these that have this chosen tag will be displayed. You can enter several tags, separated with commas.

- "Enter tag" field: There, tags belonging to the current brush, gradient, pattern, or palette are displayed. You can add another tag to the current item by clicking on one of the defined tag in the pop up list of the field. You can also create your own tag for this item by typing its name in the field. Then the new tag appears in the tag pop up list.

Figure 15.60 Example

In this example, we defined a "green" tag for the Pepper and Vine brushes. Then, we entered "green" in the Filterinput field and so, only brushes with the green tag are displayed.

> **Tip**
>
> To give several brushes the same tag at once, display brushes in List Mode, and use Ctrl- Left click on the brushes you want to select.

You can delete tags: select a brush, then select a tag in the "Enter tag" field and press the **Delete** key. When this tag has been removed from all brushes, it disappears from the list.

15.3.7   Fonts Dialog

Figure 15.61 The Fonts dialog

The "Fonts" dialog is used for selecting fonts for the Text tool. It also allows you to refresh the list of available fonts, if you add new ones to your system while GIMP is running.

15.3.7.1   Activating the Dialog

The "Fonts" dialog is a dockable dialog; see the section Section 3.2.3 for help on manipulating it.
    You can access it:

- from an image menu: Windows → Dockable Dialogs → Fonts;

- from the Tab menu in any dockable dialog by clicking on ◁ and selecting Add Tab → Fonts,

- from the Tool Options for the Text tool. If you click on the "Font" button, a Font-selector pops up. In the lower right corner is a button that, if pressed, brings up the "Fonts" dialog.

In the Windows menu, there is a list of detached windows which exists only if at least one dialog remains open. In this case, you can raise the "Fonts" dialog from the image-menu: Windows → Fonts.

15.3.7.2   Using the Fonts dialog

The most basic thing you can do is to select a font by clicking on it: this font will then be used by the Text tool. If instead of clicking and releasing, you hold down the left mouse button with the pointer positioned over the font example ("Aa"), a window showing a larger text example will pop up ("Pack my box with five dozen liquor jugs").

Grid/List modes

Figure 15.62 The Fonts dialog

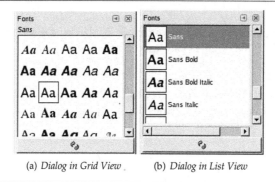

(a) *Dialog in Grid View*   (b) *Dialog in List View*

Tip

 Ctrl-F opens a search field. See View as List; View as Grid

In the Tab menu for the Fonts dialog, you can choose between View as Grid and View as List. In Grid mode, the fonts are laid out in a rectangular array. In List mode, they are lined up vertically, with each row showing an example of the appearance of the font ("Aa"), followed by the name of the font.

 Refresh font list Pressing this button at the bottom of the dialog causes the system font list to be rescanned. This may be useful if you add new fonts while GIMP is running, and want to make them accessible for the Text tool. You can also cause the font list to be rescanned by right-clicking in the font display, and selecting "Rescan Font List" from the menu that pops up (it is actually the only option in the menu).

Tip

 You can change the size of the font previews in the dialog using the "Preview Size" submenu of the dialog's Tab menu.

15.4   Image Management Related Dialogs

15.4.1   Buffers Dialog

Figure 15.63 The Buffers dialog (as a list)

Buffers are temporary repositories for image data, created when you cut or copy part of a drawable (a layer, layer mask, etc.). You can save a document in this buffer in two ways: Edit → Buffer → Copy Named or Edit → Buffer → Cut Named A dialog pops up asking you to name a buffer to store the data in. There is no hard limit on the number of named buffers you can create, although, of course, each one consumes a share of memory.

The "Buffers" dialog shows you the contents of all existing named buffers, and allows you to operate on them in several ways. It also shows you, at the top, the contents of the Global Buffer, but this is merely a display: you can't do anything with it.

Caution

  Named buffers are not saved across sessions. The only way to save their contents is to paste them into images.

15.4.1.1   Activating the Dialog

This dialog is a dockable dialog; see the section Section 3.2.3 for help on manipulating it.

You can access it:

- from an image menu: Windows → Dockable Dialogs → Buffers;

- from the Tab menu in any dockable dialog by clicking on and selecting Add Tab → Buffers.

In the Windows menu, there is a list of detached windows which exists only if at least one dialog remains open. In this case, you can raise the "Buffers" dialog from the image-menu: Windows → Buffers.

15.4.1.2   Using the Buffers dialog

Figure 15.64 The Buffers Menu

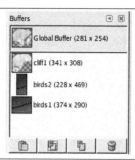

Clicking on a buffer in the display area makes it the active buffer, i. e., the one that will be used for paste commands executed with the Buffers Menu or the buttons at the bottom of the dialog. Double-clicking on a buffer causes its contents to be pasted to the active image as a floating selection; this is a quick way of executing the "Paste Buffer" command.

At the bottom of the dialog are four buttons. The operations they perform can also be accessed from the Buffers Menu that you get by right clicking on the active buffer.

Figure 15.65 The Buffers dialog (Grid View)

In the Tab menu for the "Buffers" dialog, you can choose between View as Grid and View as List. In Grid mode, the buffers are laid out in a rectangular array. In List mode, they are lined up vertically, with each row showing a thumbnail of the contents of the buffer, its name, and its pixel dimensions.

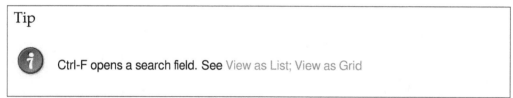

Tip

Ctrl-F opens a search field. See View as List; View as Grid

You can change the size of the buffer previews in the dialog using the "Preview Size" submenu of the dialog's Tab menu.

15.4.1.2.1   Buttons at the bottom   At the bottom of the dialog you find a couple of buttons:

Paste Buffer This command pastes the contents of the selected buffer into the active image, as a floating selection. The only difference between this and the ordinary Paste command is that it uses the selected buffer rather than the global clipboard buffer.

Paste Buffer Into This command pastes the contents of the selected buffer into the active image's selection, as a floating selection. The only difference between this and the ordinary Paste Into command is that it uses the selected buffer rather than the global clipboard buffer.

Paste Buffer as New This command creates a new single-layer image out of the contents of the selected buffer. The only difference between this and the ordinary Paste as New command is that it uses the selected buffer rather than the content of the global clipboard buffer.

Delete Buffer This command deletes the selected named buffer, no questions asked. You cannot delete the Global Buffer.

Figure 15.66 The "Buffers" context menu

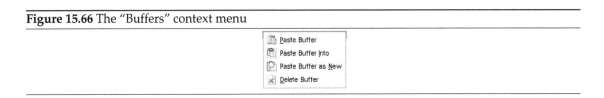

15.4.1.2.2   Context menu   These commands are explained above with Buttons.

15.4.2   Images Dialog

Figure 15.67 The Images dialog

The "Images" Dialog displays the list of open images on your screen; each of them is represented with a thumbnail. This dialog is useful when you have many overlapping images on your screen: thus, you can raise the wanted image to foreground.

15.4.2.1   Activating the dialog

The "Images" dialog is a dockable dialog; see the section Section 3.2.3 for help on manipulating it.
    You can access it:

- from the image menu: Windows → Dockable Dialogs → Images;

- from the Tab menu in any dockable dialog by clicking on 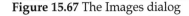 and selecting Add Tab → Images.

In the Windows menu, there is a list of detached windows which exists only if at least one dialog remains open. In this case, you can raise the "Images" dialog from the image-menu: Windows → Images.

15.4.2.2   Using the Images dialog

In multi-window mode, at the top of the dialog, a drop-list of open images appears if the "Show Image Selection" option is checked in the Tab Menu.
    At center, open images appear, as a list or a grid, according to the selected mode. The current image is highlighted in list mode, outlined in grid mode. With a double click on an image name, you raise this image to the foreground of your screen. With a simple click you select this image so that the buttons of the dialog can act on it.

Grid and List modes, preview size In the Tab menu for the "Images" dialog, you can choose between View as Grid and View as List. In Grid mode, the images are laid out in a rectangular array. In List mode, they are lined up vertically, with each row showing a thumbnail of the contents of the image, its name, and its pixel dimensions.

> **Tip**
>
> Ctrl-F opens a search field. See View as List; View as Grid

You can change the size of the image previews in the dialog using the "Preview Size" submenu of the dialog's Tab menu.

Buttons Three buttons at the bottom of the dialog allow you to operate on the selected image. These buttons are present if the "Show button bar" is checked in the tab dialog. You can get the same commands through the pop menu by right-clicking on the dialog.

Raise this image displays The selected image appears at the foreground of your screen. If this image has another view, this view also is raised but remains behind the original. The same option in the pop-up menu, that you get by right-clicking, is called "Raise views "

Create a new display for this image Duplicates the image window (not the image) of the selected image.

Delete This command works only on a image which is loaded without any window. Though images can be opened by the New Window command, if the image has been already loaded without window by a primitive procedure command (such as `gimp-image-new`, `file-png-load`, etc.), it can not be unloaded even if its windows are closed to the last. Then use this command to close it.

15.4.3 Document History Dialog

Figure 15.68 Document History dialog

The History Dialog displays the list of the documents you have opened in previous sessions. It is more complete than the list you get with the "Open Recent" command.

15.4.3.1 Activating the Dialog

The "History" dialog is a dockable dialog; see the section Section 3.2.3 for help on manipulating it.
You can access it:

- From an image menu: Windows → Dockable Dialogs → Document History.

- From the Tab menu in any dockable dialog by clicking on ◄ and selecting Add Tab → Document History.

- From the image Menu bar through: File → Open Recent → Document History.

15.4.3.2 Using the Document History dialog

The scroll bar allows you to browse all images you have opened before.

In the Tab menu for the "Document History" dialog, you can choose between View as Grid and View as List. In Grid mode, the documents are laid out in a rectangular array. In List mode, they are lined up vertically, with each row showing a thumbnail of the contents of the image, its name, and its pixel dimensions.

Tip

   Ctrl-F opens a search field. See View as List; View as Grid

---

Use the *Open the selected entry* 🖻 button or Open Image command of the dialog's context menu, to open the image you have selected. With the **Shift** key pressed, it raises an image hidden behind others. With the **Ctrl** key pressed, it opens the Open Image dialog.

Use the *Remove the selected entry* ➖ button or Remove Entry command of the dialog's context menu, to remove an image from the History dialog. The image is removed from the recently open images list also. But the image itself is not deleted.

Use the *Clear the entire file history* 🧹 button or Clear History command of the dialog's context menu, to remove all the files from the history.

Use the *Recreate Preview* 🔄 button or Recreate Preview command of the dialog's context menu, to update preview in case of change. With **Shift** key pressed, it acts on all previews. With **Ctrl** key pressed, previews that correspond to files that can't be found out, are deleted.

15.4.4 Templates Dialog

Figure 15.69 The Templates dialog

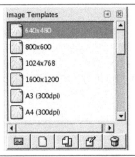

Templates are templates for an image format to be created. GIMP offers you a lot of templates and you can create your owns. When you create a New image, you can access to the list of existing templates but you can't manage them. The "Templates" dialog allows you to manage all these templates.

15.4.4.1 Activating the dialog

The "Templates" dialog is a dockable dialog; see the section Section 3.2.3 for help on manipulating it. You can access it:

- from the image menu: Windows → Dockable Dialogs → Templates.

- from the Tab menu in any dockable dialog by clicking on 🔽 and selecting Add Tab → Templates.

15.4.4.2 Using the Templates dialog

You select a template by clicking on its icon. Right clicking reveals a local menu that offers the same functions as buttons.

15.4.4.2.1 Grid/List modes In the Tab menu for the "Templates" dialog, you can choose between View as Grid and View as List. In Grid mode, templates are laid out in a rectangular array of identical icons (unless you gave them a particular icon, as we will see later). Only the name of the selected template is displayed. In List mode, they are lined up vertically; icons are identical too; all names are displayed.

In this Tab menu, the Preview Size option allows you to change the size of thumbnails.

Tip

Ctrl-F in a list view opens a search field. See View as List; View as Grid

---

15.4.4.2.2 Buttons at the bottom The buttons at the bottom of the dialog allow you to operate on templates in several ways:

 Create a new image from the selected template Clicking on this button opens the dialog Create a new image on the model of the selected template.

Create a new template Clicking on this button opens the New template dialog, identical to the Edit Template dialog, that we will see below.

 Duplicate the selected template Clicking on this button opens the Edit Template dialog that we are going to study now.

Edit the selected template Clicking on this button opens the Edit Template dialog.

Delete the selected template Guess what?

Tip

Every template is stored in a `templaterc` file at your personal GIMP directory. If you want to restore some deleted templates, you can copy or append template entries to your file from the master `templaterc` file at the `etc/gimp/2.0` directory of the GIMP's system folder.

15.4.4.3 Edit Template

Figure 15.70 The Edit Template dialog

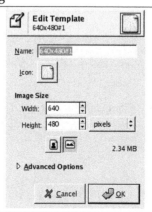

The dialog allows you to set the specifications of the selected template.

You can access this editor by clicking on the Edit Template button at the bottom of the dialog. Options

Name In this text box, you can modify the displayed template name.

Icon By clicking on this icon, you open a list of icons. You can choose one of them to illustrate the selected template name.

Image size Here you set the width and height of the new image. The default units are pixels, but you can switch to some other unit if you prefer, using the adjoining menu. If you do, note that the resulting pixel size will be determined by the X and Y resolution (which you can change in the Advanced Options), and by the setting of "Dot for Dot", which you can change in the View menu.

Note

 Please keep in mind, that every Pixel of an image is stored in the memory. If you're creating large files with a high density of pixels, GIMP will need some time for every function you're applying to the image.

Portrait/Landscape buttons These buttons toggle between Portrait and Landscape mode. Concretely, their effect is to exchange the values for Width and Height. If the X and Y resolutions are different (in Advanced Options), then these values are exchanged also. On the right, image size, image resolution and color space are displayed.

Advanced Options

Figure 15.71 The "Advanced Options" dialog

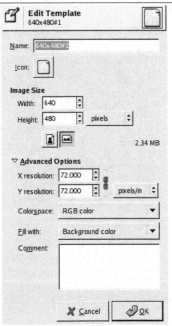

These are options that will mainly be of interest to more advanced users.

X and Y resolution These values come into play mainly in relation to printing: they do not affect the size of the image in pixels, but they determine its size on paper when printed. They can also affect the way the image is displayed on the monitor: if "Dot for Dot" is switched off in the View menu, then at 100% zoom, GIMP attempts to display the image on the monitor at the correct physical size, as calculated from the pixel dimensions and the resolution. The display may not be accurate, however, unless the monitor has been calibrated. This can be done either when GIMP is installed, or from the Display tab of the Preferences dialog.

Colorspace You can create the new image as either an RGB image or a grayscale image. You cannot create an indexed image directly in this way, but of course nothing prevents you from converting the image to indexed mode after it has been created.

Fill You have four choices for the solid color that will fill the new image's background layer:

- Foreground color, as shown in the Main Toolbox.
- Background color, as shown in the Main Toolbox.
- White, the more often used.
- Transparent. If this option is chosen, then the Background layer in the new image will be created with an alpha channel; otherwise not.

Comment You can write a descriptive comment here. The text will be attached to the image as a "parasite", and will be saved along with the image by some file formats (but not all of them).

15.5 Misc. Dialogs

15.5.1 Tool Presets Dialog

In GIMP-2.6, tool presets were not easy to use. You had to click on a tool first, and then click on the Restore Presets... button in the button bar at the bottom of the Tool options dialog... if you had not disabled this button bar in the Tab menu to make place on your desk! Now, with GIMP-2.8, a dockable Tool Presets Dialog is available where you just have to click on a preset to open the corresponding tool with its saved options.

Figure 15.72 The Tool Presets Dialog

15.5.1.1 Activating the Dialog

The "Tool Presets Dialog" is a dockable dialog; see the section Section 3.2.3 for help on manipulating it. You can access it:

- from an image menu: Windows → Dockable Dialogs → Tool Presets;
- or, as a tab in Toolbox window, through Tab Menu → Add Tab → Tool Presets.

15.5.1.2 Using the Tool Presets Dialog

This dialog comes with a list of predefined presets. Each of them has an icon representing the tool presets will be applied to and a name.

Presets can be tagged so that you can arrange presets display as you want. Please see Section 15.3.6 for more information about tagging.

Double-clicking on a preset icon opens the Tool Preset Editor.
Double-clicking on preset name allows you to edit this name.
At the bottom of the dialog appear four buttons:

- Edit this tool preset: clicking on this button opens the Tool Preset Editor for the selected preset. You can actually edit presets you have created; predefined presets options are all grayed out and inactive. But you can create a new preset from a predefined preset and edit its options.

The Tool Preset Editor is described in Section 15.5.2.

- Create a new tool preset: before clicking on this button, you can either select an existing preset, or select a tool in Toolbox, for example the Healing Tool which is not in the presets list. A new preset is created at the top of the dialog and the Tool Preset Editor is opened. Please see Section 15.5.2.

- Delete this tool preset: this button is active only for presets you have created.

- Refresh tool presets: If you have added a preset manually in gimp/2.0/tool-presets folder, you have to click on this button to include it in the presets list.

Note

 With GIMP-2.8, tool presets are saved in a new format (.gtp). To use your 2.6 presets, you have to convert them using `http://wiki.gimp.org/index.php/Mindstorm:Preset_converter`, until it is included in GIMP.

15.5.1.3   The Tool Presets Dialog Context Menu

Right-clicking on the Presets Dialog opens a context menu where you find some commands already described with buttons: Edit tool preset, New tool preset, Refresh tool presets. You also find two new commands:

- Duplicate Tool Preset: this command is always disabled. It is not necessary since, as we saw above, a duplicate is automatically created when you create a new preset from an existing preset.

- Copy Tool Preset Location: this command copies the path to the tool preset file into clipboard.

15.5.2   Tool Preset Editor

Figure 15.73 The Tool Preset Editor

15.5.2.1   Activating the Dialog

You can access this dialog through:

- a click on the Edit this tool preset button in the button bar of the Tool Presets Dialog.

- a double-click on a preset icon in the Tool Presets Dialog.

- a right-click on a preset in the Tool Presets Dialog to open a context menu and then click on the Edit Tool Preset command.

15.5.2.2   Using the Tool Preset Editor

You can edit presets you have created only; all options of predefined presets are grayed out and disabled. In this dialog you can:

- **edit preset name** in text box,

- **change preset icon** by clicking on preset icon. This opens a window where you can choose a new icon.

- **select resources to be saved** by clicking on check boxes.

15.5.3   Device Status Dialog

Figure 15.74 The "Device Status" Dialog

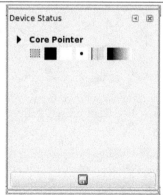

This window gathers together the current options of Toolbox, for each of your input devices: the mouse (named "Core pointer") or either the tablet, if you have one. These options are represented by icons: foreground and background colors, brush, pattern and gradient. Excepted for colors, clicking on an icon opens the window which lets you select another option; the tool-box will be updated when changing. You can drag and drop items to this dialog.

The "Save device status" button 🖫 at the bottom of the window, seems to have the same action as the "Record device status now" option in the Input Devices section in preferences.

15.5.3.1 Activating the Dialog

The device status dialog is a dockable dialog; see the section Section 3.2.3 for help on manipulating it. It can be activated in two ways:

- From an image menu : Windows → Dockable Dialogs → Device Status.

- From the Tab menu in any dialog : Add a Dock → Device Status

15.5.4 Error Console

The Error console offers more possibilities than the single "GIMP Message". This is a log of all errors occurring while GIMP is running. You can save all this log or only a selected part.

15.5.4.1 Activating the Dialog

The "Error Console" dialog is a dockable dialog; see the section Section 3.2.3 for help on manipulating it.

You can access it:

- from an image menu: Windows → Dockable Dialogs → Error Console;

- from the Tab menu in any dockable dialog by clicking on ◁ and selecting Add Tab → Error Console.

15.5.4.2 The "Error Console" Dialog

Figure 15.75 "Error Console" Dialog window

🖉 **Clear errors**   This button lets you delete all errors in the log.

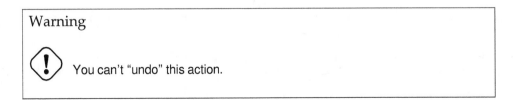

Warning

⚠ You can't "undo" this action.

Save all errors This button lets you save the whole log. You can also select a part of the log (by click-and-dragging the mouse pointer or by using the Shift-Arrow keys key combination) and save only this selected part by pressing the **Shift** key.

A dialog window Save Error Log to File lets you choose the name and the destination directory of this file:

Figure 15.76 "Save Error Log to file" Dialog window

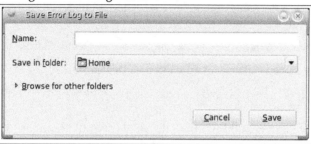

> Tip
>
> You will as well find these button actions in the dialog tab menu by clicking on , or in the context menu you get by right-clicking on the dialog window.

15.5.5   Save File

The Save command saves your image to disk. With GIMP-2.8, this command saves in XCF format only. If you try to save to a format other than XCF, you get an error message:

Starting from GIMP-2.8.8, the error dialog sports a link that jumps directly to the export command dialog. Please see Section 6.1.1.

If you have already saved the image, the previous image file is overwritten with the current version. If you have not already saved the image, the Save command opens the Save Image dialog.

If you quit without having saved your image, GIMP asks you if you really want to do so, if the "Confirm closing of unsaved images" option is checked in the Environment page of the Preferences dialog.

Figure 15.77 Save Image Dialog

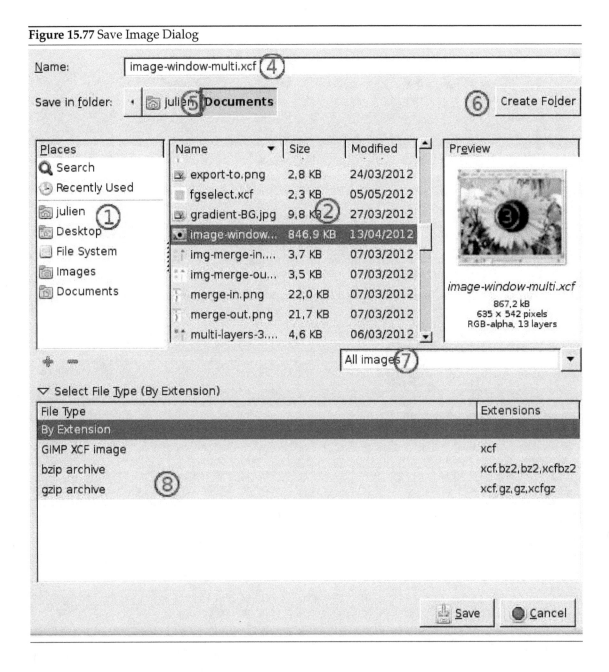

15.5.5.1 Activate the Dialog

- You can access this command in the image menu bar through File → Save,

- or from the keyboard by using the shortcut Ctrl-S.

- Use Ctrl-Shift-S to save the opened image with a different name.

15.5.5.2 The Save Image Dialog

With this file browser, you can edit filename directly in name box (default is "Untitled.xcf") or by selecting a file in name list. We repeat that only XCF format is permitted. You must also fix the image destination in Save in Folder. You can create a new folder if necessary.

Select File Type If you develop this option, you can select a compressed format for your XCF file:

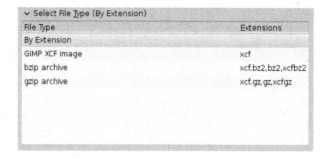

15.5.6   Export File

With GIMP-2.8, the Save command saves images in XCF format only. The Export command is now used to save images to various file formats.

You can access to this command through File → Export As..., or from the keyboard by using the shortcut Ctrl-Shift-E.

Figure 15.78 Export Image Dialog

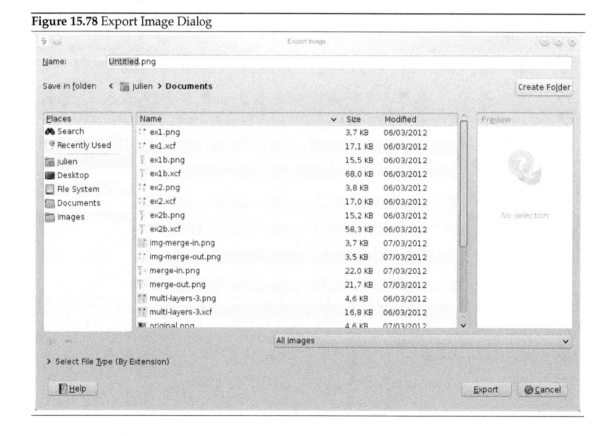

15.5.6.1   The Export Image Dialog

With this file browser, you can edit filename and extension directly in name box (default is "Untitled.png") or by selecting a file in name list. You must also fix the image destination in Save in Folder. You can create a new folder if necessary.

Select File Type If you develop this option, you can select an extension in the drop-down list for your file:

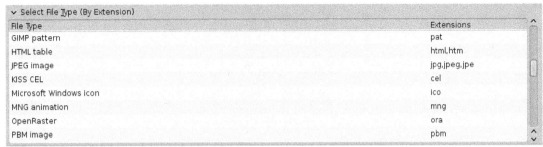

File formats dialogs are described in Section 6.1.

15.5.6.2 Exporting

When file name and destination are set, click on Export. This opens the export dialog for the specified file format.

If you have loaded a non-XCF file, a new item appears in File menu, allowing you to to export file in the same format, overwriting the original file.

If you modify an image that you already have exported, the **Export** command in File menu is changed, allowing you to export file again in the same format.

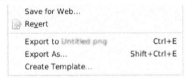

15.5.7 Sample Points Dialog

While the Color Picker can display color information about one pixel, the "Sample Points" dialog can display the data of four pixels of the active layer or the image, at the same time. Another important difference is that the values of these points are changed in real time as you are working on the image.

15.5.7.1 Activating the dialog

The "Sample Points" dialog is a dockable dialog; see the section Section 3.2.3 for help on manipulating it.

You can access it:

- from the image menu: Windows → Dockable Dialogs → Sample Points.

- from the Tab menu in any dockable dialog by clicking on ⊲ and selecting Add Tab → Sample Points.

15.5.7.2 Using sample points

To create a sample point, **Ctrl**-click on one of the two measure rules of the image window and drag the mouse pointer. Two perpendicular guides appear. The sample point is where both guides intersect. You can see its coordinates in the lower left corner and the information bar of the image window. Release the mouse button.

The reticle you get Ctrl + click-and-dragging from a rule.

By default, this sample point comes with a round mark and an order number. You can cancel these marks by unchecking the Show Sample Points option in the View menu.

The "Sample Points" dialog should automatically open when you create a sample point. This is not the case; you have to open it manually.

You can delete a sample point, as you do with guides, by click-and-dragging it up to a rule. Order numbers are automatically re-arranged in the dialog window; the most recent are moved one rank up.

By default, sampling is performed on all layers. If you want to sample on the active layer only, uncheck the Sample merged option in the tab menu:

Figure 15.79 The "Sample Point" menu

15.5.7.3 "Sample Points" dialog description

Figure 15.80 Sample points dialog

The information about four sample points is displayed in this window. You can create more, which will be existing and not shown. To show them, you have to delete displayed points.

The color of the sampled point is displayed in a swatch box.

In the drop-down list, you can choose between:

Pixel This choice displays the *Red, Green, Blue* and *Alpha* values of the pixel, as numbers between 0 and 255.

RGB This choice displays the *Red, Green, Blue* and *Alpha* values of the pixel, as percentages. It also shows the hexadecimal value of the pixel's color.

HSV This choice displays the *Hue*, in degrees, as well as the *Saturation, Value* and *Alpha* of the pixel, as percentages.

CMYK This choice displays the *Cyan*, *Magenta*, *Yellow*, *Black* and *Alpha* values of the pixel, as percentages.

Data are supplied for every channel in the chosen color model. The Alpha is present only if the image holds an Alpha channel.

Hexa appears only with the RGB mode. That's the hexadecimal code of the HTML Notation.

15.5.8 Pointer Dialog

Figure 15.81 Pointer dialog

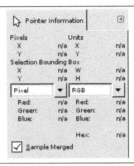

This dialog offers you, in a same window, in real time, the position of the mouse pointer, and the channel values of the pointed pixel, in the chosen color model.

15.5.8.1 Activating the dialog

The "Pointer" dialog is a dockable dialog; see the section Section 3.2.3 for help on manipulating it.
You can access it:

- from the image menu: Windows → Dockable Dialogs → Pointer.

- from the Tab menu in any dockable dialog by clicking on ◀ and selecting Add Tab → Pointer.

15.5.8.2 "Pointer" dialog options

Pixels Shows the position of the pointed pixel, in X (horizontal) and Y (vertical) coordinates, stated in pixels from the origin (the upper left corner of the canvas).

Units Shows the distance from the origin, in inches.

Pointer Bounding Box This information is active when a selection exists. X and Y are the coordinates of the upper left corner of the rectangular frame that bounds rectangular and ellipse selections. H and W are the height and width of this box.

This information also exits for the other selections, but they are of less interest and the bounding box is not visible.

This information concerning the selection remains unchanged when you use another tool, while pointer coordinates vary.

Channel values The channel values for the selected color model are shown below. Both pulldown menus contain the same choices, which makes it easier for you to compare the color values of a particular pixel using different color models. "Hex" is the HTML Notation of the pixel color, in hexadecimal. The choices on the pulldown menus are (Pixel is the default):

Pixel The RGB channel values. This choice displays the *Red*, *Green*, *Blue* and *Alpha* values of the pixel, as numbers between 0 and 255.

RGB The RGB channel values. This choice displays the *Red*, *Green*, *Blue* and *Alpha* values of the pixel, as percentages. It also shows the hexadecimal value of the pixel's color.

HSV The HSV components. This choice displays the *Hue*, in degrees, as well as the *Saturation*, *Value* and *Alpha* of the pixel, as percentages.

CMYK The CMYK channel values. This choice displays the *Cyan*, *Magenta*, *Yellow*, *Black* and *Alpha* values of the pixel, as percentages.

Sample Merged If this option is checked (default), sampling is performed on all layers. If it is unchecked, sampling is performed on the active layer only.

Part VIII

GNU Free Documentation License

Note that any translations of the GNU Free Documentation License are not published by the Free Software Foundation, and do not legally state the distribution terms for software that uses the GNU FDL-only the original English text of the GNU FDL does that.

The GIMP Documentation Team

Copyright (C) 2000,2001,2002 Free Software Foundation, Inc. 59 Temple Place, Suite 330, Boston, MA 02111-1307 USA. Everyone is permitted to copy and distribute verbatim copies of this license document, but changing it is not allowed.

.11 PREAMBLE

The purpose of this License is to make a manual, textbook, or other functional and useful document "free" in the sense of freedom: to assure everyone the effective freedom to copy and redistribute it, with or without modifying it, either commercially or noncommercially. Secondarily, this License preserves for the author and publisher a way to get credit for their work, while not being considered responsible for modifications made by others.

This License is a kind of "copyleft", which means that derivative works of the document must themselves be free in the same sense. It complements the GNU General Public License, which is a copyleft license designed for free software.

We have designed this License in order to use it for manuals for free software, because free software needs free documentation: a free program should come with manuals providing the same freedoms that the software does. But this License is not limited to software manuals; it can be used for any textual work, regardless of subject matter or whether it is published as a printed book. We recommend this License principally for works whose purpose is instruction or reference.

.12 APPLICABILITY AND DEFINITIONS

This License applies to any manual or other work, in any medium, that contains a notice placed by the copyright holder saying it can be distributed under the terms of this License. Such a notice grants a world-wide, royalty-free license, unlimited in duration, to use that work under the conditions stated herein. The "Document", below, refers to any such manual or work. Any member of the public is a licensee, and is addressed as "you". You accept the license if you copy, modify or distribute the work in a way requiring permission under copyright law.

A "Modified Version" of the Document means any work containing the Document or a portion of it, either copied verbatim, or with modifications and/or translated into another language.

A "Secondary Section" is a named appendix or a front-matter section of the Document that deals exclusively with the relationship of the publishers or authors of the Document to the Document's overall subject (or to related matters) and contains nothing that could fall directly within that overall subject. (Thus, if the Document is in part a textbook of mathematics, a Secondary Section may not explain any mathematics.) The relationship could be a matter of historical connection with the subject or with related matters, or of legal, commercial, philosophical, ethical or political position regarding them.

The "Invariant Sections" are certain Secondary Sections whose titles are designated, as being those of Invariant Sections, in the notice that says that the Document is released under this License. If a section does not fit the above definition of Secondary then it is not allowed to be designated as Invariant. The Document may contain zero Invariant Sections. If the Document does not identify any Invariant Sections then there are none.

The "Cover Texts" are certain short passages of text that are listed, as Front-Cover Texts or Back-Cover Texts, in the notice that says that the Document is released under this License. A Front-Cover Text may be at most 5 words, and a Back-Cover Text may be at most 25 words.

A "Transparent" copy of the Document means a machine-readable copy, represented in a format whose specification is available to the general public, that is suitable for revising the document straightforwardly with generic text editors or (for images composed of pixels) generic paint programs or (for drawings) some widely available drawing editor, and that is suitable for input to text formatters or for automatic translation to a variety of formats suitable for input to text formatters. A copy made in an otherwise Transparent file format whose markup, or absence of markup, has been arranged to thwart or discourage subsequent modification by readers is not Transparent. An image format is not Transparent if used for any substantial amount of text. A copy that is not "Transparent" is called "Opaque".

Examples of suitable formats for Transparent copies include plain ASCII without markup, Texinfo input format, LaTeX input format, SGML or XML using a publicly available DTD, and standard-conforming simple HTML, PostScript or PDF designed for human modification. Examples of transparent image formats include PNG, XCF and JPG. Opaque formats include proprietary formats that can be read and edited only by proprietary word processors, SGML or XML for which the DTD and/or processing tools are not generally available, and the machine-generated HTML, PostScript or PDF produced by some word processors for output purposes only.

The "Title Page" means, for a printed book, the title page itself, plus such following pages as are needed to hold, legibly, the material this License requires to appear in the title page. For works in formats which do not have any title page as such, "Title Page" means the text near the most prominent appearance of the work's title, preceding the beginning of the body of the text.

A section "Entitled XYZ" means a named subunit of the Document whose title either is precisely XYZ or contains XYZ in parentheses following text that translates XYZ in another language. (Here XYZ stands for a specific section name mentioned below, such as "Acknowledgements", "Dedications", "Endorsements", or "History".) To "Preserve the Title" of such a section when you modify the Document means that it remains a section "Entitled XYZ" according to this definition.

The Document may include Warranty Disclaimers next to the notice which states that this License applies to the Document. These Warranty Disclaimers are considered to be included by reference in this License, but only as regards disclaiming warranties: any other implication that these Warranty Disclaimers may have is void and has no effect on the meaning of this License.

.13 VERBATIM COPYING

You may copy and distribute the Document in any medium, either commercially or noncommercially, provided that this License, the copyright notices, and the license notice saying this License applies to the Document are reproduced in all copies, and that you add no other conditions whatsoever to those of this License. You may not use technical measures to obstruct or control the reading or further copying of the copies you make or distribute. However, you may accept compensation in exchange for copies. If you distribute a large enough number of copies you must also follow the conditions in section 4.

You may also lend copies, under the same conditions stated above, and you may publicly display copies.

.14 COPYING IN QUANTITY

If you publish printed copies (or copies in media that commonly have printed covers) of the Document, numbering more than 100, and the Document's license notice requires Cover Texts, you must enclose the copies in covers that carry, clearly and legibly, all these Cover Texts: Front-Cover Texts on the front cover, and Back-Cover Texts on the back cover. Both covers must also clearly and legibly identify you as the publisher of these copies. The front cover must present the full title with all words of the title equally prominent and visible. You may add other material on the covers in addition. Copying with changes limited to the covers, as long as they preserve the title of the Document and satisfy these conditions, can be treated as verbatim copying in other respects.

If the required texts for either cover are too voluminous to fit legibly, you should put the first ones listed (as many as fit reasonably) on the actual cover, and continue the rest onto adjacent pages.

If you publish or distribute Opaque copies of the Document numbering more than 100, you must either include a machine-readable Transparent copy along with each Opaque copy, or state in or with each Opaque copy a computer-network location from which the general network-using public has access to download using public-standard network protocols a complete Transparent copy of the Document, free of added material. If you use the latter option, you must take reasonably prudent steps, when you begin distribution of Opaque copies in quantity, to ensure that this Transparent copy will remain thus accessible at the stated location until at least one year after the last time you distribute an Opaque copy (directly or through your agents or retailers) of that edition to the public.

It is requested, but not required, that you contact the authors of the Document well before redistributing any large number of copies, to give them a chance to provide you with an updated version of the Document.

.15 MODIFICATIONS

You may copy and distribute a Modified Version of the Document under the conditions of sections 3 and 4 above, provided that you release the Modified Version under precisely this License, with the Modified Version filling the role of the Document, thus licensing distribution and modification of the Modified Version to whoever possesses a copy of it. In addition, you must do these things in the Modified Version:

A. Use in the Title Page (and on the covers, if any) a title distinct from that of the Document, and from those of previous versions (which should, if there were any, be listed in the History section of the Document). You may use the same title as a previous version if the original publisher of that version gives permission.

B. List on the Title Page, as authors, one or more persons or entities responsible for authorship of the modifications in the Modified Version, together with at least five of the principal authors of the Document (all of its principal authors, if it has fewer than five), unless they release you from this requirement.

C. State on the Title page the name of the publisher of the Modified Version, as the publisher.

D. Preserve all the copyright notices of the Document.

E. Add an appropriate copyright notice for your modifications adjacent to the other copyright notices.

F. Include, immediately after the copyright notices, a license notice giving the public permission to use the Modified Version under the terms of this License, in the form shown in the Addendum below.

G. Preserve in that license notice the full lists of Invariant Sections and required Cover Texts given in the Document's license notice.

H. Include an unaltered copy of this License.

I. Preserve the section Entitled "History", Preserve its Title, and add to it an item stating at least the title, year, new authors, and publisher of the Modified Version as given on the Title Page. If there is no section Entitled "History" in the Document, create one stating the title, year, authors, and publisher of the Document as given on its Title Page, then add an item describing the Modified Version as stated in the previous sentence.

J. Preserve the network location, if any, given in the Document for public access to a Transparent copy of the Document, and likewise the network locations given in the Document for previous versions it was based on. These may be placed in the "History" section. You may omit a network location for a work that was published at least four years before the Document itself, or if the original publisher of the version it refers to gives permission.

K. For any section Entitled "Acknowledgements" or "Dedications", Preserve the Title of the section, and preserve in the section all the substance and tone of each of the contributor acknowledgements and/or dedications given therein.

L. Preserve all the Invariant Sections of the Document, unaltered in their text and in their titles. Section numbers or the equivalent are not considered part of the section titles.

M. Delete any section Entitled "Endorsements". Such a section may not be included in the Modified Version.

N. Do not retitle any existing section to be Entitled "Endorsements" or to conflict in title with any Invariant Section.

O. Preserve any Warranty Disclaimers.

If the Modified Version includes new front-matter sections or appendices that qualify as Secondary Sections and contain no material copied from the Document, you may at your option designate some or all of these sections as invariant. To do this, add their titles to the list of Invariant Sections in the Modified Version's license notice. These titles must be distinct from any other section titles.

You may add a section Entitled "Endorsements", provided it contains nothing but endorsements of your Modified Version by various parties-for example, statements of peer review or that the text has been approved by an organization as the authoritative definition of a standard.

You may add a passage of up to five words as a Front-Cover Text, and a passage of up to 25 words as a Back-Cover Text, to the end of the list of Cover Texts in the Modified Version. Only one passage of Front-Cover Text and one of Back-Cover Text may be added by (or through arrangements made by) any one entity. If the Document already includes a cover text for the same cover, previously added by you or by arrangement made by the same entity you are acting on behalf of, you may not add another; but you may replace the old one, on explicit permission from the previous publisher that added the old one.

The author(s) and publisher(s) of the Document do not by this License give permission to use their names for publicity for or to assert or imply endorsement of any Modified Version.

.16 COMBINING DOCUMENTS

You may combine the Document with other documents released under this License, under the terms defined in section 5 above for modified versions, provided that you include in the combination all of the Invariant Sections of all of the original documents, unmodified, and list them all as Invariant Sections of your combined work in its license notice, and that you preserve all their Warranty Disclaimers.

The combined work need only contain one copy of this License, and multiple identical Invariant Sections may be replaced with a single copy. If there are multiple Invariant Sections with the same name but different contents, make the title of each such section unique by adding at the end of it, in parentheses, the name of the original author or publisher of that section if known, or else a unique number. Make the same adjustment to the section titles in the list of Invariant Sections in the license notice of the combined work.

In the combination, you must combine any sections Entitled "History" in the various original documents, forming one section Entitled "History"; likewise combine any sections Entitled "Acknowledgements", and any sections Entitled "Dedications". You must delete all sections Entitled "Endorsements".

.17 COLLECTIONS OF DOCUMENTS

You may make a collection consisting of the Document and other documents released under this License, and replace the individual copies of this License in the various documents with a single copy that is included in the collection, provided that you follow the rules of this License for verbatim copying of each of the documents in all other respects.

You may extract a single document from such a collection, and distribute it individually under this License, provided you insert a copy of this License into the extracted document, and follow this License in all other respects regarding verbatim copying of that document.

.18 AGGREGATION WITH INDEPENDENT WORKS

A compilation of the Document or its derivatives with other separate and independent documents or works, in or on a volume of a storage or distribution medium, is called an "aggregate" if the copyright resulting from the compilation is not used to limit the legal rights of the compilation's users beyond what the individual works permit. When the Document is included in an aggregate, this License does not apply to the other works in the aggregate which are not themselves derivative works of the Document.

If the Cover Text requirement of section 4 is applicable to these copies of the Document, then if the Document is less than one half of the entire aggregate, the Document's Cover Texts may be placed on covers that bracket the Document within the aggregate, or the electronic equivalent of covers if the Document is in electronic form. Otherwise they must appear on printed covers that bracket the whole aggregate.

.19 TRANSLATION

Translation is considered a kind of modification, so you may distribute translations of the Document under the terms of section 5. Replacing Invariant Sections with translations requires special permission from their copyright holders, but you may include translations of some or all Invariant Sections in addition to the original versions of these Invariant Sections. You may include a translation of this License, and all the license notices in the Document, and any Warranty Disclaimers, provided that you also include the original English version of this License and the original versions of those notices and disclaimers. In case of a disagreement between the translation and the original version of this License or a notice or disclaimer, the original version will prevail.

If a section in the Document is Entitled "Acknowledgements", "Dedications", or "History", the requirement (section 5) to Preserve its Title (section 2) will typically require changing the actual title.

.20 TERMINATION

You may not copy, modify, sublicense, or distribute the Document except as expressly provided for under this License. Any other attempt to copy, modify, sublicense or distribute the Document is void, and will automatically terminate your rights under this License. However, parties who have received copies, or rights, from you under this License will not have their licenses terminated so long as such parties remain in full compliance.

.21 FUTURE REVISIONS OF THIS LICENSE

The Free Software Foundation may publish new, revised versions of the GNU Free Documentation License from time to time. Such new versions will be similar in spirit to the present version, but may differ in detail to address new problems or concerns. See http://www.gnu.org/copyleft/.

Each version of the License is given a distinguishing version number. If the Document specifies that a particular numbered version of this License "or any later version" applies to it, you have the option of following the terms and conditions either of that specified version or of any later version that has been published (not as a draft) by the Free Software Foundation. If the Document does not specify a version number of this License, you may choose any version ever published (not as a draft) by the Free Software Foundation.

.22 ADDENDUM: How to use this License for your documents

To use this License in a document you have written, include a copy of the License in the document and put the following copyrightand license notices just after the title page:

> Copyright (c) YEAR YOUR NAME. Permission is granted to copy, distribute and/or modify this document under the terms of the GNU Free Documentation License, Version 1.2 or any later version published by the Free Software Foundation; with no Invariant Sections, no Front-Cover Texts, and no Back-Cover Texts. A copy of the license is included in the section entitled "GNU Free Documentation License".

If you have Invariant Sections, Front-Cover Texts and Back-Cover Texts, replace the "with...Texts." line with this:

> with the Invariant Sections being LIST THEIR TITLES, with the Front-Cover Texts being LIST, and with the Back-Cover Texts being LIST.

If you have Invariant Sections without Cover Texts, or some other combination of the three, merge those two alternatives to suit the situation.

If your document contains nontrivial examples of program code, we recommend releasing these examples in parallel under your choice of free software license, such as the GNU General Public License, to permit their use in free software.

www.ingramcontent.com/pod-product-compliance
Lightning Source LLC
LaVergne TN
LVHW060133070326
832902LV00018B/2771